天天读英语

小故事大道理全集

(英汉对照)

青 闰 ⊙ 主 编
张连亮 ⊙ 副主编

台海出版社

图书在版编目(CIP)数据

英汉双语小故事大道理全集 / 青闰主编. -- 北京：
台海出版社, 2018.5（2022.7重印）
ISBN 978-7-5168-1883-1

Ⅰ.①英… Ⅱ.①青… Ⅲ.①英语—汉语—对照读物
②人生哲学—通俗读物 Ⅳ.① H319.4：B

中国版本图书馆 CIP 数据核字 (2018) 第 092498 号

英汉双语小故事大道理全集

主　　编：青闰		
责任编辑：高惠娟　赵旭雯	装帧设计：	同人阁文化传媒·书装设计
版式设计：同人阁文化传媒·书装设计	责任印制：蔡　旭	

出版发行：台海出版社
地　　址：北京市东城区景山东街 20 号　　邮政编码：100009
电　　话：010 — 64041652（发行，邮购）
传　　真：010 — 84045799（总编室）
网　　址：www.taimeng.org.cn/thcbs/default.htm
E - m a i l：thcbs@126.com

经　　销：全国各地新华书店
印　　刷：香河县宏润印刷有限公司
本书如有破损、缺页、装订错误，请与本社联系调换

开　　本：710mm×1000mm	1/16
字　　数：379 千字	印　　张：22
版　　次：2018年9月第1版	印　　次：2022年7月第2次印刷
书　　号：ISBN 978-7-5168-1883-1	
定　　价：68.80 元	

版权所有　　翻印必究

前　　言

　　《小故事大道理全集》是让人获得自信的心灵密码，是按摩情感的心灵圣经，也是温暖千万心灵、改变千万人生的传世宝典。本书所选篇章以英汉对照形式编排，原汁原味，新颖独特，系统全面，贴近实际，贴近时代，贴近生活，所选内容发人深省、引人入胜、耐人寻味、励人奋进。

　　《小故事大道理全集》分为悟人生的真谛、人生的价值、大自然的爱、人生的恩惠、母亲的爱、永远的父爱、相信爱就会有奇迹和只要心中有爱等八卷，涉及心态、宽容、尊重、亲情、爱情、友谊、善良、感恩、幸福、做人、做事、挫折、成功等一系列人生课题。这些文章既可以使读者感到心灵震撼，又可以从容自信，端正人生态度，找到生活方向，成就美满人生。

　　朋友，每当华灯初上，白天的喧哗与骚动渐渐平息，伴着明月清风，和着舒缓旋律，携一卷美文，品一杯香茗，坐在属于自己的空间，体验文字带给你的优美、睿智、灵动与流畅，感受时间从指缝间飘然而去，体味一种纯净、充实和有趣的生活，是何等美妙和惬意！

　　我们奉献给你的正是这样一种精神享受。她们像一只只神奇灵动的手拨动着你的心弦，使你如沐春风、如逢甘霖。她们就像鲜花一样芬芳，月色一样柔和，微风一样清新，春雨一样滋润。

　　朋友，请走进我们营造的精神家园，这里有你的青春，有你的记忆，有你的梦想,还有你的爱情和希望。让我们在此相会,让我们的人生得到心灵的滋润,提升人生的品位。

本书由焦作大学青闰主编、翻译和统稿,焦作大学外语学院张连亮副主编并参与部分翻译。

目 录

第一卷　悟人生的真谛

Life Is an Opportunity / 人生是一次机遇 ·········· 2
The Three Boxes of Life / 人生的三只箱子 ·········· 2
The Orientation of Life / 人生的定位 ·········· 4
The Philosophy of a Mirror / 一面镜子的人生哲理 ·········· 5
The Art of How to Hold Life / 把握人生的艺术 ·········· 6
The Law of Life Grandma Taught Me / 奶奶教给我的人生准则 ·········· 7
The Best Time of My Life / 我一生中最好的时光 ·········· 9
The Inquiry of Life / 人生的疑问 ·········· 10
First Change Yourself / 改变从自己做起 ·········· 14
The Ebb and Flow of Life / 人生的涨落 ·········· 15
The Journey of Life Starts from the Set Goal / 人生之旅从选定目标开始 ·········· 17
Position Your Life / 定位你的人生 ·········· 19
Life Is a Symphony / 人生是一曲交响乐 ·········· 20
Sense Life / 感悟人生 ·········· 22
The Splashes of Life / 人生的波纹 ·········· 24
Do not Meddle / 莫管闲事 ·········· 25

The Fish I Didn't Catch / 那条我没钓到的鱼 ⋯⋯⋯⋯⋯⋯⋯⋯⋯ 31
Behind Time / 为时晚矣 ⋯⋯⋯⋯⋯⋯⋯⋯⋯⋯⋯⋯⋯⋯⋯⋯ 33
Control Your Temper / 请君制怒 ⋯⋯⋯⋯⋯⋯⋯⋯⋯⋯⋯⋯ 36
The Artist Surprised / 一鸣惊人的艺术家 ⋯⋯⋯⋯⋯⋯⋯⋯ 37

第二卷 人生的价值

You Have Only One Life / 你只有一次生命 ⋯⋯⋯⋯⋯⋯⋯ 48
A Promise of Flowers / 鲜花的承诺 ⋯⋯⋯⋯⋯⋯⋯⋯⋯⋯ 49
Life Is the Cookie / 生命就是小甜饼 ⋯⋯⋯⋯⋯⋯⋯⋯⋯⋯ 52
The Worth of Life / 生命的价值 ⋯⋯⋯⋯⋯⋯⋯⋯⋯⋯⋯⋯ 53
Life Is like a Piece of Cake / 生活就像一块蛋糕 ⋯⋯⋯⋯⋯ 55
The Only Attitude Is Gratitude / 感激是唯一的态度 ⋯⋯⋯ 55
The Meaning of Life / 人生的意义 ⋯⋯⋯⋯⋯⋯⋯⋯⋯⋯⋯ 57
Human Beings Have Choices / 人生可以选择 ⋯⋯⋯⋯⋯⋯ 58
The Boys and the Sticks / 男孩与木棍 ⋯⋯⋯⋯⋯⋯⋯⋯⋯ 59
The Mahogany Piano / 一架桃花心木钢琴 ⋯⋯⋯⋯⋯⋯⋯ 60
The Boy and the Nail / 男孩和钉子 ⋯⋯⋯⋯⋯⋯⋯⋯⋯⋯ 64
The Next Step to Life / 人生的第二步 ⋯⋯⋯⋯⋯⋯⋯⋯⋯ 64
Schemes of Life often Illusory / 人生的规划 ⋯⋯⋯⋯⋯⋯ 68

第三卷 大自然的爱

Feathers in the Wind / 风中的羽毛 ⋯⋯⋯⋯⋯⋯⋯⋯⋯⋯ 74
When the Wind Blows / 当起风时 ⋯⋯⋯⋯⋯⋯⋯⋯⋯⋯⋯ 76
Talking with a Flower / 与花儿私语 ⋯⋯⋯⋯⋯⋯⋯⋯⋯⋯ 78
A Maple / 一棵枫树 ⋯⋯⋯⋯⋯⋯⋯⋯⋯⋯⋯⋯⋯⋯⋯⋯⋯ 80
The Catch of Lifetime / 一生的收获 ⋯⋯⋯⋯⋯⋯⋯⋯⋯⋯ 82
The Roses and Thorns / 玫瑰与荆棘 ⋯⋯⋯⋯⋯⋯⋯⋯⋯⋯ 83
When the Moon Follows Me / 月随人走 ⋯⋯⋯⋯⋯⋯⋯⋯ 84
A Big Tree and a Young Tree / 大树和小树 ⋯⋯⋯⋯⋯⋯ 87
A Young Apple Tree / 一棵小苹果树 ⋯⋯⋯⋯⋯⋯⋯⋯⋯ 87
The Power of a Bee / 一只蜜蜂的威力 ⋯⋯⋯⋯⋯⋯⋯⋯⋯ 88

The Boy and the Walnuts / 男孩与核桃 …………………… 91
First Snow / 第一场雪 …………………………………… 91
The Revelation of Lilacs / 紫丁香的启示 ………………… 94
Mahogany / 桃花心木 …………………………………… 96
A Picture of Human Life / 人生风景画 …………………… 97

第四卷　人生的恩惠

A Lesson for Living / 人生的教训 ……………………… 104
The Sculpture of Life / 人生的雕塑 …………………… 105
Don't Quit / 不要停 …………………………………… 106
Enjoy What You Have / 享受自己所有 ………………… 107
A Wonderful Present / 神奇的礼物 …………………… 108
The Grace of Life / 人生的恩惠 ……………………… 112
The Tiger's Whisker of Life / 人生的虎须 ……………… 113
One-dollar Tip / 一美元小费 …………………………… 117
Are You a Carrot, an Egg or Coffee Beans / 你是胡萝卜、鸡蛋还是咖啡豆 119
What Is the Best in Life / 人生最美好的是什么 ………… 120
Mary's Smile / 玛丽的微笑 …………………………… 123
It Is As You Will / 你来决定 …………………………… 124
Love of a Lifetime / 一生的爱 ………………………… 125
What Will Matter in Life / 人生重要的是什么 ………… 126
The Teacher and Sick Scholar / 老师和生病的学生 …… 127

第五卷　母亲的爱

Mother's Hands / 母亲的手 …………………………… 136
A Rose for Her Mother / 送给母亲的玫瑰 ……………… 137
A Daughter's Love for Her Mother / 母女情怀 ………… 139
Mom Charged Zero Dollar / 妈妈只收零美元 ………… 141
Prayer for My Mother / 为母亲祈祷 …………………… 143
You Thanked Mother / 报答母亲 ……………………… 143
Mother's Strength / 母亲的力量 ……………………… 147

For the Love of Mother / 献给母亲的爱 ········· 148
Mother Love in the Dress / 连衣裙里的母爱 ········· 150
Mum Who Wrote Family Letters / 爱写家书的妈妈 ········· 152
A Mother's Letter to the World / 一位母亲写给世界的信 ········· 156
Mother's Final Gift / 母亲最后的礼物 ········· 157
Singing with Mom / 与妈妈同唱 ········· 161
A Boy with a Mission / 男孩的使命 ········· 163
The Voice of Love / 爱的声音 ········· 168
Love Is a Thread / 爱是一根线 ········· 170
Squeeze My Hand / 握住我的手 ········· 172
My Mother's Grave / 母亲的坟墓 ········· 174

第六卷　永远的父爱

Love in Bloom / 爱在盛开 ········· 180
A Dance with Dad / 与爸爸共舞 ········· 182
A Violin / 一把小提琴 ········· 185
A Box of Kisses / 一盒子吻 ········· 191
Lesson From a Penguin / 爱心企鹅 ········· 192
Dad's Kiss / 爸爸的吻 ········· 194
My Father's Crocus / 父亲的藏红花 ········· 196
The Confession from a Father / 一位父亲的忏悔 ········· 199
Penance after 50 Years / 50年后的忏悔 ········· 202
Love Is a Two-Way Street / 爱是一条双行道 ········· 207
I Hear the Love / 我听到了爱 ········· 208
Homework of Love / 爱的作业 ········· 209
Daddy's Advice / 爸爸的忠告 ········· 210
My Father's Music / 父亲的音乐 ········· 212
The Unlighted Candle / 点不亮的蜡烛 ········· 216

第七卷　相信爱就会有奇迹

Love Is Understanding / 爱就是谅解 ········· 220

Roses for Paradise / 天堂玫瑰 …… 221
The Unopened CD / 没有打开的CD …… 223
A Gift of Light / 光明的礼物 …… 225
Love Is a Telephone / 爱情是一部电话 …… 228
The Red Rose and the White Rose / 红玫瑰与白玫瑰 …… 230
At the Small Café / 相约小咖啡馆 …… 233
I'm Going with You / 跟你一起走 …… 236
Salty Coffee / 咸咖啡 …… 238
Words from the Heart / 爱，就要说出来 …… 240
The Shared Love / 同心爱 …… 242
See How Much I Love You / 知道我有多么爱你 …… 243
The Wings of Love / 爱的翅膀 …… 246
100/0 Love / 100比0的爱 …… 250
The Essence of Love / 爱的真谛 …… 252
A Letter to Sophie / 写给索菲的信 …… 253
The Sign Language of Love / 爱的手语 …… 254
Written in the Stars / 命中吉星 …… 256

第八卷　只要心中有爱

The Remembrance of Lilacs / 紫丁香的回忆 …… 262
The Envelope on Christmas Morning / 圣诞节早晨的信封 …… 265
The Heart-Shaped Pillow / 心形枕头 …… 268
The Seed of Love / 爱的种子 …… 270
Tomorrow Shining Ahead / 明天就在眼前 …… 273
Christmas Present / 圣诞礼物 …… 277
Don't Wait Till the Flowers Wilt / 莫等到花儿都谢了 …… 278
I Love the Blue Flowers / 我 爱 蓝 花 …… 280
Grandma's Love Letters / 外婆的情书 …… 281
The Sweet Memory / 甜蜜的回忆 …… 284
A Letter to Grandpa / 写给爷爷的信 …… 286
Tommy's Essay / 汤米的随笔 …… 288
The Love of a Full Moon / 满月情 …… 290

Love Notes / 爱的纸条 …………………………………………… 293
Love Is Not a Single Act / 爱不是一场独角戏 ………………… 295
Greet This Day with Love / 用爱迎接今天 ……………………… 297
The Old Man with Flowers / 手持鲜花的老人 ………………… 299
The Chain of Love / 爱的链条 …………………………………… 301
Saving Happiness / 储存幸福 …………………………………… 304
As Long As You Have Love in Your Heart / 只要心中有爱 …… 306
Make the Love Grow in the Heart / 让爱在心中成长 ………… 308
Bobby's Gift / 博比的礼物 ……………………………………… 309
What Is Love / 爱是什么 ………………………………………… 312
The Wallet of Love / 爱的钱包 ………………………………… 314
Rudy's Angel / 鲁迪的天使 ……………………………………… 319
"I Pity Them" / "我同情他们" ………………………………… 321
An Old-fashioned Girl / 守旧的女孩 …………………………… 323
The Tea Rose / 茶玫 ……………………………………………… 327
The Machinist's Return / 机械工回家 ………………………… 332
The Best Kind of Revenge / 最好的报复 ……………………… 336

第一卷

悟人生的真谛

Life Is an Opportunity

Life is an opportunity. A chance to influence someone else's life by your daily example.

I have experienced loss, gain, hope and sorrow. My experiences have made me into the person I am today. Yes, I could wallow in the despair that comes with the loss of a loved one or the failure of a venture, but why choose sorrow when you can choose joy?

When my dear friend and mentor Debbie passed away, my family and I took it very hard. She was a wonderful person, an inspiration to everyone she met. I was devastated when I found out that she had cancer. I prayed, cried, and was very angry for a long time. She should not deserve this! When I went to visit her she looked pale. I did everything I could to hold back my tears. There before me was a beautiful and handsome woman who did so much for so many, as a teacher and a friend. She was obviously in a great deal of pain, but she smiled. I'll never forget it. In her weakness she reached out to me. She chose to have a good outlook on her life.

She chose to be strong. She chose to live, and so do I.

人生是一次机遇

人生是一次机遇。是一次用你的日常典范去影响他人生活的机会。

我曾经历过失败、收获、希望和悲伤。我这些经历使我成了今天这样的人。是的，我可以沉迷在痛失我爱的绝望中或沉迷在冒险的失败中，但在你可以选择快乐时，为什么要去选择悲伤？

我的良师益友黛比去世时，我和家人都很难接受。黛比是一个了不起的人，她鼓舞着每一个遇到的人。发现她患癌症时，我不知所措。我祈祷过，哭泣过，而且愤怒了很长时间。她不该得到这种结局！我去看望她时，她面无血色，我竭尽全力忍住眼泪。我面前的是一位美丽大方的女人，她既是老师又是朋友，为这么多人做了这么多事。显然她剧痛难忍，但她面带微笑。这情景我永远难忘。她虚弱地向我伸出手。她选择快乐地面对生活。

她选择坚强。她选择活下去，我也要这样。

The Three Boxes of Life

A rich man lives in his enormous villa, enjoying the extremely luxurious life. Every day there are some strangers who take away a couple of boxes from his home. The rich man decided to follow them and came to a mysterious valley. Seeing they were about to throw the three boxes in the abyss, he demanded with surprise, "Please tell me what's in boxes."

The strangers answered indifferently, "They are the feelings that you have abandoned."

"No, it's impossible!" The rich man disbelieved them and opened them.

In the first box there was his beloved one walking alone slowly along the beach at night.

His close friend was in the second box. After bankruptcy, his friend was longing for help and consolation from him.

His parents were seen in the third box. They have prepared a table of delicious food for dinner, waiting for him to reunion.

Seeing them, he felt that his heart was lashed by a burning whip full of misery and guilt. He begged the strangers, "Please give them back to me. I have a lot of money. You can take as much as you want!"

However, the strangers told him with a serious look, "It's too late to take them back. The woman you loved never showed up again at charming night; your friend, having endured the long daytime, finally made out the stars with different distance; your parent bought a dog and found love and warmness from it."

After finishing their words, they threw the three boxes down to the abyss and disappeared.

With a lonely look, the rich man stood there still, gazing at the hollow of the valley in front of him…

人生的三只箱子

富翁住在巨大的别墅里，享受着非常豪华的生活。

每天都有几个陌生人从他家里搬走几只箱子。富翁决定跟踪他们，随后来到了一个神秘的山谷。他看到这些人正准备把三只箱子扔进深渊，便吃惊地问道："请告诉我，这些箱子里装的是什么。"

陌生人冷冷地回答说："它们是你抛弃的那些感情。"

"不，这不可能！"富翁不相信他们的话，就打开了那三只箱子。

第一只箱子里装的是他心爱的人夜晚独自在海滩慢慢地走着。

第二只箱子里装的是他的密友。公司破产后，密友渴望富翁的帮助和安慰。

第三只箱子里装的是他的父母亲。他们做了一桌美餐等待他回家团聚。

看完后，他感到心像被火辣辣的鞭子抽打了一般，充满了痛苦和愧疚。

他哀求陌生人说:"请把它们还给我吧。我有的是钱,你们要多少都可以拿去!"

然而,陌生人一脸严肃地告诉他说:"太晚了,无法收回了。你爱的女人在迷人的夜晚再也没有出现。你的朋友熬过长长的白天后,终于看清了那些远近不一的星星。你的父母买了一条狗,从它身上找到了爱和温暖。"

说完,陌生人把三只箱子扔下了山谷,就消失了。

富翁神情孤独,站在那里一动不动,凝望着眼前空荡荡的山谷……

The Orientation of Life

In 1957, in an Arkansas primary school, there were two good friends: one was named Bill, the other John. Once, they lay basking on the lawn. After drinking a coke, John said to Bill as if he suddenly discovered the New World, "Originally, Roosevelt who led the Americans to win World War II was handicapped!"

"Yes, he is my idol!" Bill said. "His spirit of perseverance is worth studying for us."

"He is my idol, too!" John said. "I think the most important point of his success is his adversity!"

Later, John stubbornly amputated his legs because he wanted to create the same adversity for himself as Roosevelt and became a great man like Roosevelt. However, he did not become the President of the United States, but only won a medal in the Games for the Disabled.

Bill learned Roosevelt's industrious character and indomitable spirit. Finally, he became master of the White House. His name was Bill Clinton.

人生的定位

1957年,在美国阿肯色州一所小学里有一对好朋友,一个叫比尔,一个叫约翰。一次,两人躺在草坪上晒太阳。约翰喝了一口可乐后,突然像发现新大陆似的对比尔说:"原来带领美国人赢得二战胜利的罗斯福是一个残疾人呀!"

"是的,他是我的偶像!"比尔说,"他做事执着的精神值得我们学习。"

"他也是我的偶像!"约翰说,"我认为他成功的最重要一点是他的不幸!"

后来,约翰固执地锯掉了双腿,因为他想给自己创造一个和罗斯福一样的逆境，成为像罗斯福一样的伟人。不过，他并没有成为总统，只是在一届残疾人运动会上拿到了一枚奖牌。

比尔则学习罗斯福刻苦勤奋的品格和不屈不挠的精神。最后，他成了美国白宫的主人。他的名字叫比尔·克林顿。

The Philosophy of a Mirror

"Dr. Papaderos, what is the meaning of life?" I asked.

Papaderos looked at me for a long time, and taking his wallet out of his hip pocket, he fished into a leather billfold and brought out a very small round mirror, about the size of a quarter.

And what he said went like this, "When I was a small child, during the war, we were very poor living in a remote village. One day, on the road, I found the broken pieces of a mirror. A German motorcycle had been wrecked in that place.

"I tried to find all the pieces and put them together, but it was not possible, so I kept only the largest piece. By polishing it on a stone, I made it round. I began to play with it as a toy and became fascinated by the fact that I could reflect light into dark places where the sun would never shine—in deep holes and crevices and dark closets. It became a game for me to get light into the most inaccessible places I could find.

"As I became a man, I grew to understand that this was not just a child's game but a metaphor for what I might do with my life. I came to understand that I am not the light or the source of light. But light—truth, understanding, knowledge—is there, and it will shine in many dark places as long as I reflect it.

"I am a fragment of a mirror whose whole design and shape I do not know. Nevertheless, with what I have I can reflect light into the dark places of this world—into the black places in the hearts of men—and change some things in some people. Perhaps others may see and do likewise. This is what I am about. This is the meaning of life."

一面镜子的人生哲理

"帕帕德罗斯博士，人生的意义是什么？"我问。

帕帕德罗斯看了我好一阵子，然后从裤子后面的口袋里掏出一只皮夹，拿出了一块非常小的圆镜，大概有25分硬币大小。

随后，他这样说道："战争期间，我还很小的时候，我们很穷，住在一个偏僻的村里。有一天，我在路上发现了一块镜子的那些碎片，是一辆德国摩托车在那个地方发生了事故。

"我设法找到所有的碎片,把它们拼在一起,但那不可能做到,所以我只保留了最大的那块碎片。我在一块石头上打磨,使它变圆。我开始把它当玩具玩,渐渐着迷,发现自己可以用它把光线反射到太阳永远照不到的暗处:深洞、裂缝和黑暗的壁橱。这渐渐成了我的一种游戏,把光线照到我能找到的那些最难接近的地方。

"随着我渐渐长大,我慢慢明白了这不只是一个孩子的游戏,而且对我的人生是一种象征。我最终明白自己既不是光,也不是光源,但真理、理解和知识这些光就在那里,只要我反射,它就会照亮许多黑暗的地方。

"我是镜子的一块碎片,我并不知道整个镜子的图案和形状。不过,我尽力把光照射到世界上那些黑暗的地方,照射到人们心灵的黑暗处,让一些人有所改变。说不定其他人看到,也会这样做。这就是我的看法,这就是人生的意义。"

The Art of How to Hold Life

The art of life is to know when to hold fast and when to let go. For life is paradox: it gives us many gifts, but eventually it will take them back. Someone said in this way, "A man comes to this world with his fists clenched, but when he dies, his hands are open."

Surely we ought to hold fast to life, for it is wondrous. We know that this is so, but all too often we recognize this truth only in our backward glance and then suddenly realize that it is no more.

A recent experience re-taught me this truth. Due to a severe heart attack I was hospitalized for several days.

One morning I had to have some additional tests, so I had to be wheeled across the courtyard. As we emerged from our ward, the sunlight hit me. I looked to see whether anyone else relished the sun's golden glow, but everyone was hurrying to and fro, most with eyes fixed on the ground. Then I remembered how often I, too, had been indifferent to the grandeur of each day.

So we should be reverent before each dawning day. Embrace each hour. Seize each minute.

Hold fast to life, but not so fast that you cannot let go. This is the second side of life's coin, the opposite pole of its paradox: we must accept our losses, and learn how to let go.

At every stage of life we sustain losses and grow in the process.

把握人生的艺术

生活的艺术是知道何时抓紧、何时放手。因为生活自相矛盾：它赐给我们很多礼物，但最终会——收回。有人这样说道："人紧握拳头来到世间，离世时却两手张开。"

的确，我们应该紧紧抓住生活，因为生活非常精彩。尽管我们知道如此，但我们常常是在回首的那一刻才认识到这个真理，随后突然明白一切都不复存在。

最近的一次经历又教给了我这个真理。由于严重心脏病，我住院治疗了好几天。

一天早上，我必须做一些额外的体检，所以必须坐轮椅穿过院子。我们刚一出病房，阳光就照在了我身上。我看了看周围，看其他人是不是也喜欢太阳的金色光芒，但每个人都来去匆匆，大部分人眼睛盯着地面。随后，我想起了自己平时对每天的壮观景象也是无动于衷。

所以，我们要虔诚地对待每个黎明，拥抱每个小时，抓住每一分钟。

紧紧抓住生命，但不能抓得太紧而无法放手。这就是生活的另一面，也是生活矛盾体的另一面：我们必须接受失去、学会放手。

在生命的每个阶段，我们既忍受失去，又在这个过程中成长。

The Law of Life Grandma Taught Me

Two years ago my grandma left this earth. It wasn't until she died that I truly recognized how much she meant to me. She was my friend, my teacher and my inspiration. She taught me things that became my own personal laws of life, which have helped me get through each day with a smile, have made me aware of my strong points as well as my weaknesses, and helped me overcome those weaknesses. They are true lessons to live by, and I hope I will never forget them.

As we each let our own light shine, through our talents and ideas, we unconsciously give others permission to do the same. Just think about what our world could be like if each and every one of us let our own light shine through. I think it would be a better place.

One lesson my grandma taught me was to always go for my dreams and never give up. She once told me, "Shoot for the moon because even if you fall, you'll land among the stars."

I have never heard anything truer in all my life. I have tried to live by these words, and have figured out that it is very important to go for your dreams and never let anything get in your way. Even if you have had a bitter experience in the past, never limit your view of life by that experience. I believe that life is constantly testing our commitment, and I am convinced life's greatest rewards are reserved for those who show a never-ending commitment to act until they achieve. This kind of determination can accomplish miracles, but it must be continual and consistent. Simple as this may sound, it is still the common denominator separating those who live their dreams from those that live in regret.

Another great lesson my grandma taught me was, "Never let anyone come to you without coming away better and happier." Everyone should see goodness in your face, in your eyes, in your smile. Too often we underestimate the power of such things: a touch, a smile, a kind word, a listening ear, an honest compliment, or even the smallest act of caring. All have the potential to turn a life around.

My grandma is no longer present here on earth, but she will always remain present in my heart. Her words and personality have affected my life. Her lessons on life have become a part of me, and have made me a better person. I will never forget the great love my grandma shared with everyone. She is my idol. My grandma's laws of life will live in me forever.

奶奶教给我的人生准则

两年前，奶奶离开了这个世界。她去世后，我才真正认识到，她对我有多么重要。她是我的朋友、我的老师和我的灵感。她教给我的东西渐渐成了我个人生活的准则。这些准则帮助我微笑度过每一天，使我认识到自己的优点与缺点，并帮助我克服那些弱点。它们是我赖以为生的真正训诫，我希望自己永远不要忘记它们。

当我们各自通过自己的才能和思想让自己发光时，我们无意中就同意别人也这样做。试想一下，如果每个人都让自己的光照亮别人，我们的世界会是什么景象。我想那会是一个更加美好的地方。

奶奶教给我的一个训诫是，要永远追逐自己的梦想、绝不放弃。她曾告诉我说："争取摘到月亮，因为即使你坠落，也会落在群星间。"

我一生从来没有听过比这更真实的事情。我努力按照这些话去生活，而且明白这对追逐梦想非常重要，永远不要让任何事情阻挡你的道路。即使过去曾有过惨痛经历，也永远不要让那种经历限制自己的人生观。我相信，生活总在考验我们的责任感，而且我确信，生活最大的奖赏就是为那些不懈奋斗，直至成功的人而准备。这种决心可以成就奇迹，但必须始终如一。尽管这听起来可能简单，但仍是区分追逐梦想者和懊悔过去者的共同点。

奶奶教给我的又一大训诫是："离开时不能给人留下更幸福、更美好的印象，千万不要让任何人到你身边来。"每个人都应该从你的脸上、你的眼里和你的微笑中看到善意。我们常常会低估一次抚摸、一个微笑、一句善言、一只倾听的耳朵、一声真诚的赞美甚或最小的一个关爱之举这些东西的力量。所有这些都有转变人生的可能。

尽管奶奶已不在人世，但她会永远活在我的心里。她的话语和人格魅力已经影响了我的人生。她对人生的训诫已经成为我的一部分，使我更加出色。我永远不会忘记奶奶和每个人分享的大爱。她是我的偶像，奶奶的人生准则将永远活在我的心里。

The Best Time of My Life

It was June 15, and in two days I would be turning thirty. I was insecure about entering a new decade of my life and feared that my best years were now behind me.

My daily routine included going to the gym for a workout before going to work. Every morning I would see my friend Nicholas at the gym. He was seventy-nine years old and in terrific shape. As I greeted Nicholas on this particular day, he noticed I wasn't full of my usual vitality and asked if there was anything wrong. I told him I was feeling anxious about turning thirty. I wondered how I would look back on my life once I reached Nicholas's age, so I asked him, "What was the best time of your life?"

Without hesitation, Nicholas replied, "Well, Joe, this is my philosophical answer to your philosophical question.

"When I was a child in Austria and everything was taken care of for me and I was nurtured by my parents, that was the best time of my life.

"When I was going to school and learning the things I know today, that was the best time of my life.

"When I got my first job and had responsibilities and got paid for my efforts, that was the best time of my life.

"When I met my wife and fell in love, that was the best time of my life.

"The Second World War came, my wife and I had to flee Austria to save our lives. When we were together and safe on a ship bound for North America, it was the best time of my life.

"When we came to Canada and started a family, that was the best time of my life.

"When I was a young father, watching my children grow up, that was the best time of my life.

"And now, Joe, I am seventy-nine years old. I have my health, I feel good and I am in love with my wife just as I was when we first met. This is the best time of my life."

我一生中最好的时光

那天是6月15日,再过两天我就要30岁了。我对要进入生命中又一个新的10年没有把握,害怕自己最好的时光现在就会远去。

我每天上班前都要去体育馆锻炼一会儿。每天早上,我都会在体育馆见到我的朋友尼古拉斯。他79岁了,身材特棒。那天我跟他打招呼时,他注意到我不像往常那样充满活力,便问我是不是有什么不舒服。我对他说我对自己快要30岁感到担忧。我不知道自己到了尼古拉斯的岁数会怎么回顾一生,就问他:"你一生中最好的时光是什么时候?"

尼古拉斯毫不犹豫地回答说:"噢,乔,这是我对你的哲理问题做出的哲理回答。

"小时候我在奥地利时,一切都被照顾得很好,我被父母抚养成人,那是我一生中最好的时光。

"我上学时学会了我现在熟悉的那些事情,那是我一生中最好的时光。

"我找到第一份工作,承担职责并因努力而拿到报酬时,那是我一生中最好的时光。

"当我遇到妻子并坠入爱河时,那是我一生中最好的时光。

"二次大战来临,我和妻子为了活命,不得不逃离奥地利。当我们一起平安坐上驶向北美洲的一艘轮船时,那是我一生中最好的时光。

"当我们来到加拿大建立家庭时,那是一生中最好的时光。

"当我成了一位年轻的父亲,看着自己的孩子长大时,那是我一生中最好的时光。

"而现在,乔,我都79岁了。我身体健康,感觉良好,和我们初次相遇时一样爱我的妻子。这是我一生中最好的时光。"

The Inquiry of Life

During my junior year in high school, Mr. Reynolds, my English teacher, handed each student a list of thoughts or statements written by other students, then gave us a creative writing assignment based on one of those thoughts.

At 17, I was beginning to wonder about many things, so I chose the statement, "I wonder why things are the way they are?" That night, I wrote down in the form of a story all the questions that puzzled me about life. I realized that many of them were hard to answer, and perhaps others could not be answered at all.

When I turned in my paper, I was afraid that I might fail the assignment because I had not answered the question, "I wonder why things are the way they are?" I had no answers. I had only written questions.

The next day Mr. Reynolds called me to the front of the class and asked me to read my story for the other students. He handed me my paper and sat down in the back of the room. The class became quiet as I began to read my story:

Mommy, Daddy…Why?

Mommy, why are the roses red?
Mommy, why is the grass green and the sky blue?
Why does a spider have a web and not a house?
Daddy, why can't I play in your toolbox?
Teacher, why do I have to read?
Mother, why can't I wear lipstick to the dance?
Daddy, why can't I stay out until 12 : 00? The other kids can.
Mother, why do you hate me?
Daddy, why don't the boys like me?
Why do I have to be so skinny?
Why do I have braces and wear glasses?
Why do I have to be 16?
Mom, why do I have to graduate?
Dad, why do I have to grow up?
Mom, Dad, why do I have to leave?
Mom, why don't you write more often?
Dad, why do I miss my old friends?
Dad, why do you love me so much?
Dad, why do you spoil me?
Your little girl is growing up.
Mom, why don't you visit me?
Mom, why is it hard to make new friends?
Dad, why do I miss being at home?
Dad, why does my heart skip a beat when he looks in my eyes?
Mom, why do my legs tremble when I hear his voice?
Mother, why is being "in love" the greatest feeling in the world?
Daddy, why don't you like to be called "Gramps"?
Mother, why do my baby's tiny fingers cling so tightly to mine?

Mother, why do they have to grow up?
Daddy, why do they have to leave?
Why do I have to be called "Grannie"?
Mommy, Daddy, why did you leave me? I need you.
Why did my youth slip past me?
Why does my face show every smile that I have ever given to a friend or a stranger?
Why does my hair glisten shiny silver?
Why do my hands quiver when I bend to pick a flower?
Why are the roses red?

At the conclusion of my story, my eyes locked with Mr. Reynolds' eyes, and I saw a tear slowly sliding down his cheek. It was then that I realized that life is not always based on the answers we receive, but also on the questions that we ask.

人生的疑问

我上初中时,英语老师雷诺先生给每位同学发了一个其他同学写的各种想法或说法的清单。随后,他要我们据此写一篇有创意的作文。

17岁的我对很多事都想知道,所以就选了"我想知道为什么事情是这样?"这个题目。那天晚上,我以故事形式写下了我对人生的所有困惑。我知道很多问题很难回答,也许有些问题根本无法回答。

交过作文后,我担心作业可能过不了关,因为我没有回答"我想知道为什么事情是这样?"这个问题。我找不到答案,只写出了问题。

第二天,雷诺先生让我到堂前,让我把自己的作文念给其他同学听。他把我的作业递给我,在教室后面坐下来。我开始念自己的故事时,全班鸦雀无声:

妈妈、爸爸……为什么?

妈妈,为什么玫瑰是红的?
妈妈,为什么草是绿的、天是蓝的?
为什么蜘蛛有网、没有房?
爸爸,为什么我不能在你的工具箱里玩耍?
老师,为什么我得读书?
妈妈,为什么我不能抹口红参加舞会?
爸爸,为什么我不能在外面待到12点?别的小孩都可以。
妈妈,为什么你讨厌我?

爸爸，为什么男生不喜欢我？
为什么我得那样骨感？
为什么我要系背带、戴眼镜？
为什么我得过16岁？
妈，为什么我得毕业？
爸，为什么我得长大？
妈，爸，为什么我得离开家？
妈，为什么您不常写信来？
爸，为什么我想老朋友？
爸，为什么您这样爱我？
爸，为什么您这样宠我？
您的小女儿渐渐长大。
妈，为什么您不来看我？
妈，为什么交新朋友这样难？
爸，为什么我想在家的日子？
爸，为什么每次他看着我的眼睛时我就怦然心动？
妈，为什么听到他的声音我就双腿打战？
妈妈，为什么"堕入爱河"是世界上最美妙的感觉？
爸爸，为什么您不喜欢有人叫您"外公"？
妈妈，为什么我宝宝的小手指那样紧地抓住我的手？
妈妈，为什么他们得长大？
爸爸，为什么他们得离开家？
为什么要有人叫我"奶奶"？
妈妈、爸爸，为什么你们要离我而去？我需要你们呀！
为什么我的青春悄悄从我的身边溜走？
为什么我要对朋友和陌生人面带微笑？
为什么我的头发银光闪闪？
为什么我弯腰摘花时双手颤抖？
为什么玫瑰是红的？

我念完故事，望着雷诺先生，雷诺先生也望着我。我看到一颗泪珠正慢慢地滑过他的脸颊。就在那时，我意识到，生活并不总是以我们得到的答案为基础，而且也以我们提出的问题为基础。

First Change Yourself

A man hired a taxi outside the airfield. The cab had a woolen carpet with brilliant laces. On the grass partition that shielded the driver's seat was a replica of a famous painting. Its windows were all clean.

The passenger was surprised very much and said to the driver, "I've never seen a nicer cab."

"Thank you for your praise," the driver answered smilingly.

"How did it occur to you to decorate your car?" asked the passenger.

"The car isn't mine," said the driver. "It belongs to the company. I used to be a cleaner of cabs. When they returned, all of them were as dirty as garbage cans with cigarette butts and rubbish scattered here and there. On the seats and doorhandles could be found something sticky like peanut sauce or chewing gum. Why so? I thought if the car itself were very clean, the passengers would mostly likely be considerate and refrain from littering.

"So when I got a license to be a taxi-driver, I began to put my idea into practice-to tidy and decorate the car. Now before a new passenger gets on my car, I'd make a check and be sure it is in good order. When my car returns after a day's work, it always remains spotless."

When doing a thing, one makes efforts and wants to see the result. To change others, one has to make twice the effort but get half the result. To change oneself is the other way round. One had better ask oneself why one makes demands on others much more than on oneself. If you take enough care to do as best you can for other people's sake, your efforts will yield results. If you look into the inner world of your own, examine yourself and wipe out the dust and dirt, instead of fixing your eyes on other people, you will find a cheerful mood for yourself and create a pleasant environment for others.

改变从自己做起

一个人在机场租了一辆出租车。出租车铺着绣有鲜艳花边的羊毛地毯，保护司机座的玻璃隔板上是一幅名画的复制品，车窗都非常干净。

乘客非常惊讶，对司机说："我从未见过这样漂亮的出租车。"

"谢谢你的赞扬。"司机笑着回答说。

"你为什么要装饰你的车呢？"乘客问道。

"车不是我的，"他说，"车是公司的。我以前是出租公司的清洁工。

每当出租车回来时，都像垃圾桶一样脏，地板上到处都是烟蒂和垃圾，座位上或车门把手上还有花生酱、口香糖之类的粘东西。为什么会这样？我当时想，如果车本身很干净，乘客们十有八九都会体谅我们，不乱扔东西。

"所以，我取得出租车驾驶执照后，就开始把自己的想法付诸行动——收拾并装饰车子。现在每位乘客上车前，我都要检查，确保车子井然有序。经过一天工作，我的车子回公司时仍然一尘不染。"

有人做一件事付出努力，就想看到结果。改变别人是事倍功半，改变自己则事半功倍。一个人最好扪心自问，为什么要求别人的多，要求自己的少。如果你尽最大可能去关心别人的利益，你的努力就会产生效果。如果你审视自己的内心世界，检查自我，打扫干净其中的尘埃，而不是眼睛盯着别人，你会发现，在自己愉快的同时，也为别人创造了舒适的环境。

The Ebb and Flow of Life

During my first year in Japan I took a hitchhiking trip and went to numerous fishing villages on the west coast of Japan.

In one village I had the privilege of meeting a very special man. He was in his sixties and walked with a noticeable limp. He told me that as a youth he was very involved in karate, but at the age of twenty-five he was injured while working on his father's fishing boat, and he had been limping ever since.

We sat out on a small wooden dock one night as he told me about his life. He said once he realized he would no longer be able to actively take part in karate, he made up his mind to use his life as a fisherman to further his martial arts studies. He read various martial arts books and then applied what he read to his work life.

"One of the most important things I have learned," he said. "is to create a rhythm with your presence, movements, and breathing, which matches the rhythm of nature. This is a phrase numerous martial arts masters wrote about in the books I have read."

As we sat by the water, he asked me to notice the ebb and flow of the ocean and the sounds of the tide lapping against the pillings of the pier. "As you notice your movements and breathing, you can sense the movement and sounds of the ocean, and realize how you go with the rhythm of this flow."

I began to do as he suggested, and I quickly felt I was being drawn into a parallel world, that I was somehow usually ignoring, or simply not noticing.

"Feel the life force of the ocean," he said. "And breathe with the ocean. Feel the life force of the ocean, and without doing anything, allow yourself to move with the ocean…Breathe, move, and feel your heartbeat…Invite your heartbeat to synchronize with the heartbeat of the ocean."

Now you are becoming one with the water, and the fluid inside your body begins to become a tiny powerful ocean that ebbs and flows throughout your system.

Now, like the ocean, you can begin to feel the power of flowing without resisting. Flowing without fighting against.

The water surrounds and moves past all obstacles. There is no forcing, and no need for strength. Only flow…The power is in the flow, and each drop of water is pliant and soft. No one drop of water is powerful on its own.

We sat there together for a while. The man, myself, and the ocean. I felt the power and presence of the ocean, myself, and the fisherman. Not separate, but together. And I knew very clearly that all this power was really one.

The one tiny drop of water that you are.

The ebb and flow of your life mirrors the ebb and flow of all life. When you calm yourself, slow down, and become one with your surroundings, you realize that nature offers you a parallel understanding of life. The tiny drop of water known as "me" is an integral part of the ocean of life, and your power manifests most gracefully when you join your individual spirit with the spirit of all creation.

Breathe deeply, calm yourself, and begin to notice and appreciate the ebb and flow of the world around you…You will discover the power of the universe is the power that nurtures your life.

人生的涨落

在日本的第一年，我搭便车旅行，到过日本西海岸的无数渔村。

我在一个村里有幸遇到了一个非常特别的人。他年过花甲，走路明显一瘸一拐。他告诉我说，他年轻时热衷空手道，但他25岁时在父亲的渔船上干活时受伤，从那以后就一直一瘸一拐。

一天夜里，我们坐在外面的一个木制小码头上，他对我说起了自己的人生。他说，一旦意识到自己再也不能积极参加空手道，他就下定决心这辈子做个渔民，进一步研究武术。他阅读了各种武术书籍，然后把看到的知识运用到了工作生活中去。

"我学到的最重要的一件东西，"他说，"就是创造一种与自然韵律协调一致的自身、运动和呼吸的节奏。这是我看过的书里许多武术大师都写道的一个用语。"

我们坐在水边，他让我注意大海的涨落和潮水拍打码头木桩的声音。

"就像你注意自己的运动和呼吸一样，你可以感受到大海的运动和声音，然后领悟到你怎样和这流水的节奏保持一致。"

我开始像他建议的那样去做，很快就感到自己正被引入一个常常忽视或根本没有注意过的相似世界。

"感受大海的生命力，"他说，"和大海一起呼吸。感受大海的生命力，什么也不做，让自己和大海一起运动……呼吸，运动，感受自己的心跳……让自己的心跳和大海的心跳保持同步。"

现在你渐渐和海水融为一体，体内的液体开始变成在你全身涨落、威力无穷的小小海洋。

现在，像大海一样，你能渐渐感受到没有阻挡的流动力量，没有对抗的流动力量。

海水包围并流过了一切障碍。没有强迫，无须用力。只是流动……力量就在流动中，每一滴水都顺从温柔。哪一滴水本身都不强大。

我们一起坐了一会儿。老人、我自己和大海。我感受到了大海、我自己和渔民的力量与存在。不是各自孤立，而是合为一体。而且我非常清楚所有这力量其实都是一体的。

你就是那小小的一滴水。

你的生命涨落反映了所有生命的涨落。当你平静下来，放慢速度，与周围环境融为一体时，就会认识到大自然为你提供了对生命的相似理解。被称为"我"的小小水滴是生命海洋的一个完整部分。当你自己的精神和天地万物的精神合在一起时，你的力量才会最优美地呈现出来。

深呼吸，保持平静，开始注意和欣赏你周围世界的涨落……你会发现宇宙的力量正是滋养你生命的力量。

The Journey of Life Starts from the Set Goal

Bissel is a small village of the West Sahara. It lies next to a patch of 1. 5-square-kilometer oasis, from where three days and nights are generally required to go out of the desert. However, before Ken Levin discovered it in 1926, none of the people had walked out of the desert. Reportedly, they were not reluctant to leave this barren land, but had no way to walk out of it after they had tried many times.

As an academician of the British Royal College of Sciences, Ken Levin, of course, did not believe this viewpoint. He asked the reason of the people here. As a result, the answer of each was the same: To whichever direction they went from here, they would eventually return to this place. To prove this parlance, he did an experiment. He went north from Bissel Village and finally walked out from it in three and a half days.

Why couldn't the Bissel villagers walk out of it? Ken Levin was very puzzled. In the end, he had to employ a Bissel villager to lead the way and wanted to find out the reason. They prepared the water that could be used for half a month and two camels while only leaning on a stick, Ken Levin put away the compass and other facilities, following the man.

Ten days later, they walked for about 800 miles. On the 11th morning, an oasis came into their view. They really came back again to Bissel. This time, Ken Levin came to understand: the Bissel people couldn't walk out of the desert because they had no knowledge of the North Star.

In the boundless desert, if a person goes forward relying on his or her sense, he or she will make lots and lots of circles of different sizes, and the final footprints will be most likely the shape of a tape. Bissel Village was in the middle of the immense desert with more than one thousand square kilometers, so without a compass, it was indeed impossible to walk out of the desert.

Leaving Bissel Village, Ken Levin brought a young man called Argutel, who was the man who had cooperated with him last time. He told the young man, "As long as you rest in the daytime and walk towards the brightest star at night, would be able to walk out of the desert." Argutel did as he was told. Three days later, he, sure enough, came to the edge of the desert.

Now in the West Sahara Bissel has been a bright pearl, where tens of thousands of tourists come here. As the pioneer of Bissel, Argutel's bronze statue stands in the center of the town. On the base of the bronze statue the following line were engraved, "A new life starts from the fixed direction."

人生之旅从选定目标开始

比塞尔是西撒哈拉沙漠中的一个小村庄，它靠在一片1.5平方公里的绿洲旁，从这里走出沙漠一般需要三个昼夜。可是，在肯·莱文1926年发现它之前，这里的人没有一个走出过大沙漠。据说，他们不是不愿意离开这块贫瘠的地方，而是尝试过很多次都没有走出来。

作为英国皇家学院的院士，肯·莱文当然不相信这种说法。他用手语向这里的人问其原因，结果每个人的回答都是一样的：从这里无论向哪个方向走，最后都还要转回到这个地方。为了证实这种说法，他做了一次试验。从比塞尔村向北走，结果三天半就走了出来。

比塞尔人为什么走不出来呢？肯·莱文非常纳闷。最后，他只得雇一个比塞尔人，让他带路，看看到底是怎么回事。他们准备了能用半个月的水，牵上两匹骆驼，肯·莱文收起指南针等设备，只挂了一根木棍，跟在后面。

十天过去了，他们走了大约800英里的路程，第11天早晨，一块绿洲出现在眼前，他们果然又回到了比塞尔。这一次肯·莱文终于明白了，比塞尔人之所以走不出大沙漠，是因为他们根本就不认识北极星。

在一望无际的沙漠里，一个人如果凭感觉往前走，会走出许许多多、大小不一的圆圈，最后的足迹十有八九是一把卷尺的形状，比塞尔村处在浩瀚的沙漠中间，方圆上千公里，没有指南针，想走出沙漠，确实是不可能的。

离开比塞尔村时，肯·莱文带了一个叫阿古特尔的青年，这个青年就是上次和他合作的人。他告诉这个青年说："只要你白天休息，夜晚朝着北面那颗最亮的星星走，就能走出沙漠。"阿古特尔照着去做，3天后果然来到了大漠边缘。

现在比塞尔已是西撒哈拉沙漠中的一颗明珠，每年有数以万计的旅游者来到这里。阿古特尔作为比塞尔的开拓者，他的铜像竖立在小城中央，铜像底座上刻着一行字："新生活从选定方向开始。"

Position Your Life

Everyone has two natures. One wants us to advance and the other wants to pulls us back. The one that we cultivate and concentrate on decides what we are at the end. Both natures are trying to gain control. The will alone decides the issue. A man by one supreme effort of the will may change his whole career and even create miracles. You may be that man if you will, for will can find a way or make one.

You alone can decide when the turning point will come. He is the director of his life if he wills to be. What we are to do is the result of our training. We can be completely controlled by our will power.

Habit is a matter of acquirement. You hear people say, "He comes by this or that naturally, a chip off the old block," meaning that he is only doing what his parents did. This is quite often the case, but there's no reason for it, for a person can break a habit just the moment he masters the "I will." A man may have been a "good-for-nothing" all his life up to this very minute, but from this time on he begins to amount to something. Even old men have suddenly changed and accomplished wonders.

"I lost my opportunity," says one. That may be true, but by sheer force of will, we can find a way to bring us another opportunity. There is no truth saying that opportunity knocks at our door but once in a lifetime. The fact is, opportunity never seeks us; we must seek it. What usually turns out to be one man's opportunity was another man's loss. In this day one man's brain is matched against another's. It is often the quickness of brain action that determines the result.

Many people read good books, but say they do not get much good out of them. They don't realize that the knowledge of books can awaken their potentials; to stimulate them to use their will power. A sage said, "You can lead him to the fountain, but you can't make him drink."

定位你的人生

每个人都有两种天性，一种想让我们前进，另一种想拉我们后退。我们创造并培养的那种天性决定我们最终会成为什么样的人。这两种天性都在设法得到控制权，只有意志决定这个问题。一个意志坚强、竭诚努力的人可以改变整个事业，甚至可以创造奇迹。只要你愿意，就可能成为那种人，因为意志能找到方法或创造方法。

只有你能决定转折点何时会来。只要愿意，他就可以成为生活的主人。我们要做什么，是看我们训练的结果，完全是由自己的意志力控制。

习惯是慢慢养成的一种东西。你常常听人们说："他生来就是这样，活像他的父母。"这意味着他父母亲做什么他也会做什么。事情常常就是这样，但绝不是原因，因为一个人只要把握"我一定会行"，就能打破一种习惯。一个人也许一直到此刻都一无是处，但从这一刻起，他会开始有所作为。就是老年人也会突然发生改变，创造奇迹。

有人常常说："我错失了良机。"那也许没错，但凭借绝对的毅力，我们可以找到给我们带来另一次机遇的方法。说机遇一辈子只敲我们的门一次，根本没有事实依据。其实，机遇根本不会寻找我们，我们必须寻找机遇。通常的结果是，一个人得到的机遇正是另一个人错失的良机。当今时代，一个人的大脑与另一个人的大脑不相上下，常常是反应迅速的大脑决定最后的结果。

尽管许多人曾看过好书，但又说自己并没有从中获得多少好处。他们没有意识到书里的知识能唤醒自己的潜能，激励他们运用自己的毅力。一位智者说过："你可以把他领到泉水边，但你不能强迫他喝。"

Life Is a Symphony

The symphony is a symbol for life, especially in a community. The blend of each instrument gives the symphony its unique sound. This is also true in life and the world we live. Individuals bring in their own influence. A symphony orchestra is composed of a variety of brass, woodwind, percussion and stringed instruments.

Each of these instruments has its own unique sound but when played together they complement each other. Like a symphony and its instruments, the world is composed of many races and cultures. They are uniquely different but can have an influence on each other even if it is not intentional.

Individuality is an important part of the symphony. Each player has his or her own part to perform. These parts can be played on their own but do not have the same effect as when they are combined with the other parts of the orchestra. They blend into a harmonious piece of music. In other words, you can hear what each person has to contribute and how each performer works together. In life, each person has a talent that they are particularly good at. When they work together, it accentuates their talent.

Carnegie said that individuality was important, but should not be taken so far that it separates everyone from each other. Each person should contribute their own ideas that better help the community as a whole.

Another similarity between life and the symphony is that a performer may not have the melody but will accompany someone who does. In life, everybody has their moments of glory although they may go unnoticed like the accompanist. This does not mean, however, that they are any less important than anyone else. The melody doesn't stay with one instrument for the whole song but moves throughout the orchestra. As in life, everyone eventually has their moment to shine and their chance to be in the spotlight.

When preparing for a concert, the musicians are reminded by their conductor to stagger their breathing. They can, of course, breathe when they need to but they have to try not to breathe at the same time as the person sitting next to them. If everyone breathed at the same time, there would be a noticeable moment of silence in the song. This is yet another example that can be applied to life.

The orchestra continues to play. It moves together as a group yet separately. Each musician is an active member of the symphony. In life, we contribute what we have to offer from day to day as active members in our community. The orchestra plays their last note and the song is over. There is a moment of silence that is broken by the thunderous applause of the audience.

人生是一曲交响乐

交响乐是生命的象征，尤其是在团队中。各种乐器交织在一起，使交响乐发出独一无二的声音。我们的人生和居住的世界也是这样，每个人都会带来各自的影响。交响乐队由多种不同的铜乐器、木管乐器、打击乐器和弦乐器组成，每种乐器都有其独特的声音，但一起演奏时，它们总是互补。像交响乐和它的乐器一样，世界也是由许多种族和文化组成。尽管它们各不相同，但能在不经意间相互影响。

每个人都是交响乐中重要的一部分。每个演奏者都有其演奏的片段。尽管这些片段都可以独自演奏，但和交响乐团中的其他部分合奏时，它们会产生不同的效果，合成为一首和谐曲。换句话说，你可以听到每个人都得独奏，也可以听到每个演奏者怎样一起合奏。在生活中，每个人都拥有各自的特长，他们一起合作时，各自的天赋就会更加突出。

卡耐基认为个性非常重要，但不应该和他人偏离太远。每个人都应该贡献自己的观点，这更有助于整个社会。

生活和交响乐的另一个相似点是，演奏者不可能总是演奏出优美的旋律，但可以为演奏出优美旋律的人伴奏。在人生中，每个人都有其辉煌的时刻，尽管他们也许会像伴奏者那样不引人注目。然而，这并不意味着他们没有别人重要。整首歌曲的优美旋律不会停留在一种乐器上，而是要通过整个乐队演奏。人生也是这样，每个人最终都会有发光的时刻，也会有聚焦的机会。

准备一场音乐会时，乐队指挥会提醒音乐家们交错呼吸。需要呼吸时，他们当然可以呼吸，但必须尽量不要和邻座的人同时呼吸。如果大家同时呼吸，音乐中就会出现明显寂静的时刻。这是实用于人生的另一个例子。

乐队继续演奏。他们既是一个团体，又是分离的个体。每个音乐家都是交响乐中发挥作用的一名成员。在生活中，作为社会中发挥作用的成员，我们每天都贡献自己的一切。乐队演奏完最后的音符，乐曲结束，观众们雷鸣般的掌声便会打破片刻的宁静。

Sense Life

I've learned that sometimes all a person needs a hand to hold and a heart to understand.

I've learned that we didn't do it all in one day.

I've learned that love, not time, heals all wounds.

I've learned that everyone you meet deserves to be greeted with a smile.

I've learned that there's nothing sweeter than sleeping with your babies and feeling their breath on you cheeks.

I've learned that no one is perfect until you fall in love with them.

I've learned that opportunities are never lost; someone will take the ones you miss.

I've learned that when you harbor bitterness, happiness will dock elsewhere.

I've learned that I wish I could have told my mom that I love her one more time before she passed away.

I've learned that one should keep his words both soft and tender because tomorrow he may have to eat them.

I've learned that a smile is an inexpensive way to improve your looks.

I've learned that I can't choose how I feel, but I can choose what I do about it.

I've learned that everyone wants to stand on top of the mountain, but all the happiness and growth occurs while you're climbing it.

I've learned that it is best to give advice in only two circumstances: when it is requested and when it is a life-threatening situation.

I've learned that the less time I have to work with, the more things I get done.

感 悟 人 生

我已经明白了，有时一个人想要的只是一只可握的手和一颗明白的心。

我已经明白了，一天做不完所有的事情。

我已经明白了，治愈一切创伤的是爱，而不是时间。

我已经明白了，你相遇的每一个人都值得你笑脸相迎。

我已经明白了，没有比和宝宝睡在一起并感受到他们的呼吸吹在你脸上更甜蜜的事情。

我已经明白了，只有爱一个人时才会认为他/她十全十美。

我已经明白了，机会从来不会失去，有人会抓住你错过的机会。

我已经明白了，当你心怀痛苦时，幸福就会停靠到别的地方。

我已经明白了，我本应在妈妈去世前再对她说一次我爱她。

我已经明白了，一个人应该信守诺言，因为明天他可能不得不自食其言。

我已经明白了，微笑是改善容貌的一种容易的方式。

我已经明白了，我无法选择自己的感觉，但我可以选择做事的方式。

我已经明白了，每个人都想站在山顶，但所有的幸福和成长都发生在爬山的过程中。

我已经明白了，最好只在两种情况下提出忠告：别人要求时和生命攸关时。

我已经明白了，工作时间越少，工作效率越高。

The Splashes of Life

My grandfather took me to a fish pound on the farm when I was about seven, and he told me to throw a stone into the water and watch the circles created by the stone. Then he asked me to think of myself as that stone.

"You may create lots of splashes in your life, but the waves that come from those splashes will disturb the peace of all your fellow creatures," he said.

"Remember that you are responsible for what you put in your circle and that circle will also touch many other circles.

"You will need to live in a way that allows the good that comes from your circle to send the peace of that goodness to others. The splash that comes from anger or jealousy will send those feelings to other circles. You are responsible for both."

That was the first time I realized that each person creates the inner peace or discord that flows out into the world. We can't create world peace if we are riddled with inner conflict, hatred, doubt, or anger.

We radiate the feelings and thoughts that we hold inside, whether we speak them or not. Whatever is splashing around inside of us is spilling out into the world, creating beauty or discord with all other circles of life.

人生的波纹

我大约7岁那年，祖父带我来到农场的一个鱼塘边。他让我把一个石子扔进水里，吩咐我观察石子激起的一圈圈波纹，然后让我把自己当成那个石子。

他说："你在人生中也许能激起许多波纹，但你激起的波纹会打破别人的平静。

"记住，你要对自己激起的波纹负责，你的波纹会触及其他许多的波纹。

"你需要让自己波纹中善的一面传播给他人和平。来自愤怒或嫉妒的波纹会把这些情绪传给其他的波纹，你要对双方负责。"

这是我第一次认识到，每个人内心的平静或不和，都会流向世界。如果我们内心充满了冲突、仇恨、疑虑或愤怒，就无法创造世界和平。

无论说不说，我们都会传播内心的感觉和想法。无论我们内心激起的是什么波纹，它们都会流向世界，创造美或与人生的其他所有波纹产生影响。

Do not Meddle

About twenty years ago there lived a singular gentleman in the Old Hall among the elm trees. He was about three-score years of age, very rich, and somewhat odd in many of his habits, but for generosity and benevolence he had no equal.

No poor cottager stood in need of comforts, which he was not ready to supply; no sick man or woman languished for want of his assistance; and not even a beggar, unless a known impostor, went empty-handed from the Hall. Like the village pastor described in Goldsmith's poem of "The Deserted Village,"

"His house was known to all the vagrant train;
He chid their wand'rings, but relieved their pain;
The long-remembered beggar was his guest,
Whose beard descending swept his aged breast."

Now it happened that the old gentleman wanted a boy to wait upon him at table, and to attend him in different ways, for he was very fond of young people. But much as he liked the society of the young, he had a great aversion to that curiosity in which many young people are apt to indulge. He used to say, "The boy who will peep into a drawer will be tempted to take something out of it; and he who will steal a penny in his youth will steal a pound in his manhood."

No sooner was it known that the old gentleman was in want of a boy than twenty applications were made for the situation; but he determined not to engage anyone until he had in some way ascertained that he did not possess a curious, prying disposition.

On Monday morning seven lads, dressed in their Sunday clothes, with bright and happy faces, made their appearance at the Hall, each of them desiring to obtain the situation. Now the old gentleman, being of a singular disposition, had prepared a room in such a way that he might easily know if any of the young people who applied were given to meddle unnecessarily with things around them, or to peep into cupboards and drawers. He took care that the lads who were then at Elm Tree Hall should be shown into this room one after another.

And first, Charles Brown was sent into the room, and told that he would have to wait a little. So Charles sat down on a chair near the door. For some time he was very quiet, and looked about him; but there seemed to be so many curious things in the room that at last he got up to peep at them.

On the table was placed a dish cover, and Charles wanted sadly to know what was under it, but he felt afraid of lifting it up. Bad habits are strong things; and, as

Charles was of a curious disposition, he could not withstand the temptation of taking one peep. So he lifted up the cover.

This turned out to be a sad affair; for under the dish cover was a heap of very light feathers; part of the feathers, drawn up by a current of air, flew about the room, and Charles, in his fright, putting the cover down hastily, puffed the rest of them off the table.

What was to be done? Charles began to pick up the feathers one by one; but the old gentleman, who was in an adjoining room, hearing a scuffle, and guessing the cause of it, entered the room, to the consternation of Charles Brown, who was very soon dismissed as a boy who had not principle enough to resist even a slight temptation.

When the room was once more arranged, Henry Wilkins was placed there until such time as he should be sent for. No sooner was he left to himself than his attention was attracted by a plate of fine, ripe cherries. Now Henry was uncommonly fond of cherries, and he thought it would be impossible to miss one cherry among so many. He looked and longed, and longed and looked, for some time, and just as he had got off his seat to take one, he heard, as he thought, a foot coming to the door; but no, it was a false alarm.

Taking fresh courage, he went cautiously and took a very fine cherry, for he was determined to take but one, and put it into his mouth. It was excellent; and then he persuaded himself that he ran no risk in taking another; this he did, and hastily popped it into his mouth.

Now, the old gentleman had placed a few artificial cherries at the top of the others, filled with Cayenne pepper; one of these Henry had unfortunately taken, and it made his mouth smart and burn most intolerably. The old gentleman heard him coughing, and knew very well what was the matter. The boy that would take what did not belong to him, if no more than a cherry, was not the boy for him. Henry Wilkins was sent about his business without delay, with his mouth almost as hot as if he had put a burning coal in to it.

Rufus Wilson was next introduced into the room and left to himself; but he had not been there ten minutes before he began to move from one place to another. He was of a bold, resolute temper, but not overburdened with principle; for if he could have opened every cupboard, closet, and drawer in the house, without being found out, he would have done it directly.

Having looked around the room, he noticed a drawer to the table, and made up his mind to peep therein. But no sooner did he lay hold of the drawer knob than he set a large bell ringing, which was concealed under the table. The old gentleman immediately answered the summons, and entered the room.

Rufus was so startled by the sudden ringing of the bell, that all his impudence could not support him. He looked as though anyone might knock him down with a feather. The old gentleman asked him if he had rung the bell because he wanted anything. Rufus was much confused, and stammered, and tried to excuse himself, but all to no purpose, for it did not prevent him from being ordered off the premises.

George Jones was then shown into the room by an old steward; and being of a cautious disposition, he touched nothing, but only looked at the things about him. At last he saw that a closet door was a little open, and, thinking it would be impossible for anyone to know that he had opened it a little more, he very cautiously opened it an inch farther, looking down at the bottom of the door, that it might not catch against anything and make a noise.

Now had he looked at the top, instead of the bottom, it might have been better for him; for to the top of the door was fastened a plug, which filled up the hole of a small barrel of shot. He ventured to open the door another inch, and then another, till, the plug being pulled out of the barrel, the leaden shot began to pour out at a strange rate. At the bottom of the closet was placed a tin pan, and the shot falling upon this pan made such a clatter that George was frightened half out of his senses.

The old gentleman soon came into the room to inquire what was the matter, and there he found George nearly as pale as a sheet. George was soon dismissed.

It now came the turn of Albert Jenkins to be put into the room. The other boys had been sent to their homes by different ways, and no one knew what the experience of the other had been in the room of trial.

On the table stood a small round box, with a screw top to it, and Albert, thinking it contained something curious, could not be easy without unscrewing the top; but no sooner did he do this than out bounced an artificial snake, full a yard long, and fell upon his arm. He started back, and uttered a scream which brought the old gentleman to his elbow. There stood Albert, with the bottom of the box in one hand, the top in the other, and the snake on the floor.

"Come, come," said the old gentleman, "one snake is quite enough to have in the house at a time; therefore, the sooner you are gone the better." With that he dismissed him, without waiting a moment for his reply.

William Smith next entered the room, and being left alone soon began to amuse himself in looking at the curiosities around him. William was not only curious and prying, but dishonest, too, and observing that the key was left in the drawer of a bookcase, he stepped on tiptoe in that direction. The key had a wire fastened to it, which communicated with an electrical machine, and William received such a shock as he was not likely to forget. No sooner did he sufficiently recover himself to walk, than he was told to leave the house, and let other people lock and unlock their own drawers.

The other boy was Harry Gordon, and though he was left in the room full twenty minutes, he never during that time stirred from his chair. Harry had eyes in his head as well as the others, but he had more integrity in his heart; neither the dish cover, the cherries, the drawer knob, the closet door, the round box, nor the key tempted him to rise from his feet; and the consequence was that, in half an hour after, he was engaged in the service of the old gentleman at Elm Tree Hall. He followed his good old master to his grave, and received a large legacy for his upright conduct in his service.

莫管闲事

20多年前，有一位脾气古怪的老绅士住在有很多榆树环绕的古老庄园里。他大约60多岁，是个富翁，性格孤僻古怪，但他的慷慨仁慈却无人能及。

对需要安慰的穷苦佃农，对需要他帮助的病人，甚至对乞丐，当然不包括那些冒名顶替的人，他总是慷慨解囊，没有人空着手离开他的庄园，就像村里的牧师在一首名为《被遗弃的村庄》里描述的：

　　所有流浪的队伍都知道他的住处，
　　他斥责他们的流浪，却纾解他们的痛苦；
　　他总是记得他招待过的那位乞丐，
　　乞丐的白须飘在苍老的胸前。

现在，这位老绅士想找一个男孩服侍他的饮食起居，帮助他做些事情，因为他非常喜欢年轻人。虽然他对年轻人的世界很感兴趣，可是他非常厌恶年轻人难以自拔的好奇心。他经常说："向抽屉里偷看的孩子，总会禁不住诱惑。俗话说：'小时偷针，大时偷金。'"

人们得知老绅士要找侍童的消息后，都想得到这个职位，很快老绅士就收到了20多封求职信。但是老绅士已经决定，一定要找一位没有好奇心、不爱管闲事的人。

在一个星期一的早晨，7个身着盛装、打扮光亮的小伙子出现在庄园里，每个人都暗下决心，一定要得到这份工作。这位脾气古怪的老绅士准备了一个房间，以便观察哪个年轻人喜欢管闲事，或喜欢往壁橱、抽屉里偷看。他做好安排之后，让榆树庄园里的这些小伙子逐个进入这个房间。

首先，查尔斯·布朗被叫到房间里，老绅士请他在这里等一会儿。于是查尔斯在门旁的一个椅子上坐下。开始一段时间他非常安静，坐在椅子上向四周看着。但是他发现房间里有很多非常稀罕的东西，他终于站起来，偷偷窥探。

桌子上放着一个罩子,查尔斯非常想知道下面是什么,但是他又不敢掀起罩子。坏习惯对人的影响是非常大的,而查尔斯的性格又是非常好奇的,他怎么也忍不住想看个究竟,于是他掀起了罩子。

结果真是令人沮丧,罩子下面是一堆非常轻的羽毛。有些羽毛被流动的空气带起来,飞到房间里。查尔斯非常害怕,匆匆把罩子放下,可这下桌子上其余的羽毛也被吹到了地上。

这可怎么办?查尔斯一根一根地把羽毛捡起来。老绅士一直待在隔壁的房间,他听到这里的动静,猜到发生了什么事情,就走进房间,正好看到查尔斯·布朗慌乱的样子。他很快就把查尔斯打发走了,因为他确定查尔斯连最小的诱惑都抵制不了。

老绅士又重新布置了房间,然后叫进亨利·威尔金斯。当房间只剩下亨利一个人时,他的目光就被一盘诱人而熟透的樱桃吸引了。其实,亨利特别爱吃樱桃,而且他想,这里有这么多樱桃,就是吃掉一个,老绅士也不会发觉。他看看想想,想想看看,就在他从椅子上站起来想拿一个的时候,他似乎听到门口有脚步声。不过还好,是他听错了。

亨利又重新鼓足勇气,小心翼翼地站起来,拿起一个特别好的樱桃放进嘴里,他当时下定决心就只拿一个。太好吃了!他想,再吃一个也没关系。于是他又拿起一个,匆匆塞进嘴里。其实,老绅士在樱桃中间放了几个假樱桃,假樱桃里面全是辣椒。不幸的是,亨利凑巧拿了一个假樱桃,他的嘴立刻辣得刺痛起来,想着了火一样。老绅士听到他在咳嗽,明白了怎么回事。这个孩子不仅会拿樱桃,还会拿别的不属于他的东西,这个孩子当然是老绅士不喜欢的。亨利·威尔金斯也被打发走了,他的嘴热辣辣的,就好像刚向里面投进一块炭。

接下来,鲁弗斯·威尔森被叫了进来,自己待在房间里。但是他在里面待了不到十分钟,就开始摸摸这儿,碰碰那儿。他鲁莽而倔强,也没有什么原则,如果他能打开房间里的每个壁橱、储藏室和抽屉,而不被人发现的话,他会毫不犹豫地这么做。

他看了看四周,发现桌子上有一个抽屉,就想窥探一下里面。但是他刚把手放在抽屉把手上,一阵铃声响起。原来桌子下面藏着一个响铃。老绅士听到铃声,赶忙走进房间。

鲁弗斯被突然的铃声吓了一跳,虽然他的脸皮很厚,可是这时也开始觉得羞愧，他看上去脆弱不堪。老绅士问他，他打铃是不是因为想要什么东西，鲁弗斯非常困惑，结结巴巴地试图道歉，但是这一点用也没有，他从候选名单上被剔除了出去。

然后，乔治·琼斯被一名老管家领到房间里。他的性格比较谨慎，什么也没有碰，只是向四下里看着。最后，他发现一扇壁橱的门有些虚掩着。他想，如果他再把门打开些，肯定不会有人发现。于是他看着门的下方，以免碰到什么东西引起响动，小心地把门打开了一英寸。如果他看上面，而不是看下面，那就好了。因为门上系着一个小塞子，塞子堵住了一个小桶，小桶里盛满了小铅球。他冒险又将门打开了一英寸，又一英寸，直到塞子被拽了出来，小铅球蹦了出来。壁橱的底部放着一个锡盘，小铅球落在锡盘上，发出很大的响声，乔治吓得魂飞魄散。

老绅士很快出现，看看是怎么回事。他看到乔治的脸像纸一样苍白，就把他打发走了。

现在轮到阿尔伯特·詹金斯了。其他的男孩被各自送回家，没人知道这些人在房间里的经历。

桌子上有一个小圆盒子，盒子有个旋盖。阿尔伯特断定里面的东西很奇怪，他坐立不安，非常想拧开盒盖。但是他刚刚打开，盒子里就跳出一条假蛇，它足有一码长，缠绕在他的胳膊上。他往后退去，尖叫了一声。叫声引来了老绅士，他看到阿尔伯特一手拿着盒子，一手拿着盖子，蛇掉在地板上。

"起来，起来，"老绅士说，"屋里有一条蛇就够了，你还是快出去吧。"他就这样打发了这个男孩，连任何解释都没有听。

接下来，威廉·史密斯走进了房间，老绅士离开房间以后，他就开始好奇地左看右看。威廉不仅好奇、爱管闲事，还不诚实。他发现书柜的抽屉上还挂着钥匙，就踮着脚尖走过去。钥匙上系着一段金属线，金属线与一台电机相连，威廉被狠狠地击中，这下可够他受的。他刚刚恢复神志可以行走，老绅士就告诉他，以后最好还是让抽屉的主人亲自开锁或上锁，并让他离开了房间。

最后一个男孩叫哈里·戈登。他独自在房间里待了足足有20分钟，但是他安静地坐在椅子上，从未离开。哈里虽然也能看见有趣的东西，但是他的心灵正直。罩子、樱桃、抽屉把手、壁橱门、圆盒子或钥匙都没能引诱他离开座位。结果，半个小时后，他被录用了，留在榆树庄园为老绅士服务。他一直服侍老绅士，直到他离开人世，并因为他的正直而从老绅士那里得到了一大笔遗产。

The Fish I Didn't Catch

Our bachelor uncle who lived with us was a quiet, genial man, much given to hunting and fishing; and it was one of the pleasures of our young life to accompany him on his expeditions to Great Hill, Brandy-brow Woods, the Pond, and, best of all, to the Country Brook. We were quite willing to work hard in the cornfield or the haying lot to finish the necessary day's labor in season for an afternoon stroll through the woods and along the brookside.

I remember my first fishing excursion as if it were but yesterday. I have been happy many times in my life, but never more intensely so than when I received that first fishing pole from my uncle's hand, and trudged off with him through the woods and meadows. It was a still, sweet day of early summer; the long afternoon shadows of the trees lay cool across our path; the leaves seemed greener, the flowers brighter, the birds merrier, than ever before.

My uncle, who knew by long experience where were the best haunts of pickerel, considerately placed me at the most favorable point. I threw out my line as I had so often seen others, and waited anxiously for a bite, moving the bait in rapid jerks on the surface of the water in imitation of the leap of a frog. Nothing came of it. "Try again," said my uncle. Suddenly the bait sank out of sight. "Now for it," thought I; "here is a fish at last."

I made a strong pull, and brought up a tangle of weeds. Again and again I cast out my line with aching arms, and drew it back empty. I looked at my uncle appealingly. "Try once more," he said; "we fishermen must have patience."

Suddenly something tugged at my line, and swept off with it into deep water. Jerking it up, I saw a fine pickerel wriggling in the sun. "Uncle!" I cried, looking back in uncontrollable excitement, "I've got a fish!" "Not yet," said my uncle. As he spoke there was a plash in the water; I caught the arrowy gleam of a scared fish shooting into the middle of the stream, my hook hung empty from the line. I had lost my prize.

We are apt to speak of the sorrows of childhood as trifles in comparison with those of grown-up people; but we may depend upon it the young folks don't agree with us. Our griefs, modified and restrained by reason, experience, and self-respect, keep the proprieties, and, if possible, avoid a scene; but the sorrow of childhood, unreasoning and all-absorbing, is a complete abandonment to the passion. The doll's nose is broken, and the world breaks up with it; the marble rolls out of sight, and the solid globe rolls off with the marble.

So, overcome with my great and bitter disappointment, I sat down on the nearest hassock, and for a time refused to be comforted, even by my uncle's assurance that there were more fish in the brook. He refitted my bait, and, putting the pole again in my hands, told me to try my luck once more.

"But remember, boy," he said, with his shrewd smile, "never brag of catching a fish until he is on dry ground. I've seen older folks doing that in more ways than one, and so making fools of themselves. It's no use to boast of anything until it's done, nor then, either, for it speaks for itself."

How often since I have been reminded of the fish that I did not catch. When I hear people boasting of a work as yet undone, and trying to anticipate the credit which belongs only to actual achievement, I call to mind that scene by the brookside, and the wise caution of my uncle in that particular instance takes the form of a proverb of universal application: "NEVER BRAG OF YOUR FISH BEFORE YOU CATCH HIM."

那条我没钓到的鱼

我们的单身汉叔叔和我们住在一起,他是个安静而和蔼的人,他喜欢狩猎和钓鱼,和他一同去山里、树林、池塘等,是我们的一大乐趣。我们到过格瑞特山、布兰迪山坡树林、大湖和康瑞河,那是我们最喜欢去的地方。我们总是很高兴去玉米地或干草堆那儿干活,忙完在这个季节必须要做的工作,好有一个下午的时间和他一起去树林或小溪边散步。

我还记得我的第一次探险好像还是在昨天发生的事。我的人生中有许许多多的趣事,但是都没有我从叔叔手里接过我的第一根鱼竿更能让我感到快乐。我记得那是夏天一个风和日丽的日子,大树的阴影投射在道路上,显得格外的凉爽,叶子更绿了,花儿也更漂亮了,鸟儿的叫声比以往更动听了。

叔叔经验丰富,他知道哪里是捕获小梭鱼的最佳场所,他把我放在了捕小梭鱼的最佳位置。我像其他钓鱼的人一样,抛出了鱼线,然后焦急地等待它上钩。我用青蛙在水上跳跃的方式,把鱼饵提出水面,并快速地让它在水面上来回抽动,但是什么也没有出现。"再试一次。"叔叔说。突然鱼漂沉入了水底。"就是现在,拉起来,"我想,"这回终于有鱼了。"

我用力把鱼漂拉了回来,却是一些杂草。我一次又一次地用酸痛的胳膊抛出鱼饵,可每次都是无功而返。我可怜巴巴地看着我的叔叔,"再试一次,"他说,"我们钓鱼的人必须要有耐心。"

突然,我感觉有什么东西在拉我的鱼线,很快,鱼线沉入水底,我猛地把鱼饵拉起来,看到一条大梭鱼在金灿灿的阳光下摆动尾巴。"叔叔!"我难以控制激动的情绪,大叫道,"我钓到了大鱼!""还没呢。"叔叔说。我看到这条受了惊吓的鱼像箭一般地冲进小河,我的鱼钩上面空了,钓到的大鱼就这么跑了。

我们总是愿意把童年琐事所带来的悲伤和成年后所遭受的悲痛做比较,尽管童年时的懊恼不值一提,但年轻人不同意我们的观点。成年后的悲痛,受到理性、经验还有自尊的调整和制约,要尊重社会传统习俗,而且还要尽可能避免当众出丑。但是孩童时期的悲痛是毫无理由的,沉湎其中而难以化解,这是任由激情放纵的表现。比如,一个玩具娃娃的鼻子坏了,就觉得这个世界抛弃了自己;弹珠滚丢了,整个天也觉得塌陷了。

于是,我在巨大的失落感的支使下,一屁股坐在了离我最近的草丛里,并且拒绝别人的安慰,即使是我叔叔肯定地告诉我,这小溪里还有数不清的鱼也无济于事。他重新弄好我的鱼饵,并把鱼竿再一次放在我手上,并且跟我说,再试试运气。

"不过,要记住,孩子,"他露出了狡猾的微笑说,"永远不要在鱼被拽上岸之前,炫耀自己钓到了鱼。我看到过的老钓手都这么干,结果总是让自己出丑。所以说,在一件事情做完之前就夸耀是没有用的;而且,即使事情成功了,也没必要炫耀,因为那时候你的成功是大家有目共睹的。"

从那以后,每当我听到有人在没做完事就开始炫耀自己的时候,我就会想起那条我没有钓到的鱼。小溪边的场景在我的脑海里还历历在目,我叔叔那次对我的教诲可以换成一句全球通用的谚语:"在鱼到手之前,绝不要吹嘘自己钓到了鱼。"

Behind Time

A railroad train was rushing along at almost lightning speed. A curve was just ahead, beyond which was a station where two trains usually met. The conductor was late, —so late that the period during which the up train was to wait had nearly elapsed; but he hoped yet to pass the curve safely. Suddenly a locomotive dashed into sight right ahead. In an instant there was a collision. A shriek, a shock, and fifty souls were in eternity; and all because an engineer had been behind time.

A great battle was going on. Column after column had been precipitated for eight hours on the enemy posted along the ridge of a hill. The summer sun was sinking in the west; reenforcements for the obstinate defenders were already in sight; it was necessary to carry the position with one final charge, or everything would be lost.

A powerful corps had been summoned from across the country, and if it came up in season all would yet be well. The great conqueror, confident in its arrival, formed his reserve into an attacking column, and ordered them to charge the enemy. The whole world knows the result. Grouchy failed to appear; the imperial guard was beaten back; and Waterloo was lost. Napoleon died a prisoner at St. Helena because one of his marshals was behind time.

A leading firm in commercial circles had long struggled against bankruptcy. As it had large sums of money in California, it expected remittances by a certain day, and if they arrived, its credit, its honor, and its future prosperity would be preserved. But week after week elapsed without bringing the gold. At last came the fatal day on which the firm had bills maturing to large amounts. The steamer was telegraphed at daybreak; but it was found, on inquiry, that she brought no funds, and the house failed. The next arrival brought nearly half a million to the insolvents, but it was too late; they were ruined because their agent, in remitting, had been behind time.

A condemned man was led, out for execution. He had taken human life, but under circumstances of the greatest provocation, and public sympathy was active in his behalf. Thousands had signed petitions for a reprieve; a favorable answer had been expected the night before, and though it had not come, even the sheriff felt confident that it would yet arrive. Thus the morning passed without the appearance of the messenger.

The last moment was up. The prisoner took his place, the cap was drawn over his eyes, the bolt was drawn, and a lifeless body swung revolving in the wind. Just at that moment a horseman came into sight, galloping down hill, his steed covered with foam. He carried a packet in his right hand, which he waved frantically to the crowd. He was the express rider with the reprieve; but he came too late. A comparatively innocent man had died an ignominious death because a watch had been five minutes too late, making its bearer arrive behind time.

It is continually so in life. The best laid plans, the most important affairs, the fortunes of individuals, the weal of nations, honor, happiness, life itself, are daily sacrificed, because somebody is "behind time." There are men who always fail in whatever they undertake, simply because they are "behind time." There are others who put off reformation year after year, till death seizes them, and they perish unrepentant, because forever "behind time."

为 时 晚 矣

一辆列车以闪电般的速度飞驰，前面是一段弯路，弯路前是一个车站，通常两列列车会在这里汇合。列车长迟到了，前面的那辆列车应该早已出发了，但他还是希望在前面的弯道处减速。这时，后面的火车冲了过来，两辆列车相撞了。一声尖叫之后，50人丧生，然而这一切仅仅是因为列车长误时了。

一场激烈的战争正在进行，足足8小时，一队又一队的战士冲向敌人占领的山冈。夏日的太阳将要西沉，不远处，顽固的守卫者的援兵快要到了，因此，必须进行最后一次冲锋，否则之前的努力都是徒劳。

一支强大的军队接到派遣命令，如果他们及时赶到，一切都会非常顺利。这位伟大的统治者自信地将剩余的兵力组成进攻纵队，命令他们向敌人发起进攻。全世界的人都知道这场战争的结果，葛罗奇没有出现，皇家军队被击退，滑铁卢失陷了。拿破仑成了一个囚犯，他死在了圣赫勒拿，就因为他的一位将军误时了。

一个商业界的龙头企业，面临破产危机，一直挣扎着。这家公司在加利福尼亚有一笔巨额钱款，他们预计这笔资金会及时汇过来，那样，公司的名誉就可以得到挽救，以后的发展前景也是相当可观的。但时间一周一周地过去了，那笔钱一直没有汇过来。最后公司的大量账单已经到期，汽船在拂晓时刻到达，但一经询问，它并没有带来资金，就这样，公司破产了。然而，下一艘汽船却给那群破产的人带来了将近五十万的资金，但这一切都晚了，就因为代理商在汇款的时候误时了。

一个被宣判有罪的人被押往刑场。他杀了人，但那是在他受到极端挑衅的时候才这么做的。公众都非常同情他，上千人为他签了一份请愿书，请求对他缓刑。前一天晚上，人们本以为会得到一个肯定的答复，虽然没有等到答复，但就连法官也坚信会得到答复。可是第二天，上午慢慢过去了，但迟迟不见送信使者的身影。

最后的时刻到了，囚犯站在了他应该站的位置，有人用帽子遮住了他眼睛，扎栓落下了，没有了生命的身体在风中旋转着。就在这时，一个骑马的人出现在人们的视野中，他飞奔过山冈，胯下的马已经累得口吐白沫。他的右手高举一个包裹，冲着人群疯狂地挥舞。缓刑的答复带来了，但来得太晚了。仅仅因为钟表走慢了五分钟，送信人误时了，导致一个本来清白的人死于非命。

生活中有很多事都是如此，本来完美的计划、最重要的事情、个人的命运、国家的福祉、个人的荣誉和快乐，甚至生命本身，每天都会因为有人"误时"而牺牲。有些人不论干什么都会失败，仅仅是因为他"误时"了，另一些人年复一年地推迟着，直到死亡也不愿改变，他们遭到万劫不复的毁灭，因为他们永远都在"误时"。

Control Your Temper

No one has a temper naturally so good, that it does not need attention and cultivation, and no one has a temper so bad, but that, by proper culture, it may become pleasant. One of the best disciplined tempers ever seen, was that of a gentleman who was naturally quick, irritable, rash, and violent; but, by having the care of the sick, and especially of deranged people, he so completely mastered himself that he was never known to be thrown off his guard.

The difference in the happiness which is received or bestowed by the man who governs his temper, and that by the man who does not, is immense. There is no misery so constant, so distressing, and so intolerable to others, as that of having a disposition which is your master, and which is continually fretting itself. There are corners enough, at every turn in life, against which we may run, and at which we may break out in impatience, if we choose.

Look at Roger Sherman, who rose from a humble occupation to a seat in the first Congress of the United States, and whose judgment was received with great deference by that body of distinguished men. He made himself master of his temper, and cultivated it as a great business in life. There are one instance which show this part of his character in a light that is beautiful.

One day, after having received his highest honors, he was sitting and reading in his parlor. A roguish student, in a room close by, held a looking-glass in such a position as to pour the reflected rays of the sun directly in Mr. Sherman's face. He moved his chair, and the thing was repeated. A third time the chair was moved, but the looking-glass still reflected the sun in his eyes. He laid aside his book, went to the window, and many witnesses of the impudence expected to hear the ungentlemanly student severely reprimanded. He raised the window gently, and then shut the window blind!

请 君 制 怒

没有人天生就是好脾气，它并不需要你多么专注或多么有教养；当然，也没有人生来就是坏脾气。不过，只要你接受的是正确的文化传统，你就能成为一个讨人喜欢的人。我所见过的最好的、最有规矩的情感来自一位绅士，他生性急躁、爱发脾气、做事鲁莽，却能照顾那些生病的人，特别是那些精神病患者，在照顾这些人的时候，他能完全控制住自己的情绪。

一个能控制自己情绪的人所能感受到的快乐，和一个不能控制自己情绪的人所能感受到的快乐相比，是存在巨大差异的。这个世上没有永恒的、令人烦恼的痛苦，这种痛苦让旁人难以忍受。你应该控制自己的情绪，然而你的情绪却又在不停地阻挠自己。生活中总会有不开心的事，它会阻挡我们前进，也会让我们失去耐心。

看看罗杰·谢尔曼，从一事无成到成为美国第一届国会议员，那些声名显赫的人会恭恭敬敬地接受他的裁决。他懂得如何控制自己的情绪，并把它当作至关重要的素养，专门对此进行精心培养。下面的故事，能够突显他高尚的人格光辉。

一天，当他接受了最高的荣誉之后，坐在客厅里看书，一个坐在他附近的淘气学生拿着镜子，摆好角度，直接把太阳光反射到罗杰·谢尔曼的脸上。他挪了挪位置，但是，那个男孩又把阳光射到了他的脸上。罗杰·谢尔曼再一次挪动了自己的椅子，但是，那个男孩还是用镜子把太阳光反射到他的脸上。于是，他放下书，走到窗户旁边，那些看到此情此景的傲慢学生都希望这个不懂礼貌的同学能够受到严厉的训斥。然而，罗杰·谢尔曼轻轻地提起窗户，把它关上了。

The Artist Surprised

It may not be known to all the admirers of the genius of Albert Durer, that that famous engraver was endowed with a "better half," so peevish in temper, that she was the torment not only of his own life, but also of his pupils and domestics. Some of the former were cunning enough to purchase peace for themselves by conciliating the common tyrant, but woe to those unwilling or unable to offer aught in propitiation. Even the wiser ones were spared only by having their offenses visited upon a scapegoat.

This unfortunate individual was Samuel Duhobret, a disciple whom Durer had admitted into his school out of charity. He was employed in painting signs and the coarser tapestry then used in Germany. He was about forty years of age, little, ugly, and humpbacked; he was the butt of every ill joke among his fellow disciples, and was picked out as an object of especial dislike by Madame Durer. But he bore all with patience, and ate, without complaint, the scanty crusts given him every day for dinner, while his companions often fared sumptuously.

Poor Samuel had not a spice of envy or malice in his heart. He would, at any time, have toiled half the night to assist or serve those who were wont oftenest to laugh at him, or abuse him loudest for his stupidity. True, he had not the qualities of social humor or wit, but he was an example of indefatigable industry. He came to his studies every morning at daybreak, and remained at work until sunset. Then he retired into his lonely chamber, and wrought for his own amusement.

Duhobret labored three years in this way, giving himself no time for exercise or recreation. He said nothing to a single human being of the paintings he had produced in the solitude of his cell, by the light of his lamp. But his bodily energies wasted and declined under incessant toil. There was none sufficiently interested in the poor artist, to mark the feverish hue of his wrinkled cheek, or the increasing attenuation of his misshapen frame.

None observed that the uninviting pittance set aside for his midday repast, remained for several days untouched. Samuel made his appearance regularly as ever, and bore with the same meekness the gibes of his fellow-pupils, or the taunts of Madame Durer, and worked with the same untiring assiduity, though his hands would sometimes tremble, and his eyes become suffused, a weakness probably owing to the excessive use he had made of them.

One morning Duhobret was missing at the scene of his daily labors. His absence created much remark, and many were the jokes passed upon the occasion. One surmised this, and another that, as the cause of the phenomenon; and it was finally agreed that the poor fellow must have worked himself into an absolute skeleton, and taken his final stand in the glass frame of some apothecary, or been blown away by a puff of wind, while his door happened to stand open. No on thought of going to his lodgings to look after him or his remains.

Meanwhile, the object of their mirth was tossing on a bed of sickness. Disease, which had been slowly sapping the foundations of his strength, burned in every vein; his eyes rolled and flashed in delirium; his lips, usually so silent, muttered wild and incoherent words. In his days of health, poor Duhobret had his dreams, as all artists, rich or poor, will sometimes have. He had thought that the fruit of many years' labor, disposed of to advantage, might procure him enough to live, in an economical way, for the rest of his life. He never anticipated fame or fortune; the height of his ambition or hope was, to possess a tenement large enough to shelter him from the inclemencies of the weather, with means enough to purchase one comfortable meal per day.

Now, alas! however, even that one hope had deserted him. He thought himself dying, and thought it hard to die without one to look kindly upon him, without the words of comfort that might soothe his passage to another world. He fancied his bed surrounded by fiendish faces, grinning at his sufferings, and taunting his inability to summon power to disperse them. At length the apparition faded away, and the patient sunk into an exhausted slumber.

He awoke unrefreshed; it was the fifth day he had lain there neglected. His mouth was parched; he turned over, and feebly stretched out his hand toward the earthen pitcher, from which, since the first day of his illness he had quenched his thirst. Alas! it was empty! Samuel lay for a few moments thinking what he should do. He knew he must die of want if he remained there alone; but to whom could he apply for aid?

An idea seemed, at last, to strike him. He arose slowly, and with difficulty, from the bed, went to the other side of the room, and took up the picture he had painted last. He resolved to carry it to the shop of a salesman, and hoped to obtain for it sufficient to furnish him with the necessaries of life for a week longer. Despair lent him strength to walk, and to carry his burden. On his way, he passed a house, about which there was a crowd. He drew nigh, asked what was going on, and received for an answer, that there was to be a sale of many specimens of art, collected by an amateur in the course of thirty years. It has often happened that collections made with infinite pains by the proprietor, have been sold without mercy or discrimination after his death.

Something whispered to the weary Duhobret, that here would be the market for his picture. It was a long way yet to the house of the picture dealer, and he made up his mind at once. He worked his way through the crowd, dragged himself up the steps, and, after many inquiries, found the auctioneer. That personage was a busy man, with a handful of papers; he was inclined to notice somewhat roughly the interruption of the lean, sallow hunchback, imploring as were his gesture and language.

"What do you call your picture?" at length, said he, carefully looking at it.

"It is a view of the Abbey of Newburg, with its village and the surrounding landscape," replied the eager and trembling artist.

The auctioneer again scanned it contemptuously, and asked what it was worth. "Oh, that is what you please; whatever it will bring," answered Duhobret.

"Hem! it is too odd to please, I should think; I can promise you no more than three thalers."

Poor Samuel sighed deeply. He had spent on that piece the nights of many months. But he was starving now; and the pitiful sum offered would give bread for a few days. He nodded his head to the auctioneer, and retiring took his seat in a corner.

The sale began. After some paintings and engravings had been disposed of, Samuel's was exhibited. "Who bids at three thalers? Who bids?" was the cry. Duhobret listened eagerly, but none answered. "Will it find a purchaser?" said he despondingly, to himself. Still there was a dead silence. He dared not look up; for it seemed to him that all the people were laughing at the folly of the artist, who could be insane enough to offer so worthless a piece at a public sale.

"What will become of me?" was his mental inquiry. "That work is certainly my best;" and he ventured to steal another glance. "Does it not seem that the wind actually stirs those boughs and moves those leaves! How transparent is the water! What life breathes in the animals that quench their thirst at that spring! How that steeple shines! How beautiful are those clustering trees!" This was the last expiring throb of an artist's vanity. The ominous silence continued, and Samuel, sick at heart, buried his face in his hands.

"Twenty-one thalers!" murmured a faint voice, just as the auctioneer was about to knock down the picture. The stupefied painter gave a start of joy. He raised his head and looked to see from whose lips those blessed words had come. It was the picture dealer, to whom he had first thought of applying.

"Fifty thalers," cried a sonorous voice. This time a tall man in black was the speaker. There was a silence of hushed expectation. "One hundred thalers," at length thundered the picture dealer.

"Three hundred!" "Five hundred!" "One thousand!"

Another profound silence, and the crowd pressed around the two opponents, who stood opposite each other with eager and angry looks.

"Two thousand thalers!" cried the picture dealer, and glanced around him triumphantly, when he saw his adversary hesitate. "Ten thousand!" vociferated the tall man, his face crimson with rage, and his hands clinched convulsively. The dealer grew paler; his frame shook with agitation; he made two or three efforts, and at last cried out "Twenty thousand!"

His tall opponent was not to be vanquished. He bid forty thousand. The dealer stopped; the other laughed a low laugh of insolent triumph, and a murmur of admiration was heard in the crowd. It was too much for the dealer; he felt his peace was at stake. "Fifty thousand!" exclaimed he in desperation. It was the tall man's turn to hesitate. Again the whole crowd were breathless. At length, tossing his arms in defiance, he shouted "One hundred thousand!" The crestfallen picture dealer withdrew; the tall man victoriously bore away the prize.

How was it, meanwhile, with Duhobret, while this exciting scene was going on? He was hardly master of his senses. He rubbed his eyes repeatedly, and murmured to himself, "After such a dream, my misery will seem more cruel!" When the contest ceased, he rose up bewildered, and went about asking first one, then another, the price of the picture just sold. It seemed that his apprehension could not at once be enlarged to so vast a conception.

The possessor was proceeding homeward, when a decrepit, lame, and humpbacked invalid, tottering along by the aid of a stick, presented himself before him. He threw him a piece of money, and waved his hand as dispensing with his thanks. "May it please your honor," said the supposed beggar, "I am the painter of that picture!" and again he rubbed his eyes.

The tall mall was Count Dunkelsback, one of the richest noblemen in Germany. He stopped, took out his pocketbook, took out a leaf, and wrote on it a few lines. "Take it, friend," said he; "it is a check for your money. Adieu."

Duhobret finally persuaded himself that it was not a dream. He became the master of a castle, sold it, and resolved to live luxuriously for the rest of his life, and to cultivate painting as a pastime. But, alas, for the vanity of human expectation! He had borne privation and toil; prosperity was too much for him, as was proved soon after, when an indigestion carried him off. His picture remained long in the cabinet of Count Dunkelsback, and afterward passed into the possession of the King of Bavaria.

一鸣惊人的艺术家

也许,并不是所有仰慕阿尔伯特·杜勒才华的人都知道这位著名的雕刻家拥有一位"贤内助",由于他脾气暴躁,因此不但她在他自己的生活中受尽了折磨,而且还殃及他的学生和家庭。他以前的学生非常圆滑,他们会以安抚这位共同暴君的方式给自己换来和平;然而对于那些倒霉鬼来说,他们不乐意或是没办法拿出任何可以让他满意的东西。甚至更明智的人也只有利用嫁祸替罪羊的方式,来宣泄内心的不爽。

这个不幸的人就是塞缪尔·杜霍布赖特。杜勒因为可怜他才将他招致门下,让他负责在标志牌和粗制绒绣毯上涂颜色,然后再把它们运到德国。他大约四十岁,身体单薄,相貌丑陋,还有些驼背,因此杜勒的一些学生总是恶毒地嘲笑他。阿尔伯特·杜勒夫人尤其讨厌他,可以说他就是她的眼中钉。但是他十分有耐心,且毫无怨言,尽管他每天的晚饭只是一些面包屑,而同伴们的饭菜要比他的丰盛得多。

可怜的塞缪尔心里没有丝毫的嫉妒或怨恨。任何时候,他都是卖力劳动到半夜,为那些嘲笑他并大声辱骂他愚笨的人服务。是的,他不具备社交幽默或者才智,但他是不知疲倦、勤勤恳恳的模范。每天,他总是在天刚蒙蒙亮的时候就开始学习,直到日落黄昏。然后他会只身来到自己的小屋里休息,逗自己开心。

塞缪尔以这种方式吃了三年的苦头,既没有任何练习的时间,也没有放松神经的机会。他没有向任何人讲他独自一人在小屋子里凭借昏暗的灯光思考绘画的事情。但是,这样长年累月的辛劳将他身体里的能量都耗干了。没有人关注这个可怜的艺术家,也没有谁注意他满是皱纹的脸上泛出的病态的红晕,他那畸形的身躯日益变得瘦弱。

没有人注意到他的薪水几乎买不了一顿午饭,此后数天都是如此。塞缪尔像往常一样出现,忍受同学的嘲讽,或者是来自阿尔伯特·杜勒夫人的嘲弄,继续毫不松懈地努力工作,有时他的手会颤抖,眼睛遍布血丝,他畸形的身躯大概就是因为过度辛劳而导致的。

一天早上，塞缪尔没来画室，人们对他的旷工议论纷纷，很多人更是冷嘲热讽。大家互相猜测他为什么会旷工，或者细细研究产生这种事情的原因，最终大家一致认为那个可怜的家伙一定是死了，变成了一具骷髅，正在某个药剂师的玻璃框架里面做展示，或者是他家的大门碰巧没关上，从屋外刮进来的大风把他给吹走了。总之，没有人愿意去他家探望，看看他到底出了什么事。

与此同时，大家取乐的对象塞缪尔已经卧床不起，疾病慢慢地吞噬着他的身体，阻塞他的每一条血管；他的眼睛开始打转，并且因为兴奋而闪亮无比；他平常不怎么说话的嘴巴此时有些语无伦次地说着什么。在身体健康的时候，可怜的塞缪尔做过各种各样的美梦，要么是成了一位大艺术家，要么是成了一个非常富有的人，或者又变成了一个贫苦的穷人。他本打算依靠自己多年的辛苦劳动，认为只要保持勤俭节约的方式就能生活下去，那么他以后就不会为了生活而忧愁。他从来不期望自己有很大的名气或者很有钱；他的期望或者希望，就是拥有一所足够大的房子来躲避恶劣的天气，有足够的钱来买每天必需的食物。

然而，现在所有的愿望都离他而去，他觉得自己快死了，但是他不想就这么轻易死掉，因为还没有人好好地照看过他，也没有人说过一些安慰他的话，让他安心去另一个世界。他想象到，自己的床周围都是恶魔般的脸孔，对他的不幸遭遇进行冷嘲热讽，他无力驱散这些邪恶的面孔，最终那些面孔消失了，他很快陷入了疲惫的沉睡。

他醒来时，觉得一点精神都没有，他已经在这里躺了五天五夜，但就是没有人来看他。他十分口渴，翻了个身，虚弱地把手伸向陶制水壶。从生病一开始，他就用这个水壶止渴。啊！水壶里竟然是空的！塞缪尔躺了几分钟，心想接下来该怎么做。他知道如果他被遗弃在这里，他就会被口渴折磨致死。但是谁能帮助他呢？

终于，一个突发奇想触动了他。他缓慢地直起身来，挣扎着从床上下来，走到屋子的另一边，取出自己最近一次创作的油画，决定把画带到画商的店里，希望用这幅画获取能够让他再活一个礼拜的生活必需品。绝望在驱使他前进，同时肩负着沉甸甸的担子。在去商店的路上，他从一所房子边走过，看到那里聚集着一大群人，于是他凑过去，问道："这里发生了什么事？"他得到的回答是这里要进行一场艺术品拍卖会，这些艺术品是一位业余收藏家花费30年时间收集起来的。通常这些作品都是作者本人花费巨大努力才画成的，然后在这些画家死去之后，这些作品会被毫不怜惜或不加区分地以低价变卖出去。

一些人的谈话传到了机警的塞缪尔的耳朵里，他认为在这里可以把自己的画卖出去，况且从这里到商店还有很长的一段路要走；于是他做出了决定，穿过人群，在询问了几个人之后，他找到了拍卖商。拍卖商正在忙得不可开交，手里拿着一堆文件，注意到了这个衣衫褴褛、瘦弱并且驼背的人，所以就用手势和话语试探了他一下。

"你怎么看你的画？"终于，拍卖商在仔细看过这幅画之后说。

"这幅画画的是纽伯格大修道院，背景是它所在的村落和周围的景色。"画家急切而有些颤抖地说。

拍卖商再次用轻蔑的眼神看起这幅画来，问他打算卖多少钱。"噢，你觉得多少钱合适，就多少钱拿走吧。"塞缪尔答道。

"哼！太蹩脚了，还真没法给价啊。不过，我可以向你保证，这画最多值三泰勒。"

可怜的塞缪尔深深地叹了口气。他想不到自己花费数个夜晚完成的这幅画才值这么点钱。但是他现在饥饿难耐，即使可怜的三泰勒也能买到足够维持数天的面包。他冲拍卖商点点头，便在拍卖场的一处角落坐下来。

拍卖开始了。在拍卖商拍卖了几幅油画和雕刻品之后，塞缪尔的作品被展示出来。"谁出3泰勒？有谁愿出价？"拍卖商大声喊道。塞缪尔急切地听着，但是没有人回答。"会有人买吗？"他沮丧地对自己说道。拍卖会上仍然一片死寂。他都不敢抬头看了，因为在他看来，在场的所有人都在嘲笑画这幅画的作者有多么愚蠢。因为他太过疯狂，竟然在公开拍卖会上拍卖如此毫无价值的作品。

"我的作品会怎么样？"他扪心自问，"这是我画得最好的作品。"他鼓起勇气偷看了一下。"没有人注意到风激起了那些树枝，吹动了那些树叶！画里面的水是多么的清澈啊！在泉水旁喝水的动物生活得多么自在啊！那尖塔是多么的闪亮啊！那些树是多么的美丽啊！"这是这位艺术家自尊心即将消亡的最后悸动。悲剧的寂静仍在继续，塞缪尔的心里感到十分痛苦，他把头埋在了手心。

就在拍卖商取下这幅画的时候，突然传来一个微弱的声音："我出21泰勒。"塞缪尔目瞪口呆，开始兴奋起来。他抬起了头，想看看究竟是谁开的尊口。那个喊价的是一名画商，他之前就认为这个人会首先喊价。

"50泰勒！"一个响亮的声音传来。这次是一位身着黑色上衣、手拿扬声器的大高个儿。在充满期望的寂静过后，"100泰勒！"终于，画商大声喊道。

"300泰勒！"

"500泰勒！"

"1000泰勒！"

场上再一次陷入了寂静，众人都围在这两个竞争者之间，他们面对面坐着，脸上都带着既热情又胜券在握的表情，怒目相视。

"2000泰勒！"画商叫道，当他看到竞争对手犹豫了，便炫耀似地打量着他。"10000泰勒！"那个高个儿喊道，他的脸由于愤怒而变得通红，双手紧握，犹如痉挛一般。画商的脸变得苍白起来，他的身躯因激动而开始抖动，在竞拍了两三次之后，终于他大叫道："两万泰勒！"

那个高个儿的竞争对手并没有因此而屈服。他出价四万泰勒，画商不再出价了；那个高个儿用充满轻蔑的笑声炫耀他的胜利，人群里传来了低声的赞叹。对于画商来说，这样的声音太刺耳了，他感到自己没法再保持平稳的心态了。"五万泰勒！"画商充满绝望地吼道。这次轮到那个高个儿的出价者犹豫了。人群再一次陷入了令人难以呼吸的紧张氛围之中。终于，高个儿蔑视地举起手，拼尽全力高喊："十万泰勒！"那位画商终于望而却步，高个儿拿着那幅画，胜利而归。

与此同时，面对这样激动人心的时刻，塞缪尔的心情又是怎样的呢？在拍卖结束之后，塞缪尔无法控制自己的情感。他反复擦拭自己的眼睛，对自己小声说："做过这样的梦之后，我的痛苦将变得更加残酷！"当拍卖结束的时候，他充满疑惑地站起来，接连打听了好几个人，问他们刚才那幅画卖了多少钱。很显然，他还无法理解10万泰勒到底是多少钱。

当那个苍老、虚弱并且驼着背的塞缪尔拄着拐杖踉跄地朝前走的时候，那个高个儿的出价者正在回家的路上。塞缪尔走到他前面，刚打算做自我介绍，高个儿给塞缪尔扔了一块钱，还没等他说谢谢，就急忙摆手。"谢谢您的慷慨，"塞缪尔说，"我是这幅画的作者。"说着，他再一次擦了擦自己的眼睛。

这个高个儿就是敦克尔巴克伯爵，德国最有钱的绅士之一，他停了下来，拿出支票簿，从里面撕下来一张支票，在上面写了几行字。"拿着，我的朋友，"他说，"这是张支票，里面是你应得的钱。再会！"

最终，塞缪尔说服了自己这不是一场梦。他买下了一座城堡，后来，又把城堡卖了，并且下定决心，在剩下的后半生要过奢侈的生活，并且把绘画当作消遣。真是让人唏嘘，人类的期望竟是如此的空虚！他家境贫困，受尽折磨，对他来说富有竟然难以承受，正如后来的事实所证明的那样，他因奢侈的生活而丧了命。他的那幅作品一直放在敦克尔巴克伯爵的陈列室里，之后又流落到巴伐利亚国王手中。

人生的价值

You Have Only One Life

The best kind of friend is the kind you can sit on a porch swing with, never say a word, and then walk away feeling like it was the best conversation you've ever had.

Don't go for looks; they can deceive. Don't go for wealth; even that fades away. Go for someone who makes you smile because it takes only a smile to make a dark day seem bright.

Dream what you want to dream; go where you want to go; be what you want to be, because you have only one life and one chance to do all the things you want to do.

A careless word may kindle strife; a cruel word may wreck a life; a timely word may level stress; a loving word may heal and bless.

A sad thing in life is when you meet someone who means a lot to you, only to find out in the end that it was never meant to be and you just have to let go.

Always put yourself in the other's shoes. If you feel that it hurts you, it probably hurts the person, too.

The happiest of people don't necessarily have the best of everything, they just make the most of everything that comes along their way.

When you were born, you were crying and everyone around you was smiling. Live your life so that when you die, you're the one smiling and everyone around you is crying.

To see a world in a grain of sand.

And a heaven in a wild flower.

Hold infinity in the palm of your hand.

And eternity in an hour.

Let's write that letter we thought of writing "one of these days".

Don't cry because it is over;

Smile, because it happened.

And forever has no end.

你只有一次生命

最好的朋友就是那种你可以促膝而坐,默默无语,分别时却感到这是你曾有过的最好的交谈。

不要追求容貌,它们可能蒙骗人。不要追求财富,那会渐渐消散。追求能让你微笑的人吧,因为仅仅一个微笑就能使黑天变得光明。

做你想做的梦,到你想去的地方,做你想做的人吧,因为你只有一次生命、一个机会去做你想做的一切。

一句粗心的话可能引发冲突，一句无情的话可能毁灭生命，一句适时的话可能消除压力，一句关爱的话可能愈合伤口、带来祝福。

生命中的一件伤心事是你遇到了一个对你至关重要的人，最终却发现有缘无分，你不得不放手。

总是要设身处地为别人着想。如果你感到受伤，很可能别人也会受伤。

最幸福的人不见得胜过一切，他们只是充分利用顺其自然的一切。

你出生时，哇哇大哭，你身边的每个人都在微笑。好好生活吧，这样你去世时，你就能一人含笑，身边的每个人都号啕大哭。

一沙一世界，

一花一天堂。

把握掌中无限，

把握瞬间永恒。

我们原想着"有一天"去写的那封信，现在就写。

不要因为结束而哭泣。

要因发生而微笑。

而且永无止境。

A Promise of Flowers

Early in the spring, about a month before my grandpa's stroke, I began walking for an hour every afternoon. Some days I would walk four blocks south to see Grandma and Grandpa. At eighty-six, Grandpa was still quite a gardener, so I always watched for his earliest blooms and each new wave of spring flowers.

I was especially interested in flowers that year because I was planning to landscape my own yard and I was eager to get Grandpa's advice. I thought I knew pretty much what I wanted—a yard full of bushes and plants that would bloom from May till November.

It was right after the first rush of purple violets in the lawns and the sudden blaze of forsythia that spring that Grandpa had a stroke. It left him without speech and with no movement on his left side. The whole family gathered around Grandpa. We all spent many hours by his side. Some days his eyes were eloquent—laughing at our reported mishaps, listening alertly, revealing painful awareness of his inability to care for himself. There were days, too, when he slept most of the time, overcome with the weight of his approaching death.

As the months passed, I watched the growing earth with Grandpa's eyes. Each time I was with him, I gave him a garden report. He listened, gripping my hand. But he could not answer my questions. The new flowers would blaze, peak, fade, and die before I knew their names.

Grandpa's illness held him through the spring and on, week by week, through summer. I began spending hours at the local nursery, studying and choosing seeds and plants. It gave me special joy to buy plants I had seen in Grandpa's garden and give them humble starts in my own garden. I discovered Sweet William, which I had admired for years in Grandpa's garden without knowing its name. And I planted it in his honor.

As I waited and watched in the garden and by Grandpa's side, some quiet truths emerged. I realized that Grandpa loved flowers that were always in bloom; he kept a full bed of roses in his garden. But I noticed that Grandpa left plenty of room for the brief highlights. Not every nook of his garden was constantly in bloom. There was always a treasured surprise tucked somewhere.

I came to see, too, that Grandpa's garden mirrored his life. He was a hard worker who understood the law of the harvest. But along with his hard work, Grandpa knew how to enjoy each season, each change.

In July, Grandpa worsened. One hot afternoon arrived when no one else was at his bedside. He was glad to have me there, and reached out his hand to pull me close.

I told Grandpa what I had learned—that few flowers last from April to November. Some of the most beautiful bloom for only a month at most. To really enjoy a garden, you have to plant corners and drifts and rows of flowers that will bloom and grace the garden, each in its own season.

His eyes listened to every word: "If I want a garden like yours, Grandpa, I'm going to have to work." His grin laughed at me.

"Grandpa, in your life right now the chrysanthemums are in bloom. Chrysanthemums and roses." Tears clouded both our eyes. Neither of us feared this last flower of fall, but the wait for spring seems longest in November. We knew how much we would miss each other.

Grandpa and I wept together.

It was the end of August when Grandpa died, the end of summer. As we were choosing flowers from the florist for Grandpa's funeral, I slipped away to Grandpa's garden and walked with my memories of columbine and Sweet William. Only the tall lavender and white phlox were in bloom now, and some baby's breath in another corner.

On impulse, I cut the prettiest strands of phlox and baby's breath and made one more arrangement for the funeral. When they saw it, friends and family all smiled to see Grandpa's flowers there. We all felt how much Grandpa would have liked that.

The October after Grandpa's death, I planted tulip and daffodil bulbs, snowdrops, crocuses, and bluebells. Each bulb was a comfort to me, a love sent to Grandpa, a promise of spring.

鲜花的承诺

初春时节,大约在爷爷中风前的一个月,我开始每天下午散步一小时。有一段日子,我常常向南步行4个街区,去看望爷爷奶奶。86岁的爷爷仍是个了不起的花匠,所以我总是留意他那些最早盛开的鲜花和春天新开的每一片花海。

因为那年我打算美化自己的院子,所以对花特别感兴趣,渴望听到爷爷的建议。我以为自己非常清楚需要什么——满院子花草树丛,从5月一直开到11月。

爷爷就是那年春天在草坪里第一丛紫罗兰出现和连翘突然盛开后中风的。他无法言语,身体左半侧也无法动弹。家里所有人都聚到了爷爷身边。我们都花了很多时间守在他身边。有几天,他的眼睛炯炯有神——他一边笑我们报告的不幸,一边留意倾听,露出了他生活不能自理的痛苦。有一段日子,他大多数时间都处于睡眠状态,死亡随时都会向他逼近。

几个月过去了,我像爷爷一样望着地上的东西渐渐长大。我每次和他在一起,都要向他汇报花园的情况。他一边听,一边紧握着我的手。可是,他无法回答我的问题。很多新的花朵常常绽放、憔悴、枯萎,还没等我知道它们的名字就死去了。

从春天开始,爷爷周复一周疾病缠身,一直持续到夏天。我开始泡在当地的苗圃,研究、选种和栽培。我买了一些曾在爷爷的花园里见过的幼苗,恭恭敬敬地种在自己的花园里,这让我感到特别开心。我在爷爷的花园里发现了自己喜欢多年的美洲石竹,以前一直不知道它的名字,而且我以爷爷的名义栽下了它。

我待在花园、守在爷爷身边时,一些真理悄悄涌现出来。我知道爷爷爱那些怒放的鲜花;他在花园里种了满满一苗圃的玫瑰。可是,我注意到爷爷留了很多空当,让光线暂时照进来。他的花园并不是每个角落都经常鲜花怒放,总有某个珍藏的惊喜躲在某个地方。

我最终明白爷爷的花园是他一生的写照。他是一个勤劳的人,明白收获的规律。但说起辛勤劳动,爷爷知道如何享受每一个季节、每一种变化。

7月,爷爷病情恶化。一个炎热的下午,其他人都不在他身边,只有我在那里,他很高兴,就伸出一只手将我拉近。

我把自己学到的告诉了爷爷:能从4月开到11月的花寥寥无几。大部分花最多只开一个月。为了真正欣赏花园,你必须在各个角落都种上花,美化花园,一丛丛一行行,鲜花开放,四季如春。

他用目光听着我的每一个字:"爷爷,如果想要一个像你的一样的花园,我必须得去工作。"他咧开嘴对我笑了笑。

"爷爷,在您的人生中,现在菊花正在开放。菊花和玫瑰花。"泪水模糊了我们的眼睛。我们俩都不害怕秋天的最后一朵花,但在11月等待春天似乎太长,我们都知道我们会多么想念对方。

我和爷爷都泪流满面。

8月底、夏末之际,爷爷撒手而去。当大家都在花店为爷爷的葬礼选花时,我悄然离去,来到爷爷的花园。我一边走,一边回忆着那些耧斗菜和美洲石竹。现在只有高高的熏衣草和白色夹竹桃在开花,另一个角落还有一些水香花菜。

我一时冲动,剪下了最漂亮的几束夹竹桃和水香花菜,又给爷爷的葬礼装点了一番。看到这些花,亲友们都露出了微笑。我们都知道爷爷一定会多么喜欢。

爷爷去世后的10月,我种了一些郁金香、水仙花、雪花莲、藏红花和蓝铃花。对我来说,每一棵花根都是一种安慰,都是送给爷爷的一份爱,都是春天的一份承诺。

Life Is the Cookie

One of my patients, a successful businessman, tells me that before his cancer he would become depressed unless things went a certain way. For him, happiness was "having the cookie." If you had the cookie, things were good. If you didn't have the cookie, life wasn't worth a damn. Unluckily, the cookie kept changing. Sometimes it was money, sometimes power, sometimes sex. At other times, it was the new car, the biggest contract, the most prestigious address. A year and a half after his diagnosis of prostate cancer he sits shaking his head ruefully. "It's like I stopped learning how to live after I was a kid. When I give my son a cookie, he is happy. If I take the cookie away or it breaks, he is unhappy. But he is two and a half and I am forty-three. It's taken me this long to understand that the cookie will never make me happy for long. The minute you have the cookie it starts to crumble or you start to worry about it crumbling or about someone trying to take it away from you. You know, you have to give up a lot of things to take care of the cookie, to keep it from crumbling and be sure that no one takes it away from you. You may not even get a chance to eat it because you are so busy just trying not to lose it. Having the cookie is not what life is about."

My patient laughs and says cancer has changed him. For the first time he is happy whether his business is doing well or not, whether he wins or loses at golf. "Two years ago, cancer asked me, 'What is important? What is really important?' Well, life is important. Life. Life any way you can have it, life with the cookie, life without the cookie. Happiness does not have anything to do with the cookie; it has to do with being alive. But who can make the time go back?" He pauses thoughtfully. "I guess life is the cookie."

生命就是小甜饼

我的一个病人是一名成功商人，他告诉我说，他患癌症前，如果事情没有按照某种确定的方式发展，他就会情绪低落。对他来说，幸福就是"拥有小甜饼"。如果你拥有小甜饼，事情就一帆风顺。如果你没有小甜饼，生活就一文不值。不幸的是，小甜饼总是不断变化，有时是金钱，有时是权力，有时是性。在其他时候，它则是新车、数额最大的合同、享有声望的演讲。诊断出患有前列腺癌一年半后，他坐在那里，悲伤地摇了摇头。"长大后，我好像不去学如何生活了。当我送给儿子一块小甜饼时，他就开心。如果我拿走小甜饼或小甜饼破碎，他就不开心。但他才两岁半，我已经43岁了。我花了这么长时间才明白，小甜饼并不能使我长久幸福。你一拥有小甜饼，它就开始破碎，或者你就开始担心它会破碎，要么担心别人会从你手里拿走。你知道，你不得不放弃很多东西来看护好小甜饼，防止它破碎，并确保别人不会从你手里抢走。因为你忙着尽力不失去它，所以说不定都没有机会去吃它。拥有小甜饼并不是生活的全部。"

我的病人笑着说癌症已经改变了他。无论他的生意是否一帆风顺，无论他在打高尔夫时是输是赢，他第一次感到幸福。"两年前，癌症问我：'什么重要？什么才真正重要？'对，生命重要。生命，生命，无论你拥有什么样的生命，无论有没有小甜饼，幸福和小甜饼没有任何关系，而是和活着有关。可谁又能让时间倒回去呢？"他若有所思地停顿了一下，"我想生命就是小甜饼。"

The Worth of Life

A well-known speaker started his speech by holding up a $20 bill. In the room of 200 people, he asked, "Who would like this $20 bill?"

Hands started going up. He said, "I am going to give this $20 to one of you—but first, let me do this."

He proceeded to crumple the 20-dollar note up. He then asked, "Who still wants it?" Still the hands were up in the air.

"Well," he replied, "what if I do this?" He dropped it on the ground and started to grind it into the floor with his shoe. He picked it up, now crumpled and dirty. "Now, who still wants it?"

Still the hands went into the air.

"My friends, you have all learned a very valuable lesson. No matter what I did to the money, you still wanted it because it did not decrease in value. It was still worth $20.

"Many times in our lives, we are dropped, crumpled, and ground into the dirt by the decisions we make and the circumstances that come our way. We feel as though we are worthless; but no matter what happened or what will happen, you will never lose your value. Dirty or clean, crumpled or finely creased, you are still priceless to those who love you.

"The worth of our lives comes, not in what we do or who we know, but by WHO YOU ARE.

"You are special—don't ever forget it."

生命的价值

一位著名的演说家举着一张20美元的钞票开始了演讲。他在一个200人的房间里问道:"谁想要这20美元的钞票?"

人们的手都举了起来。他说:"我准备把这张钞票给你们其中一个人,但首先让我这样做。"

他接着把20美元的钞票揉了揉,举了起来,然后问道:"谁还想要?"那些手仍然举向了空中。

"好,"他回答说,"如果我这样做会怎么样?"他把钞票扔在地上,开始用鞋使劲在地板上踩。随后,他拾起钞票,现在钞票又皱又脏,"现在,谁还想要?"

那些手仍然举向空中。

"我的朋友们,你们都已经学到了非常宝贵的一课。无论我对这钱做了什么,你们都仍然想要它,因为它没有降低价值。它仍然是20美元。

"我们生命中会多次遇到挫折、坎坷,并让我们做出的决定和周围的环境逼到卑微的境地。我们感到自己似乎毫无价值。但无论发生什么和将会发生什么,你都永远不会失去自己的价值。无论是肮脏还是干净,无论是被揉成一团还是整齐折叠,在爱你的人看来,你都极其珍贵。

"我们的价值不在于我们做了什么或者认识谁,而在于你是谁。"

"你与众不同——永远别忘记这一点。"

Life Is like a Piece of Cake

A little boy is telling his grandma how everything is going wrong. Meanwhile, Grandma is baking a cake. She asks her grandson if he would like a snack, which, of course, he does.

"Here, have some cooking oil." "Yuck," says the boy. "How about a couple of raw eggs?" "Disgusting, Grandma!" "Would you like some flour then? Or maybe baking soda?" "Grandma, those are all yucky!"

Grandma replies, "Yes, all those things seem bad all by themselves. But when they are put together in the right way, they make a wonderfully delicious cake! Many times we wonder why it would let us go through such difficult times. But when it puts these things all in his order, they always work for good! We just have to trust it. Eventually, they will all make something wonderful! I hope your day is a piece of delicious cake."

生活就像一块蛋糕

小男孩正在对他的奶奶说一切都不顺心。此刻,奶奶正在烤蛋糕。她问孙子是不是想吃一块蛋糕。他当然想吃。

"喂,来点儿油。""呸,"男孩说,"来几个生鸡蛋怎么样?""恶心,奶奶!""那你喜欢面粉?或者喜欢发酵粉吗?""奶奶,那些东西都令人恶心!"

奶奶回答说:"是的,所有那些东西单独看起来似乎并不好,但当它们以适当方式放在一起时,就成了美味无比的蛋糕!很多时候,我们抱怨它常常让我们经历这样的艰难时刻。当它以自己的顺序把这些东西在一起时,它们总是会发挥作用。我们得相信它。最终,它们就会成为美妙的东西!我希望你的每一天都是一块美味可口的蛋糕。"

The Only Attitude Is Gratitude

Around twenty years ago I was living in Seattle and going through hard times. I could not find satisfying work and I found this especially difficult as I had a lot of experience and a Masters degree. To my shame I was driving a school bus to make ends meet and living with friends. I had lost my apartment. I had been through five interviews with a company and one day between bus runs they called to say I did not get the job. I went to the bus barn like a zombie of disappointment.

Later that afternoon, while doing my rounds through a quiet suburban neighborhood I had an inner wave—like a primal scream—arise from deep inside me and I thought"Why has my life become so hard?" "Give me a sign, I asked…"

Immediately after this internal scream I pulled the bus over to drop off a little girl and as she passed she handed me an earring saying I should keep it in case somebody claimed it. The earring was stamped metal, painted black and said, "BE HAPPY". At first I got angry—yeah, yeah, I thought. Then it hit me. I had been putting all of my energies into what was wrong with my life rather than what was right! I decided then and there to make a list of 50 things I was grateful for.

At first it was hard, then it got easier. One day I decided to up it to 75. That night there was a phone call for me at my friend's house from a lady who was a manager at a large hospital. About a year earlier I had submitted a syllabus to a community college to teach a course on stress management. She asked me if I would do a one-day seminar for 200 hospital workers. I said yes and got the job.

My day with the hospital workers went very well. I got a standing ovation and many more days of work. To this day I know that it was because I changed my attitude to gratitude.

Incidentally, the day after I found the earring the girl asked me if anyone had claimed it. I told her no and she said, "I guess it was meant for you then."

I spent the next year conducting training workshops all around the Seattle area and then decided to risk everything and go back to Scotland where I had lived previously. I closed my one-man business, bought a plane ticket and got a six-month visa from immigration. One month later I met my wonderful English wife and best friend of 15 years now. We live in a small beautiful cottage, two miles from a paved road in the highlands of Scotland.

"THE ONLY ATTITUDE IS GRATITUDE" has been my motto for years now and completely changed my life.

感激是唯一的态度

大约20年前，我住在西雅图，正经历着坎坷。我经验丰富，拥有硕士学位，却找不到满意的工作，感到特别难受。让我羞愧的是，当时我驾驶一辆校车勉强度日，和朋友住在一起。要知道，我失去了自己的房子。我应聘一家公司，经历了五轮面试。一天，我就要出车时，对方打来电话说我没应聘上。我向车库走去时，失魂落魄。

那天下午晚些时候，我开着校车转到一片安静的郊区的居民区时，内心闪过了一个念头——像精神病患者的早期治疗——来自我的内心深处。我想："为什么自己的生活变得如此艰难？""给我一个征兆，我请求过……"

很快，我把车停住，一个小姑娘要下车。她经过我身边时，递给我一只耳饰，说保管住，以防有人认领。耳饰上面压有金属印，被漆了黑色，写的是"一定要幸福"。起初，我很生气——是啊，是啊，我想。接着，它让我忽然明白了。我一直一门心思用在想我的生活出的问题上，而不是我的生活的美好！我当即决定列出50件感激的事情。

一开始，很难列出来，后来就变得容易了。我决定将这个习惯坚持到75岁。有天晚上，一个电话打到了我朋友的家中要求找我，是一家大医院的女经理打来的。大约一年前，我向一所社区大学递交过一份课程提纲，要求去教一门成功应对压力的课程。她问我是否愿意给200名医院职工做一场为期一天的讲习会。我答应了，得到了这份工作。

我跟那家医院的职工们相处得很融洽。我受到了长期欢迎，获得了更多天的工作。直到今天，我都非常清楚，那全是因为我转变为感激生活的态度。

顺便提一下，我找到那个耳饰后第二天，那个小姑娘问我是否有人认领。我告诉她没有，她说："我猜当时它是为你准备的。"

接下来的一年，我一直都在西雅图各地给车间工人们做培训，后来决定冒着一切风险回到我以前生活过的苏格兰。我关掉了只有我一个人的生意，买了一张飞机票，从移民局获得了半年签证。一个月后，我见到了我那漂亮的英国妻子和交了15年的挚友。现在我们住在一所漂亮的小别墅，距离苏格兰高地的一条道路两英里。

多年来，"感激是唯一的态度"已经成为我的座右铭，彻底改变了我的人生。

The Meaning of Life

An eight-year-old boy approached an old man in front of a wishing well, looked up into his eyes, and asked: "I understand you're a very wise man. I'd like to know the secret of life."

The old man looked down at the youngster and replied, "I've though a lot in my lifetime, and the secret can be summed up in four words:

"The first is think. Think about the values you wish to live your life by.

"The second is believe. Believe in yourself based on the thinking you've done about the values you're going to live your life by.

"The third is dream. Dream about the things that can be, based on your belief in yourself and the values you're going to live by.

"The last is dare. Dare to make your dreams become reality, based on your belief in yourself and your values."

And with that, Walter E. Disney said to the little boy: Think, believe, dream and dare.

人生的意义

一个8岁的小男孩走到一眼许愿井旁边的一位老人身边,抬头望着他的眼睛问道:"我知道你是一个非常有智慧的人,我想知道人生的真谛。"

老人看着小男孩答道:"我在一生中想了很多,生活的真谛可以概括为四个词:

"首先是思考,思考你生活的价值观。

"其次是信任,对自己的信任基于你已经找到自己一生依赖生存的价值观。

"其三是梦想,梦想那些可以基于你一生遵循的价值观和对自己的信任的事情。

"最后是勇敢,在你的价值观和对自己信任的基础上,勇敢地让梦想变成现实。"

最后,沃尔特·E.迪士尼对这个小男孩说:思考、信任、梦想和勇敢。

Human Beings Have Choices

It takes both rain and sunshine to create a rainbow. Lives are no different. There is happiness and sorrow. There is the good and the bad; dark and bright spots. If we can handle adversity, it only strengthens us. We cannot control all the events that happen in our lives, but we can decide how we deal with them.

Richard Blechnyden wanted to promote Indian tea in St. Louis World Fair in 1904. It was very hot and no one wanted to sample his tea. Blechnyden saw that all the other iced drinks were doing flourishing business. It dawned on him to make his tea into an iced drink, mix in sugar and sell it. He did and people love it. That was the introduction of iced tea to the world.

When things go wrong, as they sometimes will, we can react responsibly or resentfully.

Human beings are not like an acorn which has no choice. An acorn cannot decide whether to become a giant tree or to become food for the squirrels. Human beings have choices. If nature gives us a lemon, we have a choice: either cry for grace or make lemonade.

人生可以选择

彩虹是雨和阳光共同创造的。生活也是这样,有喜有悲、有好有坏、有明有暗。如果我们能战胜不幸,就会增强我们的力量。尽管我们无法控制生活中发生的所有事情,但可以决定如何处理它们。

1904年,理查德·布莱克尼登在圣路易斯世界博览会上推销印度茶。当时天气很热,没人想品尝他的茶。布莱克尼登看到其他冰镇饮料都生意兴隆,于是就想到了一个主意,将茶做成冰镇饮料,加上糖,再卖。他这样做后,人们非常喜欢。冰茶就是这样介绍给世人的。

事情有时会出错,我们既可以积极回应,也可以愤愤不平。

人不像无从选择的橡子。一粒橡子无法决定是长成参天大树,还是成为松鼠的食物。人则有选择的余地。如果大自然给我们一颗柠檬,那我们就可以做出选择:要么感恩而泣,要么将它做成柠檬汁。

The Boys and the Sticks

A father's sons were always fighting. He had no way to stop them, so he decided to teach them a lesson.

He told his sons to bring him a bunch of sticks. He took the sticks, gave them to his eldest son and asked him to break them. The eldest son tried with all his might but was not able to do it. The other sons tried their best and were also unsuccessful.

The father then separated the sticks and put one into each son's hand. He asked his sons again to try and break the sticks. They broke them easily.

The father said, "My sons, if you are of one mind, and unite to assist each other, you will be like these sticks together; but if you are divided among yourselves, you will be broken as easily as a single stick."

男孩与木棍

父亲的一群孩子总喜欢吵架,但他想不出什么办法来阻止他们,于是决定给他们上一课。

他吩咐孩子们抱来一捆木棍。他拿起这捆木棍，递给大儿子，让他把它们折断。大儿子用尽全力，也没能做到。其他的儿子努力了半天，也没有成功。

于是，父亲把那些木棍分开，将它们各自放进了每个儿子的手里。他再次要求他们用力折断那些木棍。这次，他们轻而易举便将它们折断了。

父亲说："儿子们，要是齐心协力、团结互助，你们就会像这捆木棍一样；但要是各自为政，你们就会像这单根木棍一样容易折断。"

The Mahogany Piano

Many years ago, when I was a young man in my twenties, I worked as a salesman for a St. Louis piano company. We sold our pianos all over the state by advertising in small town newspapers and then, when we had received sufficient replies, we would load our little trucks, drive into the area and sell the pianos to those who had replied.

Every time we would advertise in the cotton country of Southeast Missouri, we would receive a reply on a postcard which said, "Please bring me a new piano for my little granddaughter. It must be red mahogany. I can pay $10 a month with my egg money." The old lady scrawled on and on and on that postcard until she filled it up, then turned it over and even wrote on the front—around and around the edges until there was barely room for the address.

Of course, we could not sell a new piano for $10 a month. No finance company would carry a contract with payments that small, so we ignored her postcards.

One day, however, I happened to be in that area calling on other replies, and out of curiosity I decided to look up the old lady. I found pretty much what I expected: The old lady lived in a one-room sharecroppers cabin in the middle of a cotton field. The cabin had a dirt floor and there were chickens in the house. Obviously, the old lady could not have qualified to purchase anything on credit—no car, no phone, no real job, nothing but a roof over her head and not a very good one at that. I could see daylight through it in several places. Her little granddaughter was about 10, barefoot and wearing a feed sack dress.

I explained to the old lady that we could not sell a new piano for $10 a month and that she should stop writing to us every time she saw our ad. I drove away heartsick, but my advice had no effect—she still sent us the same postcard every six weeks. Always wanting a new piano, red mahogany, please, and swearing she would never miss a $10 payment. It was sad.

A couple of years later, I owned my own piano company, and when I advertised in that area, the postcards started coming to me. For months, I ignored them—what else could I do?

But then, one day when I was in the area something came over me. I had a red mahogany piano on my little truck. Despite knowing that I was about to make a terrible business decision, I delivered the piano to her and told her I would carry the contract myself at $10 a month with no interest, and that would mean 52 payments. I took the new piano in the house and placed it where I thought the roof would be least likely to rain on it. I admonished her and the little girl to try to keep the chickens off of it, and I left—sure I had just thrown away a new piano.

But the payments came in, all 52 of them as agreed—sometimes with coins taped to a 3×5 inch card in the envelope. It was incredible!

So, I put the incident out of my mind for 20 years.

Then one day I was in Memphis on other business, and after dinner at the Holiday Inn, I went into the lounge. As I was sitting at the bar having an after-dinner drink, I heard the most beautiful piano music behind me. I looked around, and there was a lovely young woman playing a very nice grand piano.

Being a pianist of some ability myself, I was stunned by her virtuosity, and I picked up my drink and moved to a table beside her where I could listen and watch. She smiled at me and asked for requests. When she took a break she sat down at my table.

"Aren't you the man who sold my grandma a piano a long time ago?"

It didn't ring a bell, so I asked her to explain.

She started to tell me, and I suddenly remembered. My God, it was her! It was the little barefoot girl in the feed sack dress!

She told me her name was Elise and since her grandmother couldn't afford to pay for lessons, she had learned to play by listening to the radio. She said she had started to play in church where she and her grandmother had to walk over two miles, and that she had then played in school, had won many awards and a music scholarship. She had married an attorney in Memphis and he had bought her that beautiful grand piano she was playing.

Something else entered my mind. "Elise," I asked. "It's a little dark in here. What color is that piano?"

"It's red mahogany," she said. "Why?"

I couldn't speak.

Did she understand the significance of the red mahogany? The unbelievable audacity of her grandmother insisting on a red mahogany piano when no one in his right mind would have sold her a piano of any kind? I think not.

And then the marvelous accomplishment of that beautiful, terribly underprivileged child in the feed sack dress? No, I'm sure she didn't understand that either.

But I did, and my throat tightened.

Finally, I found my voice. "I just wondered," I said. "I'm proud of you, but I have to go to my room."

And I did have to go to my room, because men don't like to be seen crying in public.

一架桃花心木钢琴

很多年前，我还是20多岁的小伙子，当时我是圣路易斯钢琴公司的一名推销员。我们的钢琴销售遍及整个州，我们通常是先在各小镇的报纸上做广告，然后等到收到足够的回单，我们就给我们的一辆辆小卡车装货，开到那个地方，把钢琴卖给那些回单的人。

每次在密苏里州东南部棉花产地打广告，我们都会收到一张明信片，上面写着："请给我的小孙女带一架新钢琴。必须是红色桃花心木的。我可以用每月卖鸡蛋的钱支付10美元。"这位老太太字迹潦草，直到写满了一张明信片，甚至写到了正面——边边角角都写满了，直到差不多没地方写地址为止。

当然，我们不会把一架把钢琴分期每月卖10美元，没有哪家信贷公司会以这么小的分期付款签合同，所以我们没有理睬她的那些明信片。

然而，有一天，我碰巧要在那个地方拜访其他客人。出于好奇，我决定去探访那位老太太。我发现大大出乎我的意料：老太太住在棉花田中央的一个佃农单间小屋里。小屋是泥土地面，而且还养了鸡。显然，老太太没有资格赊购任何东西：她没有车，没有电话，没有真正的工作，只有头上的房顶，就连房顶也不是很好。我可以看到有好几处地方漏光。她的小孙女大约10岁，赤着双脚，身穿饲料袋改做的衣服。

我向老太太解释说，我们不能以每月10美元分期出售新钢琴，她不要再每次看到广告给我们写信了。我驱车离开时，感到心痛，但我的建议没有奏效——她仍然每隔6周就给我们寄去一张相同的明信片。总是想买一架新钢琴，红色桃花心木的，求求你们了，她还发誓绝不遗漏每次10美元付款。这真让人伤心。

两三年后，我拥有了自己的钢琴公司；而当我去那个地方打广告时，那些明信片开始源源不断地寄给我。有好几个月，我都对它们熟视无睹。我还能做什么呢？

但后来有一天，我在那个地区活动时萌发了想法。我的小卡车上装了一架红色桃花心木钢琴。尽管我知道这是一桩糟糕的买卖，但我还是把这架钢琴运到了她家,并告诉她我亲自签署这个每月付10美元没有利息的合同,而这将意味着要付52次款。我把钢琴送进屋里,把它放在一个最不可能淋到雨的地方,告诫她和小女孩尽量让鸡远离钢琴,随后我便离开了——我肯定是扔掉了一架新钢琴。

可是,那些钱一笔一笔地寄来了,正如合同上约定的那样,整整52笔——有时硬币粘在信封里一张3.5英寸大的卡片上。真不可思议!

于是,我便把这件事忘在了脑后,转眼就是20年。

后来有一天,我在孟菲斯做其他买卖。我在防洪堤上的假日旅馆吃完饭后,走进了休闲室。我坐在酒吧里喝餐后饮料时,听到身后传来最美妙的钢琴曲。我环顾四周,看见一个可爱的年轻女子弹奏一架非常漂亮的大钢琴。

我总是自信有钢琴家的才干,一下子被她的精湛演技震住了。我端起饮料,走到她身边的一张桌子,我在那里可以倾听欣赏。她朝我微微一笑,发出了邀请。她中场休息时,在我这张桌边坐下。

"你不就是很久以前卖给我祖母一架钢琴的那个人吗?"

我一时想不起来,于是便请她解释一下。

她开始向我说起来,我突然想起来了。我的天啊,是她!是那个赤着脚、穿着饲料袋改做的衣服的小女孩!

她告诉我她的名字叫伊莉斯,因为她的祖母没有钱供她上钢琴课,所以她学弹钢琴是靠听收音机。她说她开始演奏是在教堂里,她和祖母要步行两英里走到那里。她后来在学校演奏,多次获奖,还获得了一次音乐奖学金。她嫁给了孟菲斯的一位律师,刚才弹奏的那架漂亮的大钢琴就是他给她买下的。

这时,我想到了别的东西。"伊莉斯,"我问道,"这里光线有点儿暗,你那架钢琴是什么颜色?"

"是红色桃花心木的,"她说,"怎么了?"

我说不出话来。

她明白红色桃花心木的意义吗?她明白她祖母是怎样执意要买一架红木钢琴而做出的那些惊人举动吗?当时头脑正常的人不会把钢琴卖给她。我想不会。

还有,那个取得非凡成就的漂亮而穷困的小女孩呢?不,我确信她也不会明白。

但我明白,我的喉咙哽咽了。

最后,我又能说话了。"我当时只是好奇,"我说,"我为你感到骄傲，但我得去自己的房间了。"

我确实得去自己的房间，因为男人们是不喜欢当众流泪的。

The Boy and the Nail

Once there was a little boy who had a bad temper. His father gave him a bag of nails and told him that every time he lost his temper, he must hammer a nail into the fence.

The first day the boy hammered 37 nails into the fence. Over the next few weeks, as he learned to control his anger, the number of nails hammered daily dwindled down. He discovered it was easier to hold his temper than to drive those nails into the fence.

Finally the day came when the boy didn't lose his temper at all. He told his father about it and the father suggested that the boy now pull out one nail for each day that he was able to hold his temper.

The days passed and one day the young boy told his father that all the nails were gone. The father took his son by the hand and led him to the fence. The fence would never be the same. "When you say things in anger, they leave a scar just like those nails," his father said.

男孩和钉子

从前，有一个小男孩，他的脾气很坏。他的父亲送给他一袋钉子，告诉他说，他每发一次火，就必须将一颗钉子钉在栅栏上。

第一天，男孩将37颗钉子钉进了栅栏。又过了几周，随着他学会控制自己的怒火，钉子的数目日益减少。他发现控制自己的脾气要比往栅栏上钉那些钉子容易。

最后，男孩再也不发火的日子终于来了。他把这件事告诉了他的父亲。他的父亲建议他现在每天能控制住自己的脾气，就拔掉一颗钉子。

又过去了好几天。有一天，男孩对他的父亲说，所有的钉子都没有了。男孩的父亲拉住他的手，将他领到了栅栏边。栅栏再也不是从前的样子了。"当你生气地说出事情时，它们就像那些钉子一样留下了伤疤。"他的父亲说。

The Next Step to Life

"A journey of a thousand miles must begin with a first step," a Chinese sage once said. Our first step was to rent a pop-up trailer so our family of five could try camping. The trip was a success. To pull the trailer on subsequent trips, we had to buy a bigger station wagon. Sundry equipments followed: sleeping bags, stove, lantern, grill, pup tent, cooler and so on. Eventually, when we went camping, we looked like the Grand Army of the Republic.

Now we were clamoring for a canoe. I placed an ad in the paper: "Wanted, canoe for young family on limited budget. Please call after 6 p. m."

We waited for days by a silent phone. Then one night came—THE CALL. "Are you the family looking for a canoe?" asked an elderly voice.

"Yes, we are, ma'am." I replied.

"I may have what you are looking for. First, tell me about your family and your plans for the canoe."

So I told her how our family had enjoyed camping that summer, and how we especially liked remote places near lakes. I told her that a canoe seemed like the next step for us.

Apparently I'd said the right things, for the woman invited us to come to look at a canoe. On the following Sunday, the whole family drove to her house. We rang the bell, and a frail woman with white hair invited us in.

Once we were seated around the kitchen table, she proceeded to engage each of us in conversation. She made it clear that the canoe was special to her. She wanted it to go to a family with love and care.

It seems we passed the test, because she invited us out to the garage. It was empty, except for a wooden rack on which rested—THE CANOE.

It was 18 feet long, with high, curved bow and stern; green-painted canvas seats, one with a cedar backrest; and two cushions stuffed with balsam-fir needles. A portrait of an Indian chief had been wood-burned on a hand-carved paddle.

The canoe was magnificent. It was almost too much to hope that such a glorious thing could be ours.

Dazzled, we followed the woman back to the house. She opened an old album and showed us a picture of a smiling couple on a porch swing. We recognized our hostess. The young man was handsome.

She turned the page, and we recognized the canoe. The young man was in the stern, holding the Indian head paddle. In the bow sat a young woman wearing a straw hat. "My husband courted me in that very canoe," the woman explained. She told us about some of the outings they had enjoyed long ago.

We feared the canoe was beyond our grasp. My wife and I had agreed that we could go as high as $100. This canoe was clearly worth more than that. Timidly we inquired how much she was asking.

"How much will you prepare to spend?" she asked.

"Seventy-five dollars," I stammered, leaving room for negotiation.

"Tsk," said the woman. "With your young family, I couldn't possibly accept more than $35." We shook hands fervently.

Our treasured canoe has taken us on many adventures—island-hopping on a Maine lake, blueberrying expeditions, moonlit paddles to listen for loons. True to our word, we have treated it with love and care.

When our children outgrew family camping, my daughter took the canoe to college. At the campus woodworking shop, she made a new center thwart to replace the old one.

A workman there pointed out a small brass plaque, which we had overlooked for years. Thus we found out that our canoe had been manufactured in 1907 by the Morris Canoe Company in Veazie, Maine. A fire a few years later put Morris out of business.

So today our canoe is a collector's item, valued in the thousands of dollars. But the real value, for us, lies in the adventures our family had, and the memories we now treasure. We'll never forget our friend, the woman who shared her memories and helped us take the next step to life.

人生的第二步

中国一位圣人曾经说过："千里之行，始于足下。"我们的第一步是从租赁一辆蹩脚的拖车开始的，这样一家5口便可一块去野营了。旅行取得了成功。在后来的旅行中，为了拉那辆拖车，我们不得不买了一辆旅行车。接下来是各种各样的装备：睡袋、炉子、提灯、烤肉架、三角小帐篷、冷却器等。最终出去野营时，我们浩浩荡荡，看上去就像共和国大军。

现在，我们家嚷嚷着想要一条独木舟。我在报纸上刊登了一条广告："征求启事：年轻家庭欲购独木舟，资金有限。请下午6点后打电话。"

我们等了好几天都不见有电话。后来有一天夜里，电话突然响了起来："是你们家想要独木舟吗？"一个苍老的声音问道。

"是的，是我们家，太太。"我回答说。

"我也许有你们要找的那种独木舟。首先，给我谈谈你们家的情况和你们要独木舟的打算。"

于是，我就把那年夏天我们家野营的事儿告诉了她，同时还告诉她说，我们尤其喜欢湖附近的偏远地方。我对她说，独木舟好像是我们下一步计划的关键。

显然，我的话正中下怀，因为老太太邀请我们去看独木舟。第二个星期天，我们全家驱车赶到了她的家。我们按响门铃，随后一位白发苍苍、弱不禁风的老妇人将我们迎了进去。

我们一在她的餐桌边落座,她就开始跟我们每个人攀谈了起来。她明确表示说,独木舟对她不同寻常,她想要独木舟归属到一个充满爱心和关怀的家庭。

似乎我们通过了考试,因为她请我们进了她的车库。那里空荡荡的,只有一个木架,上面放着一条独木舟。

独木舟长18英尺,船头和船尾弯弯的高高翘起;绿色油漆帆布座,其中一个座上带有雪松木靠背;而且两个垫子装有胶枞针叶;一幅印第安首领的头像浇铸在雕花船桨上。

独木舟美观大方,简直难以想象这样一件贵重的东西会归我们所有。

我们晕晕乎乎跟随老太太回到屋里。她打开一本旧相册,让我们看一张一对夫妇面带笑容坐在门廊秋千上的照片。我们认出了我们的女主人。那个小伙子非常英俊。

她翻过那页,然后我们就看到了那条独木舟。那个小伙子手握那只刻着印第安首领头像的船桨坐在船尾。一个年轻姑娘头戴草帽坐在船头。"我的丈夫就是在那只独木舟上向我求婚的。"老太太解释说。她给我们说起了多年前他们外出郊游的情景。

我们担心买不起这条独木舟。我和妻子商定最高出价100美元。独木舟明显不止这个价。我们不好意思问她要价多少。

"你们准备花多少钱?"她问。

"75美元。"我结结巴巴地说,留下了砍价的余地。

"啧啧,"老太太说,"像你们这样年轻的家庭,超过35美元我是不可能接受的。"我们热情地握了握手。

这条心爱的独木舟曾载着我们经历过许多次的冒险——在缅因州一个湖上越岛作战,去冒险采摘过蓝莓,在月光下泛舟湖倾听潜鸟的吟唱。说实在话,我们对独木舟充满了爱心和关怀。

当我们的子女都长大不适合家庭野营时,我们的女儿将独木舟带到了大学。在学校的木工店,她做了一块新的中横坐板,换下了那块旧板。

店里的木匠无意间发现了一个小铜饰板,这么多年我们一家人谁也没有注意到。于是,我们发现我们的独木舟是1907年由缅因州维基市莫里斯轻舟公司生产的。几年后的一场大火使该公司变成了一片废墟。

因此,眼下我们的独木舟摇身一变,价值几千美元,成了收藏品。但对我们来说,独木舟的真正价值在于,我们家共同分享过的奇趣和珍藏在心间的回忆。我们将终生难忘我们的朋友——那位老太太，她不仅自己留下了点点滴滴的回忆，而且帮助我们走向了人生的第二步。

Schemes of Life often Illusory

Omar, the son of Hassan, had passed seventy-five years in honor and prosperity. His house is filled with gold and silver; and whenever he appeared, the benedictions of the people proclaimed his passage.

Terrestrial happiness is of short continuance, The brightness of the flame is wasting its fuel; the fragrant flower is passing away in its own odors. The vigor of Omar began to fail; the curls of beauty fell from his head; strength departed from his hands, and agility from his feet. He sought no other pleasure for the remainder of life than the converse of the wise and the gratitude of the good.

The powers of his mind were yet unimpaired. His chamber was filled by visitants, eager to catch the dictates of experience, and officious to pay the tribute of admiration. Caleb, the son of the viceroy of Egypt, entered every day early, and retired late. He was beautiful and eloquent; Omar admired his wit, and loved his docility.

"Tell me," said Caleb, "thou to whose voice nations have listened, and whose wisdom is known to the extremities of Asia, tell me, how I may resemble Omar the prudent? The arts by which thou hast gained power and preserved it, are to thee no longer necessary or useful; impart to me the secret of thy conduct, and teach me the plan upon which thy wisdom has built thy fortune."

"Young man," said Omar, "it is of little use to form plans of life. When I took my first survey of the world, in my twentieth year, having considered the various conditions of mankind, in the hour of solitude I said thus to myself, leaning against a cedar which spread its branches over my head: 'seventy years are allowed to man; I have yet fifty remaining.'

"Ten years I will allot to the attainment of knowledge, and ten I will pass in foreign countries; I shall be learned, and therefore I shall be honored; every city will shout at my arrival, and every student will solicit my friendship. Twenty years thus passed will store my mind with images which I shall be busy through the rest of my life in combining and comparing. I shall revel in inexhaustible accumulations of intellectual riches; I shall find new pleasures for every moment, and shall never more be weary of myself.

"I will not, however, deviate too far from the beaten track of life; but will try what can be found in female delicacy. I will marry a wife as beautiful as the houries, and wise as Zobeide; and with her I will live twenty years within the suburbs of Bagdad, in every pleasure that wealth can purchase, and fancy can invent.

"I will then retire to a rural dwelling, pass my days in obscurity and contemplation; and lie silently down on the bed of death. Through my life it shall be my settled resolution, that I will never depend on the smile of princes; that I will never stand exposed to the artifices of courts; I will never pant for public honors, nor disturb my quiet with the affairs of state. Such was my scheme of life, which I impressed indelibly upon my memory.

"The first part of my ensuing time was to be spent in search of knowledge, and I know not how I was diverted from my design. I had no visible impediments without, nor any ungovernable passion within. I regarded knowledge as the highest honor, and the most engaging pleasure; yet day stole upon day, and month glided after month, till I found that seven years of the first ten had vanished, and left nothing behind them.

"I now postponed my purpose of traveling; for why should I go abroad, while so much remained to be learned at home? I immured myself for four years, and studied the laws of the empire. The fame of my skill reached the judges: I was found able to speak upon doubtful questions, and I was commanded to stand at the footstool of the caliph. I was heard with attention; I was consulted with confidence, and the love of praise fastened on my heart.

"I still wished to see distant countries; listened with rapture to the relations of travelers, and resolved some time to ask my dismission, that I might feast my soul with novelty; but my presence was always necessary, and the stream of business hurried me along. Sometimes, I was afraid lest I should be charged with ingratitude; but I still proposed to travel, and therefore would not confine myself by marriage.

"In my fiftieth year, I began to suspect that the time of my traveling was past; and thought it best to lay hold on the felicity yet in my power, and indulge myself in domestic pleasures. But, at fifty, no man easily finds a woman beautiful as the houries, and wise as Zobeide. I inquired and rejected, consulted and deliberated, till the sixty-second year made me ashamed of wishing to marry. I had now nothing left but retirement; and for retirement I never found a time, till disease forced me from public employment.

"Such was my scheme, and such has been its consequence. With an insatiable thirst for knowledge, I trifled away the years of improvement; with a restless desire of seeing different countries, I have always resided in the same city; with the highest expectation of connubial felicity, I have lived unmarried; and with an unalterable resolution of contemplative retirement, I am going to die within the walls of Bagdad."

人生的规划

奥尔马是哈桑的儿子，他在人们的爱戴和尊敬中度过了75年的岁月。他异常富有，无论何时，无论他走到哪里，总有人欢呼喝彩，向他祝福。

幸福终究只是暂时的，灯火通明也需要燃料的维持；繁花也不可能百日红艳——它们终有一天会枯萎凋谢。现在的奥尔马已是步入老年，精力不像当年那么旺盛。一缕白发从他的头上掉落，曾经强有力的手已不再有力，曾经敏捷的双脚也已步履蹒跚。权力和欲望已经不再是他所追求的事物，他现在只渴求理智与宽怀。

但奥尔马的才智并没有因为他的年迈体迈而减弱。在他的客厅里，总是高朋满座，他们都希望老奥尔马能够面授机宜，传授给他们一些经验和知识。他们对奥尔马充满了崇敬之情。埃及总督的儿子卡勒卜每天早早来到大厅，很晚才离开。他年轻英俊，善于雄辩。奥尔马欣赏他的才智，喜欢他的温顺与机敏。

"请您告诉我，"卡勒卜说，"许多国家都能听到您的声音，您的智慧为亚洲最远的国家所知。请您告诉我，我如何才能像您那样充满智慧，像您那样稳健、博学，而且为世人所敬仰呢？您获得并保持影响力的方法，对您来说已不再有用，那么您可不可以把这些秘密都告诉我，把您用聪明才智获得大量财富的计划都教给我？"

"年轻人，"奥尔马说，"制订生活计划是没有用的。当我二十几岁，第一次审视这个世界时，我是用孤独的眼光来观察人类的各种变化的。我靠着一株枝繁叶茂的柏树，自言自语道：'一个人活70岁就算是高龄，我还剩下50年的人生。'

"于是，我打算用十年时间来获得知识，丰富自己的头脑，另外再用十年时间到国外旅行。这样，我就能明白一个道理，而且我将以此为豪。每个城市都会因为我的到来而欢呼，每个学生都将寻求我的友谊。这20年的时间，也让我产生这样的体会：我的余生将会忙于对各种事情的联合和比较。我将迷醉于无穷无尽的知识财富的积累，生活中的每一刻我都会找到乐趣，永远不会感到厌倦、疲劳。

"当然，我也不会偏离生活的轨道和足迹，去尝试女性的雅致所包含的真谛。我将娶一位像佐贝德那样美丽如仙、聪明伶俐的姑娘。她陪伴我在巴格达的郊区度过快乐的20年时光，享受所有能够用财富买来的快乐，尝试所有能够想出来的奇妙的想法。

"然后，我将隐居山林，过着低调且沉思的日子，一直到自己安静地离开人世。这会是我最后的归宿，我将不再依赖王子的微笑生存，我也不会在宫廷的虚伪中颤抖，我不再渴望公众对我的尊崇，也不会为了国家的事情扰乱平静的内心。这就是我的生活目标和规划，我将它们镌刻在我的记忆之中。

"首先要做的就是掌握知识，我不知道自己是如何偏离了当初的设计。我既没有可以看得见的障碍，也没有难以控制的热情。我把寻求知识看成是最崇高的事业，也是最开心的快乐。然而随着时间的流逝，我发现，我最开始的十年中，有7个年头全都被荒废了。

"现在，我只好推迟旅游计划，因为国内就有很多东西需要学习，我为什么还要去国外呢？我将自己禁闭了4年，在这4年间，我研究了帝国的法律。我拥有的知识已经比得上法官了，发现自己能解决许多疑难问题，于是，我被派去为哈里发服务。我开始用内心倾听，自信地说出自己的想法，获得称赞的喜悦之情很快占满了我的内心。

"我仍然希望远游他国，高兴地聆听旅行归来的人们谈论他们的所见所闻。我多次请求解除我的职务，这样我就可以享受新鲜事物的奇妙了。但是公务让我始终难以脱身，繁忙的事务总是源源不断地向我涌来。有时我害怕被人指责忘恩负义，缺乏感恩之情。但我还是希望能够出国旅游，因此，我不会让自己被婚姻束缚住。

"等到我50岁的时候，我开始意识到自己旅行的期望终将无法实现；虽然我将自己一生的岁月都用来追逐由影响力所产生的幸福，却未能享受到家庭的快乐。不过，50岁的人已经很难找到貌美如仙、聪明如佐贝德那样的姑娘了。我四处寻找，可每次都遭到拒绝，直到62岁时，我为自己这么一大把年纪还想结婚而感到羞愧。到这个时候，我一事无成，只能隐居。然而，我一直没有时间隐居，直到疾病迫使我辞去公职。

"这就是我的人生规划，这就是我的人生规划所产生的结果：对知识抱有永不满足的渴求，却浪费了自我提高和完善的时间；总是难以抑制地想周游列国，但是始终孑然一身一直生活在同一座城市；对幸福美满的婚姻怀有最高的愿望，但是一辈子没娶妻；坚定信念想隐居山林过宁静的生活，可现在我却只能在巴格达的高墙里遗憾终老。"

第三卷

大自然的爱

Feathers in the Wind

A good woman one day said something that hurt her best friend of many years. She regretted it immediately and would have done anything to take the words back. But they were said in a moment of thoughtlessness, and as close as she and her friend were, she didn't consider the effects of her words beforehand.

What she said hurt her friend so much that this good woman was herself hurt for the pain she caused. In an effort to undo what she had done, she went to an older, wiser woman, explained her situation, and asked for advice.

The older woman listened patiently in an effort to determine just how sincere the younger woman was, how far she was willing to go to correct the situation. She explained that sometimes, in order to put things back in order, great efforts must be made.

She then asked, "Just what would you be willing to do to repair the harm done?"

The answer was heartfelt, "Anything!"

Listening to her, the older woman sensed the younger woman's distress and knew she must help her. She also knew she could never lessen her pain, but she could teach, if the younger woman would first listen and then learn.

She knew the outcome would depend solely on the character of the younger woman. She said, "There are two things you need to do to make amends. The first of the two is extremely difficult.

"Tonight, take your best feather pillows and open a small hole in each one. Then, before the sun rises, you must put a single feather on the doorstep of each house in town.

"When you are through, come back to me. If you've done the first thing completely, I'll tell you the second."

The younger woman hurried home to prepare for her chore, even though the pillows were very dear and very expensive.

All night long, she labored alone in the wind. She went from doorstep to doorstep, taking care not to overlook a single house. Her fingers were frozen, the wind was so sharp it caused her eyes to water, but she ran on through the darkened street, thankful there was something she could do to put things back the way they once were.

Finally as the sky was getting light, she placed the last feather on the steps of the last house. Just as the sun rose, she returned to the older woman.

She was exhausted but relieved that her efforts would be rewarded.

"My pillows are empty. I placed a feather on the doorstep of each home."

"Now," said the wise woman, "Go back and refill your pillows. Then everything will be as it was before."

The young woman was stunned. "You know that's impossible! The wind blew away each feather as fast as I placed them on the doorsteps! You didn't say I had to get them back! If this is the second requirement, then things will never be the same."

"That's true," said the older woman. "Never forget. Each of your words is like a feather in the wind. Once spoken, no amount of effort, regardless of how heartfelt or sincere, can never return them to your mouth. Choose your words well and guard them most of all in the presence of those you love."

风中的羽毛

有一天，一个好女人无意间说了几句话，伤害了她交往多年的一位好友。她马上就感到后悔，愿意不惜一切收回自己说过的那些话。这些话都是她未经思索脱口说出的，而且她跟这位朋友情同姐妹，因此她事先根本就想不到自己说的话会有什么样的后果。

她的话深深地伤害了她的朋友，所以她自己也因为造成这样的伤害而备受折磨，心神不安。她想尽力与朋友重修旧好，就去找了一位长者，向长者解释了她目前的处境，并想虚心求教。

长者耐心地听着，以确定这个年轻女士的心有多诚，要弥补过失的愿望有多强。听完之后，长者解释说，有时为了恢复原状，需要付出巨大努力。

接下来，长者问："请问，为了重修旧好，你愿意做什么？"

年轻女士的回答发自肺腑："什么都愿意做。"

听着年轻女士的回答，长者知道年轻女士心里有多么痛苦，知道自己必须帮助她，同时也知道自己永远也无法减轻她的痛苦，但只要年轻女士愿意先听后学，她可以言传身教。

她知道结果如何完全取决于这个年轻女士的性格。她说："要重修旧好，有两件事情你需要去做。其中第一件非常难做。

"今晚，带上你最好的羽毛枕头，每个枕头上都打开一个小孔。然后，在太阳出来之前，你必须在镇上每一家房前的台阶上放上一根羽毛。

"你做完后，再回到我这里。如果你善始善终做完了第一件事，我会告诉你第二件事怎么做。"

年轻女士匆忙回到家里准备起来，纵使那些枕头非常昂贵，而且她爱不释手。

整整一夜，她独自一人在寒风中忙活着。她在一家一家房前的台阶上放着羽毛，小心翼翼唯恐漏掉一家。天寒地冻，她的手指冻僵了；寒风呼号，她眼睛不停地流着泪，但她仍然坚持穿过黑黢黢的街道，谢天谢地，不管怎样，她可以做一些力所能及的事情来将功补过了。

最后，天渐渐放亮，她终于在最后一家的门阶上放上了最后一根羽毛。这个时候，太阳刚好升起。她又回到了那位长者的身边。

尽管筋疲力尽，但她如释重负，心里想着自己的努力终会有所回报。

"我那些枕头都空了。我在每一家门阶上都放上了一根羽毛。"

长者说："现在，回去把那些羽毛再填进枕头里去，然后一切都会回到原状。"

年轻女士一下子目瞪口呆："你知道那是不可能的事儿！我一把羽毛放在台阶上，风就飞快地把它们吹跑了！你没有说过我必须得把它们装回去呀！如果这就是第二个要求，那事情再也无法回到原状了。"

"你说得没错，"长者说，"切勿忘记。你说过的每一句话就像风中的羽毛一样。话一出口，任何的努力——无论这种努力是多么发自肺腑、真心实意——都不能再将这些话收回去了。在你所爱的人面前，说话要注意分寸，才能有备无患。"

When the Wind Blows

Years ago a farmer owned a land along the Atlantic seacoast. He constantly advertised for hired hands. Most people were reluctant to work on farms along the Atlantic. They dreaded the awful storms that raged across the Atlantic, wreaking havoc on the buildings and crops. As the farmer interviewed applicants for the job, he received a steady stream of refusals.

Finally, a short, thin man, well past middle age, approached the farmer. "Are you a good farmhand?" the farmer asked him.

"Well, I can sleep when the wind blows," answered the little man.

Although puzzled by this answer, the farmer, desperate for help, hired him. The short man worked well around the farm, busy from dawn to dusk, and the farmer felt satisfied with the man's work.

Then one night the wind howled loudly in from offshore. Jumping out of bed, the farmer grabbed a lantern and rushed next door to the hired hand's sleeping quarters. He shook the short man and yelled, "Get up! A storm is coming! Tie things down before they blow away!"

The short man rolled over in bed and said firmly, "No sir. I told you, I can sleep when the wind blows."

Enraged by the response, the farmer was tempted to fire him on the spot. Instead, he hurried outside to prepare for the storm. To his amazement, he discovered that all of the haystacks had been covered with tarpaulins. The cows were in the barn, the chickens were in the coops, and the doors were barred. The shutters were tightly secured. Everything was tied down. Nothing could blow away.

The farmer then understood what his hired hand meant, so he returned to his bed to also sleep while the wind blew.

When you're prepared spiritually and physically, you have nothing to fear.

当起风时

几年前,一个农场主在大西洋沿岸拥有一块土地,他经常打广告雇人。多数人都不愿在大西洋岸边的农场上干活,他们害怕横扫大西洋严重破坏建筑和庄稼的可怕风暴。这个农场主招工面试时,收到的是一连串坚定的拒绝。

最后,一名个子矮瘦、已过中年的男人走近农场主。"你是个干农活的能手吗?"农场主问他。

"是的,起风时我可以睡觉。"矮个子回答说。

尽管对这个回答感到迷惑,但农场主急需帮手,就雇用了他。这个矮个子在农场干活很卖劲,从早忙到晚。所以,农场主对他的工作非常满意。

后来,有一天夜里,从海面上呼呼刮来了大风。农场主从床上一跃而起,飞快提起灯笼,向隔壁雇工睡的地方跑去。他晃着那个矮个子大声喊道:"起来!风暴来了!趁还没刮跑,快把东西捆好!"

矮个子在床上翻了个身,口气坚定地说道:"不,先生,以前我告诉过你,刮风时我可以睡觉。"

听到这个回答,农场主勃然大怒,禁不住想把他当场解雇。不过,他没有这样做,而是赶紧跑出去应对暴风雨。让他惊愕的是,他发现所有的干草垛都已经盖上了防水油布,牛都在牲口棚里,小鸡待在鸡笼里,而且门闩也好了,百叶窗关得严严实实的,一切都拴牢了,什么东西都无法刮走。

农场主这才明白了雇工的话意。于是,当风刮起时,他也回自己的床上睡觉去了。

当你身心都做好准备时,就会无所畏惧。

Talking with a Flower

I stood in front of a flower growing alone in a deserted garden, located in a courtyard on the desert. The flower felt isolated, or it was what I imagined it like that. There was nothing but her in this place. I had thought she must be longing to have a green friend to comfort her solitude in the endless space.

I said to her, "Good morning! You are the most beautiful flower in here!"

She said, "What's the meaning of 'the most beautiful'?"

I knew that she was so modest that she didn't know she herself was beautiful. The law of the creator that the flowers all followed surprised me. I asked her again, "When you open up the path in the dark and heavy earth, what are you thinking about? Do you feel painful?"

The flower asked, "What is 'the pain'?"

I came to see that the pain only existed in the human life, so she didn't understand what pure beauty was.

I asked her again, "I'm so sorry. What are you thinking about now?"

She said, "I'm thinking about sending the fragrant moment to the air."

I asked her, "Do you like the air to such a degree?"

She said, "The sun is the reason."

I asked, "Have you fallen in love with the sun?"

The flower answered, "The sun gives me the energy and the heaven permits the sun to give me the energy that makes me full of fragrance, which will stay in my heart all the time. So I think, when the fragrance flows from me and into the air around me. And it is what is happening."

I asked, "O Flower, what will you get from your devotion?"

The flower answered, "I don't think it over. Nor do I care about what I will get but give."

I told her, "I expect you to answer my question. Think it over again, what kind of compensation and repayment from your giving?"

The flower said, "What is the repayment?"

I told her, "I appear to be talking with you in another language. I'm so sorry. What is your dream now?"

The flower answered, "Wither and fall and then go to the tranquil of old age. How wonderful the creation falls down the earth! It gives fragrance, leaving wisdom."

与花儿私语

我站在一株花面前。它孤零零地生长在一座荒弃的花园里。花园坐落在沙漠中的一个庭院里。花儿感到孤寂,或者我是这样想象的。在这个地方没有任何别的东西,只有她。我以为她一定渴望着一个绿色伙伴,来慰藉她那无边空旷中的孤独。

我对她说:"早上好!你是这里最美丽的花朵!"

她说:"'最美丽'是什么意思?"

我明白了,她太谦虚了,谦虚到这种程度——不知道自己是美丽的。造物主的法则——花儿们都顺从这法则——使我感到惊奇。我又问她:"你在泥土的黑暗和沉重中开辟道路时,想着什么?你感到很痛苦吗?"

花儿说:"什么叫'痛苦'?"

我明白了,痛苦只存在于人类的生活中,而纯美也是她所不了解的。

我又问她:"我很遗憾,你现在想些什么?"

她说:"我在想给空气送去芬芳的时刻。"

我问她:"你喜欢空气到这种程度吗?"

她说:"太阳是原因。"

我说:"你陷入对太阳的爱了吗?"

花儿说:"太阳给我能量,上天恩准太阳给我能量,使我充满了馨香。这馨香将一直留在我的内心。所以,我想,何时芳香将从我溢出,散发在我周围的空气中。而这就是正在发生的事情。"

我问:"花儿哟,对你的奉献,你将得到什么?"

花儿说:"我不考虑这些。我不问将获得什么,我只给予。"

我对她说:"我希望你回答我的问题。再想一想,对你的给予你将得到何种补偿、何种回报?"

花儿说:"什么叫'回报'?"

我对她说:"我似乎在和你用另一种语言说话。我很遗憾。你现在的梦想是什么?"

花儿说:"凋谢,走向老年的平静。创造物落于大地,这多么美妙啊!它给予馨香,留下智慧。"

A Maple

My neighbor Mrs. Gargan first told me about it. "Have you seen the tree?" she asked as I was sitting in the back yard enjoying the October twilight.

"The one down at the corner," she explained. "It's a beautiful tree—all kinds of colors. Cars are stopping to look. You ought to see it."

I told her I would, but I soon forgot about the tree. Three days later, I was jogging down the street, my mind swimming with petty worries, when a splash of bright orange caught my eye. For an instant, I thought someone's house had caught fire. Then I remembered the tree.

As I approached it, I slowed to a walk. There was nothing remarkable about the shape of the tree, a medium-sized maple. But Mrs. Gargan had been right about its colors. Like the messy whirl of an artist's palette, the tree blazed a bright crimson on its lower branches, burned with vivid yellows and oranges in its center, and simmered to deep burgundy at its top. Through these fiery colors cascaded thin rivulets of pale-green leaves and blotches of deep-green leaves, as yet untouched by autumn.

Edging closer—like a pilgrim approaching a shrine—I noticed several bare branches near the top, their black twigs scratching the air like claws. The leaves they had shed lay like a scarlet carpet around the trunk.

With its varied nations of color, this tree seemed to become a globe, embracing in its broad branches all seasons and continents; the spring and summer of the Southern Hemisphere in the light and dark greens, the autumn and winter of the Northern in the blazing yellows and bare branches. The whole planet seemed poised on the pivot of this pastiche.

As I marveled at this all-encompassing beauty, I thought of Ralph Waldo Emerson's comments about the stars. If the constellations appeared only once in a thousand years, he observed in"Nature," imagine what an exciting event it would be. But because they're up there every night, we barely give them a look.

I felt the same way about the tree. Because its majesty will last only a week, it should be especially precious to us. And I had almost missed it.

Once when Emily Dickinson's father noticed a brilliant display of northern lights in the sky over Massachusetts, he tolled a church bell to alert townspeople. That's what I felt like doing about the tree. I wanted to become a Paul Revere of autumn, awakening the countryside to its wonder.

I didn't have a church bell or a horse, but as I walked home, I did ask each neighbor I passed the same simple but momentous question Mrs. Gargan had asked me: "Have you seen the tree?"

一 棵 枫 树

起初，这件事是我的邻居贾根太太告诉我的。"你看到那棵树了吗？"当我坐在后院观赏10月的黄昏景色时，她问。

"街角那棵，"她解释道，"那是一棵美丽的树——五颜六色的。好多车子都停下来看呢。你应该去看一下才是。"

我告诉她说我会去看的，但很快我便将那棵树给忘到了脑后。3天后，我因一些鸡毛蒜皮的烦心事而心神不定，正懵懵懂懂地沿着大街慢跑。突然，一道鲜橙色彩映入了我的眼帘。一瞬间，我还以为是谁家的房子着火了呢。随后，我才想起了那棵树。

我走近那棵树时，放慢了脚步。那是一棵不高不低的枫树，外形毫无突出显眼之处。但是，贾根太太所说的颜色倒是不错。那棵枫树像画家的颜色斑斓的调色板一般，下枝鲜亮粉红，中部鲜黄与橙黄交相辉映，顶端渐至深红。通过这些火焰般的色泽，只见深深浅浅斑斑点点、尚未被秋天触摸的绿叶，小溪般涓涓流下。

我慢慢地向前移动脚步，像朝圣者走近圣殿一般。这时，我注意到在接近树顶的地方有几根秃枝，黑黢黢的枝条虬曲着指向天空，枝条上掉落的树叶如鲜红的毯子一般聚拢在树干四周。

这棵树色彩斑斓，变化多端，仿佛成了我们的地球，以其博大的枝蔓拥抱五洲和四季：那深深浅浅的绿色代表南半球的春夏季节，那耀眼夺目的黄色和秃枝则象征北半球的秋冬风光。整个地球似乎都落在了这只五光十色的制品的主轴上。

我惊叹其包罗万象的美的同时，想起了拉尔夫·瓦尔多·爱默生对星辰的有关论述。他在《自然》一书中说道，倘若星辰一千年仅出现一次，试想一下那该是何等激动人心的情景。但因为它们每天晚上都在夜空中出现，所以我们几乎对它们不屑一顾。

由此，我想到了那棵树。由于它的辉煌仅持续一周，因此它对我们应该是极其珍贵的。而我差点儿错失良机。

有一次，艾米丽·狄金森的父亲注意到马萨诸塞州上空北极光辉煌展现，便敲响教堂的钟声以警示市民。我想对那棵树也应该那样做。我想成为秋天的保罗·里维尔，去唤醒世人对美的发现。

我既没有教堂的钟,也没有保罗的马。但当我步行回家时,还是将贾根太太问我的那个简单而又重要的问题向遇到的每个邻居提了出来:"你看到那棵树了吗?"

The Catch of Lifetime

He was eleven years old and went fishing every chance he got from the dock as his family's cabin on an island in the middle of a New Hampshire's lake.

On the day before the bass season opened, he and his father were fishing early in the evening, catching sunfish and perch with worms. He tied on a small silver lure and practiced casting. The lure struck the water and caused golden ripples in the sunset, then silver ripples as the moon rose over the lake.

When his pole doubled over, he knew something huge was on the other end. His father watched with admiration as the boy skillfully worked the fish alongside the dock.

Finally, he very gingerly lifted the exhausted fish from the water. It was the largest one he had ever seen, but it was a bass.

The boy and his father looked at the handsome fish, gills playing back and forth in the moonlight. The father lit a match and looked at his watch. It was 10 p. m. two hours before the season opened. He looked at the fish, then at the bay.

"You'll have to put it back, son," he said.

"Dad!" cried the boy.

"There will be other fish," said the father.

"Not as big as this one," cried the boy.

He looked around the lake. No other fishermen or boats were nowhere around in the moonlight. He looked again at his father. Even though no one had seen them, nor could anyone ever know what time he caught the fish, the boy could tell by the clarity of his father's voice that the decision was not negotiable. He slowly worked the hook out of the lip of the huge bass and lowered it into the black water.

The creature swished its powerful body and disappeared. The boy suspected that he would never again see such a great fish.

That was 34 years ago. Today, the boy is a successful architect in New York City. His father's cabin is still there on the island in the middle of the lake. He takes his own son and daughter fishing from the same dock.

And he was right. He has never again caught such a magnificent fish as the one he landed that night long ago. But he does see that same fish—again and again—every time he comes up against a question of ethics.

一生的收获

他已经11岁了。只要一有机会,他就会到新汉普郡湖心岛上他家小屋的码头钓鱼。

鲈鱼季节开放前的那天晚上,他和父亲早早地开始垂钓,用蠕虫作诱饵钓太阳鱼和鲈鱼。他系上银色的小诱饵,练习抛线。诱饵击在水面,在夕阳中荡起金色的涟漪。随后,当月亮冉冉升上湖面时,涟漪又变成了银色。

当鱼竿向下弯时,他知道线的另一端一定钓到了一条大鱼。父亲看着他动作熟练地在码头边钓鱼,眼中露出了赞赏的神情。

最后,他小心翼翼地将筋疲力尽的鱼拎出了水面。这是他见过的最大的一条鱼,但是一条鲈鱼。

男孩和父亲看着这条漂亮的鱼,鱼鳃在月光下一张一合的。父亲点燃一根火柴,看了看手表。已经是夜里10点了,离开放还有两个小时。他看了看鱼,然后又瞧了瞧男孩。

"儿子,你得把它放回去。"他说。

"爸爸!"男孩叫道。

"还会有其他鱼的。"父亲说。

"不会有这条大的。"男孩叫道。

他看了看湖四周。月光下没有其他的渔民或船只。他又看了一眼父亲,从父亲明白无误的口气中,他知道这个决定没有商量余地,即使没有人看到他们,也无从得知他们什么时候钓到了这条鱼。他慢慢地将鱼钩从大鲈鱼的嘴唇上取下来,然后将它放回了黑幽幽的水里。

鱼摆动着有力的身躯,消失在了水里。男孩想,他可能再也见不到这么大的一条鱼了。

那是34年前的事了。如今,男孩是纽约市一位功成名就的建筑师。他父亲的小屋仍在湖心岛上。他常常带着自己的儿女在同一个码头钓鱼。

而且他想得没错,他再也没有见过很久以前那天夜里钓到的那么大的鱼。但他每次面临道德难题时,他的眼前总是一次次浮现出那条鱼。

The Roses and Thorns

The twin sisters went into the rose garden. Soon afterwards, one of the girls ran back to her mother and said, "Mama, this is a bad place!"

"Why, my child?"

"Because there're thorns below each flower."

After a while, the other girl ran to her mother and said, "Mama, this is a good place."

"Why, my child?"

"Because there're flowers on each thorn in here."

On hearing this, the mother was lost in thought.

Everything in the world both has a good side and a bad side; the key lies in from which point of view you will look at it.

玫瑰与荆棘

一对孪生小姑娘走进玫瑰园。不多久,其中一个小姑娘跑回来对母亲说:"妈妈,这里是个坏地方!"

"为什么呢,我的孩子?"

"因为这里的每朵花下面都有刺。"

不一会儿,另一个小姑娘跑来对母亲说:"妈妈,这里是个好地方。"

"为什么呢,我的孩子?"

"因为这里的每丛刺上都有花。"

母亲听了,沉思起来。

世间万物既有好的一面又有坏的一面,关键在于你从哪个角度去看。

When the Moon Follows Me

Each of my sons made the discovery early. We would be riding in the car at night, and the little voice would call out from the back seat, "Hey, the moon is following us!" I would explain that the moon was not actually gliding along with our car. There would be another period of critical observation and the final verdict, delivered more quietly this time: "But it really is moving. I can see it."

I thought of that one evening as I was driving. The moon, one day short of fullness, rode with me, first gliding smoothly, then bounding over the bumpy stretches, now on my right, then straight ahead, the silver light washing over dry grasses in open fields, streaking along through black branches, finally disappearing as the road wound its way through the hills.

When I crested the hill in the village, there it was again—grown suddenly immense, ripe, flooding the town with a sprawling light so magical I began to understand why it is said to inspire "looniness." I could hardly wait to get back home to show the boys.

Robert was in the bathtub, so I grabbed John. "Close your eyes and come see what followed me home," I said, hoping to increase the dramatic impact. I led him out into the night. "Okay. Open! Isn't it beautiful?"

John blinked a few times and looked at me as if I might be loony. "Mom, it's just the moon. Is this the surprise?" I suppose he was hoping for a puppy.

I should have realized that, being only ten, he was probably too young to know how much we sometimes need the magic and romance of moonlight—a light that is nothing like the harsh glare of the sun that it reflects. Moonlight softens our faults; all shabbiness dissolves into shadow. It erases the myriad details that crowd and rush us in the sunlight, leaving only sharp outlines and highlights and broad brushstrokes—the fundamental shape of things.

Often in the soothing, restorative glow we stare transfixed, bouncing out ambitions and hopes and plans off this great reflector. We dream our dreams; we examine the structure of our lives; we make considered decisions. In a hectic, confusing world, it helps to step out into a quiet, clear swash of moonlight, to seek out the fundamentals and eschew the incidentals.

The night after I showed John the moon, he burst breathlessly through the door, calling, "Mom, come out for a minute!" This time, he led me, coatless and shivering. The driveway gravel crunched underneath our sneakers. From somewhere in the woods beyond the pond, the plaintive calls of geese honked and died away.

Past the row of pine trees that line the road, the sky opened up with the full moon on it, suspended so precariously close that it might come hurtling toward us—incandescent, even larger and more breathtaking than the night before, climbing its motionless climb over the molten silver of our pond. Even a ten-year-old could see this wasn't just the moon. This was The Moon.

When I turned around, John was grinning, expectant, studying my face intently to see if he had pleased me. He had. I knew that now the moon was following him too.

月 随 人 走

我的每个儿子早就发现了。我们夜里驾车回家，后座常常传来一声叫喊，"嘿，月亮在跟着我们！"我向他们解释说，月亮并不是真的随着我们的车子滑行。孩子又经过了一段时间的审慎观察，做出了最后的裁定。这次声音更平静了："它真的在移动。我可以看得到。"

我记得那天晚上我驾车的情景。那是一轮亏月，始终伴我前行，起初是平稳滑行,然后在崎岖不平的路上开始跳跃,时而在我右侧,时而又在我正前方,银色的月光洒在空旷的草地上,飞快地穿过黑黢黢的树枝。最后,当道路沿着群山蜿蜒盘行时,月亮便消失了。

我到达村里的山顶时,月亮再次出现,这次突然变得硕大、圆满,月光匍匐着洒满了整个镇子,是那样变幻莫测,我才开始明白了为什么月亮能激发"狂想"。我迫不及待想赶回家让孩子们观看。

罗伯特正在浴缸里洗澡,所以我飞快地拎起约翰。"闭上眼睛,看看谁跟着我一起回家了,"我说,希望增加戏剧性的效果。我领着他走进了夜幕。"好了,睁开吧!是不是漂亮极了?"

约翰眨了几下眼睛,然后看着我,好像我是个疯子。"妈妈,这不过是一轮月亮罢了,有什么大惊小怪的?"我猜他希望是一只小狗。

我早该意识到,他才10岁,年纪还太小,无法知道有时我们是多么需要月光的魅力和浪漫——一道太阳折射出的耀眼光芒。月光减轻了我们的过失;所有的罪孽都溶解在月影之中。它擦去了阳光下充斥我们的无数细枝末节,仅留下了鲜明的轮廓、强光部分和宽宽的线条——事物基本的形态。

我们常常沐浴在心旷神怡的光里,目不转睛地看着,将我们的抱负和希望从这个大反射器上跳开。我们异想天开;我们审视生活结构;我们深思熟虑做出决定。在这个熙来攘往的世界,月光帮助我们步入了宁静亮堂的地带,寻找生活真谛,避开繁文缛节。

我领着约翰看过月亮后的那天夜里,他从门口气喘吁吁地喊道:"妈妈,出来一会儿!"这次,他领着未穿外衣、瑟瑟发抖的我。我们的运动鞋踩在车道的沙砾上嘎吱嘎吱响个不停。从池塘边的树林里传来一群大雁的鸣叫,然后又渐渐消失了。

穿过路边的那排松树,天空开阔,中天悬挂着一轮满月。月亮近在咫尺,岌岌可危,像要冲我们猛撞过来——闪闪发亮,比昨晚的更大、更惊人,笼罩着整个池塘,波光粼粼,犹如熔化的银子。就连一个10岁的孩子都能看出这不仅仅是一轮月亮。这是一个月球。

我转过身后,只见约翰笑眯眯的,充满了期待,热切地注视着我,看看是否让我感到高兴。他如愿以偿。我知道现在月亮也在跟着他了。

A Big Tree and a Young Tree

A young father asked an elderly neighbor how strict parents should be with their children.

The old man pointed to a rope between a big tree and a young one, saying, "Untie the rope."

The young father did so and at once the young tree bent. Then the old man asked the young man to tie it again, and immediately the young tree stood upright as it used to.

Now the old man said, "There, it is the same with children. You must be strict with them for their healthy growth. But sometimes you must let them stand alone to see if they are strong enough. Being strict with them is for the sake of their independence development."

大树和小树

一位年轻父亲问一位上年纪的邻居，父母亲应该如何严格对待自己的孩子。

老人指着一根绑在一棵大树和一棵小树之间的绳子说："解开绳子。"

年轻父亲解开绳子，小树马上弯下了腰。随后，老人让年轻父亲又绑好了绳子，小树马上又像先前那样站得笔直了。

这时，老人说道："瞧，这和养孩子一样。为了他们健康成长，你必须严格要求他们。但有时，你必须让他们自立，看他们是否足够强壮。严格要求他们，是为了他们独立发展。"

A Young Apple Tree

A poor farmer had a friend who was famous for the wonderful apple he grew.

One day, his friend gave the farmer a young apple tree and told him to take it home and plant it. The farmer was pleased with the gift, but when he got home he did not know where to plant it.

He was afraid that if he planted the tree near the road, strangers would steal the fruit. If he planted the tree in one of his field, his neighbors would come at night and steal some of the apples. If he planted the tree near his house, his children would take the fruit. Finally he planted the tree in his wood where no one could see it. But without sunlight and good soil, the tree soon died.

Later the friend asked the farmer why he had planted the tree it such a poor place. "What's the difference?" the farmer said angrily. "If I had planted the tree near the road, strangers would have stolen the fruit. If I had planted the tree in one of my fields, my neighbors would have come at night and stolen some of the apples. If I had planted it near my house, my own children would have taken the fruit."

"Yes," said the friend, "but at least someone could have enjoyed the fruit. Now you not only have robbed everyone of the fruit, but also you have destroyed a good apple tree!"

一棵小苹果树

一个穷困的农夫有一个朋友,这个朋友因为种了神奇的苹果树而远近闻名。

有一天,农夫的这个朋友送给他一棵小苹果树。农夫对这个礼物非常高兴。但当他回到家时,却不知道将它栽在什么地方。

他担心如果把苹果树栽在路边,陌生人就会偷树上的苹果;如果把树栽在自己的一块地里,邻居们夜里就会过来偷苹果;如果把树栽在自己的房边,他的孩子们就会摘苹果。最后,他把那棵树栽在了林子里,那里没人能看见。但没有阳光和沃土,树不久就死了。

后来,朋友问农夫他为什么把树栽在那样贫瘠的地方。"那有什么不一样?"农夫生气地说,"我把苹果树栽在路边,陌生人就会偷树上的苹果。我把树栽在自己的一块地里,邻居们夜里就会过来偷苹果。我把树栽在自己的房边,我的孩子们就会摘苹果。"

"是的,"他的朋友说,"但至少可能有人来分享这些果实。现在你不仅剥夺了每个人的果实,也毁了一棵好苹果树!"

The Power of a Bee

One afternoon a few summers ago, I had been clearing brush in the mountains for several hours and decided to reward myself with lunch. Sitting on a log, I unwrapped a sandwich and surveyed the rugged scenery. Two turbulent streams joined to form a clear, deep pool before roaring down a heavily wooded canyon.

My idyll would have been perfect had it not been for a persistent bee that began buzzing around me. The bee was of the common variety that plagues picnickers. Without thinking, I brushed it away.

Not the least intimidated, the bee came back and buzzed me again. Now, losing patience, I swatted the pest to the ground and crunched it into the sand with my boot.

Moments later I was startled by a minor explosion of sand at my feet. My tormentor emerged with its wings buzzing furiously. This time I took no chances. I stood up and ground the insect into the sand with all my 210 pounds.

Once more I sat down to my lunch. After several minutes I became aware of a slight movement near my feet. A broken but still living bee was feebly emerging from the sand.

Beguiled by its survival, I leaned down to survey the damage. The right wing was relatively intact, but the left was crumpled like a piece of paper. Nevertheless, the bee kept exercising the wings slowly up and down, as though assessing the damage. It also began to groom its sand-encrusted thorax and abdomen.

Next the bee turned its attention to the bent left wing, rapidly smoothing the wing by running its legs down the length. After each straightening session, the bee buzzed its wings as if to test the lift. This hopeless cripple thought is could still fly!

I got down on my hands and knees to better see these futile attempts Closer scrutiny confirmed the bee was finished—it must be finished. As a veteran pilot, I knew a good deal about wings.

But the bee paid no attention to my superior wisdom. It seemed to be gaining strength and increasing the tempo of its repairs. The bent veins that stiffened the gossamer wing were nearly straight now.

At last the bee felt sufficiently confident to attempt a trial flight. With an audible buzz it released its grip on the earth—and flew into a rise in the sand not more than three inches away. The little creature hit so hard that it tumbled. More frantic smoothing and flexing followed.

Again the bee lifted off, this time flying six inches before hitting another mound. Apparently the bee had regained the lift in its wings but had not mastered the directional controls. Like a pilot learning the peculiarities of a strange airplane, it experimented with short hops that ended ignominiously. After each crash the bee worked furiously to correct the newly discovered structural deficiencies.

Once more it took off, this time clearing the sand but heading straight toward a stump. Narrowly avoiding it, the bee checked its forward speed, circled and then drifted slowly over the mirror-like surface of the pool as if to admire its own reflection. As the bee disappeared, I realized that I was still on my knees, and I remained on my knees for some time.

一只蜜蜂的威力

几年前夏天的一个下午，我在清理山上的灌木丛，连续干了好几个小时后，决定吃午饭犒劳一下自己。我坐在一根圆木上，打开一块三明治，观察着层峦叠嶂的山景，只见两条汹涌的小溪呼啸着流过林木茂密的峡谷后汇合成一泓清澈见底的深潭。

要不是一只固执的蜜蜂一直在我身边嗡嗡乱叫，我的田园生活情趣本应是非常完美的。这是那种干扰野餐者的普通蜜蜂，我不假思索就将它赶跑了。

蜜蜂毫不畏惧，又飞回来朝我嗡嗡叫了起来。这次，我失去耐心，猛地把这个害虫拍到地上，并用靴子将它踩进了沙地里。

过了一会儿，发现脚下沙地微微响了一声，我吃了一惊，折磨我的这个东西拼命扇着翅膀又钻了出来。这次，我不再给它机会了。我站起来，用我210磅的体重将这只昆虫踩进了沙地里。

我再次坐下来吃午饭。几分钟后，我感到脚边又微微动了一下。只见那只受伤却仍活着的蜜蜂又从沙里有气无力地钻了出来。

我被它的生命力迷住了，弯下腰去查看它受的伤势。右边的翅膀相对完整，但左边的翅膀被压得像一张纸一样。不过，这只蜜蜂一直在慢慢地上下拍动着翅膀，好像要确定一下自己的伤势。同时，它也开始修整起沙土包裹的胸部和腹部。

接下来，蜜蜂把注意力转向了左边被弄弯了的翅膀，迅速用腿在翅膀上滑动抚平翅膀。每抚一段时间后，蜜蜂就嗡嗡嗡扇动翅膀，似乎要测试它的提升力。这只没有希望的瘸子还以为自己能飞呢！

为了更好看清它无效的努力，我双膝两手趴在地上；进一步细查之后，证实这个蜜蜂完了，它肯定不行了。作为一名富有经验的飞行员，我对翅膀了如指掌。

但蜜蜂对我的超人智慧并不在意。它似乎在积蓄力量，并加快了修复的速度。由于翅脉弯曲，使它轻而薄的翅膀变得僵硬，但现在几乎又平展起来了。

最后，蜜蜂感觉有足够的信心可以试飞一次了。随着一阵清晰可闻的嗡嗡声，它离开了地面，然后飞到了距离不足3英寸的一个沙丘上。小东西撞得太猛，所以翻滚了几下。接着是拼命抚翅和收缩屈伸。

蜜蜂再次飞起，这次飞了6英寸，然后撞到了另一个土墩上。显然，蜜蜂已经得到了启动翅膀的力量，但还掌握不住方向。像飞行员在学习掌握一架奇怪飞机的特性一样，它在试飞几个短途，最后落得很不光彩。每次坠落后，蜜蜂都拼命动作，以纠正新发现的结构上的不足。

它再次起飞，这次清除了身上的沙子，径直朝着一个树桩飞去。它偏了一点，躲过树桩，检查了前飞的速度，绕了一圈，慢慢地飞过镜子般明亮的湖面，仿佛是要欣赏自己的倒影。蜜蜂消失后，我才意识到自己仍跪在地上，并且跪了好一阵子。

The Boy and the Walnuts

A boy once found a jar full of walnuts and raisins in his mother's kitchen and he put his hand in to help himself to hold as many as he could. When he tried to take his hand out of the jar, however, he found that the opening was too small for his clenched fist to pass through.

"What shall I do?" he wailed. "My hand will be stuck in this jar for ever."

Just then his mother came in.

"Really," she said. "there's nothing to make such a fuss about. Try taking half as many as walnuts and raisins you have in your hand and you'll find it will come out of the jar quite easily."

男孩与核桃

有一次，一个小男孩在他妈妈的厨房里发现了一个装满核桃和葡萄干的罐子，便将手伸进去，想尽可能多抓一把。然而，他设法抽出手时，却发现罐口太小，他抓着核桃的手怎么也出不去。

"我怎么办呢？"他大声哭道，"我的手会永远被卡在这个罐子里的。"

正在这时，他的妈妈走了进来。

"其实，"她说，"这没有什么可大惊小怪的。试着抓一半的核桃和葡萄干，你的手轻而易举就会出来了。"

First Snow

He wasn't sure what had awakened him. Perhaps the child had made some small noise in his sleep. But as he peeked from beneath the covers, his gaze was drawn not to the cradle but to the window.

It was then that he realized what had sneaked through the shield of his slumbers. It was the sense of falling snow.

Quietly, so as not to disturb the child's mother, he rose from the bed and inched toward the cradle. Reaching down, he gently lifts the warm bundle to his shoulder. Then, as he tiptoed from the bedroom, she lifted her head, opened her eyes and—

daily does of magic—smiled up at her dad.

He carried her downstairs, counting the creaks on the way. Together, they settled in at the kitchen table, and adult in him slipped away. Two children now, they pressed their noses against the glass.

The light from the street lamp on the corner filtered down through the birch trees, casting a glow as green as a summer memory upon the winter-brown backyard. From the distance can the endless echo of the stoplight, flashing in ruby message, teasing like a dawn that would not come.

The flakes were falling thick and hard now, pouring past window, a waterfall of mystery. Occasionally, one would stick to the glass, as if reluctant to tumble to its fate. Then, slowly, slipping and sliding down the glass, it would melt, its beauty fleeting gone.

Within an hour, a white table was spread up on the lawn. And as gray streaks of dawn unraveled along the bleak seam of the distant hills, father and daughter watched the new day ripple across the neighborhood.

A porch light came on. A car door slammed. A television flickered.

Across the street, a family scurried into gear. But this day was different. Glimpsed through undraped windows as they darted from room to room, the slim figures of the children seemed to grow ever father until, finally, the kitchen door flew open and out burst three awesomely bundled objects that set instantly to rolling in the snow.

He wonders where they had learned this behavior. Even the littlest one, for whom this must have been the first real snowfall, seemed to know instinctively what to do.

They rolled in it, they tasted it, they packed it into balls and tossed it at one another. Then, just when he thought they might not know everything, they set about shaping a snowman on the crest of the hill.

By the time the snowman's nose was in place, the neighborhood was fully awake. A car whined in protest, but skidded staunchly out of its driveway. Buses ground forward like Marines, determined to take the hill. And all the while, the baby sat secure and warm in his arms.

He knew, of course, that she wouldn't remember any of this. For her there would be other snowfalls to recall. But for him, it was her first. Their first. And the memory would stay, cold and hard, fresh in his thoughts, long after the snowman melted.

第一场雪

他拿不准是什么把他从睡梦中唤醒的，也许是孩子在梦里发出的一些小小的声响吧。但当他从被子下面探出头悄悄向外看时，吸引他的目光的不是摇篮，而是窗户。

这时,他才意识到是什么偷偷穿过了自己的梦境。是他感觉到了落雪纷飞。

为了不惊醒孩子的母亲,他默默地从床上起来,一步一步走向摇篮,俯下身轻轻地抱起暖烘烘的襁褓,然后蹑手蹑脚走出卧室,她抬起头,睁开眼睛,对爸爸露出了微笑,她每天都这样妙不可言。

他抱着她下楼,小心翼翼,唯恐弄出响声。他们一起在厨房的餐桌边停下来。他心中那种成人感悄悄溜走。现在是两个孩子将鼻子贴在玻璃上。

街角路灯的光透过白桦树照下来,犹如在冬天褐色的后园投下一道夏日记忆一样的绿光。红色尾灯从远处源源不断地照过来,闪动着红宝石般的讯号,就像迟迟不来的黎明在逗人。

现在雪花越下越密、越下越大了,纷纷扬扬飘过窗户,就像神秘的瀑布似的。有时,一片雪花会粘在玻璃上,好像是不甘于命运,于是顺着玻璃慢慢滑落、融化,它的美丽转瞬即逝。

不到一小时,草坪就铺上了一块雪白的台布。随后,一道道灰蒙蒙的曙光沿着远山黯淡的接缝铺散开来,父女俩目不转睛地望着新的一天波纹状穿过街坊四邻。

一盏门廊灯亮了起来,一扇车门咚地关上,一台电视闪了起来。

街对面的一家匆匆拉开了窗帘。但今天不一样,透过拉开窗帘的窗户,只见那家的几个孩子在几个房间里跑来跑去,瘦小的身影似乎变得越来越胖,最后厨房门飞快地打开,突然蹦出来3个包裹得严严实实的东西,立刻在雪地里打起滚来。

他不知道他们是在哪里学的这种举止。即便是那个最小的孩子似乎本能地知道该干什么,因为这肯定是他真正经历的第一场降雪。

他们在雪地里打滚,他们把雪放在嘴里品尝,他们团起雪球打起了雪仗。随后,正在他想他们不可能什么都知道时,他们开始在斜坡顶上堆起了雪人。

待他们堆好雪人的鼻子时,邻居们全都醒了。一辆汽车呜呜叫着,以示抗议,但还是坚定地滑到了一边。公共汽车像舰队似的旋转向前,决定爬上前面的斜坡。而他的宝宝却一直安全可靠暖暖地坐在他的怀里。

当然,他知道,她不会记住这一切。对她来说,还会有别的雪景去回忆。但对他来说,这是她的第一场雪,是他们的第一场雪。就算那个雪人融化后很久,这场雪也会带着阵阵寒意,让他记忆犹新。

The Revelation of Lilacs

"I can't believe it. These blooms have lasted so long this year," my wife said.

"I hadn't really thought about it, but you are right. As much as I love lilacs, they come and go so fast," I said.

It has been incredibly exciting this year here in my backyard. Our lilac tree has produced the most blooms I have ever seen. The scent is so wonderful that I spend a lot of time just standing on our small deck breathing it all in.

Many of the branches are hollow and cracked leaving me to believe it has seen many springs. A few winters ago one of the biggest branches crashed to the ground under the weight of melting snow. It broke my heart. I guess I wasn't expecting much from the old thing this year. But it is magnificent!

Since we have been experiencing so much rain lately the flowers have become heavier. The once tall bush seems to be under a lot of pressure. I can relate to that.

Sadly, today I noticed the first bunch of flowers turning brown. It won't be long until they are all gone. But here's what I've learned from it.

Some people are like fragrant flowers. They come into our lives ever so briefly and leave behind a scent that remains embedded in our being. They brighten your day by just having had contact with them even if for a moment. If kindness would have scent it would remind you of them.

Like when I smell pine, all the best Christmas memories rush through my mind. When I smell roses I think of romantic, moon-filled evenings.

Some people, having given so much to you, remain a part of who you are forever. You cannot possibly go through a day without thinking about them. Their beautiful spirit gently nudges your heart each time you hear their name. The very thought of them stirs within your soul like the sweet fragrance of a thousand roses.

Loved ones who have passed on, having given their lives to you, having stayed in bloom through a lifetime of eternal spring, are like these lilacs. Although my heart is saddened having discovered that they are dying, I will not remember them that way. I will forever see a thousand blooms each time I think of them. In the coldest, darkest days of the winter of my life, the memory of them will get me through it all. Even the slightest fragrance will bring a smile to my face and my heart will pound remembering the love.

I'm thankful every day not only for the beauty of the people in my life, but for the lingering fragrance and everlasting memories of ever having loved them at all.

Loving them and life means I will have spring forever in my heart.

紫丁香的启示

"我无法相信,今年这些花开了这么久。"妻子说。

"我确实没有想过,但你说得对。我喜欢紫丁香,它们来去匆匆。"我说。

今年我家后院的景象让人无比兴奋,我们的紫丁香树从来没有开过这么多花。紫丁香芬芳四溢,好多时候我都站在小露台上尽情呼吸它的香气。

紫丁香的好多枝条已经中空裂开,这使我相信这棵紫丁香树已经历了好多个春天。几年前的一个冬天,由于积雪融化,这棵树上最大的一个枝条被压落到了地上,这让我很伤心。我以为今年这棵老树没有多大指望了,但它太棒了!

我们这里最近雨水一直很多,所以紫丁香花开得越来越多。从前高大的树丛似乎承受了很大压力。我能理解那种情况。

让我伤心的是,今天我注意到第一丛花渐渐变成了褐色,过不了多久它们就会全部凋谢。但我从中也有所领悟。

有些人就像芬芳的鲜花。他们在我们的生活中是那样短暂,却留下一缕清香,深深地嵌入我们的生命。即使和他们只有瞬间的接触,这些人也会照亮我们的人生。如果友善具有芳香,它会使你想起这些人。

就像我一闻到松树的香气,圣诞节最美好的回忆便会一下子涌上心头。我闻到玫瑰的芳香时,便会想起月华满天的浪漫之夜。

有些人给了你这么多便成了你永恒的一部分。如果你不想他们,就可能过不了某一天。每次听到他们的名字,他们美丽的灵魂都会轻轻触及你的心灵。你灵魂深处对他们的想念犹如千朵玫瑰那样甜蜜芬芳。

那些你爱的把生命传给你的人绽放在生命永恒的春天里,就像这些紫丁香一样。尽管我发现这些花快要凋谢,感到伤心,但我不会那样回忆它们。每次想起它们时,我都会永远看到百花绽放的情景。在生命里最寒冷、最黑暗的冬天,一想起它们,我就会挺过去。哪怕是最细微的芳香,也能让我露出笑脸,让我在怦然心动中想起爱。

我每天充满感激,不仅是因为我身边那些好人,也因为爱他们而产生的袅袅芳香和永久回忆。

爱他们、爱人生,就意味着我将在心里拥有永恒的春天。

Mahogany

The open ground in front of my home in the countryside was leased to the other to plant mahogany seedlings. After the seedlings planted, the man who planted the trees would always water them every other day. The number of days he came had no rules, sometimes three days, sometimes five days, sometimes more than ten days. The quantity of watering was not steady, sometimes more, sometimes less. The mahogany sometimes suddenly withered, so when he came, he always brought some seedlings to replant.

Initially, I thought he was so lazy that he would water the trees as a long time passed. But how would a lazy man know how many trees had withered? He said, "Planting the trees is the foundation of 100 years, so the trees have to learn to find the water in the earth. I water, just to imitate God's rain that is not exactly calculated. If they cannot grow in this uncertainty by drawing water, the seedlings will naturally wither. But as long as they find the water in this uncertainty and struggle to take roots, they will grow into the trees of 100 years out of question," the man said in earnest. "If I pour a certain amount of water every day, the seedlings will become dependent on me, and their roots will grow on the surface and cannot go deep into the ground, so once I stop watering, the seedlings will wilt even more. The seedlings that have survived will collapse when they encounter a violent storm."

What he said moved me very much. I think that it is not only a tree, but also human beings. In the uncertainty, we will develop an independent mind, turn the tiny nutrients into the huge energy and try to grow.

桃 花 心 木

乡下老家前面的空地租给人家种桃花心木的树苗。树苗种下来后，植树人总是隔几天才来浇水。他来的天数并没有规则，有时三天，有时五天，有时十几天来一次。浇水的量也不一定，有时浇得多，有时浇得少。桃花心木有时就莫名地枯萎了，所以他来时总会带几株树苗补种。

我起先认为他太懒，隔那么久才为树浇水。但懒的人怎么会知道有几棵树枯萎了呢？他说："种树是百年基业，所以树木自己要学会在土地里找水源。我浇水只是模仿老天下雨，老天下雨是算不准的。如果无法在这种不确定中汲水生长，树苗很自然就枯萎了。但只要在不确定中找到水源、拼命扎根，长成百年的大树就不成问题了，"种树人语重心长地说，"如果我每天都来定量浇水，树苗就会养成依赖的心，根就会浮生在地表上，无法深入地底，一旦我停止浇水，树苗会枯萎得更多。幸而可以存活的树苗，遇到狂风暴雨，也是一吹就倒了。"

植树者言，使我非常感动，想到不只是树，人也是一样。在不确定中，我们会养成独立自主的心，把很少的养分转化为巨大的能量，努力生长。

A Picture of Human Life

  Obidah, the son of Abnesina, left the caravansary early in the morning, and pursued his journey through the plains of Hindostan. He was fresh and vigorous with rest; he was animated with hope; he was incited by desire; he walked swiftly forward over the valleys, and saw the hills gradually rising before him.

  As he passed along, his ears were delighted with the morning song of the bird of paradise; he was fanned by the last flutters of the sinking breeze, and sprinkled with dew by groves of spices; he sometimes contemplated towering height of the oak, monarch of the hills; and sometimes caught the gentle fragrance of the primrose, eldest daughter of the spring; all his senses were gratified, and all care was banished from his heart.

  Thus he went on, till the sun approached his meridian, and the increasing heat preyed upon his strength; he then looked round about him for some more commodious path. He saw, on his right hand, a grove that seemed to wave its shades as a sign of invitation; he entered it, and found the coolness and verdure irresistibly pleasant. He did not, however, forget whither he was traveling, but found a narrow way, bordered with flowers, which appeared to have the same direction with the main road, and was pleased, that, by this happy experiment, he had found means to unite pleasure with business, and to gain the rewards of diligence without suffering its fatigues.

  He, therefore, still continued to walk for a time, without the least remission of his ardor, except that he was sometimes tempted to stop by the music of the birds, which the heat had assembled in the shade, and sometimes amused himself with picking the flowers that covered the banks on each side, or the fruits that hung upon the branches. At last, the green path began to decline from its first tendency, and to wind among the hills and thickets, cooled with fountains, and murmuring with waterfalls.

  Here Obidah paused for a time, and began to consider whether it was longer safe to forsake the known and common track; but, remembering that the heat was now in its greatest violence, and that the plain was dusty and uneven, he resolved to pursue the new path, which he supposed only to make a few meanders, in compliance with the garieties of the ground, and to end at last in the common road.

  Having thus calmed his solicitude, he renewed his pace, though he suspected he was not gaining ground. This uneasiness of his mind inclined him to lay hold on every new object, and give way to every sensation that might soothe or divert him. He listened to every echo, he mounted every hill for a fresh prospect, he turned aside to every cascade, and pleased himself with tracing the course of a gentle river that rolled among the trees, and watered a large region, with innumerable circumvolutions.

In these amusements, the hours passed away uncounted; his deviations had perplexed his memory, and he knew not toward what point to travel. He stood pensive and confused, afraid to go forward lest he should go wrong, yet conscious that the time of loitering was now past. While he was thus tortured with uncertainty, the sky was overspread with clouds, the day vanished from before him, and a sudden tempest gathered round his head.

He was now roused by his danger to a quick and painful remembrance of his folly; he now saw how happiness is lost when ease is consulted; he lamented the unmanly impatience that prompted him to seek shelter in the grove, and despised the petty curiosity that led him on from trifle to trifle. While he was thus reflecting, the air grew blacker and a clap of thunder broke his meditation.

He now resolved to do what remained yet in his power; to tread back the ground which he had passed, and try to find some issue where the wood might open into the plain. He prostrated himself upon the ground, and commended his life to the Lord of nature. He rose with confidence and tranquillity, and pressed on with his saber in his hand; for the beasts of the desert were in motion, and on every hand were heard the mingled howls of rage, and fear, and ravage, and expiration; all the horrors of darkness and solitude surrounded him; the winds roared in the woods, and the torrents tumbled from the hills.

Thus, forlorn and distressed, he wandered through the wild without knowing whither he was going or whether he was every moment drawing nearer to safety or to destruction. At length, not fear but labor began to overcome him; his breath grew short, and his knees trembled, and he was on the point of lying down, in resignation to his fate, when he beheld, through the brambles, the glimmer of a taper. He advanced toward the light, and finding that it proceeded from the cottage of a hermit, he called humbly at the door, and obtained admission. The old man set before him such provisions as he had collected for himself, on which Obidah fed with eagerness and gratitude.

When the repast was over, "Tell me," said the hermit, "by what chance thou hast been brought hither; I have been now twenty years an inhabitant of this wilderness, in which I never saw a man before." Obidah then related the occurrences of his journey, without any concealment or palliation.

"Son," said the hermit, "let the errors and follies, the dangers and escapes, of this day, sink deep into your heart. Remember, my son, that human life is the journey of a day. We rise in the morning of youth, full of vigor, and full of expectation; we set forward with spirit and hope, with gayety and with diligence, and travel on awhile in the straight road of piety toward the mansions of rest. In a short time we remit our fervor, and endeavor to find some mitigation of our duty, and some more easy means of obtaining the same end.

"We then relax our vigor, and resolve no longer to be terrified with crimes at a distance, but rely upon our own constancy, and venture to approach what we resolve never to touch. We thus enter the bowers of ease, and repose in the shades of security. Here the heart softens, and vigilance subsides; we are then willing to inquire whether another advance can not be made, and whether we may not at least turn our eyes upon the gardens of pleasure. We approach them with scruple and hesitation; we enter them, but enter timorous and trembling, and always hope to pass through them without losing the road of virtue, which we for a while keep in our sight, and to which we propose to return.

"But temptation succeeds temptation, and one compliance prepares us for another; we, in time, lose the happiness of innocence, and solace our disquiet with sensual gratifications. By degrees we let fall the remembrance of our original intention, and quit the only adequate object of rational desire. We entangle ourselves in business, immerge ourselves in luxury, and rove through the labyrinths of inconstancy till the darkness of old age begins to invade us, and disease and anxiety obstruct our way. We then look back upon our lives with horror, with sorrow, and with repentance; and wish, but too often vainly wish, that we had not forsaken the paths of virtue.

"Happy are they, my son, who shall learn, from thy example, not to despair, but shall remember that though the day is past, and their strength is wasted, there yet remains one effort to be made; that reformation is never hopeless, nor sincere endeavors ever unassisted; that the wanderer may at length return after all his errors; and that he who implores strength and courage from above, shall find danger and difficulty give way before him. Go now, my son, to thy repose: commit thyself to the care of Omnipotence; and when the morning calls again to toil, begin anew thy journey and thy life."

人生风景画

阿比尼西的儿子奥比达一大清早就离开了商队旅馆，开始了他穿越印度斯坦高原的旅程。休息一晚上之后，他感觉神清气爽、精力旺盛，他满怀希望，被欲望激励着，轻快地走过山谷，面前渐渐有山峰出现。

当他一路行走的时候，耳边传来清晨鸟儿阵阵婉转的晨歌。最后，一股柔和的晨风迎面吹来，时不时还会有林间的露珠洒在他身上。他有时会注视那高耸的橡树，那是山丘上的君主；有时他会闻到樱草花的香气，那是春天的长女；他的感官得到了极大的满足和享受，他所有的忧虑全都抛到了脑后。

他继续向前走，直到太阳升到他的头顶，他感到越来越热，这使他筋疲力尽，所以他停下来审视四周，希望可以找到一条更怡人的路。在他的右手边，有一个树林似乎在以它的阴凉召唤他到那儿一游。他走进去，发现那儿又凉快又清新，环境宜人，让人不想离开；但是他没有忘记这次旅行的目的地，所以他选择了一条路边开着小花的路，这条小路似乎和大道的方向相同；更让他高兴的是，通过这件事他找到了折中的乐趣和解决问题的方法。这样他既能享受勤奋的成果，又不用忍受路途中的劳累。

所以，他继续往前走了一段时间。他的热情没有丝毫减退，有时他会被因为炎热而躲在树荫下的小鸟的叫声吸引，驻足欣赏一会儿它们美妙的歌喉；或者有时候他会摘下河边的小花或树枝上的果实，自娱自乐一会儿。最后，那绿色小道的地势慢慢下降了，并且在山丘和灌木丛中蜿蜒而去，一路上只见清泉生凉，水瀑呜咽。

奥比达在此停留了片刻，他考虑到，离开那熟悉的大道会不会不安全，但一想到现在正是酷热淫威最盛的时候，他决定还是走这条新发现的小路。他想，这条路应该是根据地形的变化转一些弯，最终它会与大道会合的。

就这样平息了顾虑之后，他又重新上路了，尽管他怀疑自己好像并没有向前行进。这种不安的心情促使他不放过任何一个新鲜事物，并且一产生什么能让他感到欣慰和愉悦的念头，他就立刻照着这个念头去做。他倾听每一个回声，攀登每一座山丘来查看方向。他朝着每个瀑布的方向走去，然后跟着潺潺流动的溪流向前走，只见溪流蜿蜒流过树林，浇灌到一大片区域，在那里又延伸出无数弯弯曲曲的分支。

时间不知不觉在欢快的旅行中过去了，他这样七转八弯地走着，弄得自己也记不清走过的路了，他不知道接下来该去哪儿。他忧郁而困惑地站在那儿，因为怕走错路，所以站在那里不敢往前去，但是此刻他很明白，闲逛的时候已经过去了，现在该一心赶路了。正当他犹豫不决、非常苦恼的时候，天空被乌云遮住了，天色很快就暗了下来，一团突如其来的云团在他的头顶上迅疾积聚。

现在所面临的危险让他对自己的愚蠢行为进行了一次快速而痛苦的检讨。这时他明白了为什么贪图安逸会导致幸福丧失。他为自己的娇气和急躁感到悲伤，是它们促使他去树林中寻求庇护，他也嘲笑自己为了小小的好奇心就在细小的枝节上纠缠不清。在他反省的时候，天色变得更暗了，一声响雷打断了他的思绪。

他现在决定去做一件他力所能及的事情：按原路返回，同时找找看，有没有从树林通向平原的出口。他全身伏倒在地，把自己的命运交给大自然主宰。爬起来的时候，他内心充满了自信和平静。他把刀紧紧地握在手中，因为沙漠中的野兽已经开始出没了，到处都充满着愤怒、恐惧、蹂躏的气息。恐惧、黑暗和孤独包围着他，狂风在林间吼叫，洪流从山上滚滚而下。

他就这样无助而沮丧地在树林里穿行，不知道自己走向哪个方向，也不知道随着时间的流逝，他走向安全之地还是毁灭之地。最终，不是恐惧而是疲惫，使他承受不住了。他的呼吸开始变得急促，膝盖也开始颤抖起来，就在他将要倒下、听天由命的时候，他看到一点蜡烛的微光透过荆棘传过来。他向那点微光走去，发现那来自于一个隐士的小屋。他谦卑地叩门，得到进门的允许。那位隐士将他储存的食物放在他面前，奥比达带着感激之情，狼吞虎咽地吃了起来。

等那些食物都吃完了，隐士发话了："告诉我，你是怎么到这里来的？我在这荒郊野外住了20年，还从来没看见有人从这里经过。"奥比达详细叙述了他在旅途中的遭遇，没有任何隐瞒和掩饰。

"孩子，"那个隐士说，"就让今天的错误和愚蠢、危险和侥幸都深深地埋藏在你的内心深处吧。记住，我的孩子，人的一生就是一天的旅行。我们早上起来的时候精力旺盛，充满希望，就像是在我们年轻的时候；我们带着信念和希望出发，那时我们欢乐而勤奋，所以在通向栖息之所的阳光大道上前行。但是过了一段时间，我们就会不甘平淡，重拾热情，然后努力着想要减轻一点我们的职责，期望能够更轻松地到达我们的目的地。

"然后，我们变得松懈了，我们决心不再为远处的罪恶行径而恐惧，我们觉得能克制自己，在茫茫的世事中始终保持不变。所以我们就开始冒险，靠近我们从来没接触过的东西。这样我们就走进了安逸的树林，开始在树荫下休息。就是在这里，我们的心被麻痹了，渐渐地失去了警惕性，然后就会很自然地问自己：难道非要向前进吗？就不可以停下来欣赏欣赏这乐园里的美景吗？我们犹豫不决地接近那个乐园。走进去了却依然感到胆怯和不安，我们总是希望我们能在不偏离大道的前提下穿越这个乐园，我们时不时也会见到那条大道出现在面前，而我们会安抚自己说：总有一天会回到那条路上去的。

"但是诱惑接踵而至，第一次的屈服就为第二次打下了基础，时间一长，我们就会失去天真的快乐，只会用物质上的享受平息我们的不安。逐渐地，我们忘了我们的天性，放弃了我们唯一可以理智追求的目标。我们事务缠身，花天酒地，在反复无常的迷宫里徘徊，一直到年迈的黑暗开始侵蚀我们，疾病和忧虑让我们举步维艰。然后我们回首一生，感到惊恐、悲痛、悔恨。尽管通常是徒劳的，但我们还是会希望，我们从没放弃那条人间正道。

"我的孩子，真正幸福的人，是那些能够吸取教训，却从不绝望的人；是那些尽管明白光阴已经虚度，青春已经挥霍，却依然坚持并付诸行动的人；是那些相信悔过总不至于绝望，真诚努力总会有所收获的人；是那些坚信浪子回头金不换的人。去吧，去休息吧，我的孩子。当早晨的铃声再次响起的时候，你就可以开始你新的旅程和人生了。"

第四卷

人生的恩惠

A Lesson for Living

"Everything happens for the best," my mother said whenever I faced disappointment. "If you carry on, one day something good will happen."

Mother was right, as I discovered after graduating from college in 1932, I had decided to try for a job in radio, then work my way to a sports announcer. I hitchhiked to Chicago and knocked on the door of every station and got turned down every time.

In one studio, a kind lady told me that big stations couldn't risk hiring an inexperienced person. "Go find a small station that'll give you a chance," she said.

I thumbed home to Dixon, Illinois. While there were no radio-announcing jobs in Dixon, my father said Montgomery Ward had opened a store and wanted a local athlete to manage its sports department. Since Dixon was where I had played high-school football, I applied. The job sounded just right for me. But I wasn't hired.

My disappointment must have shown. "Everything happens for the best," Mom reminded me. Dad offered me the car to job hunt. I tried WOC Radio in Davenport, Iowa. The program director, a wonderful Scotsman named Peter MacArthur, told me they had already hired an announcer.

As I left his office, I asked aloud, "How can a fellow get to be a sports announcer if he can't get a job in a radio station?"

I was waiting for the elevator when I heard MacArthur calling, "What was that you said about sports? Do you know anything about football?" Then he stood me before a microphone and asked me to broadcast an imaginary game.

The preceding autumn, my team had won a game in the last 20 seconds with 65-yard run. I did a 15-minute build-up to that play, and Peter told me I would be broadcasting Saturday's game!

On my way home, as I have many times since, I thought of my mother's words: "If you carry on, one day something good will happen."

I often wonder what direction my life might have taken if I'd gotten the job at Montgomery Ward.

人生的教训

"一切都会好的，"每当我面临失望时，母亲都会说，"如果你坚持下去，总有一天好事会出现。"

1932年大学毕业时，我才发现母亲说得没错。当时，我决定在电台找一份工作，然后通过奋斗，当一名体育播音员。我搭便车来到芝加哥，敲了每一家电台的门,每次都被拒之门外。

在一家演播室,一位好心的女士告诉我说,大电台都不可能冒风险去聘用没有经验的人。"找一家小电台,它会给你一个机会的。"她说。

我搭便车回到家乡伊利诺伊州迪克森。迪克森没有无线电播音的工作。父亲告诉我说,蒙哥马利·沃德开了一家商店,想在当地聘用一位运动员管理体育部。因为迪克森是我中学曾打过橄榄球的地方,所以我就提出了申请。这份工作对我正合适,但我还是没被雇用。

我的失望之情一定是露了出来。"一切都会好的。"妈妈提醒我说。爸爸将车给我,让我去找工作。我去了艾奥瓦州达文波特WOC电台试了试。节目主管是一个名叫彼得·麦克阿瑟的了不起的苏格兰人,他告诉我说他们已经雇用了一名播音员。

我离开他的办公室时,大声问道:"一个在广播电台都找不到工作的人怎么能成为一名体育播音员呢?"

我等电梯时,听到麦克阿瑟朝我喊道:"你说的体育是怎么回事?你知道橄榄球吗?"于是,他让我站在麦克风前,请我为一场假想的比赛解说。

在前一年的秋天,我的球队在最后20秒以65码的距离赢得了一场球。我对那场球赛做了15分钟的精彩解说。彼得告诉我可以为星期六的比赛解说!

在回家的路上,我想到了母亲的那番话,从此多次都是这样:"一切都会好起来的。如果你坚持不懈,好事总有一天会到来。"

我常常想,如果得到了蒙哥马利·沃德的那份工作,我的人生会通向何方。

The Sculpture of Life

A sculptor was absorbed in his work in which he was carving and polishing an unshaped marble with the graver in his hand while a small boy close by was looking at him with curiosity.

After a while, the sculpture gradually took shape: head, shoulders, arms, limbs, then hair, eyes, nose, mouth…A beautiful woman appeared before them.

The small boy felt extremely surprised and asked the sculptor, "How did you know she hid in it?"

The sculptor told the boy with a haw-haw, "There was nothing in the stone. I just moved the woman in my heart here with my graver."

人生的雕塑

一位雕刻家正在全神贯注地工作，用手中的刻刀一刀一刀地琢磨一块尚未成形的大理石。一个小男孩好奇地在一旁看着他。

不一会儿，雕像逐渐成形：头部、肩膀、手臂、身躯，接着头发、眼睛、鼻子、嘴巴……一个美丽的女人出现在了面前。

小男孩万分惊讶，问雕刻家："你怎么知道她藏在里边的呢？"

雕刻家哈哈大笑，对孩子说："石头里原本什么也没有，只不过是我把我心中的女人用刻刀给搬到这里来了。"

Don't Quit

Wishing to encourage her young son's progress on the piano, a mother took her boy to a Paderewski concert.

After they were seated, the mother spotted a friend in the audience and walked down the aisle to greet her. Seizing the opportunity to explore the wonders of the concert hall, the little boy rose and eventually explored his way through a door marked"NO ADMITTANCE".

When the house lights dimmed and the concert was about to begin, the mother returned to her seat and discovered that the child was missing. Suddenly, the curtains parted and spotlights focused on the impressive Steinway on stage. In horror, the mother saw her little boy sitting at the keyboard, innocently picking out"Twinkle, Twinkle Little Star."

At that moment, the great piano master made his entrance, quickly moved to the piano and whispered in the boy's ear, "Don't quit. Keep playing." Then, leaning over, Paderewski reached down with his left hand and began filling in the bass part. Soon his right arm reached around to the other side of the child and he added a running obbligato.

Together, the old master and the young novice transformed the frightening situation into a wonderfully creative experience. And the audience were mesmerized.

Whatever our situation in life and history, there is the voice deep within our beings, "Don't quit. Keep playing. You are not alone. Together we will transform the broken patterns into a masterwork of my creative art. Together, we will mesmerize the world."

不 要 停

一位母亲想鼓励小儿子好好练琴,就带着他去看帕德列夫斯基的音乐会。

他们坐好后,这位母亲在观众席里发现了一位朋友,便走过去和她打招呼。小男孩抓住这个机会,离开了座位,好奇地走进了音乐厅一扇标有"禁止入内"的门。

当观众席的照明灯暗下来、音乐会就要开始时,这位母亲回到了自己的座位,发现孩子不见了。突然,帷幕拉开了,聚光灯照在了舞台上那架显眼的施泰韦钢琴上。这位母亲惊恐地发现自己的小儿子坐在键盘边,凭记忆天真地弹奏起了《闪闪小星星》。

此时,那位伟大的钢琴师入场,快步走到钢琴边,低声对小男孩说道:"不要停,接着弹。"随后,帕德列夫斯基弯下腰,伸出左手,开始补全低音部分。不久,他的右臂绕到了小男孩的另一侧,补全了伴奏部分。

年长的大师和年幼的新手一起将那令人担心的情景变成了极具创意的演出。而且观众们如痴如醉。

无论我们现在和过去的境遇如何,我们的内心深处总会有一个声音说:"不要停,接着弹。你不是独自一人。我们一起将破碎的音符变成具有创意的杰作。我们一起倾倒整个世界。"

Enjoy What You Have

People who are satisfied appreciate what they have in life and don't worry about how it compares to what others have. Valuing what you have over what you do not or cannot have leads to greater happiness.

Four-year-old Alice runs to Christmas tree and sees wonderful presents beneath it. No doubt she has received fewer presents than some of her friends, and probably she has not received some of the things she most wanted. But at that moment, she doesn't stop to think why aren't there more presents or to wonder what she may have asked for that she didn't get. Instead, she marvels at the treasures before her.

When we think about our lives, too often we think about what we don't have and what we didn't get. But such a focus denies us pleasure. You wouldn't sit next to the Christmas tree and remind Alice that there were presents she didn't receive. Why remind yourself of the things in life you don't have when you could remind yourself of what you do have?

People who have the most are only as likely to be happy as those who have the least. People who like what they have, however, are twice as likely to be happy as those who actually have the most.

享受自己所有

知足的人感激生活中拥有的一切，不会因为和别人比较而担心。珍惜自己拥有的东西胜于自己没有或不能拥有的东西，将会给你带来更大的快乐。

4岁的爱丽丝跑到圣诞树边，看到了树下漂亮的礼物。毫无疑问，她收到的礼物比她的一些朋友的要少，而且也许没有收到她最想要的一些东西。但此时此刻，她想得到的并不是这里为什么没有更多的礼物，或者自己还能得到什么未曾拥有的东西。相反，她对眼前的这些宝物感到惊奇。

我们在回想生活时，常常回想自己并未得到的东西。但这种专注会让我们失去快乐。你不会坐在圣诞树边提醒爱丽丝她没有收到有些礼物。当你能让自己想起眼前拥有的东西时，为什么又要提醒自己去想那些不曾拥有的东西呢？

最富的人可能和最穷的人一样快乐。然而，喜欢自己所拥有的人可能比实际最富有的人快乐一倍。

A Wonderful Present

It was a cold December afternoon. A girl of about eight or nine stood in front of a shop on a small street. Her face was close to the shop window. Inside the window there were lots and lots of beautiful things. With large and serious eyes, the girl looked at the jewels and carefully studied each of them. Then a smile came across her face, and she stepped back from the window and entered the shop.

There was not much light inside the shop. But the girl could see that the shop was full of wonderful things. In the counter, there were more jewels. And there were also many other things for which she did not even know their names.

Pete Richards was standing behind the counter when the girl came in. He was about thirty years old. He looked very lonely. His eyes were cold as he looked at the little girl. "Please," she said to Pete, "would you let me look at the necklace in the window?"

Pete took the necklace from the window and held it up for the girl to see. It was a very beautiful necklace. It was a string of blue beads.

"It is just right," said the girl. "Will you wrap it up in pretty paper for me please?" Pete looked at the girl with cold eyes. "Are you buying it for someone?" he asked. "For my sister. She takes care of me. You see, this will be the first Christmas since our mother died. I've been looking for a wonderful present for her."

"How much money do you have?" asked Pete. From the pocket of her coat, the girl took a handful of pennies and put them on the counter. "This is all I have," she explained simply. "I have been saving money for my sister's present."

For a moment Pete Richards was silent. He looked at the girl again. She was a pretty girl. Her hair was yellow as the sunlight, and her eyes were blue as the sea. And now there was a happy look in her blue eyes. It struck him. Then he removed the price mark on the necklace so that the girl could not see it. How could he tell her the price?

"Just a moment," Pete went to the back of the shop. "What is your name, little girl?" he called out to her as he was busy about something.

"Jean Grace," answered the girl.

When Pete returned, he held a package in his hand. It was wrapped in pretty Christmas paper and tied with green ribbon. "There you are," he said. "Don't lose it on the way home."

The girl smiled happily at him, and then turned and ran out of the shop. Through the big shop window Pete watched her until she was lost among crowds of people. Jean Grace reminded Pete of his old grief. A few years ago, Pete loved a girl. Her hair and eyes were of the same colors as Jean Grace. And the necklace was meant for her. But on a rainy night, the girl was knocked down and killed in a car accident. Pete was filled with grief and began to live a lonely life. Sometimes he talked with the people who came to his shop, but after the business hours he was left alone with his grief.

Now the blue eyes of Jean Grace made him remember again all that he had lost. The pain was so great that sometimes he even wanted to run away from the people who came to buy Christmas presents in his shop in the next ten days.

Christmas Eve came. The last customer left his shop. Pete sat down behind his counter and soon was deep in thought.

All at once the door opened and a young woman came in. Pete looked up and was surprised. He felt he had seen this woman somewhere before. Her hair was sunlight yellow and her eyes were sea blue.

The young woman came up to Pete Richards, and without saying anything she put on the counter a package wrapped in pretty Christmas paper. From her pocket she took some green ribbon and put it with the package. When Pete opened the package he saw the string of blue beads.

"Did this come from your shop?" she asked.

"Yes," Pete answered.

"Are the stones real?"

"Yes. They are not the best in the world, but they are real."

"Can you remember to whom you sold them?"

"A small girl. Her name was Jean Grace. She wanted the necklace for her sister's Christmas present."

"How much was it?"

"Sorry, I can't tell you that," Pete said. "The seller never tells anyone else what a buyer pays."

"But Jean Grace never had more than a few pennies. How could she pay for such a necklace?"

Pete started to wrap the necklace in the Christmas paper and tie the package with the green ribbon. He was as careful as he had been ten days earlier. Then he said to the young girl, "Jean Grace paid the biggest price she could. She gave all she had."

He handed the package to her. For a moment there was no sound in the little shop. Then somewhere in the city, the church bells began to ring. It was midnight, and the beginning of another Christmas Day.

"But why did you do it?" the girl asked.

There was no answer. It seemed Pete Richards was not listening.

"But why did you do it?" she asked again in a soft voice. "There is no one else to whom I can give a Christmas present," Pete said quietly. "It is already Christmas morning. Will you let me take you to your home? I would like to wish you and your little sister Jean Grace Merry Christmas at your door."

And so, to the sounds of church bells, Pete Richards and a young girl whose name he had not yet learned walked out. They walked out into the Christmas morning and into the hope and happiness of a new Christmas Day.

神奇的礼物

12月的一个寒冷的下午。一个大约八九岁的小女孩站在一条小街的一家商店门前。她的脸紧贴着商店橱窗。橱窗里有好多好多漂亮东西。小女孩睁着大大的眼睛认真地看着那些珠宝，仔细地一一打量着。随后，她露出了微笑，从橱窗边走开，走进了那家商店。

商店里没有多少光亮。但小女孩能看得到商店里琳琅满目。柜台里还有更多的珠宝，而且还有好多其他的东西，她甚至都叫不上它们的名字。

小女孩进来时，皮特·理查兹正站在柜台后面。他大约30岁，看上去非常孤独。他在看小女孩时，目光冰冷。她对皮特说："请你让我看看橱窗里的项链好吗？"

皮特从橱窗里拿出项链，举起来让小女孩看。这是一条非常漂亮的项链，上面串着一串蓝色的珠子。

"正合适，"小女孩说，"请你用漂亮的纸给我包一下好吗？"皮特用冰冷的目光看着小女孩，问道："你是为某个人买吗？""是为我的姐姐买的。她常常关照我。你明白，这将是我们的妈妈去世后的第一件圣诞礼物。我一直在为她找一件神奇的礼物。"

"你有多少钱？"皮特问。小女孩从上衣口袋里掏出了一把便士，将它们放在柜台上。"我就有这么多，"她简明地解释说，"我一直为给姐姐买礼物攒钱。"

皮特·理查兹沉默了一会儿。他又看了小女孩一眼，她是一个漂亮女孩，她的头发像阳光一样金黄，眼睛像大海一样湛蓝，而且蓝色的眼睛里总洋溢着快乐的神情。这一下子打动了他。随后，他将项链上的价格标签取下来，这样小女孩就看不到了。他怎么能告诉她价格呢？

"请等一会儿，"皮特走到商店的后部，"你叫什么名字，小姑娘？"他一边忙着某件事，一边向她大声问道。

"琼·格雷斯。"女孩回答说。

当皮特回来时，他一只手里拿着一个包裹。那是用漂亮的圣诞纸包着，还扎着绿丝带。"给你，"他说，"别在回家的路上丢了哟。"

小女孩冲他开心地微微一笑，然后转过身，跑出了商店。皮特透过大橱窗望着她，直到她消失在茫茫人海中。琼·格雷斯使皮特想起了他伤心的往事。几年前，皮特爱上一个女孩。她的头发和眼睛的颜色跟琼·格雷斯的一模一样，而且她也是想要那种项链。但在一个雨夜，那个女孩被一辆汽车撞死了。皮特悲伤极了，开始过起了一种孤独生活。有时他跟来商店的人说话，但下班后，他就一个人与悲伤相伴。

现在，琼·格雷斯的蓝眼睛使他又想起了他所失去的一切。痛苦是那样巨大，在接下来的10天里，他甚至想从来他的店里买圣诞礼物的人身边逃走。

圣诞节前夜来临了。最后一个顾客离开了他的商店。皮特在柜台后面坐下来，很快就陷入了沉思。

突然，门开了。一个年轻女人走了进来。皮特抬起头，吃了一惊。他感到以前曾在什么地方见过这个女人。她的头发像阳光般金黄，眼睛像大海一样湛蓝。

年轻女人走到皮特·理查兹的身边，没说一句话，将一个用漂亮的圣诞纸包着的包裹放在柜台上。她从口袋里掏出一些绿丝带，和包裹放在一起。当皮特打开包裹时，他看到了那串蓝色的珠子。

"这是你店里的东西吗？"她问。

"是的。"皮特回答说。

"这些宝石是真的吗？"

"是的。它们不是世界上最好的，但它们是真的。"

"你能记得是把它们卖给谁的吗？"

"一个小女孩，她的名字叫琼·格雷斯。她想把这条项链作为圣诞礼物送给她的姐姐。"

"这价值多少钱？"

"对不起，这我不能告诉你，"皮特说，"卖主从来不透露给别的买主付了多少钱。"

"可是，琼·格雷斯从来没有超过几便士以上的钱。她怎么能买得起这样一条项链呢？"

皮特用圣诞纸包起那条项链，并用绿丝带扎住包裹。他像10天前那样做得小心翼翼。随后，他对那个年轻女孩说："琼·格雷斯已经付了她能付的最高价格。她拿出了自己所有的积蓄。"

他将那个包裹递给她。小小的店里好一阵子没有声音。随后，在城市的某个地方，响起了教堂的钟声。现在是午夜，又一个圣诞节已经开始了。

"可是，你为什么这样做？"女孩问。

没有回音。好像皮特·理查兹没在听。

"可是，你为什么这样做？"她又柔声问道，"我没有圣诞礼物可送给别人，"皮特轻声说道。"已经是圣诞节早上了。你让我把你送回家好吗？我想在你们家门口祝你和你的小妹妹琼·格雷斯圣诞节快乐。"

于是，伴随着教堂的钟声，皮特·理查兹和一个他还不知道名字的年轻女孩走出了店门。他们走进了圣诞节的早晨，走进了一个新圣诞节的希望和幸福里。

The Grace of Life

A girl was dissatisfied with her mother's chattering, so in rage she rushed out of her home and wandered in the street alone full of grievance.

Just as she was hungry and thirsty, an old man beckoned her to his home and gave her a bowl of meal. The girl was moved to tears and told him about her grievance.

With that, the old man shook his head and said, "While you're being grateful to me for my giving you a bowl of meal, have you thought of the person who've been giving you?" the girl became speechless at once.

At times, when a person thanks the others for their offering a bit of bounty, he or she always forgets the maximum kindness he or she gets.

人生的恩惠

一个女孩子因为不满母亲的唠叨，一气之下跑出了家门，怀着满肚子委屈，孤独地走在大街上。

正当她又饥又渴时，一位老人把她叫到了自己家里，给她盛了一碗饭。女孩感激得哭了，并向他讲述了自己的委屈。

老人听后，摇了摇头说："你在感激我给你一碗饭的同时，可想过那一直给你做饭的人！"女孩顿时无言。

往往有时候，人在感激别人给自己的一点小恩惠时，却忘记了自己得到的最大恩惠。

The Tiger's Whisker of Life

A young woman by the name of Yun Ok came one day to the house of a mountain hermit to seek his help. The hermit was a sage of great renown and a maker of charms and magic potions.

When Yun Ok entered his house, the hermit said without raising his eyes from the fireplace into which he was looking. "Why are you here?"

Yun Ok said, "Oh, Famous Sage, I am in distress! Make me a potion!"

"Yes, yes, make a potion! Everyone needs potions! Can we cure a sick world with a potion?"

"Master," Yun Ok replied, "if you do not help me, I am truly lost!"

"Well, what is your story?" the hermit said, resigned at last to listen.

"It is my husband," Yun Ok said. "He is very dear to me. For the past three years he has been away fighting in the wars. Now that he has returned, he hardly speaks to me, or to anyone else. If I speak, he doesn't seem to hear. When he talks at all, it is roughly. If I serve him food not to his liking, he pushes it aside and angrily leaves the room. Sometimes when he should be working in the rice field, I see him sitting idly on top of the hill, looking toward the sea."

"Yes, so it is sometimes when young men come back from the wars," the hermit said. "Go on."

"There is no more to tell, Learned One. I want a potion to give my husband so that he will be loving and gentle, as he used to be."

"Ha, so simple, is it?" the hermit asked. "A potion! Very well, come back in three days and I will tell you what we shall need for such a potion."

Three days later, Yun Ok returned to the home of the mountain sage. "I have looked into it," he told her. "Your potion can be made. But the most essential ingredient is the whisker of a living tiger. Bring me this whisker and I will give you what you need."

"The whisker of a living tiger!" Yun Ok said. "How could I possibly get it?"

"If the potion is important enough, you will succeed," the hermit said. He turned his head away, not wishing to talk any more.

Yun Ok went home. She thought a great deal about how she would get the tiger's whisker. Then one night when her husband was asleep, she crept from her house with a bowl of rice and meat sauce in her hand. She went to the place on the mountainside where the tiger was known to live. Standing far off from the tiger's cave, she held out the bowl of food, calling the tiger to come and held out the bowl of food, calling the tiger to come and eat. The tiger did not come.

The next night Yun Ok went again, this time a little bit closer. Again she offered a bowl of food. Every night Yun Ok went to the mountain, each time a few steps nearer the tiger's cave than the night before. Little by little, the tiger grew accustomed to seeing her there.

One night Yun Ok approached to within a stone's throw of the tiger's cave. This time the tiger came a few steps toward her and stopped. The two of them stood looking at one another in the moonlight. It happened again the following night, and this time they were so close that Yun Ok could talk to the tiger in a soft, soothing voice. The next night, after looking carefully into Yun Ok's eyes, the tiger ate the food that she held out for him. After that when Yun Ok came in the night, she found the tiger waiting for her on the trail. When the tiger had eaten, Yun Ok could gently rub his head with her hand. Nearly six months had passed since the night of her first visit. At last one night, after caressing the animal's head, Yun Ok said, "Oh, Tiger, generous animal, I must have on of your whiskers. Do not be angry with me!"

And she snipped off one of the whiskers.

The tiger did not become angry, as she had feared he might. Yun Ok went down the trail, not walking but running, with the whisker clutched tightly in her hand.

The next morning she was at the mountain hermit's house just as the sun was rising from the sea. "Oh, Famous One!" she cried, "I have it! I have the tiger's whisker! Now you can make me the potion you promised so that my husband will be loving and gentle again!"

The hermit took the whisker and examined it. Satisfied that it had really come from a tiger, he leaned forward and dropped it into the fire that burned in his fireplace.

"Oh, sir!" the young woman called in anguish. "What have you done with it!"

"Tell me how you obtained it," the hermit said.

"Why, I went to the mountain each night with a little bowl of food. At first I stood afar, and I came a little closer each time, gaining the tiger's confidence. I spoke gently and soothingly to him, to make him understand I wished him only good. I was patient. Each night I brought him food, knowing that he would not eat. But I did not give up. I came again and again. I never spoke harshly. I never reproached him. And at last one night he took a few steps toward me. A time came when he would meet me on the trail and eat out of the bowl that I held in my hands. I rubbed his head, and he made happy sounds in his throat. Only after that did I take the whisker."

"Yes, yes," the hermit said, "you tamed the tiger and won his confidence and love."

"But you have thrown the whisker in the fire!" Yun Ok cried. "It is all for nothing!"

"No, I do not think it is all for nothing," the hermit said. "The whisker is no longer needed. Yun Ok, let me ask you, is a man more vicious than a tiger? Is he less responsive to kindness and understanding? If you can win the love and confidence of a wild and blood-thirsty animal by gentleness and patience, surely you can do the same with your husband?"

Hearing this, Yun Ok stood speechless for a moment. Then she went down the trail, turning over in her mind the truth she had learned in the house of the mountain hermit.

人生的虎须

一天，一个名叫云鸥的年轻女子来到山中一位隐士住的地方寻求帮助。这位隐士是一个大名鼎鼎的圣人，会施魔法、做魔液。

云鸥走进他的屋里时，隐士没抬眼睛，盯着壁炉，问道："你为什么来这里？"

云鸥说："噢，大圣人，我非常苦恼！给我做一杯魔液吧！"

"好，好，做一杯魔液！人人都需要魔液！我们能用魔液普度众生吗？"

"大师，"云鸥答道，"你若不帮我，我真要迷失方向了！"

"好吧，是什么事？"最后，隐士总算愿意听她讲了。

"是我的丈夫，"云鸥说，"他对我非常疼爱。过去3年里，他离开家，一直驰骋疆场。如今他回来了，既不怎么和我说话，也不和别人说话。就是我说话，他似乎也充耳不闻。就是他说话，也是三言两语。如果我做的饭菜不合他的口味，他就把饭菜推到一边，愤愤离开房间。有时，该下稻田干活了，我却看见他无所事事地坐在山顶上，望着大海。"

"是的，从战场回来的年轻人有时就是这样，"隐士说，"接着往下说。"

"没有要说的了，大圣人。我要魔液是想送给我的丈夫，好让他能像从前那样钟情温柔。"

"哈，这么简单，是吗？"隐士问，"一杯魔液！很好，3天后你再来，到时我会告诉你酿造这么一杯魔液需要什么。"

3天后，云鸥再次来到山中圣人的住处。"我已经研究过了，"他告诉她说。"你的魔液可以酿成。但最重要的成分是一只活虎的胡须。你要把这根胡须拿来，我就可以把你需要的东西给你。"

"活虎的胡须！"云鸥说，"我怎么可能拿到手呀？"

"如果魔液举足轻重，你就会成功。"说着，隐士转过头，不愿再多谈。

云鸥回到了家，苦思冥想，怎么才能得到老虎的胡须呢？后来有一天夜里，待丈夫睡着后，她手端一碗肉米饭悄悄出了家门，来到老虎经常出没的山腰处。她远离老虎洞站在那里，捧出了那碗肉米饭，呼唤老虎过来吃。老虎没有过来。

第二天夜里，云鸥又到了那里，这次站得离老虎洞稍微近了些。她再次捧出一碗饭。每天晚上，云鸥来山中一次，每次都要比前一天夜里靠近老虎洞几步。渐渐地，老虎对她的出现就习以为常了。

一天夜里，云鸥距离老虎洞只有几步远了。这一次，老虎朝她迈了几步，又停住了脚步。他们两个就这样站在月光下互相打量着对方。第二天晚上，出现了同样的情形，只是这一次，他们离得更近了。云鸥已经能够用软语轻声跟老虎说话。第三天夜里，待仔细看了云鸥的眼睛后，老虎吃掉了她捧上的饭食。从那以后，云鸥每次晚上过来，就会发现老虎在道上迎候她。等老虎吃过饭，她总能用手轻轻抚摸他的头。从她第一次探望老虎，将近半年过去了。终于，有一天晚上爱抚过老虎的头后，云鸥说："噢，老虎，慷慨的伙伴，我必须取你一根胡须，你可别生我的气啊！"

随后，她便剪了一根老虎的胡须。

老虎没有像她担心的那样生气。云鸥顺着山路下来了，这个时候她不是行走，而是奔跑了起来，手里紧紧攥着老虎的那根胡须。

第二天早上，她来到山中隐士住的地方，这时太阳刚好从海上冉冉升起。"噢，大圣人！"她大声喊道，"我拿到了！我有老虎的胡须了！现在你可以给我做你事先答应过的魔液了吧，这样我的丈夫就会重新钟情温柔。"

隐士接过那根胡须，仔细瞧了瞧。看到那确实是老虎的胡须，他感到非常满意，就倾身向前把那根胡须丢进了壁炉里正在燃烧的火中。

"噢，先生！"年轻女子痛苦地叫道，"你这是做什么呀！"

"告诉我你是怎么拿到的？"隐士说。

"唉，天天晚上我端一小碗饭上到山腰。起先，我远远地站在那里，后来我一次一次逐渐靠近，赢得了老虎的信任。我轻声柔语，安慰他，使他明白我对他只有好意。我很有耐心，每天晚上都给他送去食物。尽管我知道他不会吃，但我没有放弃。我跑了一趟又一趟，从不说苛刻的话，也从不责怪他。终于，有一天夜里，他向我迈了几步。有一段时间，他开始在道上迎接我，并愿意就着我端的碗吃。我轻轻地抚摸起他的头，他的喉咙里不时发出愉悦的声音。我就是这个时候取走了它的胡须。"

"好，好，"隐士说，"你驯服了老虎，赢得了他的信任和爱。"

"可你已经把那根胡须扔进了火里！"云鸥叫道，"一切都完了！"

"不，我认为一切都没有完，"隐士说，"那根胡须已经没有必要了。云鸥，我来问你，一个男人比一只老虎凶残吗？哪一个更不善解人心？如果你能通过温柔和耐心赢得一只嗜血成性的野兽的爱和信任，你肯定也能对丈夫做到吧？"

听了这番话，云鸥站在那里，默然无语。过了一会儿，她便沿着小路下山了。她一直在脑海里思考着山中隐士在屋里对她的那些点化。

One-dollar Tip

In a dirty and messy waiting room, a tired old man sat on the seat by the door. When the train pulled in, the ticket-punching began. The old man stood up in no hurry, ready to go to the ticket-punching entrance. Suddenly, a fat old lady entered the waiting room. She carried a large suitcase, obviously riding this train. But the suitcase was so heavy that she was out of breath. Seeing the old man, the fat old lady shouted at him, "Hi, old chap, carry the suitcase for me and I'll give you a tip awhile." The old man carried the suitcase and headed for the entrance with the fat old lady.

Hardly were the tickets punched and they just got on when the train had started. The fat old lady wiped off the sweat and said luckily, "Thanks to you, or I'll surely miss the train." Then, she fished out one dollar and handed it to the old man, who took it with a smile. At that moment, the conductor went along. "Hi, Mr. Rockefeller, welcome to ride this train. What can I do for you, please?"

"No, thanks, I just made a three-day hiking, and now I'm going to return to New York headquarters," the old man replied politely.

"What, Rockefeller!" the fat old lady exclaimed, "My God, I even let oil tycoon Mr. Rockefeller carry the suitcase for me and gave him one-dollar tip. What was I doing?" She hurriedly apologized to Rockefeller and pleaded him to give back the tip to her in awe.

"Madam, you needn't apologize, for you did nothing wrong at all," Rockefeller said with a smile, "this one dollar was what I earned, so I took it." With the words, Rockefeller put the dollar into his pocket solemnly.

The real great people are the ones who are at the top, but still know how to be the common people.

一美元小费

在一个又脏又乱的候车室，靠门的座位上坐着一个满脸疲惫的老人。列车进站，开始检票了。老人不急不忙地站起来，准备往检票口走。突然，候车室走进来一个胖太太，她提着一个很大的箱子，显然也是赶这班列车，可箱子太重了，累得她呼呼直喘。胖太太看到了那个老人，冲他大喊："喂，老头，你给我提一下箱子，我一会儿给你小费。"那个老人拎过箱子，就和胖太太向检票口走去。

他们刚刚检票上车，火车就启动了。胖太太抹了一把汗，庆幸地说："还真多亏了你，不然我非误车不可。"说着，她掏出一美元，递给了那个老人。老人微笑着接了过去。这时，列车长走了过来："洛克菲勒先生，您好，欢迎您乘坐本次列车，请问我能为您做点什么吗？"

"谢谢，不用了，我只是刚刚做了一个为期3天的徒步旅行，现在我要回纽约总部了。"老人客气地回答。

"什么，洛克菲勒！"胖太太惊叫起来，"上帝，我竟让洛克菲勒先生给我提箱子，居然还给了他一美元小费，我这是在干什么啊！"她忙向洛克菲勒道歉，并诚惶诚恐地请洛克菲勒把那一美元小费退给她。

"太太，你不必道歉，你根本没做错什么。"洛克菲勒微笑着说，"这一美元是我挣的，所以我收下了。"说着，洛克菲勒把那一美元郑重地放进了口袋里。

真正的大人物是那种身在高位、仍懂得如何去做平常人的人。

Are You a Carrot, an Egg or Coffee Beans

A daughter complained to her father about her life, saying everything was so difficult. She didn't know how to cope with her life, so she wanted to abandon herself to despair. She had been tired of struggle and endeavor, as if a problem was just resolved and a new problem emerged again.

Her father was a cook. He took her to the kitchen, first poured some water into the three pots, and then put them on the roaring fire to burn. Pretty soon, the water began boiling. He put some carrots into the first pot, an egg into the second one and coffee beans ground into powder into the third. He cooked them in the boiling water without a word.

His daughter smacked her lips, impatiently waiting and wondering what her father was doing. About 20 minutes later, he closed the fire, scooped the carrot out into a bowl, the egg into another bowl and coffee into a cup. After doing these, he turned to his daughter and asked, "Honey, what did you see?" "Carrots, an egg and coffee," she answered.

He let her close up and touch the carrots with her hands. After touching them, she felt they turned soft. Her father let his daughter take up the egg and break it. After shelling it, he saw it was a cooked egg. Finally, he let her drink the coffee. Tasting the savory coffee, her daughter smiled. She asked, "Father, What does this mean?"

He explained that these three things faced the same adversity—the boiled water, but their reactions were different. The carrots were strong and solid, without weakness before into the boiling water, but after into it, they softened and weakened. The egg was originally fragile, its thin shell protecting the liquid insides; but after being boiled, its insides turned hard. And the powdered coffee beans was very unique, for entering the boiling water, they changed the water. "Which one is you?" he asked his daughter. "When you encounter the adversity, how will you react? Are you a carrot, an egg or coffee beans?"

His daughter was lost in thought.

你是胡萝卜、鸡蛋还是咖啡豆

一个女儿对父亲抱怨她的生活,抱怨事事都那么艰难。她不知该如何应付生活,想要自暴自弃。她已厌倦抗争和奋斗,好像一个问题刚解决,新的问题就又出现了。

她的父亲是一位厨师，他把她带进厨房。他先往三只锅里倒入一些水，然后把它们放在旺火上烧。不久，锅里的水就烧开了。他往一只锅里放些胡萝卜，第二只锅里放只鸡蛋，最后一只锅里放入碾成粉末状的咖啡豆。他将它们浸入开水中煮，一句话也没说。

女儿咂咂嘴，不耐烦地等待着，纳闷父亲在做什么。大约20分钟后，他关了火，把胡萝卜捞出来放入一个碗里，把鸡蛋捞出来放进另一个碗里，然后又把咖啡舀到了一个杯子里。做完这些后，他才转过身问女儿："亲爱的，你看见什么了？""胡萝卜、鸡蛋、咖啡。"她回答说。

他让她靠近些，并让她用手摸摸胡萝卜。她摸了摸，注意到它们变软了。父亲又让女儿拿那只鸡蛋并打破它。她剥掉壳后，看到的是一只煮熟的鸡蛋。最后，他让她喝了咖啡。品尝到香浓的咖啡，女儿笑了。她问道："爸爸，这意味着什么？"

他解释说，这三样东西面临同样的逆境——煮沸的开水，但其反应各不相同。胡萝卜入锅之前强壮结实、毫不示弱；但进入开水后，它变软变弱。鸡蛋原来是易碎的，薄薄的外壳保护着呈液体的内脏；但经开水一煮，它的内脏变硬了。而粉状咖啡豆则很独特，进入沸水后，却改变了水。"哪个是你呢？"他问女儿，"你遇到逆境时，该如何反应？你是胡萝卜、鸡蛋还是咖啡豆？"

他的女儿陷入了沉思。

What Is the Best in Life

There was a young man who had a strange disease, he was depressed all day long.

One day, he paid a visit to a wise man for effective prescription. The wise man told him, "What do you think is the best thing that will make you happy?" He looked around and could not find the best thing. So he decided to look for it.

The young man packed his luggage, said goodbye to his family and started his journey.

The first day he met a politician, he asked, "Sir, do you know what is the best thing in the world?" The politician answered with a bureaucratic tone, "The best thing in the world is power." He reflected for a moment and found that power did not attract him much. As a result, he continued his journey.

The second day, he ran into a beggar and asked him the same question. Narrowing his eyes, the beggar said casually, "The best thing? It must be the delicious food." After consideration, he decided that he had little longing for food, so it was not the answer he wanted.

The third day he met a woman and brought forward that question once again. She blurted out joyfully, "Of course it is the upscale and beautiful garment from Paris!" He was not interested in garment and left at last.

The fourth day he saw two men in serious disease. When asked the best thing in their minds, they said with regret, "Isn't it obvious? It's health!" The man disagreed, "How come health is the best thing? I own it every day but I don't think it is the best thing."

The fifth day he met a child playing under the sunshine. When the child naively said, "The best thing is to have as many toys as I can," the man shook his head and kept on his journey.

The following days he successively ran into an old woman, a merchant, a painter, a prisoner, a mother and a young man.

The old woman said, "Youth is the best thing."

The merchant said, "Profit."

The painter said, "Color."

The prisoner said, "Freedom."

The mother said, "My precious child."

The young man said, "The smile of my beloved girl."

None of these answers had satisfied him. He kept moving forward and encountering different people. Finally, he came back to the wise man with all kinds of answers.

The wise man seemed to have known his experience and his disappointment, so he rubbed his gray beard and said, "Stop looking for the answer as you will never find a precise and unique one. Think about it. Is there anything or scene that you like most now?"

Through the long and wearisome journey the man had suffered hunger and cold with dust covered all over his body. He thought for a while and told the wise man, "I have been out for a long time. I missed my wife and lovely kids. I missed the scene that my whole family sat around the stove talking and laughing in winter nights," he could not help but sighed, "That's my favorite picture now!"

The wise man patted him on the shoulder and said, "Go home. The best thing is in your home now. It will cheer you up."

The man was not convinced, "But I left from my home!"

The wise man smiled, "You didn't know what you like before the journey, but now you must have known what you are fond of."

He was right: The best thing in the world is what we like most.

No matter what you have owned or have not, no matter it is complicated or simple, no matter it is cheap or expensive, as long as you like it, it is bound to be the best thing in the world.

人生最美好的是什么

有一个年轻人得了一种怪病：他一天到晚都郁郁寡欢。

有一天，他去拜访一位智者寻求良方。智者对他说："你认为世界上让你快乐的最好东西是什么？"年轻人环顾四周，无法找到最好的东西。于是，他决定去寻找。

年轻人打点行装，告别家人，踏上了旅途。

第一天，他遇到了一位政客，他问："先生，你知道世界上最好的东西是什么吗？"政客打着官腔说："世界上最好的东西是权力。"年轻人想了一会儿，发现权力对他没有多大吸引力。因此，他又继续寻找。

第二天，他碰到了一个乞丐，就问了同一个问题。乞丐眯起眼睛，漫不经心地说："最好的东西？那一定是美食。"年轻人想了想，认为自己对食物不太渴望，所以这不是他想要的答案。

第三天，他遇到了一个女人，又一次提出了那个问题。那个女人兴高采烈地脱口说道："当然是巴黎高档漂亮的时装了！"年轻人觉得自己对时装不感兴趣，最后就离开了。

第四天，他看到了两个重病的人。当他问他们认为世界上最好的东西是什么时，他们悔恨地说："这不明摆着吗？是健康。"年轻人不同意这个看法："健康怎么会是最好的东西呢？我每天都拥有，但我认为它不是最好的东西。"

第五天，他遇到了一个在阳光下玩耍的孩子。当那个孩子天真地说"最好的东西就是有好多好多的玩具"时，这个人摇了摇头，继续赶路。

接下来的几天，他又先后遇到了一位老太太、一个商人、一名画家、一个囚犯、一位母亲和一个年轻人。

老太太说："年轻是最好的东西。"

商人说："利润是最好的东西。"

画家说："色彩是最好的东西。"

囚犯说："自由是最好的东西。"

母亲说："我的宝贝孩子是最好的东西。"

年轻人说："我心爱姑娘的微笑是最好的东西。"

没有一个回答让他满意。他继续向前走，遇到了各种各样的人。最后，他带着五花八门的答案回到了智者身边。

智者似乎已经知道他的体验和失望,就捋着花白胡子说:"不要去寻找答案了,因为你永远找不到一个准确无二的答案。想一下,你现在有什么最喜欢的东西或情景吗?"

这个人经过长途跋涉,疲惫不堪、饥寒交迫、灰尘满身。他想了一会儿,对智者说:"我出门已经很长时间了。我想念妻子和可爱的孩子,想念全家人冬夜围着火炉谈笑风生的情景。"说到这里,他禁不住感叹道,"那是我现在最喜欢的画面!"

智者轻轻地拍了拍他的肩膀,说:"回去吧。最好的东西在你的家里。它会让你快乐起来的。"

这个人不相信:"可我就是从家里离开的!"

智者笑道:"出来前,你不知道自己喜欢什么,但现在你一定已经知道自己喜欢什么了。"

他说得对,世界上最好的东西就是我们最喜欢的东西。

无论是你拥有的还是未曾拥有的,无论它是复杂的还是简单的,无论是便宜的还是昂贵的,只要你喜欢,那它肯定就是世界上最好的东西。

Mary's Smile

When Mary opened the door, she found a man with a knife glowering at her ferociously. Mary hit a bright idea and said with a smile, "Pal, what a joke! Marketing the kitchen knife? I like it and I buy it…" she said as she let the man inside the house, then went on saying, "You're the very image of my former kindhearted neighbor. So glad to see you. Would you like coffee or tea…"

The gangster with a murderous look gradually became bashful.

He stammered, "Thank you, oh, thank you!"

At last, Mary did "buy" the shining kitchen knife; the strange man took the money, hesitated for a while and did leave her. On turning to go, he said, "Miss, you will change all my life!"

玛丽的微笑

玛丽打开门时,发现一个持刀的男人正恶狠狠地看着自己。玛丽灵机一动,微笑着说:"朋友,你真会开玩笑!是推销菜刀吧?我喜欢,我要一把……"她一边说,一边让男人进屋,接着说:"你很像我过去的一位好心的邻居,看到你真的好高兴,你要咖啡还是茶……"

本来面带杀气的歹徒渐渐腼腆了起来。

他结结巴巴地说:"谢谢,噢,谢谢!"

最后,玛丽真的"买"下了那把明晃晃的菜刀,陌生男人拿着钱迟疑一会儿,真的走了,他在转身离去时说:"小姐,你将会改变我的整个人生!"

It Is As You Will

There was once a wise old woman who lived back in the hills. All the children used to come back and ask her questions. She always gave the right answers.

There was a naughty little boy among the children. One day he caught a tiny bird and held it in his cupped hands. Then he gathered his friends around. He said, "Let's trick the old woman. I'll ask her what I'm holding in my hands. Of course, she'll answer that I have a bird. Then I'll ask her if the bird is living or dead. If she says the bird is dead, I'll open my hands and let the bird fly away. If she says the bird is alive, I'll quickly crush it and show her the dead bird. Either way, she'll be wrong."

The children agreed that this was a clever plan. Up the hill they went to the old woman's hut.

"Granny, we have a question for you," they all shouted.

"What's in my hands?" asked the little boy.

"Well, it must be a bird," replied the old woman.

"But is it living or dead?" demanded the excited boy.

The old woman thought for a moment and then replied, "It is as you will, my child."

你来决定

从前,有一位博学的老妇人,她住在后山。所有的孩子过去都经常来找她问问题。她总是有求必应。

其中有一个调皮的小男孩。有一天,他抓到一只小鸟,双手捧住,然后把伙伴们叫到身边,说:"咱们去骗一下那个老太太。我要问她我手里握着什么东西。她肯定会回答说我握的是小鸟。然后,我问她小鸟是活的还是死的。如果她说鸟是死的,我就张开手让小鸟飞走。如果她说小鸟是活的,我就马上用劲一捏,让她看到那只死鸟。不管用什么方法,她都说不对。"

孩子们都异口同声地说这是一个聪明的计划。他们爬上山,来到了老妇人的小屋。

"奶奶,我们要问您一个问题。"他们都大声说道。

"我手里是什么东西?"那个小男孩问道。

"噢,肯定是一只小鸟。"老妇人回答说。

"可是活的还是死的呢?"小男孩兴奋地问道。

老妇人想了一会儿,然后回答说:"这由你来决定,孩子。"

Love of a Lifetime

A teacher and his student lay down under the big tree near the grass. Then suddenly the student asked the teacher, "Teacher, I'm confused, how do we find our soul mate? Can you help me?"

Silent for a few seconds, the teacher then answered, "Well, it's a pretty hard and easy question."

The teacher continued, "Look that way. There is a lot of grass. Why don't you walk there? Please don't walk backwards, just walk straight ahead. On your way, try to find a blade of beautiful grass and pick it and then give it to me. But just one."

The student said, "Well, OK then…wait for me…" and walked straight ahead to the grass.

A few minutes later the student came back.

The teacher asked, "Well, I don't see a beautiful blade of grass in your hand."

The student said, "On my journey, I found quite a few beautiful blades of grass, but I thought that I would find a better one, so I didn't pick it. But I didn't realize that I was at the end of the field, and I hadn't picked any because you told me not to go back, so I didn't go back."

The teacher said, "That's what will happen in real life."

What is the message of this story?

In the story, grass is the people around you, the beautiful blade of grass is the people that attract you and the grassy field is time.

In looking for your soul mate, please don't always compare and hope that there will be a better one. By doing that, you'll waste your lifetime because time never goes back.

一 生 的 爱

一位老师和他的学生躺在草地边的大树下。这时,学生突然向老师问道:"老师,我很困惑,我们怎么找到情投意合的伴侣呢?您能帮帮我吗?"

老师沉默了一会儿,然后回答说:"噢,这是一个既很难又简单的问题。"

老师接着说:"看那边。有很多草,你何不到那里走走?请不要后退,一直向前走。路上,尽力找一棵美丽的草,把它拔下来,然后交给我。但只能拔一棵。"

学生说:"噢,好吧……等着我……"然后径直向草地走去。

几分钟后,学生返回。

老师问道:"唉,我没有看见你手里有漂亮的草呀。"

学生回答说:"我在路上发现了好多漂亮的草,但我认为自己会找到更好的草,就没有拔。但我没有意识到自己走到了地头,因为你告诉我不要后退,所以我一棵也没拔。"

老师说:"现实生活就是这样。"

这个故事的教训是什么呢?

在这个故事里,草就是你周围的人,漂亮的草就是吸引你的人,草地就是时间。

在寻找情投意合的伴侣时,请不要总是比较,希望会有更好的伴侣。如果这样做,你就会浪费一生的时间,因为时间一去不复返。

What Will Matter in Life

Ready or not, someday it will come to an end. There will be no more sunrises, no days, no hours or minutes. All the things you collected, whether treasured or forgotten, will pass to someone else.

Your wealth, fame and power will turn to irrelevance. It will not matter what you owned or what you were owed.

Your grudges, resentments, frustrations and jealousies will finally disappear. So, too, your hopes, ambitions and plans will all expire. The wins and losses that once seemed so important will fade away.

It won't matter where you came from, or on what side of the tracks you lived. It won't matter whether you were beautiful or brilliant. Your gender, skin color and race will be irrelevant.

So what will matter? How will the value of your days be measured?

What will matter is not what you bought, but what you built; not what you got, but what you gave.

What will matter is not your success, but your significance.

What will matter is not what you learned, but what you taught.

What will matter is every act of integrity, compassion, courage and sacrifice that encouraged others.

What will matter is not your competence, but your character.

What will matter is not how many people you knew, but how many will feel a lasting loss when you're gone.

What will matter is not your memories, but the memories of those who loved you.

What will matter is how long you will be remembered.

Living a life that matters doesn't happen by accident.

It's not a matter of circumstance but of choice.

Choose to live a life that matters.

人生重要的是什么

无论是否做好准备,总有一天会结束。日出、日子、时分不再会有。你搜集的所有一切,无论是值得珍惜还是应该忘记的,都会传给别人。

你的财富、名声和权力都会变得无关。你拥有的和亏欠的都不再重要。

你的怨恨、不满、沮丧和嫉妒最后都会消失。所以,你的希望、抱负和计划也会统统终止。曾对你看似非常重要的得失也会渐渐消失。

你来自哪里或曾生活在轨道的哪一边不再重要。你是美丽大方还是才华横溢不再重要。你的性别、肤色和种族也不再重要。

那什么才重要的呢?你该如何衡量自己的人生价值呢?

重要的不是你买的,而是你建立的,不是你得到的,而是你给予的。

重要的不是你的成功,而是你的意义。

重要的不是你学会了什么,而是你教会了什么。

重要的是你用正直、同情、勇气和牺牲鼓舞他人的每一次举动。

重要的不是你的能力,而是你的品质。

重要的不是你认识多少人,而是你去世时,会有多少人久久失落。

重要的不是你的记忆,而是那些爱你的人的回忆。

重要的是你会被铭记多久。

过一种重要的人生并非偶然。

那不是环境问题,而是选择问题。

选择过一种重要的人生吧。

The Teacher and Sick Scholar

Shortly after the schoolmaster had arranged the forms and taken his seat behind his desk, a small white-headed boy with a sunburnt face appeared at the door, and, stopping there to make a rustic bow, came in and took his seat upon one of the forms. He then put an open book, astonishingly dog's-eared, upon his knees, and, thrusting his hands into his pockets, began counting the marbles with which they were filled; displaying, in the expression of his face, a remarkable capacity of totally abstracting his mind from the spelling on which his eyes were fixed.

Soon afterward, another white-headed little boy came straggling in, and after him, a red-headed lad, and then one with a flaxen poll, until the forms were occupied by a dozen boys, or thereabouts, with heads of every color but gray, and ranging in their ages from four years old to fourteen years or more; for the legs of the youngest were a long way from the floor, when he sat upon the form; and the eldest was a heavy, good-tempered fellow, about half a head taller than the schoolmaster.

At the top of the first form—the post of honor in the school—was the vacant place of the little sick scholar; and, at the head of the row of pegs, on which those who wore hats or caps were wont to hang them, one was empty. No boy attempted to violate the sanctity of seat or peg, but many a one looked from the empty spaces to the schoolmaster, and whispered to his idle neighbor, behind his hand.

Then began the hum of conning over lessons and getting them by heart, the whispered jest and stealthy game, and all the noise and drawl of school; and in the midst of the din, sat the poor schoolmaster, vainly attempting to fix his mind upon the duties of the day, and to forget his little sick friend. But the tedium of his office reminded him more strongly of the willing scholar, and his thoughts were rambling from his pupils—it was plain.

None knew this better than the idlest boys, who, growing bolder with impunity, waxed louder and more daring; playing "odd or even" under the master's eye; eating apples openly and without rebuke; pinching each other in sport or malice, without the least reserve; and cutting their initials in the very legs of his desk. The puzzled dunce, who stood beside it to say his Lesson "off the book," looked no longer at the ceiling for forgotten words, but drew closer to the master's elbow, and boldly cast his eye upon the page; the wag of the little troop squinted and made grimaces (at the smallest boy, of course), holding no book before his face, and his approving companions knew no constraint in their delight. If the master did chance to rouse himself, and seem alive to what was going on, the noise subsided for a moment, and no eye met his but wore a studious and deeply humble look; but the instant he relapsed again, it broke out afresh, and ten times louder than before.

Oh! how some of those idle fellows longed to be outside, and how they looked at the open door and window, as if they half meditated rushing violently out, plunging into the woods, and being wild boys and savages from that time forth. What rebellious thoughts of the cool river, and some shady bathing place, beneath willow trees with branches dipping in the water, kept tempting and urging that sturdy boy, who, with his shirt collar unbuttoned, and flung back as far as it could go, sat fanning his flushed face with a spelling book, wishing himself a whale, or a minnow, or a fly, or anything but a boy at school, on that hot, broiling day.

Heat! ask that other boy, whose seat being nearest to the door, gave him opportunities of gliding out into the garden, and driving his companions to madness, by dipping his face into the bucket of the well, and then rolling on the grass, —ask him if there was ever such a day as that, when even the bees were diving deep down into the cups of the flowers, and stopping there, as if they had made up their minds to retire from business, and be manufacturers of honey no more. The day was made for laziness, and lying on one's back in green places, and staring at the sky, till its brightness forced the gazer to shut his eyes and go to sleep. And was this a time to be poring over musty books in a dark room, slighted by the very sun itself? Monstrous!

The lessons over, writing time began. This was a more quiet time; for the master would come and look over the writer's shoulder, and mildly tell him to observe how such a letter was turned up, in such a copy on the wall, which had been written by their sick companion, and bid him take it as a model. Then he would stop and tell them what the sick child had said last night, and how he had longed to be among them once again; and such was the poor schoolmaster's gentle and affectionate manner, that the boys seemed quite remorseful that they had worried him so much, and were absolutely quiet; eating no apples, cutting no names, and making no grimaces for full two minutes afterward.

"I think, boys," said the schoolmaster, when the clock struck twelve, "that I shall give you an extra half holiday this afternoon." At this intelligence, the boys, led on and headed by the tall boy, raised a great shout, in the midst of which the master was seen to speak, but could not be heard. As he held up his hand, however, in token of his wish that they should be silent, they were considerate enough to leave off, as soon as the longest-winded among them were quite out of breath. "You must promise me, first," said the schoolmaster, "that you'll not be noisy, or at least, if you are, that you'll go away first, out of the village, I mean. I'm sure you wouldn't disturb your old playmate and companion."

There was a general murmur (and perhaps a very sincere one, for they were but boys) in the negative; and the tall boy, perhaps as sincerely as any of them, called those about him to witness, that he had only shouted in a whisper. "Then pray don't forget, there's my dear scholars," said the schoolmaster, "what I have asked you, and do it as a favor to me. Be as happy as you can, and don't be unmindful that you are blessed with health. Good-by, all."

"Thank 'ee, sir," and "Good-by, sir," were said a great many times in a great variety of voices, and the boys went out very slowly and softly. But there was the sun shining and there were birds singing, as the sun only shines and the birds only sing on holidays and half holidays; there were the trees waving to all free boys to climb, and nestle among their leafy branches; the hay, entreating them to come and scatter it to the pure air; the green corn, gently beckoning toward wood and stream; the smooth ground, rendered smoother still by blending lights and shadows, inviting to runs and leaps, and long walks, nobody knows whither. It was more than boy could bear, and with a joyous whoop, the whole cluster took to their heels, and spread themselves about, shouting and laughing as they went. "'T is natural, thank Heaven!" said the poor schoolmaster, looking after them, "I am very glad they didn't mind me."

Toward night, the schoolmaster walked over to the cottage where his little friend lay sick. Knocking gently at the cottage door, it was opened without loss of time. He entered a room where a group of women were gathered about one who was wringing her hands and crying bitterly. "O dame!" said the schoolmaster, drawing near her chair, "is it so bad as this?" Without replying, she pointed to another room, which the schoolmaster immediately entered; and there lay his little friend, half-dressed, stretched upon a bed.

He was a very young boy; quite a little child. His hair still hung in curls about his face, and his eyes were very bright; but their light was of heaven, not of earth. The schoolmaster took a seat beside him, and, stooping over the pillow whispered his name. The boy sprung up, stroked his face with his hand, and threw his wasted arms around his neck, crying, that he was his dear, kind friend. "I hope I always was. I meant to be, God knows," said the poor schoolmaster. "You remember my garden, Henry?" whispered the old man, anxious to rouse him, for dullness seemed gathering upon the child, "and how pleasant it used to be in the evening time? You must make haste to visit it again, for I think the very flowers have missed you, and are less gay than they used to be. You will come soon, very soon now, won't you?"

The boy smiled faintly—so very, very faintly—and put his hand upon his friend's gray head. He moved his lips too, but no voice came from them, —no, not a sound. In the silence that ensued, the hum of distant voices, borne upon the evening air, came floating through the open window. "What's that?" said the sick child, opening his eyes. "The boys at play, upon the green." He took a handkerchief from his pillow, and tried to wave it above his head. But the feeble arm dropped powerless down. "Shall I do it?" said the schoolmaster. "Please wave it at the window," was the faint reply. "Tie it to the lattice. Some of them may see it there. Perhaps they'll think of me, and look this way."

He raised his head and glanced from the fluttering signal to his idle bat, that lay, with slate, and book, and other boyish property, upon the table in the room. And then he laid him softly down once more, and again clasped his little arms around the old man's neck. The two old friends and companions—for such they were, though they were man and child—held each other in a long embrace, and then the little scholar turned his face to the wall and fell asleep.

The poor schoolmaster sat in the same place, holding the small, cold hand in his, and chafing it. It was but the hand of a dead child. He felt that; and yet he chafed it still, and could not lay it down.

From "The Old Curiosity Shop" by Dickens

老师和生病的学生

就在老师安排好各年级座位，在讲台后面的椅子上坐下不久，一个头发淡黄、脸色黝黑的小男孩来到了门前，他在门口停下来，鞠了一躬，然后走进来坐下了。随后，他翻开一本相当破旧的书，把它放在自己的膝盖上，他把手插进口袋里，开始数里面装了多少弹子；尽管他目不转睛地盯着拼写本，其实从他的表情可以看出，他正在心里玩着数弹子的把戏。

很快，又有一个浅色头发的小男孩跑了进来；在他之后，又跑进来一个红头发的小男孩；随后，是一个提着淡黄色投票箱的小男孩，直到屋子里挤满了孩子。除了灰色之外，孩子们头发的颜色应有尽有，他们的年龄从四岁到十四岁，甚至更大；最小的孩子坐在自己座位上时，他的双脚和地面之间还有很大一段距离。最年长的男孩个头很大，脾气温和，他甚至比老师还要高出半个脑袋。

在一年级最前面的座位——那是学校的荣誉座位——那个位置属于一个得病的学生。在高年级那排座位的排头，坐着那些戴着帽子或习惯戴鸭舌帽的孩子，有一个座位空着。没有哪个孩子试图触犯座位或顺序的圣洁，但是其中有一个孩子偷偷摸摸地瞧着老师，并且同相邻的闲得无聊的伙伴轻声说起话来。

开始上课了，学生们开始背诵课文，他们有的小声地开着玩笑，有的玩起游戏，喧闹声和拉长声调朗读课文的声音交汇在一起。这位可怜的老师在吵闹声中绞尽了脑汁，以尽到自己应尽的责任，强迫自己忘记那个得病的孩子。但是教室里的单调乏味使他更想念那个生病的学生，他的心思早就不在这些学生身上了——他的脑海里一片空白。

再也没有人比这些最懒惰的孩子会钻空子的。当他们知道老师不会惩罚他们时，他们就变得更胆大、变得更喧闹，行为也更不计后果；他们在老师眼皮底下玩猜拳的游戏；有的甚至吃起苹果来，而且不会受到责备；他们用恶意的动作互相推搡，嬉戏打闹，没有任何防护；还有人在老师的书桌腿上刻上每个学生名字的首字母。那个让老师大伤脑筋的笨学生，则站在老师的桌子旁边说，上课的时候完全没必要看书，他也不再因为忘词而看向天花板，而是凑近老师的眼皮底下，大胆地看向那一页。这个捣蛋鬼斜着眼做起各种鬼脸（当然是冲向那个最小的孩子），而且他也没有拿起书遮挡，看到他"表演"的人大加赞赏，整个教室一片欢乐的海洋。如果老师突然醒悟过来，看到眼前所发生的一切时，喧闹就会停止，他所接触到的目光都是拼命学习和无比谦逊的。但是，当他再次陷入沉思之后，吵闹声会比之前飙高十倍。

噢！那些偷懒的孩子多么想跑到外面去啊！他们用充满渴望的眼神看向敞开的窗户，就好像他们在思考着逃离这里，钻进树林里，之后就好像变成了一群野孩子和野人似的。凉爽的小河、树荫吹到水面的池塘，都在诱惑着孩子们；尤其是那个强壮的孩子，他的衬衫领子都没扣好，领子向后敞开，仿佛立刻就要脱掉的样子，他坐在那儿不停地用拼音手册给那通红的脸扇风，希望自己是一条鲸鱼，或者一条小鱼，即便是一只苍蝇也行——什么都好，只要不是这样一动不动地待在教室，忍受那酷热难耐的天气。

真热呀！可以问问那个离门口最近的孩子。他的位置离门口最近，这给了他溜到花园的机会，他把脸扎进水桶里，然后开始在草地上惬意地翻滚。这让他的同学们近乎疯狂。如此炎热的天气，就连蜜蜂也会扎进花朵的深处隐藏起来，就好像它们决心隐退，不再采蜜了一样。一个注定让人变得慵懒的天气，躺在绿草地上，凝视着蓝天，直到明亮的光线迫使观察者想要闭上眼睛，昏昏欲睡，难道该让人憋屈在阳光照射不到的阴暗的屋子里，读那些无聊透顶的书吗？真是太荒谬了！

正课结束了，接下来该是写作的时间。这是更寂静的时刻，老师来回走动，在孩子们的背后观察，并且温和地告诉他看看那张字母表是如何写出来的，这张字母表是那个得病的男孩的临摹作品，将它当作范本挂在墙上。然后，他会停下来跟大家说，昨天晚上那个得病的孩子说了些什么话，他是多么想再次回到他们中间；那些孩子都被可怜的老师那既温柔又充满爱意的态度所感化，他们好像对让老师为自己如此操劳而感到懊悔，因此他们变得安静下来：都不再吃苹果了，没有人再刻名字了，也不再做鬼脸了，就这样一直持续了两分钟的时间。

"我想，孩子们，"老师说，此时已经十二点了，"今天下午，我给你们额外放半天假。"听到这话之后，以那个高个儿孩子为首的孩子们大声欢呼起来；老师又说了些话，但是大家听不清楚。然而，他举起了手，示意大家安静下来，孩子们非常配合，等到拖得最长的声音消失，教室便安静下来。老师说:"首先,你们必须向我保证,你们不要大声喧闹。就算是大声喧闹,也要去偏远的地方吵闹,我的意思是你们要去村子的外面。我相信你们肯定不会打扰到和自己玩耍的孩子吧。"

大家小声嘟囔着(或许很真诚,因为他们还只是孩子);那个高个子学生,或许和其他人一样真诚,让其他人作证,他只是低声地抱怨。"请不要忘记,那才是我喜欢的好孩子。"他们的老师说道,"记住并履行我说的话。尽量开心地玩,但是不要忘记,一切以身体健康为重。再见,同学们!"

"谢谢你,先生!""再见,先生!"大家用不同的腔调回答着。之后,孩子们慢慢地离开了教室。太阳投下灿烂的阳光,小鸟在枝头歌唱;只有在假期太阳才会这么灿烂,鸟儿只有在假期才会这么歌唱;小树迎风招展,示意孩子们爬上去,依偎在宽大的树枝上;干草渴望他们来到跟前,将它们在纯净的空中散开,玉米叶向木头和小溪招手;被光照和阴影覆盖的大地显得更加光滑,大地邀请他们在上面奔跑、跳跃和漫步。没人知道自己到底要去哪里。既然这样,有谁还可以强忍喜悦呢!随着一声快乐的叫喊,大家四散开来,一边叫喊着,一边飞奔。"这是再正常不过的事情,感谢上帝!"可怜的老师说,看着他们离他而去,"我很高兴,他们没有在意我说的话。"

快到晚上时,老师来到那个生病的孩子所在的农舍前,他轻轻地敲了敲农舍的门,门开了。他走进一间屋子,里面有一群女人围坐在一个年龄稍大的女人身边,她在大声地哭泣,坐在椅子上拧着自己的手,来回地摆动着:"噢,夫人!"老师走到椅子边说,"怎么变得这么糟糕?"老妇人没有回答,她用手指向了另一个房间,老师毫不犹豫地走进了那个房间:他看到那个小孩半穿着衣服,躺在一张床上。

他的年龄还很小,甚至可以说是个婴儿。他的头发在脸上卷曲着,他的眼睛非常明亮,那是来自天堂的光芒,并非来自人间。老师在他身边的椅子上坐下,把头伏在小男孩的枕头边,小声地叫着他的名字。小男孩猛地直起身子,用手摸着他的脸,之后伸出纤细的胳膊抱着他的脖子,哭喊着说,老师是他敬爱的、仁慈的朋友。"我希望我一直都是。我是说,我要做你的好朋友,上帝知道!"可怜的老师说道,"你还能想起那个花园吗,亨利?"老师低声说道,急切地想要唤醒他,因为一种压抑正在逐渐包围他,"傍晚时分真让人感到愉快啊!你应该抓紧时间再去那里看一次,我认为,那些花朵都很想念你,它们没有之前那样艳丽了。你很快就会去看的,亲爱的,你很快就会去的,对吗?"

男孩虚弱地笑了笑，非常虚弱，并且把手放在他朋友灰白的头发上。男孩蠕动着嘴唇，但是什么也没说，一点声音都没有。一切又归于寂静，远处的声音随着晚风从开着的窗户飘了进来，打破了夜晚空气的沉寂。"什么声音？"虚弱的小男孩睁开眼睛说。"是男孩们在草地上踢球的声音。"老师说。男孩从枕头下拿出了一块手绢，想在头顶挥舞，但是他虚弱的手臂无力地垂了下来。"要我帮你吗？"老师问。"请在窗户边挥舞这块手绢，"男孩虚弱地答道，"把它绑在窗户的栅格上，这样他们就能看到它了。或许他们能够想到我，然后看向这边。"

他抬起头，从迎风飘动的手绢看向和石板、书以及与其他玩具放在一起的球棒，这球棒现在没人玩，放在屋内的桌子上。随后，老师又一次把男孩轻轻地放躺下去，把那双小手绕在自己的脖子上。这两个老朋友和老伙伴——虽然一个是大人，一个是小孩，但他们确实是老朋友——久久地抱在一起，然后，男孩把脸转过来冲着墙壁，进入了梦乡。

但是，可怜的老师还在原来的位置，紧握着那只冰冷的小手，摩擦着。那是一只去世的孩子的手，他能感觉到。不过他还在不停地摩擦，迟迟不肯放下。

选自狄更斯《老古玩店》

第五卷

母亲的爱

Mother's Hands

Night after night, she came to tuck me in, even long after my childhood years. Following her longstanding custom, she'd lean down and push my long hair out of the way, then kiss my forehead.

I don't remember when it first started annoying me—her hands pushing my hair that way. But it did annoy me, for they felt work-worn and rough against my young skin. Finally, one night, I shouted out at her, "Don't do that anymore—your hands are too rough!" She didn't say anything in reply. But never again did my mother close out my day with that familiar expression of her love.

Time after time, with the passing years, my thoughts returned to that night. By then I missed my mother's hands, missed her goodnight kiss on my forehead. Sometimes the incident seemed very close, sometimes far away. But always it lurked in the back of my mind.

Well, the years have passed, and I'm not a little girl anymore. Mom is in her mid-seventies, and those hands I once thought to be so rough are still doing things for me and my family. She's been our doctor, reaching into a medicine cabinet for the remedy to calm a young girl's stomach or soothe the boy's scraped knees. She cooks the best fried chicken in the world and gets stains out of blue jeans like I never could…

Now, my own children are grown and gone. Mom no longer has Dad, and on special occasions, I find myself drawn next door to spend the night with her. So it was late on Thanksgiving Eve, as I slept in the bedroom of my youth, a familiar hand hesitantly run across my face to brush the hair from my forehead. Then a kiss, ever so gently, touched my brow.

In my memory, for the thousandth time, I recalled the night my young voice complained, "Don't do that anymore—your hands are too rough!" Catching Mom's hand in hand, I blurted out how sorry I was for that night. I thought she'd remember, as I did. But Mom didn't know what I was talking about. She had forgotten—and forgiven—long ago.

That night, I fell asleep with a new appreciation for my gentle mother and her caring hands. And the guilt that I had carried around for so long was nowhere to be found.

母 亲 的 手

夜复一夜，她都过来给我披被子，甚至在我的童年过去很久之后还是那样。这种习惯由来已久，她常常俯下身，拨开我的长发，然后吻我的前额。

我不记得最初从什么时候开始讨厌她用手拨开我的头发。但那的确让我讨厌，因为她长期劳作的手摸在我细嫩的皮肤上是那样粗糙。终于，有一天夜里，我朝她大声喊道："不要再这样做了——你的手太粗糙了！"她什么也没有说。但母亲再也没有用那种熟悉的爱的方式来结束我的一天。

光阴荏苒，日月如梭，许多年后，我的思绪又回到了那天夜里。那时我想念母亲的手，想念她留在我前额上的晚安之吻。有时这情景似乎很近，有时又似乎很远。但它总是潜伏在我的脑海深处。

噢，时光流逝，我不再是小姑娘了。母亲也已经七十四五岁了，那双我曾认为粗糙的手仍在为我和我的家庭做事。她是我们的医生，常常伸手去药箱里给我胃疼的女儿找药或为我的儿子擦伤的膝盖敷药。她能做出世界上味道最美的炸鸡，能洗掉牛仔裤上我永远洗不掉的污点……

现在，我自己的孩子都已经长大成人，离开了家。爸爸也撒手而去了。在那些特殊时刻，我常常情不自禁地走到隔壁，和她一起过夜。因此，一次感恩节前夕，到了深夜，我睡在年轻时的卧室里时，一只熟悉的手迟疑地滑过了我的脸，拨开了我前额的头发，随后一个吻触在了我的前额上，是那样轻柔。

我在记忆里无数次回想起那天夜里我年轻气盛发的牢骚："不要再那样做了——你的手太粗糙了！"我握住母亲的手，脱口说出了我是多么后悔那天夜里自己所说的话。我以为她会像我一样记得这件事，但妈妈不知道我在说什么。她早已忘记了这件事，也早已原谅了我。

那天夜里，我带着对温柔母亲和她体贴双手的新的感激之情进入了梦乡。而且我长久以来的内疚感也消失得无影无踪了。

A Rose for Her Mother

A gentleman stopped his car at the door of a flower shop. He wanted to order a bunch of flowers and asked them to deliver them to his mother. who was far in his hometown.

He saw a girl crying on the road when he was about to enter the shop. The gentleman walked to the little girl and asked her, "Little girl, why are you crying?"

"I want to buy a rose for my mother, but I haven't enough money," said the girl.

Hearing that, the gentleman felt sympathetic to the girl. "It was so…" Then he grasped the girl's hand and entered the flower shop. He first ordered the bouquet for his mother and bought a rose for the girl.

Walking out of the shop, the gentleman proposed driving the girl home.

"Would you really drive me home?"

"Of course!"

"Then drive me to my mother. But uncle, the place where my mother lives is very far from here."

Following the way the girl showed, the gentleman drove out of the urban district along the winding mountain road and finally came to the cemetery.

The little girl put the flower close to a new grave. In order to present a rose to her mother who just passed away a month ago, she took a long journey.

The gentleman drove the girl to her home, then he return to the flower shop. He cancelled the flower bunch to her mother but bought a big bunch of fresh flower instead. He drove directly to his mother's home, five-hour drive from here. He would present the flower to his mother in person.

送给母亲的玫瑰

有位绅士在花店门口停下了车,他打算向花店订一束花,请他们送去给远在故乡的母亲。

绅士正要走进店门时,发现有个小女孩坐在路上哭,便走到小女孩面前问她说:"孩子,为什么坐在这里哭?"

"我想买一朵玫瑰花送给妈妈,可我的钱不够。"孩子说。

绅士听了,感到心疼。"这样啊……"于是,绅士牵着小女孩的手走进花店,先订了要送给母亲的花束,然后给小女孩买了一朵玫瑰花。

走出花店时,绅士向小女孩提议,要开车送她回家。

"真的要送我回家吗?"

"当然啊!"

"那你送我去妈妈那里好了。可是,叔叔,我妈妈住的地方离这里很远。"

绅士照小女孩说的一直开了过去,没想到走出市区大马路之后,随着蜿蜒山路前行,竟然来到了墓园。

小女孩把花放在一座新坟旁边。她为了给一个月前刚过世的母亲,献上一朵玫瑰花,而走了一大段远路。

绅士将小女孩送回了家中,然后再次返回花店。他取消了要寄给母亲的花束,而改买了一大束鲜花,直奔离这里有5小时车程的母亲家里,他要亲自将花献给妈妈。

A Daughter's Love for Her Mother

Dear Mom,

I haven't written many letters to you before, as we've almost always been able to just pick up the phone and have a chat, so it's hard to know how to start.

Of course, all the usual things apply—we all miss you and hope you're all right wherever you are.

When you left us, it took a little for it to sink in that I would never see you again. I guess I was a bit like you being away on a trip or those times when we didn't find the time to even speak on the phone for a week or so.

I realize now there are too many things left unsaid and too many questions unasked.

Dad is finding life difficult without you and his loneliness is almost unbearable to me, as there's so little I can do to help him. I think in time he'll find some interests and make a new kind of life. But at the moment he seems only to look forward to the time when he can join you again.

Emily and I are feeling a little better each day and, in a way, your going has brought us closer together. We seem to understand each other better at the moment and maybe eventually we'll have the sort of relationship that really close sisters enjoy.

We've both found strengths in each other over the past weeks, and these are a huge comfort. Perhaps we never needed to look for them before because we had you to be strong for us.

I guess I'm lucky to have my own children to keep me so busy. I don't have much time to dwell on my sadness but sometimes I crave the peace to just have a private think about you.

For a couple of weeks after you died, my brain seemed to go crazy, searching through its memory banks for something I could keep in my heart which was special to you and me. One day it came to me—the tour we made of some special garden.

Remember the day it poured with rain the whole time but we were determined to make the most of it? I enjoyed just being with you by myself, without the children clamoring for your attention. The gardens were beautiful despite the rain and you bought me a rose I'd admired for my own garden.

For a while after your death, I expected to feel your presence around me as Dad and Emily seem to do with such ease. When I was out walking, I would look at the sky and wonder whether you could see me, or whether you were with me. At night I wondered whether you'd become a star, as some people believe.

But as time passes, I think I'm closer to finding the truth. You're with me every time I comfort one of the children or try to find the right words to gently chastise them. I listen for your words of wisdom and they come from within me because your greatest gift to me was teaching me how to be a good mother to my own children.

And although you're no longer here with us, I know in times of sadness or pain the children feel your arms around them just as I sense that I feel your arms around me, too. In years to come I hope your gift to me will be passed to my own children's children. And I know it's your voice telling me in these changing times the best thing we can give our children is love, because love is eternal and love doesn't die. So long for now, and thank you from all of us.
Happy Mother's Day, mom.

Love Carol

母女情怀

亲爱的妈妈：

　　我以前没有给您写过多少封信，因为我们几乎总能拿起电话聊天，所以很难知道怎么开始写起。

　　当然，可以用那些老生常谈——我们都想念您，希望您无论在什么地方都万事如意。

　　您离开我们时，有一小段时间我陷入了永远无法再见您的思念。我想那有点像您出门旅行了，要么就像我们有时一周左右都没时间通电话。

　　我现在意识到还有太多的话没说，还有太多的问题没问。

　　没有了您，爸爸发现生活难过，他的孤独让我几乎无法忍受，因为我几乎帮不了他什么忙。我想他最后会找到一些有兴趣的事，开始一种新的生活。但是，他现在似乎只盼望能和您再次相聚。

　　我和埃米莉的感觉渐渐好转。从某种意义上说，您的离去使我们更加亲密。我们此时似乎彼此更加了解，也许最终我们会享有亲密姐妹们享有的那种关系。

　　在过去的几周里，我们已经从彼此身上找到了力量，这是极大的安慰。也许我们以前从不需要寻求这种力量，因为我们有您做坚强后盾。

　　我想，幸运的是我自己有孩子，使我忙得团团转，没有多少时间沉湎于悲伤，但有时我渴望安静，可以私下去思念您。

　　在您去世后的两三周里，我的大脑好像发了疯似的，拼命在记忆库里寻找珍藏在我心里的某件事——某件对您我二人都特别亲密的事情。有一天，我终于想起来了——就是我们到一个特别花园进行的那次游览。

还记得那天一直大雨倾盆,但我们打定主意要尽情玩一下的情景吗?我就喜欢单独和您在一起,没有孩子们大声吵闹使您分心。尽管下着雨,但花园很美。您给我买了一枝玫瑰,我曾希望自己的花园种有这种玫瑰。

您去世后的一段时间,我期望能感到您就在我身边,因为爸爸和埃米莉好像轻松自如就能感受到。我在外面散步时,常常仰望天空,想知道您是不是能看到我,或者您是不是和我在一起。夜里,我常常想,您是不是就像有些人相信的那样变成了一颗星星。

但随着时间流逝,我想我越来越近地找到了真实的感觉。每当我安慰一个孩子或要找出合适的词语来轻轻责打他们时,您都和我在一起。如果我留神倾听您的智慧话语,它们就会从我的内心传来,因为您留给我最伟大的礼物就是教会我如何给自己的孩子当一个好妈妈。

尽管您不再和我们一起生活在这里,但我知道在悲伤和痛苦时,孩子们能感到您环抱着他们,就像我感到您环抱着我一样。在未来的岁月里,我希望把您留给我的礼物传给我的子孙们。而且我知道那是您的声音在告诉我,在这变化的时代,我们能留给我们孩子们的最好东西就是爱,因为爱是永恒的,爱不会死去。就此再见了,我们都衷心感谢您。

母亲节快乐,妈妈!

爱您的卡罗尔

Mom Charged Zero Dollar

Texas has a law: any 14-year-old children must share the household chores for the parents, such as washing dishes, scrubbing the floor and mowing the lawns.

One Sunday night, smart Tom wrote a bill to his mother:

Tom helped Mom buy the food in the supermarket, so Mom should pay five dollars;

Tom got up and folded his quilt, so Mom should pay two dollars;

Tom scrubbed the floor, so Mom should pay three dollars;

Tom is an obedient good boy, so Mom should pay 10 dollars.

The total is 20 dollars.

After that, Tom pressed the note on the table and went to bed. When his mother saw it, she smiled tolerantly, added a few lines on it and put it beside Tom's pillows.

When Tom woke up, he saw such a bill:

Mom was pregnant with Tom for 10 months, so Tom should pay 0 dollar;

Mom taught Tom to speak and walk, so Tom should pay 0 dollar;

Mom made good food for Tom every day, so Tom should pay 0 dollar;

Mom accompanied Tom to the children's playground every weekend, so Tom should pay 0 dollar;

Mom prays for Tom every day, hoping he becomes an angelic lovely little boy, so Tom should pay 0 dollar.

The total is 0 dollar.

Now this note is still treasured by Tom. It tells Tom that the real love can't be measured by money.

Mother is so generous because she loves too genuinely; Mother is so tolerant because she loves too deeply. When we have such a genuine and deep love in our hearts as Mother, we won't ask for reward, either.

妈妈只收零美元

得克萨斯州有一条法律：凡年满14岁的孩子必须为父母分担家务，比如洗碟子、擦地板和剪草坪。

一个星期天的晚上，聪明的汤姆给妈妈写下了一份账单：

汤姆帮妈妈到超级市场买食品，妈妈应付5美元；

汤姆自己起床叠被，妈妈应付2美元；

汤姆擦地板，妈妈应付3美元；

汤姆是一个听话的好孩子，妈妈应付10美元。

合计：20美元。

写完后，汤姆把纸条压在餐桌上，便上床睡觉去了。妈妈看到这张纸条后，宽容地笑了笑，随手在上面添了几行字，放到汤姆的枕边。

汤姆醒来后，看到了这样的一张账单：

妈妈怀了汤姆10个月，汤姆应付0美元；

妈妈教汤姆说话和走路，汤姆应付0美元；

妈妈每天为汤姆做好吃的食物，汤姆应付0美元；

妈妈每个周末陪汤姆去儿童乐园，汤姆应付0美元；

妈妈每天为汤姆祈祷，希望他成为天使般可爱的小男孩，汤姆应付0美元。

合计：0美元。

这张纸条至今仍被汤姆珍藏着。它告诉汤姆，真正的爱是无法用金钱计量的。

妈妈为什么如此慷慨,因为她爱得太真;妈妈为什么如此宽容,因为她爱得太深。等我们心中有了妈妈那样真那样深的爱时,我们也会不图报酬。

Prayer for My Mother

Now that I am no longer young, I have friends whose mothers have passed away. I have heard these sons and daughters say they never fully appreciated their mothers until it was too late to tell them.

I am blessed with the dear mother who is still alive. I appreciate her more each day. My mother doesn't change, but I do. As I grow older and wiser, I realize what an extraordinary person she is. How sad that I am unable to speak these words in her presence, but they flow easily from my pen.

How does a daughter begin to thank her mother for life itself? For the love, patience and just plain hard work that go into raising a child? For running after a toddler, for understanding a moody teenager, for tolerating a college student who knows everything? For waiting for the day when a daughter realizes her mother really is?

I will look as good in the eyes of my children as my mother looks in mine.

为母亲祈祷

我不再年轻,一些朋友的母亲已经去世了。我曾听这些子女们说过,他们从来没有向自己的母亲充分表示过感激之情,直到想告诉她们时为时已晚。

我庆幸自己亲爱的母亲仍然健在。我对她的感激与日俱增。母亲没有变,但我却变了。随着年龄的增长,我越来越懂事,我认识到她是一个多么非凡的人。我对自己在她面前说不出这些话感到难过,但这些话却能轻松地流诸笔端。

一个女儿如何开口感谢她的母亲给予的生命呢?是感谢她在抚养孩子时付出的爱、耐心和平常的辛劳?是感谢她跟在蹒跚学步的孩子身后奔跑,对喜怒无常的少女的理解和对一个自以为是的大学生的宽容?还是感谢她等待女儿认识到她是一位真正母亲的这一天?

在自己的孩子们的眼里,我会像母亲在我的眼里一样好。

You Thanked Mother

When you came into the world, she held you in her arms.

You thanked her by weeping your eyes out.

When you were 1 year old, she fed you and bathed you.

You thanked her by crying all night long.

When you were 2 years old, she taught you to walk.

You thanked her by running away when she called.

When you were 3 years old, she made all your meals with love.

You thanked her by tossing your plate on the floor.

When you were 4 years old, she gave you some crayons.

You thanked her by coloring the kitchen table.

When you were 5 years old, she dressed you for the holidays.

You thanked her by plopping into the nearest pile of mud.

When you were 6 years old, she walked you to school.

You thanked her by screaming, "I'm not going!"

When you were 7 years old, she bought you a baseball.

You thanked her by throwing it through the next-door-neighbor's window.

When you were 8 years old, she handed you an ice cream.

You thanked her by dripping it all over your lap.

When you were 9 years old, she paid for piano lessons.

You thanked her by never even bothering to practice.

When you were 10 years old, she drove you all day, from soccer to gymnastics to one birthday party after another.

You thanked her by jumping out of the car and never looking back.

When you were 11 years old, she took you and your friends to the movies.

You thanked her by asking to sit in a different row.

When you were 12 years old, she warned you not to watch certain TV shows.

You thanked her by waiting until she left the house.

When you were 13, she suggested a haircut that was becoming.

You thanked her by telling her she had no taste.

When you were 14, she paid for a month away at summer camp.

You thanked her by forgetting to write a single letter.

When you were 15, she came home from work, longing for a hug.

You thanked her by having your bedroom door locked.

When you were 16, she taught you how to drive her car.

You thanked her by taking it every chance you could.

When you were 17, she was expecting an important call.

You thanked her by being on the phone all night.

When you were 18, she cried at your high-school graduation.

You thanked her by staying out partying until dawn.

When you were 19, she paid your college tuition, drove you to campus, carried your bags.

You thanked her by saying good-bye outside the dorm so you wouldn't be embarrassed in front of your friends.

When you were 20, she asked whether you were seeing anyone.

You thanked her by saying, "It's none of your business."

When you were 21, she suggested certain careers for your future.

You thanked her by saying, "I don't want to be like you."

When you were 22, she hugged you at your college graduation.

You thanked her by asking whether she could pay for a trip to Europe.

When you were 23, she gave you furniture for your first apartment.

You thanked her by telling your friends it was ugly.

When you were 24, she met your fiancé and asked about your plans for the future.

You thanked her by glaring and growling, "Muuhh-ther, please!"

When you were 25, she helped to pay for your wedding, and she cried and told you how deeply she loved you.

You thanked her by moving halfway across the country.

When you were 30, she called with some advice on the baby.

You thanked her by telling her, "Things are different now."

When you were 40, she called to remind you of a relative's birthday.

You thanked her by saying you were "really busy right now."

When you were 50, she fell ill and needed you to take care of her.

You thanked her by reading about the burden parents become to their children.

And then one day she quietly died.

报 答 母 亲

你来到人世，她将你抱在怀里。

你报答她，哭得死去活来。

你1岁时，她喂你，给你洗澡。

你报答她，整夜号哭。

你2岁时，她教你走路。

你报答她，她一叫你就跑。

你3岁时，她充满爱心为你做饭。

你报答她，把盘子摔在地上。

你4岁时，她送给你几支蜡笔。

你报答她，给餐桌涂上了颜色。

你5岁时，她给你穿上节日盛装。

你报答她，扑通跌进了最旁边的泥堆里。

你6岁时，她步行送你上学。

你报答她，尖叫着："我不去！"

你7岁时，她给你买了一个棒球。

你报答她，把棒球扔到了邻居的窗户上。

你8岁时，她递给你一块冰淇淋。

你报答她，把膝盖上滴得到处都是。

你9岁时，她掏钱让你学钢琴。

你报答她，从不操心去练。

你10岁时，她整天开车，从足球场赶到健身房，又从一个生日宴会赶到另一个生日宴会。

你报答她，跳下车，头也不回。

你11岁时，她带你和朋友去影院。

你报答她，让她坐到另一排。

你12岁时，她警告你不要看某些电视节目。

你报答她，等她一离开你就去看。

你13岁时，她建议你把发型剪得体。

你报答她，对她说没有品位。

你14岁时，她掏了一个月钱送你去夏令营。

你报答她，一封信也忘了写。

你15岁时，她下班回家，渴望拥抱。

你报答她，锁住了卧室门。

你16岁时，她教你学开车。

你报答她，一有机会就开车。

你17岁，她在等一个重要电话。

你报答她，打了一夜电话。

你18岁中学毕业时，她痛哭失声。

你报答她，在外面聚会通宵达旦。

你19岁时，她为你缴纳大学学费，开车送你到校，为你拎包。

你报答她，在宿舍门外说再见，这样你就不会在朋友们面前现难堪。

你20岁时，她问你是否在约会。

你报答她，说："这不关你的事。"

你21岁时，她为你将来的事业提建议。

你报答她，说："我不想和你一样。"

你22岁大学毕业时，她拥抱你。

你报答她，问她能不能掏钱让你到欧洲兜风。

你23岁时，她为你的第一套公寓送去家具。

你报答她，告诉朋友家具难看。

你24岁时，她遇到你的未婚夫，问你们将来有什么打算。

你报答她，对她怒目而视、大声吼叫："妈——妈，求你了！"

你25岁时，她花钱帮你筹办婚礼，哭诉爱你是多么深。

你报答她，把家迁到了千里外。

你30岁时，她打电话为宝宝抚养提忠告。

你报答她，告诉她："现在情况不一样。"

你40岁时，她打电话提醒你，记住亲戚的生日。

你报答她，说你"现在实在忙"。

你50岁时，她病倒在床，需要你照顾她。

你报答她，说父母成了子女们的负担。

后来有一天，她悄然死去。

Mother's Strength

There were two warring tribes in the Andes, one that lived in the lowlands and the other high in the mountains.

One day the mountain people invaded the lowlanders, and as part of their plundering of the people, they kidnapped a baby of one of the lowlander families and took the infant with them back up into the mountains.

The lowlanders didn't know how to climb the mountain. They didn't know any clue of the path that the mountain people used, and they didn't know where to find the mountain people or how to track them in the steep terrain.

Even so, they sent out their best party of fighting men to climb the mountain and bring the baby home. The men tried first one method of climbing and then another. After several days of efforts, however, they had climbed only a couple of hundred feet. Feeling hopeless and helpless, the lowlanders decided that the cause was lost, and they prepared to return to their village below. As they were packing their gear for the descent, they saw the baby's mother walking toward them. They realized that she was coming down the mountain that they hadn't figured out how to climb. And then they saw that she had the baby strapped to her back. How could that be?

One man greeted her and said, "We, the strongest and most able men in the village, couldn't climb this mountain. How did you do this?"

The mother shrugged her shoulders and said, "It isn't your baby."

As long as you have love in your heart, no mountain you cannot climb.

母亲的力量

安第斯山有两个敌对的部落，一个部落住在低地，另一个住在高山上。

有一天，山上部落侵略山下部落。在对山下部落抢劫中，他们绑架了一户人家的婴儿，并把婴儿带上了山。

山下部落的人不知道怎么才能爬上山。他们不知道山上部落走的山道的任何线索，也不知道在哪里找到山上部落，更不知道怎样在陡峭的山地跟踪追击。

尽管如此，他们仍然派自己部落中最优秀、最勇敢的战士爬上山，把孩子抢回来。战士们尝试了一个又一个方法。然而，努力了好几天之后，他们仅仅爬了几百英尺。山下部落的战士们感到绝望无助，认为没办法爬到山上去，准备回到山下的村庄。正当他们收拾工具准备返回山下时，只见那个婴儿的母亲正朝他们走来。他们意识到她下来的那座山正是他们不知道怎样爬的那座山。随后，他们看到她背着那个婴儿。这怎么可能呢？

一个战士跟她打招呼说："我们是部落中最强壮、最能干的男人，都爬不上山。你是怎么做到的呢？"

孩子的母亲耸了耸肩，说："那不是你们的孩子。"

只要心中有爱，没有爬不过去的高山。

For the Love of Mother

When William, a 10-year-old boy who was somewhat scruffy-looking, enrolled himself to learn the piano, the music teacher was reluctant to accept him. She preferred her students to start their music lessons at a younger age when their fingers are nimble.

"William, why do you want to learn the piano?" the teacher asked.

"I want to play for my mother."

She noticed the tears in his eyes as he answered her. She had no heart to turn him down and accepted William as her student. But at each music lesson, William appeared to be in a hurry and play badly. "My mother is waiting outside for me," he would tell the teacher. She was tempted to advise William not to waste his time as he never hit the right note. But there was something about William, which she was fascinated with-the tender look of his eyes each time he mentioned "mother."

Suddenly, William stopped coming for his lessons. At the end of the semester, the music teacher decided to organize a piano recital for her students and she sent flyers to them to participate. She was surprised to find William's application that he would like to contribute a musical piece. She again had no heart to turn him down. She would put him as the last player in case he stumbled with his notes, she would come forward to remedy the situation.

The day came and William appeared with his hair uncombed and his shirt creased. He sat quietly with his eyes closed. When it was his turn to play, William bowed before the audience and said he was thankful for the music teacher's patience with him as he may not have been the best of her pupils.

"Tonight I am dedicating my music to my mother," he said. As he sat down and put his fingers on the keyboard, the most beautiful sound of music was heard. Everyone later asked why he didn't bring his mother as she would surely be proud to hear him play.

William replied, "My mother was stone deaf and she could never hear me play during her lifetime. Yet she sacrificed her time and money to let me learn the piano. This morning mother passed away. I am sure she is now happy as she can hear my piano recital. I chose a piece from Beethoven's concerto. As you all know, Beethoven was submerged with deafness at the triumph of his career. The piece released him from darkness and so was mother." Everyone was electrified to hear what William said and tears welled over their eyes.

The music teacher proudly exclaimed, "William, not only your mother but we all are proud of you. We are deeply touched by your devotion and your love for mother," as she embraced him.

献给母亲的爱

10岁男孩威廉有点儿衣衫不整，想报名学钢琴。音乐老师勉强收下了他。她更喜欢学生年龄小时上音乐课，因为这个时候他们的手指灵活。

"威廉，你为什么想学钢琴呢？"老师问。

"我想为妈妈演奏。"

她注意到，他回答她时眼里含着泪花。她不忍心拒绝，就收下了威廉。但每次音乐课，威廉好像总是匆匆忙忙，而且弹得很糟。"妈妈在外面等着我。"他常常这样对老师说。因为威廉从来没有弹准过一个音符,所以她真想建议他别再浪费时间了。但是,威廉身上有一种东西深深地吸引着她——他每次提到"母亲"时,眼里总是带着温柔的神情。

突然,威廉不再来上课了。期末时,音乐老师决定为她的学生们筹备一场钢琴独奏会。于是,她向发出传单。她吃惊地发现了威廉想演奏一曲的申请表。她还是不忍心拒绝他,就决定让他最后演奏,万一他演奏得不顺,她可以上前救场。

这一天到了,威廉头发蓬乱,衬衣起皱,来到现场,闭着眼睛静静地坐在那里。轮到威廉演奏时,他在观众面前鞠了一躬,说他感谢音乐老师对他的耐心,因为他可能不是她最好的学生。

"今天晚上,我要把自己的音乐献给我的妈妈。"说着,他坐下来,把手指放到琴键上,顿时响起了最优美的旋律。

后来,大家问他为什么不带妈妈来,因为听到他演奏,她一定会非常自豪。

威廉回答说:"我妈妈完全是个聋子,她这辈子从来都不可能听到我演奏。但是,她却牺牲时间和金钱让我学琴。今天早上,妈妈去世了。我敢肯定,她现在非常高兴,因为她能听到我的钢琴演奏了。我选了贝多芬的一首协奏曲。大家都知道,贝多芬是在事业成功时完全听不见,是这首曲子把他从黑暗中拯救了出来,我的妈妈也是这样。"听到威廉的话,每个人都激动万分、热泪盈眶。

音乐老师一边抱住他,一边骄傲地大声说道:"威廉,不仅是你的妈妈,而且我们所有的人都为你感到自豪。我们都为你对妈妈的奉献和爱深深感动。"

Mother Love in the Dress

"Do you like my dress?" with tears in her eyes, she asked of a passing stranger. "My mommy made it just for me."

"Well, I think it's very pretty, so tell me, why are you crying, little one?"

With a quiver in her voice the little girl answered, "After Mommy made me this dress, she had to go away."

"Well, now," said the lady, "with a little girl like you waiting for her, I'm sure she'll be right back."

"No, ma'am, you don't understand," said the child through her tears, "my daddy said that she's up in heaven with Grandpa."

Finally, the lady realized what the child meant and why she was crying. Kneeling down she gently cradled the child in her arms.

Suddenly the little girl did something that the lady thought was a bit strange. She stopped crying, stepped back from lady and began to sing. She sang so softly that it was almost a whisper. It was the sweetest sound the woman had ever heard, just like the song of a very small bird.

After she stopped singing, the little girl explained to the lady, "My mommy used to sing that song to me before she went away, and she made me promise to sing it whenever I started crying and it would make me stop."

"See," she exclaimed, "it did, and now my eyes are dry!"

As the lady turned to go, the little girl grabbed her sleeve. "Ma'am, can you stay just a minute? I want to show you something."

"Of course," she answered, "what do you want me to see?"

Pointing to a spot on her dress, she said, "Right here is where my mommy kissed my dress, and here," pointing to another spot, "and here is another kiss, and here, and here. Mommy said that she put all those kisses on my dress, so that I would have her kisses for every booboo that made me cry."

Then the lady realized that she was not just looking at a dress. No, she was looking at a mother…who knew that she was going away and wouldn't be there to kiss away the hurts that she knew her daughter would get.

So she took all the love she had for her beautiful little girl and put them into this dress that her child now so proudly wore.

She no longer saw a little girl in a simple dress. She saw a child wrapped in her mother's love.

连衣裙里的母爱

"你喜欢我的连衣裙吗？"她眼含着泪问一个过路的陌生人，"是妈妈为我做的。"

"噢，我想它非常漂亮。小姑娘，那你告诉我，你为什么哭？"

小女孩声音颤抖地答道："妈妈为我做完裙子后，就不得不离开了。"

"噢，好了，"那位女士说，"有一个像你这样的小女孩在等她，我相信她会回来的。"

"不，阿姨，你不明白，"小女孩哭着说道，"爸爸说她和爷爷都在天堂里。"

最后，那位女士明白了孩子的意思，也明白了她为什么在哭。她跪下来，轻轻地把孩子搂在了怀里。

突然，小女孩又做了一件让女士有点儿奇怪的事情。她停止哭泣，从女士的怀里走出来，开始唱起了歌。她唱得非常轻柔，简直是在耳语。这是那位女士听过的最甜美的声音，就像一只小小鸟的歌声。

唱完后，小女孩向那位女士解释说："妈妈走前经常给我唱这首歌，她还让我发誓，我每次要哭时就唱这首歌，这样就能让我不哭。"

"看，"她大声叫道，"这歌真行，现在我的眼里没有泪了！"

当那位女士转身要走时，小女孩抓住她的衣袖说："阿姨，你能再待一会儿吗？我想给你看一件东西。"

"当然可以，"她答道，"你想给我看什么？"

她指着裙子上的一个地方说："这里就是妈妈吻过的地方，还有这里，"她指着另一个地方，"这里是另一个吻，还有这里和这里。妈妈说她把所有的那些吻都留在我的裙子上，这样我每次受伤要哭时，就会得到她的吻。"

这时，这位女士意识到，她看到的不仅是一件连衣裙。不，她看到的是一位母亲……她知道自己即将离去，不能守候在女儿身边吻去女儿可能受到的种种伤害。

于是，她把所有给漂亮女儿的爱，都放到了孩子现在正自豪地穿在身上的这件连衣裙里。

她看到的不再是一个穿着朴素连衣裙的小女孩，而是一个包裹在母爱里的孩子。

Mum Who Wrote Family Letters

To this day I remember my mum's letters. It all started in December 1941. Every night she sat at the big table in the kitchen and wrote to my brother Johnny, who had been drafted that summer. We hadn't heard from him since the Japanese attacked Pearl Harbor.

I didn't understand why my mum kept writing to Johnny when he never wrote back.

"Wait and see—we'll get a letter from him one day," she claimed. Mum said that there was a direct link from the brain to the written word. She trusted would find Johnny.

I don't know if she said that to calm herself, dad or all of us down. But I do know that it helped us stick together, and one day a letter really did arrive. Johnny was alive on an island in the Pacific.

Mum signed her letters, "Cecilia Capuzzi." "Why don't you just write 'Mum'?" I asked.

I hadn't been aware that she always thought of herself as Cecilia Capuzzi. Not as Mum. I began seeing her in a new light.

She never wore make-up or jewelry except for a wedding ring. Her hair was fine, sleek and black and always put up in a knot in the neck. Her small silver-rimmed pince-nez only left her nose when she went to bed.

Whenever mum had finished a letter, she gave it to dad for him to post it.

Around next spring mum had got two more sons to write to. Every evening she wrote three different letters which she gave to dad and me afterwards so we could add our greetings.

Little by little the rumor about mum's letters spread. One day a small woman knocked at our door. Her voice trembled as she asked: "Is it true you write letters?"

"I write to my sons."

"And you can read too?" whispered the woman.

"Sure."

The woman opened her bag and pulled out a pile of airmail letters. "Read... please read them aloud to me."

The letters were from the woman's son who was a soldier in Europe, a red-haired boy who mum remembered having seen sitting with his brothers on the stairs in front of our house. Mum read the letters one by one and translated them from English to Italian. The woman's eyes welled up with tears. "Now I have to write to him," she said. But how was she going to do it?

"Make some coffee, Octavia," mum yelled to me in the living room while she took the woman with her into the kitchen and seated her at the table. She took the fountain pen, ink and airmail notepaper and began to write. When she had finished, she read the letter aloud to the woman.

"How did you know that was exactly what I wanted to say?"

"I often sit and look at my boys' letters, just like you, without a clue about what to write."

A few days later the woman returned with a friend, then another one and yet another one—they all had sons who fought in the war, and they all needed letters. Mum had become the correspondent in our part of town. Sometimes she would write letters all day long.

Mum always insisted that people signed their own letters, and the small woman with the grey hair asked mum to teach her how to do it. "I so much want to be able to write my own name so that my son can see it." Then mum held the woman's hand in hers and moved her hand over the paper again and again until she was able to do it without her help.

After that day, when mum had written a letter for the woman, she signed it herself, and her face brightened up in a smile.

One day when she came to us, all hope had disappeared from her eyes. Mum instantly knew what had happened. They stood hand in hand for a long time without saying a word. Then mum said: "We better go to church. There are certain things in life so great that we cannot comprehend them." When mum came back home, she couldn't get the red-haired boy out of her mind.

On one occasion mum admitted that she had always had a secret dream of writing a novel. "Why didn't you?" I asked.

She tried to explain why it absorbed her so. "All people in this world are here with one particular purpose," she said. "Apparently, mine is to write letters."

"A letter unites people. It can make them cry, it can make them laugh. There is no caress more lovely and warm than a love letter, because it makes the world seem very small, and both sender and receiver become like kings in their own kingdoms. My dear, a letter is life itself!"

Today all mum's letters are lost. But those who got them still talk about her and cherish the memory of her letters in their hearts.

爱写家书的妈妈

至今我仍记得母亲的来信。事情要从1941年12月说起。母亲每天夜里都坐在厨房的大桌边，给我哥哥约翰尼写信。那年夏天，哥哥应征入伍。自从日本袭击珍珠港以来，我们就没有听到过他的消息。

我不明白约翰尼从未回过信，母亲为什么还要一直给他写信。

"等等看——我们总有一天会收到他的回信的。"她断言说。妈妈说大脑和文字是息息相通的，她相信一定会找到约翰尼。

我不知道她这样说是不是在安慰自己、安慰爸爸或我们所有的人。但我确实知道那使我们一家人更加亲密了。而且有一天真的来了一封信，约翰尼在太平洋的一个岛上，现在还活着。

母亲总是在信上署名"塞西莉娅·卡普奇"。"为什么不直接写'妈妈'呢？"我问。

我以前没有注意到她总是把自己当成塞西莉娅·卡普奇，而不是妈妈。我开始以一种新的眼光去看妈妈。

她从来不化妆，除了手上戴的婚戒，她从不戴珠宝。她的头发乌黑柔滑，总是盘在颈后。只有在睡觉时，她才取下小银丝眼镜。

无论什么时候妈妈写完信,她都会把信交给爸爸去邮寄。

大约第二年春天,妈妈也开始给另两个儿子写信。每天晚上,她写好三封内容不同的信后交给我和爸爸,这样我们就能加上自己的问候。

渐渐地,母亲写信的事就传开了。有一天,一个矮小的女人来敲我们家的门,用颤抖的声音问道:"你真的写信了吗?"

"我是写给儿子们的。"

"那你也会读信吗?"女人小声问。

"当然会。"

那女人打开背包,掏出了一堆航空信。"念……请给我念一下。"

那些信是女人在欧洲当兵的儿子写来的,妈妈还记得那男孩的模样,他有一头红发,常和他的兄弟们坐在我们家门前的楼梯上。妈妈把信一封接一封地从英文译成意大利文读出来。那女人热泪盈眶。"现在我必须得给他写回信。"她说。可她怎么写呢?

"奥克塔维娅,去冲杯咖啡。"妈妈在客厅里向我大声说道,同时把那女人领到厨房桌边坐下。她拿出钢笔、墨水和航空信纸开始写信。写完后,她给那女人朗读了一遍。

"这正是我想说的话,你怎么知道呀?"

"我也和你一样,常坐在那里看儿子的来信,不知道该写什么。"

几天后,那女人又带来一个朋友,后来又来了一个又一个——她们都有儿子在战场上作战,都需要写信。妈妈已经成了我们镇的写信员,有时她一天到晚都在写回信。

妈妈总是坚持让那些人签上自己的名字。一位头发花白的女人要妈妈教她怎么签名。"我真想能亲手写下自己的名字,这样儿子就能看到了。于是,妈妈手把手地教她在纸上一遍一遍书写,直到她能自己签名。

那天以后,妈妈帮那个女人写好信,由她亲自签名,那女人脸上绽开了灿烂的微笑。

有一天,她来我们家时,眼里失去了所有的希望。妈妈立刻明白了是怎么回事。两人握着手,久久地站在那里,一声不吭。后来妈妈说:"我们最好去教堂。生命中有些事不同寻常,我们无法理解。"妈妈回家后,怎么也无法忘记那个红发男孩。

有一次,妈妈承认她心里总有一个写小说的梦想。"你为什么不写呢?"我问。

她试图解释她为什么对写信如此着迷。她说:"所有的人来到这个世界上都有一个特殊的目的。显然,我的目的就是写信。"

"一封信可以把人连在一起,能让人哭,让人笑。一封情书比任何爱抚都温暖动人,因为它让世界变得似乎很小,写信人和收信人都成为自己王国里的国王。亲爱的,信就是生命本身!"

今天,妈妈所有的信都已经丢失了。但那些收到信的人仍在谈论她,并把她写信的记忆珍藏在了心里。

A Mother's Letter to the World

Dear World,

My son starts school today. It's going to be strange and new to him for a while. And I wish you would sort of treat him gently. You see, up to now, he's been king of the roost. He's been boss of the backyard. I have always been around to repair his wounds, and to soothe his feelings. But now—things are going to be different.

This morning, he's going to walk down the front steps, wave his hand and start on his great adventure that will probably include wars and tragedy and sorrow.

To his life in the world he has to live in will require faith and love and courage.

So, World, I wish you would sort of take him by his young hand and teach him the things he will have to know. Teach him—but gently, if you can. Teach him that for every enemy there is a friend.

Teach him the wonders of books.

Give him quiet time to ponder the eternal mystery of birds in the sky, bees in the sun, and flowers on the green hill.

Teach him it is far more honorable to fail than to cheat.

Teach him to have faith in his own ideas.

Teach him to sell his brawn and brains to the highest bidder, but never to put a price on his heart and soul.

Teach him to close his ears to a howling mob…and to stand and fight if he thinks he's right.

Teach him gently, World, but don't coddle him because only the test of fire makes fine steel.

This is a big order, World, but see what you can do.

He's such a nice little fellow.

一位母亲写给世界的信

亲爱的世界：

我的儿子今天就要开始上学了。他会一时感到陌生新鲜。而我希望你能善待他一点儿。你明白，到目前为止，他都是家里的国王、后院的领袖。我总是在他身边为他疗伤，安慰他的情绪。可现在——事情将会截然不同。

今天早上，他就要走下门前台阶，向我挥手，开始伟大的事业，其间也许会有斗争、不幸和悲伤。

要在这个世界上生存度日，他需要信念、爱心和勇气。

所以，世界，我希望你能稍微握住他的小手，教给他必须知道的事情。教会他，但要尽可能温柔。教会他知道有敌人，就有朋友。

教会他书本的奇迹。

给他安静的时间去思考天空中的飞鸟、阳光里的蜜蜂和青山上的鲜花这样永恒的奥秘。

教会他知道，失败远比欺骗光荣。

教会他对自己的想法要有信心。

教会他将自己的体力和脑力卖给最高价竞买人，但绝不能出卖自己的良心和灵魂。

教会他要对乌合之众的嚎叫闭上耳朵……并在认为正确时挺身而战。

温柔地教他，世界，但不要溺爱他，因为只有烈火的考验才能炼出好钢。

这是一个很高的要求，世界，但请尽你所能。

他是一个这样可爱的小家伙。

Mother's Final Gift

The baggy yellow shirt had long sleeves, four extra-large pockets trimmed in black thread and snaps up the front. It was faded from years of wear but still in decent shape. I found it in 1963 when I was home from university on school recess, rummaging through bags of clothes Mom intended to give away.

"You're not taking that old thing, are you?" Mom said when she saw me packing the yellow shirt. "I wore that when I was pregnant with your brother in 1954!"

"It's just the thing to wear over my clothes during art class, Mom. Thanks!" I slipped it into my suitcase before she could object.

The yellow shirt became a part of my university wardrobe. I loved it. After graduation, I wore the shirt the day I moved into my new apartment and on Saturday mornings when I cleaned.

The next year, I married. When I became pregnant, I wore the yellow shirt during big-belly days. I missed Mom and the rest of my family, since we were living far away from them. But that shirt helped. I smiled, remembering that Mother had worn it when she was pregnant, 15 years earlier.

That Christmas, mindful of the warm feelings the shirt had given me, I patched one elbow, washed and pressed the shirt, wrapped it on holiday paper and sent it to Mom.

When Mom wrote to thank me for her "real" gifts, she said the yellow shirt was lovely. She never mentioned it again.

The next year, my husband, daughter and I stopped at Mom and Dad's to pick up some furniture. Days later, when we uncrated the kitchen table, I noticed something yellow taped to its bottom. The shirt! And so the pattern was set.

On our next visit home, I secretly placed the shirt under Mom and Dad's mattress. I don't know how long it took her to find it, but almost two years passed before I discovered it under the base of our living-room floor lamp. The yellow shirt was just I needed now while refinishing furniture. The walnut stains added character.

In 1975 my husband and I divorced. With my three children, I prepared to move back to the area where I grew up. As I packed, a deep depression overtook me. I wondered if I could succeed on my own. I wondered if I would find a job.

I tried to picture myself wearing armor, but all I saw was the stained yellow shirt. Slowly, it dawned on me. Was not my mother's love a piece of armor? My courage was renewed.

Unpacking in our new home, I knew I had to get the shirt back to Mother. The next time I visited her, I tucked it in her bottom dresser drawer. Meanwhile, I found a good job at a radio station.

A year later I discovered the yellow shirt hidden in a ragbag in my cleaning closet. Something new had been added. Embroidered in bright green across the breast pocket were the words "I BELONG TO PAT."

Not to be outdone, I got out my own embroidery materials and added an apostrophe and seven more letters. Now the shirt proudly proclaimed, "I BELONG TO PAT'S MOTHER."

But I didn't stop there. I zigzagged all the frayed seams, then had a friend mail the shirt in a fancy box to Mom from out of town. We enclosed an official-looking letter from "The Institute for the Destitute," announcing that she was the recipient of an award for good deeds.

I would have given anything to see Mom's face when she opened the box. But, of course, she never mentioned it.

Two years later, in 1978, I remarried. The day of our wedding, Harold and I put our car in a friend's garage to avoid practical jokers. After the wedding, while my husband drove us to our honeymoon suite, I reached for a pillow in the car to rest my head. It felt lumpy. I unzipped the case and found, wrapped in wedding paper, the yellow shirt. Inside a pocket was a note: "I loved you both, Mother."

The shirt was Mother's final gift. She had known for three months that she had terminal amyotrophic lateral sclerosis (ALS). Mother died the following year at age 57.

I was tempted to send the yellow shirt with her to her grave, but I'm glad I didn't, because it is a vivid reminder of the love-filled game she and I played for 16 years.

Besides, my older daughter is in university now, majoring in art. And every art student needs a baggy yellow shirt with big pockets.

母亲最后的礼物

那件宽松的黄衬衫有长长的袖子，4个特大口袋周围用黑线镶边，胸前缀有按扣。由于穿了多年，已经褪色，但外观仍然得体。我是1963年学校放假回到家后在妈妈想送人的几袋衣服里翻找时发现的。

"你不是要留那件旧衣服吧？"妈妈看到我在叠那件黄衬衫时说，"1954年我怀你弟弟时就穿着那件衬衫！"

"这正是我上艺术课时想穿在外面的衣服，妈妈。谢谢！"我没等她反对，就把它塞进了自己的衣箱。

这件黄衬衫就成了我大学衣柜里的一个组成部分。我非常喜欢它。大学毕业后，搬进新公寓那天和每星期六早上打扫卫生时，我都穿着这件衬衫。

第二年，我结婚成家。在怀孕挺着大肚子的那些日子，我穿着那件黄衬衫。我想念妈妈和家里其他人，因为我们住得相距很远。但那件衬衫帮了我的忙，我想起15年前妈妈怀孕时穿着它的样子，露出了微笑。

那年圣诞节，想起黄衬衫曾带给我的温暖感觉，我在那件衬衫的一个肘部打上补丁，洗净熨平后，用节日彩纸包好，寄给了妈妈。

妈妈写信感谢我送给她这件"真正"的礼物时，说那件黄衬衫非常漂亮。她后来再也没有提起过它。

又过了一年，我和丈夫、女儿顺路去爸妈家搬了一些家具。几天后，当我们打开饭桌的包装箱时，我注意到有一件黄东西系在桌子底部。是那件黄衬衫！母亲就这样先开了头。

第二次回家时，我悄悄地把衬衫放在了爸妈的床垫下面。我不知道妈妈多长时间才发现了它，但差不多过了两年，我才在客厅的落地灯座上发现它。现在我整修家具表面时，黄衬衫正好派上用场。它上面的胡桃色印迹使它增添了特色。

1975年，我和丈夫分道扬镳。我带着三个孩子，准备搬回从小长大的那个地方。我打点行装时，突然感到一种深深的沮丧。我不知道靠自己是不是能成功。我不知道自己会不会找到一份工作。

我尽力想象着自己穿着盔甲的情景，但我所看到的只有那件暗黄色的衬衫。慢慢地，我明白了。母亲的爱不就是一片盔甲吗？我重又获得了勇气。

在我们的新房里打开行李时，我知道自己得把衬衫还给妈妈。我又一次去看她时，将黄衬衫塞进了她的梳妆台最下面的抽屉里。其间，我在广播电台找到了一份好工作。

一年后，我发现那件黄衬衫藏在清扫用具储藏室的一只破布袋里。它上面增添了一些新东西，胸袋上用鲜绿色的线绣着"我属于帕特"这几个字。

我没有被难倒，拿出自己的绣花布料，又在后面添上了撇号和7个字母。现在，衬衫上得意地写着："我属于帕特的母亲。"

但我并没有就此打住。我用针脚弯弯曲曲将所有磨损的线缝补好，装进一个精美的盒子里，让一个朋友从城外寄给我的妈妈。我们还附上了一封"贫困协会"的公函，显示这件奖品是专门颁发她这个行善的人的。

要是能看见她打开这个盒子，我愿付出所有的一切。可是，她确实再也没有提起这件事。

两年后，1978年，我改嫁他人。婚礼那天，我和哈罗德把我们的汽车停放在一位朋友的车库里，以防恶作剧者。婚礼过后，在丈夫开车带我去我们的蜜月套房的路上，我伸手拿了车里的一个枕头，头靠在上面。枕头凹凸不平。我拉开枕套的拉链，发现了用婚礼彩纸包着的那件黄衬衫，一个口袋里还有一张字条："我爱你们俩。妈妈。"

黄衬衫是母亲最后的礼物。她3个月前就知道自己得了晚期肌萎缩性脊髓侧索硬化症（ALS）。第二年，母亲撒手人寰，时年57岁。

我禁不住想把那件黄衬衫伴送进她的坟墓，但现在我很高兴自己没有那样做，因为它栩栩如生地提醒着她和我玩了16年的那个爱意浓浓的游戏。

此外，我的大女儿现在也上了大学，学的是艺术专业。艺术专业的每个学生都需要一件带有大口袋的宽松的黄衬衫。

Singing with Mom

Mom's memory went wild after my dad died. Later on, she no longer knew me, her only living child. And yet she was always delighted to see me, and believed me completely when I said, "It's your son, John, Mom."

My 87-year-old mother's recollections of an extraordinarily vibrant life were increasingly elusive. She told me a wonderful story about a cruise she and her sister, both schoolteacher, took around Cape Horn in 1925: "We were able to save money on our small salaries because we lived very simply at home with our mother. On the ship we'd walk on the deck in the morning, play badminton, talk with other young people, nap in the afternoon and then stay up late because the nights were warm and clear and there was moonlight—and starlight. I met a lovely young man, and we had a very sweet romance, standing at the railing in the evening, singing songs together."

This was a real memory, dormant for many years. But soon Mom began to talk of an imaginary second husband. She and my father had been married only briefly, she said—though actually she and Dad were married for 50 years.

She was shocked each time I reminded her that I lived in California. She was delighted by every bit of family news I gave her—and delighted all over again if I repeated the same news a moment later. Beyond that she had almost nothing to say.

Visits became painful. I wanted to spark her memory with vivid images—"I know you remember the Christmasberry tree in the back yard…" I wanted her to remember, too, new stories about my kids and my life in the West.

She remembered none of it, sensed that she was failing me and became agitated. Sometimes visits lasted only 20 minutes: I ran through all my special news, told her I loved her, and didn't know what else to say.

A few years ago, out of desperation, I began to sing to her, quietly, shyly. I brought along the copy of the old Fireside Book of Folk Songs that used to perch on Mom's baby grand piano in the 1950s.

Sitting up straight, I sang "Loch Lomond" to my mother that day, filling my lungs, enunciating, remembering her at the piano, feeling the music glow within me.

To my astonishment Mom began to sing along, reading the words above, my finger, then singing from memory.

Mom was ecstatic as we sang, and so was I. She'd clap her hands as we finished a song, and once took my hands in hers, looked into my eyes and said, "I never knew there could be such sweetness in a human relationship."

Another time, as we rested between songs, I said '90s style, "This is kinda nice." She drew herself upright, indignant at my sloppy language. "Kinda nice? This is more than kinda nice!"

During visits after that, we did nothing but make music. On my wooden recorder I conjured up more than a hundred of the songs she had originally taught me—"Red River Valley," "The Band Played On," "I'll Take You Home Again, Kathleen" —songs Mom had learned as many as 80 years ago.

Her voice floated with my recorder's melody, two frail sopranos at play. She sang without words, her voice itself an instrument.

Once, near the top of "Danny Boy," her clear voice sailed way above my high note, but exactly right, a wild perfect harmony she broke by sailing, for a timeless instant, even higher. She stopped as though she had screamed.

Shocked at herself, she looked at me to see if what she had done was okay. Yes, I said with my eyes, as I wound down through the last chorus of "Danny Boy." Mom looked back with eyes full of wonder, as she must have looked at me on the first day of my life.

与妈妈同唱

爸爸去世后，妈妈的记忆变得越发混乱了。后来，她居然连我——她唯一活着的孩子——都不认识了。然而，见到我，她总是很高兴；而且当我说，"妈妈，我是你的儿子约翰"时，她总是对我深信不疑。

87岁高龄的妈妈对异常活跃的生活的回忆越发难以捉摸。以前她给我讲过一个非常精彩的故事。故事发生在1925年，当时她和妹妹——两人都是小学老师———道乘船绕过了合恩角："我们之所以能从微薄的薪水中省下钱来，是因为我们和母亲过得非常简朴。在船上，我们早晨常常在甲板上散步、打羽毛球、聊天，下午总是睡会儿觉，然后玩到很晚。那里的夜晚温暖清爽，月光皎洁，繁星点点。在那里，我遇到了一个可爱的年轻人。我们常常站在围栏边一块唱歌，度过了一段甜蜜的浪漫时光。"

这是一段真实的回忆，隐藏了很多年。但不久，妈妈便又开始讲起了她想象中的第二个丈夫。她说，她和爸爸的婚姻只持续了很短一段时间——尽管事实上她和爸爸在一块生活了50年。

每次我提醒她我住在加州时，她都非常震惊。但只要我告诉她家里的有关情况，她就高兴得跟什么似的——过一会儿，我要再重复一遍那件事，她还会高兴一阵子。除此以外，她几乎什么也不说。

看望她成了我一块心病。我试图用生动的形象唤起她的回忆："我知道你一定记得后院的那棵圣诞浆果树……"我还想让她记起我和我的孩子在西部生活的新故事。她什么都不记得了，只知道如果没有我在她身边，她会感到忐忑不安。有时看望她的时间只持续20分钟，我只是带给她我特别的消息，告诉她我爱她，然后就不知道还能对她说些什么了。

几年前，我抱着一线希望开始给她唱歌，轻轻地、羞涩地唱给她听。我带了一本《炉边民歌集》，那是20世纪50年代经常放在妈妈的小型卧式钢琴上的一本旧书。

那天，我挺起腰板坐在那里，对妈妈唱起了《龙梦湖》。我唱时，想起了她在钢琴弹奏的情景，顿时声情并茂，感到音乐在我的内心深处熠熠闪耀。

令我惊讶的是，母亲读着我手指指着的歌词，从记忆中找到了那首歌的曲调，开始和我一道唱了起来。

我们唱歌时，妈妈心醉神迷，我也陶醉其中。我们每唱完一首歌，她就拍手鼓掌。有一次，她抓住我的手，望着我的眼睛说："我从来不知道人和人之间的关系竟然会这样甜蜜！"

又有一次，在我们唱歌的间歇，我说起了20世纪90年代的文体："这有点儿漂亮。"她坐直身体，对我的不地道的语言感到非常愤怒。"有点儿漂亮？这不仅仅是有点点儿漂亮！"

那之后，在看望妈妈期间，我们除了唱歌什么也不做。在我的木制录音机上，我收集了100多首她原来教我唱过的歌——《红河谷》《乐队继续演奏》《凯瑟琳，我要再次带你回家》——这些歌都是妈妈80年前学会唱的。

她的声音随着录音机的旋律飞扬，两个虚弱的女高音在演唱。她唱时，没唱歌词，她的声音本身就是一种乐器。

有一次，她快唱到《男孩丹尼》高潮部分时，她的声音一下子超过了我的录音机的音调，但恰到好处，仍是那样和谐完美，高亢激越。随后，她戛然而止，好像她尖叫了起来。

她对自己感到非常震惊，望着我，看她做得是否恰当。当她唱完《男孩丹尼》的最后的合唱时，我用目光说恰当。妈妈也充满好奇地望着我，就像她生下我第一天时看我那样。

A Boy with a Mission

In 1945, a 12-year-old boy saw something in a shop window that set his heart racing. But the price—five dollars—was far beyond Reuben Earle's means. Five dollars would buy almost a week's groceries for his family. Reuben couldn't ask his father for the money. Everything Mark Earle made through fishing in Bay Roberts, Newfoundland, Canada. Reuben's mother, Dora, stretched like elastic to feed and clothe their five children.

Nevertheless, he opened the shop's weathered door and went inside. Standing proud and straight in his flour-sack shirt and washed-out trousers, he told the shopkeeper what he wanted, adding, "But I don't have the money right now. Can you please hold it for me for some time?"

"I'll try," the shopkeeper smiled. "Folks around here don't usually have that kind of money to spend on things. It should keep for a while."

Reuben respectfully touched his worn cap and walked out into the sunlight with the bay rippling in a freshening wind. There was purpose in his loping stride. He would raise the five dollars and not tell anybody.

Hearing the sound of hammering from a side street, Reuben had an idea.

He ran towards the sound and stopped at a construction site. People built their own homes in Bay Roberts, using nails purchased in hessian sacks from a local factory. Sometimes the sacks were discarded in the flurry of building, and Reuben knew he could sell them back to the factory for five cents a piece.

That day he found two sacks, which he took to the rambling wooden factory and sold to the man in charge of packing nails.

The boy's hand tightly clutched the five-cent pieces as he ran the two kilometers home.

Near his house stood the ancient barn that housed the family's goats and chickens. Reuben found a rusty soda tin and dropped his coins inside. Then he climbed into the loft of the barn and hid the tin beneath a pile of sweet-smelling hay.

It was dinnertime when Reuben got home. His father sat at the big kitchen table, working on a fishing net. Dora was at the kitchen stove, ready to serve dinner as Reuben took his place at the table.

He looked at his mother and smiled. Sunlight from the window gilded her shoulder-length blonde hair. Slim and beautiful, she was the center of the home, the glue that held it together.

Her chores were never-ending. Sewing clothes for her family on the old Singer treadle machine, cooking meals and baking bread, planting and tending a vegetable garden, milking the goats and scrubbing soiled clothes on a washboard. But she was happy. Her family and their well-being were her highest priority.

Every day after chores and school, Reuben scoured the town, collecting the hessian nail bags. On the day the two-room school closed for the summer, no student was more delighted than Reuben. Now he would have more time for his mission.

All summer long, despite chores at home weeding and watering the garden, cutting wood and fetching water—Reuben kept to his secret task.

Then all too soon the garden was harvested, the vegetables canned and stored, and the school reopened. Soon the leaves fell and the winds blew cold and gusty from the bay. Reuben wandered the streets, diligently searching for his hessian treasures.

Often he was cold, tired and hungry, but the thought of the object in the shop window sustained him. Sometimes his mother would ask: "Reuben, where were you? We were waiting for you to have dinner."

"Playing, Mum. Sorry."

Dora would look at his face and shake her head. Boys.

Finally spring burst into glorious green and Reuben's spirits erupted. The time had come! He ran into the barn, climbed to the hayloft and uncovered the tin can. He poured the coins out and began to count.

Then he counted again. He needed 20 cents more. Could there be any sacks left any where in town? He had to find four and sell them before the day ended.

Reuben ran down Water Street.

The shadows were lengthening when Reuben arrived at the factory. The sack buyer was about to lock up.

"Mister! Please don't close up yet."

The man turned and saw Reuben, dirty and sweat stained.

"Come back tomorrow, boy."

"Please, Mister. I have to sell the sacks now—please." The man heard a tremor in Reuben's voice and could tell he was close to tears.

"Why do you need this money so badly?"

"It's a secret."

The man took the sacks, reached into his pocket and put four coins in Reuben's hand. Reuben murmured a thank you and ran home.

Then, clutching the tin can, he headed for the shop.

"I have the money," he solemnly told the owner.

The man went to the window and retrieved Reuben's treasure.

He wiped the dust off and gently wrapped it in brown paper. Then he placed the parcel in Reuben's hands.

Racing home, Reuben burst through the front door. His mother was scrubbing the kitchen stove. "Here, Mum! Here!" Reuben exclaimed as he ran to her side. He placed a small box in her work-roughened hand.

She unwrapped it carefully, to save the paper. A blue-velvet jewel box appeared. Dora lifted the lid, tears beginning to blur her vision.

In gold lettering on a small, almond-shaped brooch was the word Mother.

It was Mother's Day, 1946.

Dora had never received such a gift; she had no finery except her wedding ring. Speechless, she smiled radiantly and gathered her son into her arms.

男孩的使命

1945年，一个12岁的男孩在一家商店橱窗里看到一样让他心跳加快的东西。可是，价格5美元，鲁宾·厄尔根本付不起。5美元差不多够买全家一周的食品了。

鲁宾不能向父亲要钱。马克·厄尔的每分钱都是靠在加拿大纽芬兰罗伯茨湾捕鱼挣的。鲁宾的母亲多拉为了照顾5个孩子吃穿，常常一个钱当两个钱花。

尽管如此，他还是打开商店那扇风雨剥蚀的门，走了进去。他穿着面粉袋改做的衬衫和洗得褪色的裤子，站得笔直，不卑不亢，告诉店主他想要的东西，同时补充说："可我现在没有钱。你能为我留一段时间吗？"

"我尽量吧，"店主微笑道，"这里的人通常不会花那种钱买东西的。它会留一阵的。"

鲁宾毕恭毕敬地摸了摸他的旧帽檐，走出商店。阳光下清新的微风吹得海湾泛起阵阵涟漪。鲁宾迈着大步，下定决心：他要攒够5美元，而且不告诉任何人。

听到小巷传来的铁锤声，鲁宾有了主意。

他朝响声那边跑去，在一个建筑工地停下来。人们喜欢在罗伯茨湾建房，用的钉子是从当地一家工厂买的，都装在粗麻袋里。干活时有时忙乱中会把麻袋丢在一边，鲁宾知道他可以5分钱一条把麻袋再卖给工厂。

那天，他找到了两条麻袋，拿到杂乱的木材厂，卖给负责装钉子的人。

鲁宾手里紧紧攥着两个5分硬币，跑了两公里回到了家。

他家附近有一座老谷仓，里面圈着家里的山羊和鸡。鲁宾在那里找到一个生锈的苏打罐，把两枚硬币丢了进去，然后爬上谷仓的阁楼，把铁罐藏在一堆散发着甜香味的干草下面。

晚饭时分，鲁宾回到了家里。父亲正坐在厨房大餐桌边摆弄渔网。多拉在厨灶边忙碌着，准备开饭。鲁宾在桌边坐了下来。

他望着妈妈，露出了微笑。从窗户透进的阳光将她金黄的披肩发照得金光闪闪。她身材苗条、美丽大方，是这个家的中心，是她将这个家紧紧连在了一块。

她的家务活永远也做不完。她用那台老式辛格牌踏板缝纫机为一家人缝缝补补；她要做饭、烤面包、种植、照看菜园、挤羊奶、在洗衣板上搓洗脏衣服。可是，母亲总是乐乐呵呵，全家人和他们的康乐在她心里最重要。

每天放学、做完家务事后，鲁宾就在镇上四处搜寻装钉子的粗麻袋。两间教室的学校放暑假那天，哪个学生也没有鲁宾高兴。现在他有更多时间去完成自己的使命了。

整整一个夏天，尽管在家里做家务，给菜园锄草、浇水、砍柴和打水，但鲁宾始终进行着自己的秘密任务。

转眼就到了菜园收获时，蔬菜被装罐储藏，学校也开学了。不久，树叶飘落，海湾吹来阵阵寒风。鲁宾在街头徘徊，坚持搜寻他的麻袋宝贝。

他常常饥寒交迫、疲惫不堪，但一想到商店橱窗里的那件东西，他就又坚持下去了。有时妈妈会问："鲁宾，你上哪儿去了？我们都在等你吃饭呢。"

"玩去了，妈妈。对不起。"

多拉常常看着他的脸，摇摇头。男孩就是男孩。

春天终于来了，一切都郁郁葱葱；鲁宾也精神大振。到时候了！他跑进谷仓，爬到干草棚上，打开铁罐，倒出所有硬币，开始数了起来。

随后，他又数一遍，还差20分钱。镇上哪儿还会有丢弃的麻袋呢？他得在今天结束前再找4条卖掉。

鲁宾沿着沃特街向前跑。

鲁宾赶到工厂时，厂房的影子越拉越长了。收购麻袋的人正要锁门。

"先生！请先不要关门。"

那人转过身，看到了鲁宾，只见他脏兮兮、汗津津的。

"明天再来吧，孩子。"

"求您了，先生。我必须现在卖掉麻袋——行行好。"听到鲁宾的声音颤抖，那人能断定他快要哭了。

"你为什么这样急需这钱呢？"

"这是一个秘密。"

那人接过麻袋，将手伸进口袋，掏出4个硬币，放在鲁宾的手里。鲁宾轻轻说了声"谢谢"，就向家里跑去。

随后，他紧紧搂着铁罐，奔向那家商店。

"我有钱了。"他一本正经地告诉店主。

店主走到橱窗边，取出了鲁宾要的宝贝。

他拂去灰尘，用牛皮纸小心把它包好，然后把这个小包放进了鲁宾的手里。

鲁宾飞奔到家，冲过前门。妈妈正在擦洗灶台。"给，妈妈！给！"鲁宾一边跑向她，一边大叫。他把一只小盒子放在了她因辛劳而粗糙的手里。

她小心翼翼地拆开，以免损坏包装纸。一个蓝色天鹅绒首饰盒出现在了眼前。多拉掀起盒盖，泪水渐渐模糊了双眼。

在一个小小的杏仁状胸针上用金字刻着"母亲"二字。

那是1946年母亲节。

多拉从来没有收到过这样的礼物；除了婚戒，她没有一件华丽的服饰。她默默无语，容光焕发，面带微笑，一把将儿子揽进了怀里。

The Voice of Love

Many people say their most painful moments are saying good-bye to those they love. After watching Cheryl, my daughter-in-law, through the six long months her mother suffered towards death, I think the most painful moments can be in the waiting to say good-bye. Cheryl made the two-hour trip over and over to be with her mother. They spent the long afternoons praying, soothing and retelling their shared memories.

As her mother's pain intensified and more medication was needed to ease her into sedation, Cheryl sat for hours of silent vigil by her mother's bed.

Each time she kissed her mother before leaving, her mother would say tearfully, "I'm sorry you drove so far and sat for so long and I didn't even wake up to talk with you."

Cheryl would tell her not to worry, but her mother felt she had let her down and apologized at each good-bye until the day Cheryl found a way to give her mother the same reassurance her mother had given to her so many times.

"Mom, do you remember when I made the high school basketball team?" Cheryl's mother nodded. "You'd drive so far and sit for so long and I never even left the bench to play. You waited for me after every game and each time I felt bad and apologized to you for wasting your time." Cheryl gently took her mother's hand.

"Do you remember what you would say to me?"

"I would say I didn't come to see you play, but I came to see you."

"And you meant those words, didn't you?"

"Yes, I really did."

"Well, now I say the same words to you. I didn't come to see you talk, I came to see you."

Her mother understood and smiled as she floated back into sleep.

Their afternoons together passed quietly into days, weeks, and months. Their love filled the spaces between their words. To the last day they ministered to each other in the stillness, love given and received just by seeing each other.

A love so strong that, even in this deepened silence that followed their last good-bye, Cheryl can still hear her mother's love.

爱 的 声 音

许多人说最痛苦的时刻是向自己所爱的人告别。看到儿媳妇谢丽尔经历漫长的6个月眼睁睁看着母亲经受痛苦走向死亡后,我认为最痛苦的时刻可能是等待告别。谢丽尔一次次驱车两小时来和母亲待在一起。她们常常花费漫长的下午时间祈祷、安慰和复述彼此的回忆。

当她母亲痛苦加剧、需要更多药物保持镇静时,谢丽尔会一连几个小时静静地守在她床前。

每次离开前她吻母亲时,母亲总会流着泪说:"很抱歉让你开这么远的车、坐这么久,我连清醒和你说话都不能啊。"

谢丽尔常常告诉她不要担心,但母亲还是觉得让谢丽尔失望,所以每次告别时都表示歉意。直到有一天,谢丽尔找到了让母亲放心的办法,就像母亲曾多次让她放心那样。

"妈妈,你还记得我参加中学篮球队的事吗?"谢丽尔的母亲点了点头。"你要开那么远的车过来,在我身边坐那么久,而我甚至从未离开过长椅去打球。每次比赛后你都等着我,每次我都感到糟糕,为浪费你的时间而向你道歉。"谢丽尔温柔地握住母亲的手。

"你还记得你常常对我说什么吗?"

"我常常说我不是来看你打球的,而是来看你的。"

"你说的都是真心话,对吗?"

"是,确实是。"

"那现在我也对你说同样的话。我不是来听你说话的,而是来看你的。"

她的母亲明白了,微笑着进入了梦乡。

她们一起度过的下午时光静静地流逝,一天天、一周周,然后是几个月。她们的爱填满了言语间的一个个空白。在沉静中,她们相互照顾,直到最后一天,相互凝视仅仅是我为了给予爱和接受爱。

有一种爱非常强大，即使在最后告别后最深的寂静中，谢丽尔仍能听到母爱的声音。

Love Is a Thread

Sometimes I really doubt whether there is love between my parents. Every day they are very busy trying to earn money in order to pay the high tuition for my brother and me. They don't act in the romantic ways that I read in books or I see on TV. In their opinion, "I love you" is too luxurious for them to say. Sending flowers to each other on Valentine's Day is even more out of the question. Finally my father has a bad temper. When he's very tired from the hard work, it is easy for him to lose his temper.

One day, my mother was sewing a quilt. I silently sat down beside her and looked at her. "Mom, I have a question to ask you," I said after a while. "What?" she replied, still doing her work. "Is there love between you and Dad?" I asked her in a very low voice.

My mother stopped her work and raised her head with surprise in her eyes. She didn't answer immediately. Then she bowed her head and continued to sew the quilt. I was very worried because I thought I had hurt her. I was in a great embarrassment and I didn't know what I should do. But at last I heard my mother say the following words.

"Susan," she said thoughtfully, "Look at this thread. Sometimes it appears, but most of it disappears in the quilt. The thread really makes the quilt strong and durable. If life is a quilt, then love should be a thread. It can hardly be seen anywhere or anytime, but it's really there. Love is inside."

I listened carefully but I couldn't understand her until the next spring. At that time, my father suddenly got sick seriously. My mother had to stay with him in the hospital for a month. When they returned from the hospital, they both looked very pale. It seemed both of them had had a serious illness.

After they were back, every day in the morning and dusk, my mother helped my father walk slowly on the country road. My father had never been so gentle. It seemed they were the most harmonious couple. Along the country road, there were many beautiful flowers, green grass and trees. The sun gently glistened through the leaves. All of these made up the most beautiful picture in the world.

The doctor had said my father would recover in two months. But after two months he still couldn't walk by himself. All of us were worried about him.

"Dad, how are you feeling now?" I asked him one day.

"Susan, don't worry about me," he said gently. "To tell you the truth, I just like walking with your mom. I like this kind of life." Reading his eyes, I know he loves my mother deeply.

Once I thought love meant flowers, gifts and sweet kisses. But from this experience, I understand that love is just a thread in the quilt of our life. Love is inside, making life strong and warm.

爱是一根线

有时候,我真怀疑父母之间是否有爱。他们每天忙忙碌碌拼命赚钱,为我和弟弟支付高昂的学费。他们没有像我在书里读到或在电视中看到的那样行为浪漫。他们认为,"我爱你"辞藻华丽,说不出口。情人节彼此送花就更不可能了。关键是,我父亲脾气很坏。辛苦了一天后,他筋疲力尽,动不动就发脾气。

一天,母亲正在缝被子。我静静地坐在她身边看着她。"妈妈,我想问你一个问题。"过了一会儿,我说,"什么问题?"她反问道,仍在忙着手里的活儿。"你和爸爸之间有爱情吗?"我声音很低地问道。

母亲停下手里的活,抬起头,眼里露出了吃惊的神色。她没有马上回答。随后,她低下头,继续缝起了被子。我很担心,因为我想自己伤害了她。我非常尴尬,不知道该怎么办。但最后,我听到母亲说了下面这段话。

"苏珊,"她若有所思地说,"看看这根线。有时它露出来,但大多数都藏在被子里。这些线确实让被子坚固耐用。如果生活是一条被子,那么爱就应该是一根线。不可能处处时时都看到它,但它却确实在那里。爱在里面。"

我仔细听着,但直到第二年春天才明白她的话。当时,父亲突然得了重病。母亲不得不在医院里守了他了一个月。从医院回来时,他们俩都显得非常苍白,就像他们俩都得了一场重病似的。

他们回来后,每天早晨和黄昏,母亲都会搀着父亲在乡间小路上慢慢散步。父亲从来没有那样温和过。他们就像天生的一对。乡村的路边有好多漂亮的鲜花、绿草和树木。阳光闪耀,轻轻地穿过树叶。这一切成了世界上最美的画面。

医生说我父亲两个月后康复。但两个月后,他仍然无法独自行走。我们都为他担忧。"爸爸,你现在感觉怎么样?"有一天,我问他。"苏珊,别为我担心。"他温和地说。"说实话,我就喜欢和你妈妈一块散步。我喜欢这种生活。"我读懂了他的眼神,知道他深爱我的母亲。

我曾认为爱情就是鲜花、礼物和甜吻。但从这次体验,我明白爱情只是我们生活之被里的一根线。爱情在里面，使生活变得坚固温暖。

Squeeze My Hand

Remember when you were a child and you fell and hurt yourself? Do you remember what your mother did to ease the pain? My mother, Grace Rose, would pick me up, carry me to her bed, sit me down and kiss my pain. Then she'd sit on the bed beside me, take my hand in hers and say, "When it hurts, squeeze my hand and I'll tell you that I love you." Over and over I'd squeeze her hand, and each time, without fail, I heard the words, "Mary, I love you."

Sometimes, I'd find myself pretending I'd been hurt just to have that ritual with her. As I grew up, the ritual changed, but she always found a way to ease he pain and increase the joy I felt in any area of my life. On difficult days during high school, she'd offer her favorite Hershey chocolate almond bar when I returned home. During my 20s, Mom often called to suggest a spontaneous picnic lunch at Estabrook Park just to celebrate a warm, sunny day in Wisconsin. A handwritten thank-you note arrived in the mail after every single visit she and my father made to my home, reminding me of how special I was to her.

But the most memorable ritual remained her holding my hand when I was a child and saying, "When it hurts, squeeze my hand and I'll tell you that I love you."

One morning, when I was in my late 30s, following a visit by my parents the night before, my father phoned me at work. He was always commanding and clear in his directions, but I heard confusion and panic in his voice. "Mary, something's wrong with your mother and I don't know what to do. Please come over as quickly as you can."

The 10-minute drive to my parents' home filled me with dread, wondering what was happening to my mother. When I arrived, I found Dad pacing in the kitchen and Mom lying on their bed. Her eyes were closed and her hands rested on her stomach. I called to her, trying to keep my voice as calm as possible. "Mom, I'm here."

"Mary?"

"Yes, Mom."

"Mary, is that you?"

"Yes, Mom, it's me."

I was not prepared for the next question, and when I heard it, I froze, not knowing what to say.

"Mary, am I going to die?"

Tears welled up inside me as I looked at my loving mother lying there so helpless.

My thoughts raced, until this question crossed my mind: What would Mom say?

I paused for a moment that seemed like a million years, waiting for the words to come. "Mom, I don't know if you're going to die, but if you need to, it's okay. I love you."

She cried out, "Mary, I hurt so much."

Again, I wondered what to say. I sat down beside her on the bed, picked up her hand and heard myself say, "Mom, when it hurts, squeeze my hand and I'll tell you that I love you."

She squeezed my hand.

"Mom, I love you."

Many hand squeezes and "I love you" passed between my mother and me during the next two years, until she passed away from ovarian cancer. We never know when our moments of truth will come, but I do know now that when they do, whomever I'm with, I will offer my mother's sweet ritual of love every time. "When it hurts, squeeze my hand and I'll tell you that I love you."

握住我的手

还记得你小时候跌倒摔疼的情景吗？你还记得为了减轻那份疼痛妈妈是怎么做的吗？我的妈妈格雷斯·露斯总会扶我起来，把我抱到她的床上，让我坐下，吻吻我的痛处，然后在我身边坐下来，拉住我的手说："要是疼，你就握住我的手，我会告诉你我爱你。"我曾一次又一次地握住她的手，而且我每次都必定能听到这句话："玛丽，我爱你。"

有时，我发现自己假装受伤，只是为了赢得她那份礼遇。随着我渐渐长大，那份礼遇也改变了，但她总能找到减轻疼痛的办法，让我随时随地都感到生活中增添的快乐。在上中学那段艰难日子里，每次我回家，她总会拿出她最爱吃的赫尔希牌杏仁巧克力棒。在我二三十岁这段时间，妈妈常常打来电话提议到埃斯塔布鲁克公园进行一次自发的野外午餐会，仅仅是要庆祝威斯康星这阳光温暖明媚的一天。她和爸爸每次看望我的家后，邮件里总有一小封手写的感谢信，向我提醒我对她是多么亲密。

但最难忘的礼遇仍然是我小时候她握住我的手说："要是疼，你就握住我的手，我会告诉你我爱你。"

我快40岁那年，有一天晚上，父母亲来看望我。第二天，爸爸给正在上班的我打来电话。爸爸一向威风凛凛、指挥若定，但那天我却听出他的声音里有一种疑惑和惊慌。"玛丽，你妈妈有点儿不对劲，我不知道该怎么办。请尽快过来。"

在开车前往父母亲家的10分钟的路途中，我内心充满了恐惧，不知道妈妈出了什么事。我赶到那里，发现爸爸在厨房里来回不停地踱步，妈妈躺在床上，闭着眼睛，两手放在腹部。我尽可能声音平静地向她喊道："妈妈，我来了。"

"是玛丽吗？"

"是我，妈妈。"

"玛丽，真是你吗？"

"是的，妈妈，是我。"

我没想到妈妈接下来会问那样一个问题，听到这个问题，我僵在那里，不知道该说什么。

"玛丽，我要死了吗？"

我望着慈爱的妈妈躺在那里，是那样无助，禁不住泪如泉涌。

我浮想联翩，最后我的脑海里闪过这样一个问题：妈妈会怎么说？

我停顿了一会儿，仿佛过去了一百万年，我才说出了那些话："妈妈，我不知道你是不是要死，但如果你需要，那就没事儿。我爱你。"

她大声哭道："玛丽，我好疼。"

我又一次不知道该说什么。我在床上她的身边坐下来，握住她的手，脱口而出，"妈妈，要是疼，你就握住我的手，我会告诉你我爱你。"

她握住我的手。

"妈妈，我爱你。"

在接下来的两年里，我和妈妈握了一次又一次的手，我说了一次又一次的"我爱你"，直到她因卵巢癌撒手而去。虽然我们根本无法知道考验我们的时刻何时来临，但现在我确实知道，当考验的时刻来临时，无论我和谁在一起，每次我一定会献上妈妈那种甜蜜的礼节。"要是疼，你就握住我的手，我会告诉你我爱你。"

My Mother's Grave

It was thirteen years since my mother's death, when, after a long absence from my native village, I stood beside the sacred mound beneath which I had seen her buried. Since that mournful period, a great change had come over me. My childish years had passed away, and with them my youthful character. The world was altered, too; and as I stood at my mother's grave, I could hardly realize that I was the same thoughtless, happy creature, whose cheeks she so often kissed in an excess of tenderness.

But the varied events of thirteen years had not effaced the remembrance of that mother's smile. It seemed as if I had seen her but yesterday—as if the blessed sound of her well-remembered voice was in my ear. The gay dreams of my infancy and childhood were brought back so distinctly to my mind that, had it not been for one bitter recollection, the tears I shed would have been gentle and refreshing.

The circumstance may seem a trifling one, but the thought of it now pains my heart; and I relate it, that those children who have parents to love them may learn to value them as they ought. My mother had been ill a long time, and I had become so accustomed to her pale face and weak voice, that I was not frightened at them, as children usually are. At first, it is true, I sobbed violently; but when, day after day, I returned from school, and found her the same, I began to believe she would always be spared to me; but they told me she would die.

One day when I had lost my place in the class, I came home discouraged and fretful. I went to my mother's chamber. She was paler than usual, but she met me with the same affectionate smile that always welcomed my return. Alas! when I look back through the lapse of thirteen years, I think my heart must have been stone not to have been melted by it. She requested me to go downstairs and bring her a glass of water. I pettishly asked her why she did not call a domestic to do it. With a look of mild reproach, which I shall never forget if I live to be a hundred years old, she said, "Will not my daughter bring a glass of water for her poor, sick mother?"

I went and brought her the water, but I did not do it kindly. Instead of smiling, and kissing her as I had been wont to do, I set the glass down very quickly, and left the room. After playing a short time, I went to bed without bidding my mother good night; but when alone in my room, in darkness and silence, I remembered how pale she looked, and how her voice trembled when she said, "Will not my daughter bring a glass of water for her poor, sick mother?" I could not sleep. I stole into her chamber to ask forgiveness. She had sunk into an easy slumber, and they told me I must not waken her.

I did not tell anyone what troubled me, but stole back to my bed, resolved to rise early in the morning and tell her how sorry I was for my conduct. The sun was shining brightly when I awoke, and, hurrying on my clothes, I hastened to my mother's chamber. She was dead! She never spoke more—never smiled upon me again; and when I touched the hand that used to rest upon my head in blessing, it was so cold that it made me start.

I bowed down by her side, and sobbed in the bitterness of my heart. I then wished that I might die, and be buried with her; and, old as I now am, I would give worlds, were they mine to give, could my mother but have lived to tell me she forgave my childish ingratitude. But I can not call her back; and when I stand by her grave, and whenever I think of her manifold kindness, the memory of that reproachful look she gave me will bite like a serpent and sting like an adder.

母亲的坟墓

母亲去世已经过去13年了。离开故乡多年后，我再一次站在母亲的坟墓边，我曾经亲眼看见母亲被埋葬在这里。那段让人极度悲痛的时期以后，我发现自己改变了很多。我的孩童岁月已然逝去，随之消失的还有我的青春，这个世界也改变了。站在母亲坟前的时候，我很难想象自己曾是那个天真快乐、总被慈祥的母亲亲吻脸颊的小女孩。

但是，13年的时间并没有抹去我对母亲的笑容的记忆，就好像我在昨天还看到了她的笑容，她那柔和的声音仿佛仍回荡在我的耳边。那些孩童时期的快乐梦想开始在我的脑海里浮现，倘若回忆不是悲苦的，那么我的眼泪必定是柔和且清新的。

虽然事情微不足道，但是每次只要一想起来，我的心就无比刺痛，我想讲一下自己的故事，希望那些享受父母疼爱的孩子要学会珍视这一切。我的母亲曾经长时间卧床不起，所以，我早已习惯了她那苍白的面孔和虚弱的声音，我对此并不感到担忧，孩子们都是这样的。一开始，我经常默默地哭泣，但是，日复一日，我从学校回来，发现她还是老样子，我开始相信她会陪伴在我身边，但是别人对我说她就快要死了。

一天，当我得知我的成绩在班里落后时，我沮丧地回了家。我来到母亲的房间，她的脸比往常更苍白，但她还是用充满爱意的微笑欢迎我回来。啊！当我开始回想13年前的事的时候，我发现我的心就好像是用石头做成的一样才没被融化掉。她让我下楼去给她端一杯水上来，我任性地问她，为什么不让用人去端呢？然后，她用责备的语气对我说，此刻就算我活到100岁也不会忘记，"难道我的女儿不愿意为她体弱多病的母亲端一杯水吗？"

于是，我极不情愿地下了楼，给母亲端了一杯水上来。我并没有像往常那样冲她微笑、亲吻她，而是很快放下杯子，离开了房间。然后，我便去玩了，我甚至都没有和母亲说声晚安就去睡觉了。但是，当我一个人待在黑暗的房间里时，我想起了她那苍白的脸庞，以及用颤抖的声音说出的"难道我的女儿不愿意为她体弱多病的母亲端一杯水吗"，这让我难以入睡。于是，我悄悄地来到母亲的房间请求她的原谅，此时的她已经睡着了，别人说我不能叫醒她。

我并没有跟任何人说究竟是什么在困扰着我，我悄悄地回到自己的房间，并且下定决心，在明天早上起来之后就向她道歉。当我起床的时候，太阳已经非常耀眼，于是我赶快穿好衣服，匆忙地跑到母亲的房间，但是，她已经去世了！她再也不能跟我说话了，再也不能对我微笑了。我紧紧地握住母亲的手，她曾经把手放在我的头上祝福我，现在已经变得冰冷，我惊讶极了。

我在她的床边跪下，悲痛欲绝地大哭起来。我真希望自己也能死去，和母亲葬在一起；现在的我已经不再年轻，倘若能够让母亲在生前说出她已经原谅了我小时候的忘恩的话，我宁愿用我所拥有的一切进行交换。但是，我没法让她死而复生。当我站在母亲坟前的时候，只要一想到母亲那慈祥的面容，记忆中她责备我的目光就像毒蛇一样咬着我。

第六卷

永远的父爱

Love in Bloom

I was nine when my father first sent me flowers. I had been taking tap-dancing lessons for six months, and the school was giving its yearly recital. As an excited member of the beginners' chorus line, I was aware of my lowly status.

So it was a surprise to have my name called out at the end of the show along with lead dancers and to find my arms full of long-stemmed red roses. I can still feel myself standing on that stage, blushing furiously and gazing over the footlights to see my father's grin as he applauded loudly.

Those roses were the first in a series of large bouquets that accompanied all the milestones in my life. They brought a sense of ambivalence, of being caught between please and embarrassment. I enjoy them, but was flustered by its extravagance.

Not my father. He did everything in a big way. If you sent him to a bakery for a cake, he came back with three. Once my mother told him I needed a new party dress, he brought a dozen.

His behavior often left us without funds for other more important things. After the dress incident, there was no money for the winter coat I really needed—or the new ice skates I wanted.

Sometimes I would be angry with him, but not for long. Inevitably he would buy me something to make up with me. The gift was so apparently an offering of love he couldn't verbalize that I would throw my arms around him and kiss him-an act that undoubtedly perpetuated his behavior.

Then came my 16th birthday. It was not a happy occasion. I was fat and had no boyfriend. And my well-meaning parents furthered my misery by giving me a party. As I entered the dining room, there on the table next to my cake was a huge bouquet of flowers, bigger than any before.

I wanted to hide. Now everyone would think my father had sent flowers because I had no boyfriend to do it. Sweet 16, and I feel like crying. I probably would have, but my best friend, Phyllis, whispered, "Boy, you are lucky to have a father like that."

As the years passed, other occasions—birthdays, recitals, awards, graduations—were marked with Dad's flowers. My emotions continued to seesaw between pleasure and embarrassment.

When I graduated from the college my days of ambivalence were over. I was embarking on a new career and was engaged to be married. Dad's flowers symbolized his pride, and my triumph. They evoked only great pleasure.

Now there were bright orange mums for Thanksgiving and a huge pink poinsettia at Christmas. White lilies at Easter, and velvety red roses for birthdays. Seasonal flowers in mixed bouquets celebrated the births of my children and the move to our first house.

As my fortune grew, my father's waned, but his gifts of flowers continued until he died of a heart attack a few months before his 70th birthday. Without embarrassment, I covered his coffin with the largest, reddest roses I could find.

Often in the dozen years since, I felt an urge to go out and buy a big bouquet to fill the living room, but I never did. I knew it wouldn't be the same.

Then one birthday, the doorbell rang. I was feeling blue because I was alone. My husband was playing golf, and my two daughters were away. My 13-year-old son, Matt, had run out earlier with a "see you later", never mentioning my birthday. So I was surprised to see his large frame at the door. "Forgot my key," he said, shrugging. "Forgot your birthday too. Well, I hope you like flowers, Mom." He pulled a bunch of daisies from behind his back.

"Oh, Matt," I cried, hugging him hard. "I love flowers!"

爱 在 盛 开

父亲第一次给我送花，是我9岁那年。我学踢踏舞才6个月，学校要举行一年一度的演出。初进合唱队，我兴致勃勃，但我明白自己的角色很不起眼。

所以，演出结束，和那些主舞演员一起被喊到了前台，我怀里抱满了长茎红玫瑰时，真让人吃惊。我现在还能感觉到自己站在那个舞台上，脸色羞红，越过舞台看到父亲一边咧嘴笑一边使劲鼓掌。

那是我人生里程碑中的第一束玫瑰，后来每次父亲都会相应送给我一大束。而收到那些鲜花，我总是非常矛盾：既高兴又困窘。我喜爱那些鲜花，但又为这种铺张奢侈而心慌。

父亲却不这样，他做什么事都大手大脚。你让他去面包店买一块蛋糕，他会买回来3块。有一次，母亲对他说我需要一条新舞裙，他居然买回来一打。

他这样做常常让我们没有钱去买其他更重要的东西。他买回一打舞裙后，就没钱去买我真正需要的冬装和我需要的新冰鞋。

有时我会和父亲生气，但时间都不长。他每次必定会给我买一些东西与我和好。显然，这礼物传达了他无法言表的爱。我常常搂住他，亲吻他，这种举动无疑会使他再次大手大脚。

后来到了我的16岁生日。这并不是一个快乐的节日，因为我很胖，没有男朋友。好心的父母亲为我举办了生日晚会，这更让我痛苦。我走进餐室，只见餐桌上生日蛋糕旁边有一大束鲜花，比以前的任何一束都大。

我真想藏起来。现在大家都会以为我没有男朋友送花,父亲才送的。甜蜜的16岁,我却很想大哭一场。我也许当时肯定会哭,但我最好的朋友菲利斯低声说:"噢,你有这样的父亲真幸运。"

光阴荏苒,日月如梭,其他特殊时刻——生日、演出、获奖、毕业典礼——都会有爸爸的鲜花。我的情绪仍然在高兴和困窘之间摇摆。

到大学毕业时,我那种矛盾相伴的日子结束了。我踏上了新的人生轨道,订婚成家。爸爸的鲜花是他的骄傲和我的胜利的象征。它们唤起的只有极大的喜悦。

现在感恩节都会有鲜橙色的菊花,圣诞节会有一大束粉红色的一品红,复活节会有白色的百合花,生日会有天鹅绒般的红玫瑰,孩子出生和搬到我们第一座房子时会有鲜花扎成的花束。

我好运日盛,父亲却日渐衰老,但他仍然给我送花,直到他70岁生日前几个月因心脏病而去世。我在他的灵柩上放满了我所能找到的最大、最红的玫瑰花,并不感到困窘。

在此后的12年里,我常常有一种冲动,想出去买一大束鲜花摆满客厅,但我始终没有那样做。我知道,那将不再是从前的花了。

后来有一次生日,门铃响了。那天我感到沮丧,因为只有我一个人在家。丈夫打高尔夫球去了,两个女儿到远处去了,13岁的儿子马特也早早就跑了出去,只说了声"再见",却没有提我的生日。所以,我看到马特宽大的身体站在门边,吃了一惊。"忘带钥匙了,"他耸了耸肩说,"也忘了你的生日。噢,我希望你喜欢鲜花,妈妈。"他从背后抽出了一束雏菊。

"噢,马特,"我紧紧抱住他,大声说道,"我爱鲜花!"

A Dance with Dad

I am dancing with my father at my parents' 50th-wedding-anniversary celebration. The band is playing an old-fashioned waltz as we move gracefully across the floor. His hand was on my waist is as guiding as it always was, and he hums the tune to himself in a steady, youthful way. Around and around we go, laughing and nodding to the other dancers.

We are the best dancers on the floor, they tell us. My father squeezes my hand and smiles at me. All the years that I refused to dance with him melt away now. And those early times come back.

I remember when I was almost three and my father came home from work, swooped me into his arms and began to dance me around the table. My mother laughed at us, told us dinner would get cold. But my father said, "She's just caught the rhythm of the dance! Our dinner can wait." Then he sang out, "Roll out the barrel, let's have a barrel of fun," and I sang back. "Let's get those blues on the run."

We danced through the years. We even won a dance contest at a Camp Fire Girls Round-Up. Then we learned to jitterbug at the USO downtown. Once my father caught on to the steps, he danced with everyone in the hall. We all laughed and clapped our hands for my father, the dancer.

One night when I was 15, lost in some painful, adolescent mood, my father put on a stack of records and teased me to dance with him. "C'mon," he said, "Let's get those blues on the run." When I turned away from him, my father put his hand on my shoulder, and I jumped out of the chair screaming, "don't touch me! I am sick and tired of dancing with you!" I saw the hurt on his face, but the words were out and I couldn't call them back. I ran to my room bursting into tears.

We didn't dance together after that night. I found other partners, and my father waited up for me after dances, sitting in his favorite chair, clad in his flannel pajamas. Sometimes he would be asleep when I came in, and I would wake him, saying, "If you were so tired, you should have gone to bed." "No, no," he'd say. "I was just waiting for you." Then we'd locked up the house and go to bed. My father waited up for me all through my high-school and college years while I danced my way out of his life.

Shortly after my first child was born, my mother called to tell me my father was ill. "A heart problem," she said. "Now, don't come. It's three hundred miles. It would upset your father."

A proper diet restored him to good health. My mother wrote that they had joined a dance club: "The doctor says it's good exercise. You remember how your father loves to dance."

Yes, I remember. My eyes filled up with remembering.

When my father retired, we mended our way back together again; hugs and kisses were common when we visited each other. He danced with the grandchildren, but he didn't ask me to dance. I knew he was waiting for an apology from me. I could never find the right words.

As my parents' 50th anniversary approached, my brothers and I met to plan the party. My older brother said: "Do you remember that night you wouldn't dance with him? Boy, was he mad. I couldn't believe he'd get so mad about a thing like that. I'll bet you haven't danced with him since." I didn't tell him he was right.

My younger brother promised to get the band. "Make sure they can play waltzes and polkas," I told him. I didn't tell him that all I wanted to do was dance once more with my father.

When the band began to play after dinner, my parents took the floor. They glided around the room, inviting the others to join them. The guests rose to their feet, applauding the golden couple. My father danced with his granddaughters, and then the band began to play the "Beer Barrel Polka."

"Roll out the barrel," I heard my father singing. Then I knew it was time. I wound my way through a few couples and tapped my daughter on the shoulder.

"Excuse me," I said, looking directly into my father's eyes and almost choking on my words, "but I believe this is my dance."

My father stood rooted to the spot. Our eyes met and traveled back to that night when I was 15. In a trembling voice, I sang, "Let's get those blues on the run."

My father bowed and said, "Oh, yes. I've been waiting for you."

Then he started to laugh, and we moved into each other's arms.

与爸爸共舞

在父母亲金婚纪念时，我和爸爸跳起了舞。乐队奏着一支老华尔兹舞曲，我们在舞厅中翩翩起舞。他像往常一样将手放在我的腰间领舞，嘴里和年轻人一样哼着这首曲子。我们跳了一圈又一圈，不时地笑着向其他跳舞的人点头致意。

那些人对我们说，我们是舞厅里跳得最好的一对。父亲握紧我的手，对我微笑。我多年来拒绝与他跳舞的隔膜现在渐渐淡去，早年的那些时光重新返回。

我记得，我差不多3岁那年，父亲下班回家，一把将我抱在怀里，开始和我围着桌子跳了起来。母亲对我们大声笑着，说晚饭都放凉了。但父亲说："她刚刚跟上舞蹈的节奏！晚饭可以等一等。"随后，他大声唱了起来："滚出桶子，让我们好好乐乐。"我也大声唱道："带走那些忧伤。"

我们跳了好多年。我们甚至还在篝火少女跳舞比赛得过奖呢。后来，我们又去市里的劳军联合会学跳吉特巴舞。父亲一跟上步调，就会和舞厅里的每一个人跳。我们都为我的舞迷父亲鼓掌大笑。

15岁那年的一天夜里，我正迷失在花季少女的痛苦之中，父亲却放了一堆唱片，强要我和他跳舞。"跳吧，"他说，"带走那些忧伤。"我转身离开时，父亲将手放在我的肩上。我从椅子上跳起来，冲他尖叫道："别碰我！我讨厌和你跳舞！"尽管我看到了他脸上的伤痛，但话已出口，无法收回。我跑到自己的房间放声大哭。

那夜之后，我们没再一起跳过。我找了其他舞伴，父亲总是穿着法兰绒睡衣裤坐在他最心爱的椅子上等我跳舞归来。有时我回来时，他会睡着，我便摇醒他说："你要是这么累，就该上床睡觉。""不，不，"他总是说，"我在等你呢。"随后，我们就锁上房门，上床睡觉。从中学到大学，我外出跳舞时，他就一直这样熬夜等着我。

我的第一个孩子出生后不久，母亲打电话说父亲病了。"是心脏病，"她说，"现在，不要来。有300英里呢，那会让你父亲感到不安的。"

合理的饮食调养使父亲恢复了健康。母亲写信说他们加入了一家舞蹈俱乐部："医生说这是一种很好的锻炼。你记得你父亲是多么爱跳舞。"

是的，我记得。闪现在我眼前的都是我对过去的回忆。

父亲退休时，我们再次努力想重修旧好；每次见面，我们常常拥抱和亲吻。他和外孙们跳，但他就是不找我跳。我知道他是在等我道歉，而我却怎么也找不到合适的词。

随着父母亲结婚50周年纪念日的临近，我和兄弟们聚到一起安排宴会。哥哥说："还记得你不愿和他跳舞的那个晚上吗？嗬，他跟疯了一般。我不相信会为这样一件事而那样发疯。我敢说从那以后你没和他跳过舞。"我没对他说他说得没错。

弟弟答应去请乐队。"务必要找能演奏华尔兹和波尔卡的。"我对他说。我没告诉他我所要做的就是和爸爸再跳一次。

饭后，乐队开始演奏，父母亲走进舞厅，滑着舞步绕场请其他人和他们一块跳。客人们站起来，为这一对金婚伴侣鼓掌。父亲挨个和孙女们跳着，随后乐队奏起了《啤酒桶波尔卡》。

"把桶滚出来，"我听到父亲唱道。随后，我知道是时候了。我绕过几对跳舞的客人，拍了拍女儿的肩膀。"对不起，"我直视着父亲的眼睛说，几乎把要说的话噎在了嗓子里，"但我相信这是我的舞会。"父亲像扎了根似的站在那里。我们四目相对，时光仿佛又回到了我15岁时的那个夜里。我声音颤抖地唱道："带走那些忧伤。"

父亲躬身说道："噢，是的。我一直在等着你。"

随后，他开始放声大笑，我们移动脚步，投入了对方的怀抱。

A Violin

"Wanted: Violin. Can't pay much. Call…"
Why did I notice that? I wondered, since I rarely look at the classified ads.
I laid the paper on my lap and closed my eyes, remembering what had happened

many years before, when my family struggled to make a living on our farm. I, too, had wanted a violin, but we didn't have the money…

When my older twin sisters began showing an interest in music, Harriet Anne learned to play Grandma's upright piano, while Suzanne turned to Daddy's violin. Simple tunes soon became lovely melodies as the twins played more and more. Caught up in the rhythm of the music, my baby brother danced around while Daddy hummed and Mother whistled. I just listened.

When my arms grew long enough, I tried to play Suzanne's violin. I loved the mellow sound of the firm bow drawn across the strings. Oh, how I wanted one! But I knew it was out of the question.

One evening as the twins played in the school orchestra, I closed my eyes tight to capture the picture firmly in my mind. Someday, I'll sit up there, I vowed silently.

It was not a good year. At harvest the crops didn't bring as much as we had hoped. Yet even though times were hard, I couldn't wait any longer to ask: "Daddy, may I have a violin of my own?"

"Can't you use Suzanne's?"

"I'd like to be in the orchestra, too, and we can't both use the same violin at the same time."

Daddy's face looked sad. That night, and many following nights, I heard him remind God in our family devotions, "…and Lord, Mary Lou wants her own violin."

One evening we all sat around the table. The twins and I studied. Mother sewed, and Daddy wrote a letter to his friend, George Finkle, in Columbus, Ohio. Mr. Finkle, Daddy said, was a fine violinist.

As he wrote, Daddy read parts of his letter out loud to Mother. Weeks later I discovered he'd written one line he didn't read aloud: "Would you watch for a violin for my third daughter? I can't pay much, but she enjoys much, and we'd like her to have her own instrument."

When Daddy received a letter from Columbus a few weeks later, he announced, "We'll be driving to Columbus to spend the night with Aunt Alice as soon as I can find someone to care for the livestock."

At last the day arrived, and we drove to Aunt Alice's. After we arrived, I listened while Daddy made a phone call. He hung up and asked, "Mary Lou, do you want to go with me to visit Mr. Finkle?"

"Sure," I answered.

He drove into a residential area and stopped in the driveway of a fine, old house. We walked up the steps and rang the door chime. A tall man, older than Daddy, opened the door. "Come in!" he and Daddy heartily shook hands, both talking at once.

"Mary Lou, I've been hearing things about you. Your daddy has arranged a big surprise for you!" Mr. Finkle ushered us into the parlor. He picked up a case, opened it, lifted out a violin and started to play. The melody surged and spoke like waterfalls. Oh, to play like him, I thought.

Finishing the number, he turned to Daddy. "Carl, I found it in a pawnshop for seven dollars. It's a good violin. Mary Lou should be able to make beautiful music with it." Then he handed the violin to me.

I noticed the tears in Daddy's eyes as I finally comprehended. It was mine! I stoked the violin gently. The wood was a golden brown that seemed to warm in the light. "It's beautiful," I said, barely breathing.

When we arrived back at Aunt Alice's, all eyes turned as we entered. I saw Daddy wink at Mother, and then I realized everyone had known but me. I knew Daddy's prayer, and mine, had been answered.

The day I carried my violin to school for my first lesson no one could imagine the bursting feeling in my heart. Over the months I practiced daily, feeling the warm wood fit under my chin like an extension of myself.

When I was ready to join the school orchestra, I trembled with excitement. I sat in the third row of violins and wore my white orchestra jacket like a royal robe.

My heart beat wildly at my first public performance, a school operetta. The auditorium filled to capacity and the audience buzzed while we softly tuned our instruments. Then the spotlight centered on us, and a hush fell as we started to play. I felt sure everyone in the audience was watching me. Daddy and Mother smiled proudly at their little girl who held her cherished violin for the whole world to admire.

The years seemed to run more swiftly then. And by the time my sisters graduated, I found myself in the first-violin chair.

Two years later, I graduated. I packed my cherished violin in its case and stepped into the grown-up world. Nurse's training, marriage, working in the hospital, rearing four daughters filled my years.

More years passed. My violin made every move with us, and I carefully stored it away when we unpacked—briefly remembering how much I still loved it and promising myself to play it soon.

None of my children cared about the violin. Later, one by one, they married and left home…

Now here I was with the newspaper want ads. I forced my thoughts to the present and read again the ad that had transported me back to childhood memories. Laying aside the paper, I murmured, "I must find my violin."

I discovered the case deep in the recesses of my closet. Opening the lid, I lifted the violin from where it nestled on the rose-velvet lining. My fingers caressed its golden wood. I tuned the strings, miraculously still intact, tightened the bow, and put rosin on the dry horsehairs.

And then my violin began to sing again those favorite tunes that had never left my memory. How long I played I'll never know. I thought of Daddy, who did all he could to fill my needs and desires when I was a little girl. I wondered if I had ever thanked him.

At last I laid the violin back in its case. I picked up the newspaper, walked to the phone and dialed the number.

Later in the day, an old car stopped in my driveway. A man in his 30s knocked on the door. "I've been praying someone would answer my ad. My daughter wants a violin so badly," he said, examining my instrument. "How much are you asking?"

Any music store, I knew, would offer me a nice sum. But now I heard my voice answer, "Seven dollars."

"Are you sure?" he asked, reminding me so much of Daddy.

"Seven dollars," repeated, and then added, "I hope your little girl will enjoy it as much as I did."

I closed the door behind him. Peeking out between the drapes, I saw his wife and children waiting in the car. A door suddenly opened and a young girl ran to him as he held out the violin case to her.

She hugged it against her, then dropped to her knees and snapped open the case. She touched the violin lightly as it caught the glow of the late-afternoon sun, then turned and threw her arms around her smiling father.

一把小提琴

"求购小提琴，出价不高。请打电话……"

我为什么偏偏注意这则广告呢？连我自己也搞不清楚。平时我很少注意这类广告。

我把报纸放在膝间，闭上双眼，往事便一幕幕浮现在了眼前：那时全家人含辛茹苦靠种地勉强度日。我也曾想要一把小提琴，但家里买不起……

我的两个孪生姐姐爱上了音乐。哈丽特·安妮学弹祖母留下的那台竖式钢琴，苏珊娜学拉父亲的那把小提琴。由于她们不断练习，因此没过多久简单的曲调就变成了悦耳动听的旋律。陶醉在音乐中的小弟弟禁不住随着音乐的节奏翩翩起舞，父亲轻轻哼唱，母亲也不由自主吹起了口哨，而我只是注意听着。

我的手臂渐渐长长了，也试着学拉苏珊娜的那把小提琴。我喜欢那绷紧的琴弓拉过琴弦时发出的柔媚圆润的声音。"噢，我多么希望能有一把琴啊！"但我明白这是不可能的。

一天傍晚，我的两个孪生姐姐在学校乐队演出时，我紧紧地闭上眼睛，以便把当时的情景深深地印在脑海里。"总有一天我也要坐在那里。"我暗暗发誓。

那年年景不好。收成不像我们盼望的那样好。尽管岁月如此艰难,但我还是迫不及待地问道:"爸爸,我可以有一把自己的小提琴吗?"

"你用苏珊娜那把不行吗?"

"我也想加入乐队,但我们俩不能同时用一把琴呀。"

父亲的表情显得非常难过。那天晚上以及随后的许多夜晚,我都听到他在全家人晚间祈祷时向上帝祷告:"……上帝啊,玛丽·露想要一把自己的小提琴。"

一天晚上,全家人都围坐在桌边,我和姐姐们复习功课,母亲做针线活,父亲给他在俄亥俄州哥伦布市的朋友乔治·芬科写信。父亲曾说,芬科先生是一名出色的小提琴家。

父亲一边写,一边把信的部分内容念给母亲听。几周后,我才发现信中的这一行字他没念:"请留神帮我三女儿寻一把小提琴好吗?我出不起高价,但她喜欢音乐,我们希望她能有自己的乐器。"

又过了几周,父亲收到哥伦布市的回信。他对大家说:"只要我能找到人帮忙照看家畜,我们就一起去哥伦布市,到爱丽斯姑姑家过一夜。"

这一天终于到来了。我们全家人驱车前往爱丽斯姑姑家。到那以后,父亲打了个电话,我在旁边听着。他挂上电话后问我:"玛丽·露,你想和我一起去看芬科先生吗?"

"当然想。"我答道。

父亲将车开进一个居民区,停靠在一座古色古香的楼房前的车道边上。我们登上台阶,按响了门铃。开门的是一个比我父亲年纪大的高个子的先生。"请进!"他和父亲亲切握手,两人马上攀谈了起来。

"玛丽·露,我早就听说过你的一些情况。你的父亲为你准备了一件礼物,一定会让你大吃一惊的!"说完,芬科先生将我们领进客厅,便开始拉了起来。乐曲时而激越高亢,时而像瀑布飞泻,"噢,要是像他那样拉该多好啊!"我心里想。

一曲终了,他转过身对我的父亲说:"卡尔,这是在一家当铺里找到的,才花了7美元,是一把好琴。这下玛丽·露就可以用它演奏优美的乐曲了吧。"说完,他将琴递给了我。

看到父亲眼里的泪水,我终于明白了一切。我有了自己的小提琴!我轻轻地抚摸着琴。这把琴是用金色灿烂的棕色木料制成的，在阳光的映照下显得是那样温暖。"多么漂亮啊！"我激动得透不过气来了。

当我们回到爱丽斯姑姑家时，所有人的目光都投向了我们父女俩，只见父亲正向母亲挤眼。这时，我才恍然大悟，原来只有我一个人还蒙在鼓里。我知道我和父亲的愿望已经得到了实现。

我带着那把小提琴到学校上第一堂课的那天，当时那种万分激动的心情是谁也无法想象的。随后的几个月，我天天坚持练琴，感到抵在颌下那温暖的琴木就像我身体的一部分。

加入校乐队时，我激动得浑身颤抖。我身着白色队服，俨然女王一般。我坐在小提琴组的第三排。

首次公演是学校演出的小歌剧，当时我的心狂跳不止。礼堂里座无虚席。我们乐队成员轻轻地调试音调，观众席里还在叽叽喳喳说个不停。舞台聚光灯射向我们，台下立刻鸦雀无声。我们开始了演奏。我确信观众的目光都在注视着我。我的父母亲也都在看着他们的小女儿，嘴边挂着自豪的微笑。他们的小女儿怀里抱着她那把心爱的琴，让全世界都来赞赏它。

岁月似乎过得太快了。两个姐姐双双毕业后，我便坐上了首席小提琴的席位。

两年后，我也完成了学业，将心爱的小提琴放回了琴盒，步入了成年人的世界。先是接受护士培训，然后是结婚成家。在医院工作的几年里，我先后生了4个女儿。

以后的许多年里，我们每次搬家，我都带着这把琴。每次打开行李布置居室时，我都要小心翼翼地将琴存放好，忙里偷闲时，想着我仍是多么爱它，同时对自己许愿说，用不了多久还会用这把小提琴演奏几首曲子。

我的几个孩子没有一个喜欢小提琴的。后来，她们相继结婚，离开了家。

现在我的面前摆着这张征求广告的报纸。我尽力不再去回首往事，将这则引起我对童年回忆的广告又看了一遍后，放下报纸，喃喃自语道："一定得把我的琴找出来。"

我在壁橱深处找出了琴盒，打开盖子，将安卧在玫瑰色丝绒衬里中的小提琴拿出来。我的手指轻轻地抚摸着金色的琴木，令人惊喜的是，琴弦仍然完好无损。我调试了一下琴弦，紧了紧琴弓，又往干巴巴的马尾弓上抹了点松香。

接着，小提琴又重新奏出了那些铭记在我心中最心爱的曲子。也不知究竟拉了多长时间。我想起了父亲，在我童年时代，是他竭力满足我的一切愿望和要求，对此我不知道自己是否感谢过他。

最后，我把小提琴重新放回盒子里，拿起报纸，走到电话边，拨响了那个号码。

当天晚些时候，一辆旧轿车停靠在我家的车道旁。敲门的是个30来岁的先生。"我一直都在祈祷着会有人答复我登在报纸上的那则广告。我的女儿太希望有一把属于自己的小提琴了，"他一边说，一边查看我那把琴。"要多少钱？"

我知道，不管哪家乐器行都会出好价钱的。但此时此刻，我听到自己的声音回答说："7美元。"

"真的吗？"他这一问，倒使我更多地想起了父亲。

"7美元，"我又说了一遍，接着补充道，"希望你的小女儿也会像我过去那样喜欢它。"

他走后，我随即关上门，从窗帘缝里看到他的妻子和孩子们正等候在车子里。车门突然打开，一个小姑娘迎着他双手托着的琴箱跑过来。

她紧紧地抱住琴盒，双膝跪倒在地，"吧嗒"一声打开盒子。她轻轻地抚摸着红彤彤的夕阳映照下的那把琴，转过身，搂住了面带微笑的父亲。

A Box of Kisses

A long time ago a man punished his 3-year-old daughter for wasting a roll of gold wrapping paper. Money was tight and he became very angry when the child tried to decorate a box to put under the Christmas tree.

However, the little girl brought the gift to her father the next morning and said, "This is for you, Daddy."

The father was upset by his earlier overreaction, but his anger flared again when he found out the box was empty. He yelled at her, "don't you know, when you give someone a present, there should be something inside?"

The little girl looked up at him with tears in her eyes and cried, "Oh, Daddy, it's not empty at all. I blew kisses into the box. They're all for you, Daddy."

The father was crushed. He put his arms around his little girl, and he begged for her forgiveness.

Only a short time later, an accident took the life of the child. Her father kept that gold box by his bed for many years and, whenever he was discouraged, he would take out an imaginary kiss and remember the love of the child who had put it there.

一 盒 子 吻

很久以前，一位父亲因3岁的女儿浪费了一卷金包装纸而惩罚她。当时家里钱不宽余，看到女儿想把一个包装金纸的盒子放在圣诞树下，父亲勃然大怒。

然而，第二天早上，小姑娘还是把那个礼物送给父亲说："爸爸，这是送给你的。"

那位父亲对自己先前的过激行为感到忐忑不安；可是，当发现盒子里空无一物时，他又火冒三丈，冲女儿大声嚷道："难道你不知道送别人礼物时盒子里应该放东西吗？"

小姑娘眼噙泪水望着父亲，哭道："噢，爸爸，盒子里一点也不空呀。我向里边飞了好多吻，它们都是送给你的，爸爸。"

那位父亲羞愧难当。他张开双臂抱住女儿，乞求她的原谅。

过了没多久，一场意外事故夺去了小女孩的生命。她的父亲好多年都把那个金纸包装的盒子存放在自己的床边。每当灰心丧气时，他就常常取出一个想象的吻，想起了女儿曾放在那里的爱。

Lesson From a Penguin

I've spent most of my career as a traveling salesman, and so I know that battling loneliness is an occupational hazard. But one year, my little girl Jeanne gave me the antidote for my homesickness.

It had black beady eyes, a red bow tie and orange feet—a stuffed penguin that stood about five inches tall. Attached to its left wing was a little sign bearing the hand-painted declaration"I Love My Dad!" I immediately granted the penguin a special place on my dresser.

On my next trip, I tossed the penguin in my suitcase. That night when I called home, Jeanne was upset that the penguin had disappeared. "Honey, he's here with me," I explained. "I brought him along."

From then on the penguin came with me—as essential as my briefcase or shaving kit. And we made friends along the way. In Albuquerque, I checked into a hotel, dumped out my bag and dashed to a meeting. When I returned, the maid had turned down the bed and propped the penguin on the pillow. In Boston, I found it perched in a glass on the nightstand. Once a customs agent at New York's Kennedy Airport dug the penguin out of my suitcase and, holding it up, said, "Thank God we don't charge a tax on love, or you'd owe a bundle."

One night I discovered the penguin missing, and after a frantic phone call, I learned I'd left it in my previous hotel room, where it had been rescued by a maid. I drove a hundred miles to retrieve it, and when I arrived at midnight, the penguin was waiting at the front desk. In the lobby, tired business travelers looked on at the reunion-I think with a touch of envy.

Jeanne is in college now, and I don't travel as much. The penguin sits on my dresser, a reminder that love is a wonderful traveling companion. All those years on the road, it was the one thing I never left home without.

爱 心 企 鹅

我一生大多数时间都是做旅行推销商，所以我知道战胜孤独成了一种职业病。但有一年，我的小女儿珍宁送给了我一副想家的解药。

那是一只玩具企鹅，它乌溜溜的眼睛，打着红色蝴蝶结，长着一双橘黄色的脚，大约有5英寸高。它的左腿上粘着一个小牌子，上面手绘着一条说明："我爱我爸！"我马上在我的梳妆台上给企鹅提供了一席之地。

在下一次旅行时，我就将企鹅放进了手提箱。当夜我给家里打电话时，珍宁忐忑不安，说企鹅不见了。"宝贝儿，它跟我在一块呢，"我解释说，"我把它带在了身边。"

从那以后，企鹅就跟我一路同行，就像我的公文包或剃须用具一样必不可少。而且我们一路上成了朋友。在阿尔伯克基市，我登记住进一家旅馆，倒出手提包，匆匆赶去参加一个会议。我回来时，女服务员已经铺过床，并将企鹅放在了枕头上。在波士顿，我发现它卧在床头几上的一只玻璃杯里。有一次，在纽约市肯尼迪机场，一位报关代理人从我的手提箱里搜出了企鹅，将它举起来，说："谢天谢地我们对爱是不收税的，否则你就要欠一大笔钱喽。"

有天夜里，我发现企鹅不翼而飞；而在疯狂地打了电话后，我才得知我将它忘在了先前住的旅馆房间里，旅馆的一名女服务员已经把它收了起来。我驱车100英里将它取了回来；而当我午夜赶到那里时，企鹅正在前台等着我呢。在大厅里，满脸倦容的生意人在旁边看着我们的重逢。我想，是带着一丝的嫉妒。

珍宁现已上了大学，而且我也不像以前那样经常旅行了。企鹅端坐在我的梳妆台上，它时刻提醒着我爱是妙不可言的旅伴。我出门在外在路上颠簸的那些岁月，爱是我从不离家的一件东西。

Dad's Kiss

The board meeting had come to an end. Bob started to stand up and jostled the table, spilling his coffee over his notes. "How embarrassing. I am getting so clumsy in my old age."

Everyone had a good laugh, and soon we were all telling stories of our most embarrassing moments. It came around to Frank who sat quietly listening to the others. Someone said, "Come on, Frank. Tell us your most embarrassing moment."

Frank laughed and began to tell us of his childhood. "I grew up in San River. My dad was a fisherman, and he loved the sea. He had his own boat, but it was hard making a living on the sea. He worked hard and would stay out until he caught enough to feed his family. Not just enough for our family, but also for his mom and dad and the other kids that were still at home."

He looked at us and said, "I wish you could have met my dad. He was a big man, and he was strong from pulling the nets and fighting the seas for his catch. When you got close to him, he smelled like the ocean. He would wear his old canvas, foul-weathered coat and his bibbed overalls. His rain hat would be pulled down over his brow. No matter how much my mother washed them, they would still smell of the sea and of fish."

Frank's voice dropped a bit. "When the weather was bad he would drive me to school. He had this old truck that he used in his fishing business. That truck was older than he was. It would wheeze and rattle down the road. You could hear it coming for blocks. As he would drive toward the school, I would shrink down into the seat hoping to disappear.

"Half the time, he would slam to a stop and the old truck would belch a cloud of smoke. He would pull right up in front, and it seemed like everybody would be standing around and watching. Then he would lean over and give me a big kiss on the cheek and tell me to be a good boy. It was so embarrassing for me. Here, I was twelve years old and my dad would lean over and kiss me goodbye!"

He paused and then went on, "I remember the day I decided I was too old for a goodbye kiss. When we got to the school and came to a stop, he had his usual big smile. He started to lean toward me, but I put my hand up and said, 'No, dad, '"

"It was the first time I had ever talked to him that way, and he had this surprised look on his face."

"I said, 'Dad, I'm too old for a goodbye kiss. I'm too old for any kind of kiss.'"

"My dad looked at me for the longest time, and his eyes started to well up. I had never seen him cry. He turned and looked out the windshield. 'You are right, ' he said. 'You are a big boy—a man. I won't kiss you anymore.'"

Frank got a funny look on his face, and the tears began to well up in his eyes, as he spoke. "it was not long after that when my dad went to sea and never came back. It was a day when most of the fleet stayed in, but not Dad. He had a big family to feed. They found his boat adrift with its nets half in and half out. He must have gotten into a gale."

I looked at Frank and saw that tears were running down his cheeks. Frank spoke again, "Guys, you don't know what I would give to have my dad give me just one more KISS on the cheek…to feel his rough old face…to smell the ocean on him… to feel his arm around my neck. I wish I had been a man then. If I had been a man, I would never have told my dad I was too old for a goodbye kiss."

爸爸的吻

董事会议已经结束了。鲍勃站起身时,碰了一下桌子,将咖啡溅到了他的笔记上。"真尴尬! 我老了,笨手笨脚的。"

每个人都大笑起来。过了一会儿,我们都讲起了自己最尴尬的时刻。弗兰克静静地听着别人的故事。有人说道:"快点儿,弗兰克,给我们说说你最尴尬的时刻。"

弗兰克笑了笑,开始给我们讲起了他的童年。"我在桑河边长大。爸爸是个渔民,他热爱大海。尽管他有自己的船,但很难在海上谋生。他拼命干活,每次出海捕到的鱼够家人吃才回来。他不仅要养活我们家,还要养活他的爸爸妈妈和家里其他的孩子们。"

他看了看我们,又说道:"我真希望你们能见一见我爸爸。他个子很高,因为捕鱼要拉网和跟大海搏斗,所以他的身体很壮。你走近他,就会闻到他有一股海的气味。他总是穿着又旧又脏的帆布外套和有围兜的罩衫。他的雨帽总是拉得很低,盖住眉毛。无论我妈妈洗多少遍,这些衣服还是有一股海水和鱼腥味。"

弗兰克的声音放低了点:"天气不好时,他就会开车送我上学。他用这辆旧卡车运送鱼。卡车比他的年龄还大,走在路上总是呼哧呼哧、嘎吱嘎吱响。隔几个街区你都能听到卡车驶来的声音。他每次送我上学时,我总是缩着身子坐在车座上,希望自己消失。

"通常,他都会砰地关上车门停下来,旧卡车总是喷出一股浓烟。他总是正好把车停在校门前,随后仿佛每个人都围站在那里目不转睛地看着。接着,他总是弯下腰,在我的脸颊上狠狠地亲一下,告诉我要做一个好孩子。这真让我难堪。嗨,我那时已经12岁了,爸爸总是弯下腰跟我吻别!"

他停了一下，又接着说道："我现在还记得我做出年龄太大不再吻别那个决定的那天的情景。我们到达学校停下时，他像往常一样面带灿烂的笑容，开始向我弯下腰，但我举起手说：'不，爸爸。'

"那是我第一次那样跟他说话，他脸上露出了吃惊的神情。

"我说：'爸爸，我太大了，不要再吻别了。我太大了，什么吻都不要了。'

"爸爸久久地看着我，眼睛开始流泪。我从来没有见他哭过。他转过身，透过挡门玻璃望着外面说：'你说得对，你是个大男孩，是个男子汉了。我不会再吻了。'"

弗兰克的脸上出现了奇异的表情，随后就泪如泉涌。"不久以后，爸爸出海，再也没有回来。那天，除了我爸爸，其他大多数渔船都没有出海。他有一大家人要养活啊。人们发现他的船漂浮在海面上，渔网一半在里一半在外，他肯定是遇到了大风。"

我望着弗兰克，发现泪水顺着他的脸颊滚滚而下。他接着又说道："朋友们，你们不知道我多么希望爸爸能再吻一下我的脸颊……多么希望触摸他粗糙的老脸……多么希望闻他身上的大海气味……多么希望感受他抱着我脖子的手臂。我多么希望自己当时是个男子汉。如果真是一个男子汉，我就绝不会告诉爸爸：我太大了，不要再吻别了。"

My Father's Crocus

It was an autumn morning shortly after my husband and I moved into our first house. Our children were upstairs unpacking, and I was looking out the window at my father moving around mysteriously on the front lawn. My parents lived nearby, and Dad visited us several times already. "What are you doing out there?" I called him.

He looked up, smiling. "I'm making you a surprise." Knowing my father, I thought it could be just about anything. A self-employed jobber, he was always building things out of odds and ends. When we were kids, he once rigged up a jungle gym out of wheels and pulleys. For one of my Halloween parties, he created an electrical pumpkin and mounted it on a broomstick. As guests came to our door, he would light the pumpkin and have it pop out in front of them from a hiding place in the bushes.

Today, however, Dad would say no more, and, caught up in the busyness of our new life, I finally forgot about his surprise.

Until one raw day the following March when I glanced out the windows. Dismal. Overcast. Little piles of dirty snow still stubbornly littered the lawn. Would winter ever end?

Yet was it a miracle? I strained to see what I thought was something pink, miraculously peeking out of drift, and was that a dot of blue across the yard, a small note of optimism in this gloomy sky? I grabbled my coat and headed outside for a closer look.

They were crocuses, scattered oddly throughout the front lawn. Lavender, blue, yellow and my favorite pink—little faces bobbing in the bitter wind.

Dad, I smiled, remembering the bulbs he had secretly planted last autumn. He knew that the darkness and dreariness of winter always got me down. What could have been more perfectly timed, more attuned to my needs? How blessed I was, not only for the flowers but also for him.

My father's crocuses bloomed each spring for the next four or five seasons, bringing that same assurance: Hold on, keep going, light is coming soon.

Then a spring came with only half the usual blooms. The next spring there were none. I missed crocuses, but my life was busier than ever, and I had never been much of a gardener. I would ask Dad to come over and plant new bulbs, but I never did.

He died suddenly one October day. My family grieved deeply, leaning on our faith. I missed him terribly, though I knew he would always be a part of us.

Four years passed, and on a dismal spring afternoon I was running errands and found myself feeling depressed. You've got the winter blahs again, I told myself. You get them every year.

It was Dad's birthday, and I found myself thinking about him. This was not unusual—my family often talked about him, remembering how he lived his faith. But now, in the car, I couldn't help wondering, How is he now? Where is he? Is there really a heaven?

I felt guilty for having doubts, but sometimes, I thought as I turned into our driveway, faith is so hard.

Suddenly I slowed, stopped and stared at the lawn. Muddy grass and small gray mounds of melting snow. There, bravely waving in the wind, was one pink crocus. How could a flower bloom from a bulb more than 18 years old; one that hadn't blossomed in over a decade? But there was the crocus. Tears filled my eyes as I realized its significance.

Hold on, keep going, light is coming soon. The pink crocus bloomed for only a day, but it built my faith for a lifetime.

父亲的藏红花

那是我和丈夫搬进我们的第一座房子不久后的一个秋天的早晨。我们的孩子们正在楼上打开包裹取东西。我眺望窗外，看到父亲神秘地在前草坪上走来走去。父母亲住在附近,爸爸已经来看过我们好几次了。"你在外面做什么?"我向他喊道。

他抬起头,面带微笑。"我要给你一个意外的惊喜。"我了解父亲,我想这里可能又有什么名堂。他是一名个体户,总是用零碎东西做这做那。我们小时候,他有一次曾用车轮和滑轮做了个儿童攀缘游戏立体支架。他为我的一次万圣节前夕宴会做了一只电南瓜,将它放在一把扫帚上。当客人们来到我们的门口时,他就点燃南瓜,让它从灌木丛的隐藏处蹦到他们面前"噗"的一声爆炸。

然而,父亲现在不再说什么了;而且,我对我们忙碌的新生活很感兴趣,所以就忘记了他说的让我惊喜的事儿。

直到第二年三月的一个阴天,我向窗外望去之时,黯淡、阴沉,一小堆一小堆的脏雪仍顽固不化地堆在草坪上。冬天会结束吗?

然而,它会出现奇迹吗?我睁大眼睛看着那个我认为是粉红色的东西,正好奇地从雪堆里探出。是一丝惆怅掠过庭院,还是一个小小的欢快的音符飘过阴霾的天空?我飞快地抓起大衣,跑出门外,想靠近看个究竟。

它们是藏红花,奇异地散开在前草坪。有淡紫色、蓝色、黄色和我最喜欢的粉红色——可爱的小脸在寒风中摇来晃去。

爸爸,我微笑着,回忆起他去年秋天暗地里种的那些球茎。他知道黯淡沉闷的冬天总是让我感到沮丧。还有什么能来得这样及时、这样迎合我的需要呢?我是多么幸福,不仅是为了那些花,也是为了他。

父亲的藏红花每年春天都开放,连续四五年都是这样。每次开放时总是给我们带来同一个信念:坚持不懈,继续努力,光明即将来临。

后来有一年春天,花只开了平常的一半。第二年春天,一朵也没开。尽管我想念藏红花,但我的生活比先前更忙,而且我压根就不是个好园丁。我常常想请爸爸过来栽新的球茎,但我从来没那样做过。

有一年10月的一天,爸爸突然去世。家人都悲痛万分,依靠着我们共同的信念坚持。我非常想念他,尽管我知道他总是和我们在一起。

转眼4年过去了。后来,在一个阴沉的春天的下午,我出差在外,发现自己非常沮丧。我对自己说,你又染上冬天的单调乏味了。你每年都要染上。

那天是爸爸的生日,我发现自己又想起了他。这并非什么不同寻常的事——家人常常谈起他,回忆起他是怎样依靠信念活着。但现在,待在车里,我情不自禁地想,他现在怎么样啊?他在哪里?真的有天堂吗?

尽管我对自己有这样的怀疑感到内疚，但有时我开进我们家的车道时就想，信念是这样难啊。

突然，我放慢车速，停下来，直盯盯地望着草坪。映入眼帘的是泥泞的草地和一小堆一小堆正在融化的灰色的积雪。只见那里，有一支顽强地迎风摇曳的粉红色的藏红花。一朵花怎么能从一个球茎上开放18年多啊；而且是一支在10年多时间里没有开放的花？但正是那支藏红花。我认识到它的意义时，泪水满眶。

坚持不懈，继续努力，光明即将来临。粉红色的藏红花只开放了一天，但它却建立了我终生的信念。

The Confession from a Father

Listen, son! I am saying this as you lie asleep, one little paw crumpled under your cheek and the blond curls stickily wet on your damp forehead. I have stolen into your room alone. Just a few minutes ago, as I sat reading my paper in the library, a hot, stifling wave of remorse swept over me. I couldn't resist it. Guiltily I came to your bedside.

These were the things I was thinking, son: I had been cross to you. I scolded you as you were dressing for school because you gave your face merely a dab with a towel. I took you to task for not cleaning your shoes. I called out angrily when I found you had thrown some of your things on the floor.

At breakfast, I found fault, too. You spilled things. You gulped down your food. You put your elbows on the table. You spread butter too thick on your bread. And as you started off to play and I made for my train, you turned and waved a little hand and called, "Good-bye, Papa!" and I frowned and said in reply, "Hold your shoulders back!"

Then it began all over again in the late afternoon. As I came up the road, I spied you, down on your knees, playing marbles. There were holes in your stocking. I humiliated you before your boy friends, by march on ahead of me, back to the house. Stockings were expensive—and if you had to buy them you would be more careful. Imagine that, son, from a father! It was such a stupid, silly logic.

But do you remember, later, when I was reading in the library, how you came in timidly, with a sort of hurt look in your eyes? When I glanced up over my paper, impatient at the interruption, you hesitated at the door.

"What is it you want?" I snapped.

You said nothing, but ran across the room, and threw your arms around my neck and kissed me, and your small arms tightened with an affection that God had set blooming in your heart and which even neglect couldn't wither. And then you were gone, puttering up the stairs.

Well, son, it was shortly afterwards that my paper slipped from my hands and a terrible fear came over me. Suddenly I saw myself as I really was, in all my horrid selfishness, and I felt sick at heart.

What had habit been doing to me? The habit of complaining, of finding fault, of reprimanding—all these were my rewards to you for being a boy. It was not that I didn't love you; it was that I expected too much of youth. I was measuring you by the yardstick of my own years.

And there is so much that was good, and fine, and true in your character. You didn't deserve my treatment of you, son. The little heart of you was as big as the dawn itself, over wide hills. All this was shown by your spontaneous impulse to rush in and kiss me goodnight. Nothing else matters, tonight, son. I have come to your bedside in the darkness, and I have knelt here, choking with emotion and so ashamed!

It is a feeble atonement. I know you wouldn't understand these things if I told them to you during your waking hours. Yet I must say what I am saying. I must burn sacrificial fires, alone, here in your own bedroom, and make free confession.

Tomorrow I will be a real daddy! I will chum with you and suffer when you suffer and laugh when you laugh. I will bite my tongue when impatient words come. I will keep saying, as if it were a ritual: "He is nothing but a boy—a little boy!"

I am afraid I have visualized you as a man. Yet as I see you now, son, crumpled and weary in your cot, I see that you are still a baby. Yesterday you were in your mother's arms, your head on her shoulder. I have asked too much, too much.

Dear boy! Dear little son! I kiss the little fingers, and the damp forehead, and the golden curls, and, if it were not for waking you, I would snatch you up and crush you to my breast.

Tears came and heartache and remorse and, I think, a greater, deeper love, when you ran through the library door and wanted to kiss me!

一位父亲的忏悔

听着，儿子，我要说这事儿时，你躺在那里睡觉，一只小手弯在脸颊下面，金色的鬈发湿漉漉地粘在汗津津的前额上。我独自悄悄走进你的房间。就在几分钟前，我坐在书房看报时，一阵强烈的懊悔涌遍了我的全身，使我喘不过气来。我情不自禁，怀着内疚来到了你的床边。

儿子，我之所以在想这些事儿，是因为我以前总生你的气；你穿衣服准备上学时，我大声斥责你，因为你洗脸时只用毛巾抹一下脸；我责备你，因为你没有擦净鞋；发现你把自己的一些东西扔在地板上，我总是生气地对你大叫。

早饭时，我也找碴儿。你把东西撒到了外面。你吃东西狼吞虎咽。你把胳膊肘放在了桌子上。你在面包上抹的黄油太厚。你跑出去玩，我赶火车上班，你转过头挥挥小手，喊道："爸爸，再见！"我皱了皱眉，回答说："挺起胸！"

傍晚时也一样。我走上那条路时，看见你跪在地上打弹子，你的长袜上有几个窟窿。我当着小伙伴们的面叫你出丑，让你走在我前面回家。长袜很贵——如果你自己挣钱去买，你一定会更加小心的。儿子，想想吧，父亲居然说这样的话！这是多么愚蠢的逻辑！

可是，你记得后来我在书房里看报纸时，你羞怯地走进来，眼里流露出受伤的神情的样子？我从报纸上抬起目光，对你打断我看报而不耐烦，你犹豫地站在门口。

"你想要什么？"我厉声问。

你一声不吭，但你跑过房间，搂住我的脖子，吻我，你的小手臂用爱紧紧抱住我，这是上帝让你在心里绽开的爱，即使受到冷落，也不会凋谢。随后，你就咚咚爬上楼梯，走了。

嗨，儿子，没过多久，报纸从我的手里滑落，一种可怕的恐惧袭遍了我的全身。我突然看到了真正的自己，明白了自己所有可怕的自私自利，感到心如刀绞。

恶习把我弄成了什么样子了啊？我动不动就发牢骚、找碴儿、训斥你——所有这些都是我给予你的奖赏，你还是个孩子啊。并不是我不爱你，而是我对年轻人要求太过分。我是用自己年龄的标准来衡量你。

你的性格中有那么多优良、美好、真实的品质。儿子，你不该受到我这种对待。你幼小的心灵像照亮群山的曙光一样博大。这一切表现在你情不自禁地跑进来吻我道晚安的行动上。儿子，今晚，其他一切都无关紧要。我摸黑已经来到你的床边，跪在这里，羞愧难当，强烈的感情使我说不出话来！

这是一种无力的赎罪。我知道，在你醒着时，如果我对你说这些话，你是不会明白的。然而，我必须把要说的话说出来。我必须燃起献祭之火，独自在你的房间里真诚地忏悔。

明天我会是一个真正的爸爸！我要和你成为好朋友，和你一起哭一起笑。当不耐烦的话要说出口时，我要咬住舌头。我要像举行仪式那样不断地说:"他只不过是一个孩子———一个小孩子!"

我想我已经把你想象成了男子汉。可是,儿子,当我看到你现在扭弯着疲惫地躺在小床上时,我发现你还是一个娃娃。昨天,你躺在妈妈的怀里,头靠在她的肩上。我要求你太多了、太多了。

亲爱的孩子!亲爱的小儿子!我亲吻你小小的手指、潮湿的额头和金黄色的鬈发。如果不是怕惊醒你,我会一把将你抱起,紧紧地搂在怀里。

我流泪,我心痛,我悔恨。我想,你跑过书房想吻我时,你的爱更伟大、更深厚!

Penance after 50 Years

It is in a little bookshop in the city of Lichfield, England. The floor has just been swept and the shutter taken down from the one small window. The hour is early, and customers have not yet begun to drop in. Out of doors the rain is falling.

At a small table near the door, a feeble, white-haired old man is making up some packages of books. As he arranges them in a large basket, he stops now and then as though disturbed by pain. He puts his hand to his side; he coughs in a most distressing way; then he sits down and rests himself, leaning his elbows upon the table.

"Samuel!" he calls.

In the farther corner of the room there is a young man busily reading from a large book that is spread open before him. His eyesight must be poor, for, as he reads, he bends down until his face is quite near the printed page.

"Samuel!" again the old man calls.

But Samuel makes no reply. He is so deeply interested in his book that he doesn't hear. The old man rests himself a little longer and then finishes tying his packages.

He lifts the heavy basket and sets it on the table. The exertion brings on another fit of coughing; and when it is over he calls for the third time, "Samuel!"

"What is it, father?" This time the call is heard.

"You know, Samuel," he says, "that tomorrow is market day at Uttoxeter, and our stall must be attended to. Some of our friends will be there to look at the new books they expect me to bring. One of us must go down on the stage this morning and get everything in readiness. But I hardly feel able for the journey. My cough troubles me quite a little, and you see that it is raining very hard."

"Yes, father; I am sorry," answers Samuel; and his face is again bent over the book.

"Samuel, will you not go down to the market for me this time?"

The old man is putting on his great coat.

He is reaching for his hat.

The basket is on his arm.

He casts a beseeching glance at his son, hoping that he will relent at the last moment.

"Here comes the coach, Samuel," and the old man is choked by another fit of coughing.

Samuel is still reading, and he makes no sign nor motion.

The stage comes rattling down the street.

The old man with his basket of books staggers out of the door. The stage halts for a moment while he climbs inside. Then the driver swings his whip, and all are away.

Samuel, in the shop, still bends over his book.

Out of doors the rain is falling.

Just fifty years have passed, and again it is market day at Uttoxeter.

The rain is falling in the streets. The people who have wares to sell huddle under the eaves and in the stalls and booths that have roofs above them.

A chaise from Lichfield pulls up at the entrance to the market square.

An old man alights. One would guess him to be seventy years of age. He is large and not well-shaped. His face is seamed and scarred, and he makes strange grimaces as he clambers out of the chaise. He wheezes and puffs as though afflicted with asthma. He walks with the aid of a heavy stick.

With slow but ponderous strides he enters the market place and looks around. He seems not to know that the rain is falling.

He looks at the little stalls ranged along the walls of the market place. Some have roofs over them and are the centers of noisy trade. Others have fallen into disuse and are empty.

The stranger halts before one of the latter. "Yes, this is it," he says. "I remember it well. It was here that my father, on certain market days, sold books to the clergy of the county. The good men came from every parish to see his wares and to hear him describe their contents."

He turns abruptly around. "Yes, this is the place," he repeats.

He stands quite still and upright, directly in front of the little old stall. He takes off his hat and holds it beneath his arm. His great walking stick has fallen into the gutter. He bows his head and clasps his hands. He doesn't seem to know that the rain is falling.

The clock in the tower above the market strikes eleven. The passers-by stop and gaze at the stranger. The market people peer at him from their booths and stalls. Some laugh as the rain runs in streams down his scarred old cheeks. Rain is it? Or can it be tears?

Boys hoot at him. Some of the ruder ones even hint at throwing mud; but a sense of shame withholds them from the act.

"He is a poor lunatic. Let him alone," says the more compassionate.

The rain falls upon his bare head and his broad shoulders. He is drenched and chilled. But he stands motionless and silent, looking neither to the right nor to the left.

"Who is that old fool?" asks a thoughtless young man who chances to be passing.

"Do you ask who he is?" answers a gentleman from London. "Why, he is Dr. Samuel Johnson, the most famous man in England. It was he who made the great English Dictionary, the most wonderful book of our times. He is the literary lion of England."

"Then why does he come to Uttoxeter and stand thus in the pouring rain?"

"I cannot tell you; but doubtless he has reasons for doing so," and the gentleman passes on.

At length there is a lull in the storm. The birds are chirping among the housetops.

The clock in the tower above the market strikes twelve. The renowned stranger has stood a whole hour motionless in the market place. And again the rain is falling.

Slowly now he returns his hat to his head. He finds his walking stick where it had fallen. He lifts his eyes reverently for a moment, and then, with a lordly, lumbering motion, walks down the street to meet the chaise which is ready to return to Lichfield.

We follow him through the pattering rain to his native town.

"Why, Dr. Johnson!" exclaims his hostess. "We have missed you all day. And you are so wet and chilled! Where have you been?"

"Madam," says the great man, "fifty years ago, this very day, I tacitly refused to oblige or obey my father. The thought of the pain which I must have caused him has haunted me ever since. To do away the sin of that hour, I this morning went in a chaise to Uttoxeter and did do penance publicly before the stall which my father had formerly used."

The great man bows his head upon his hands and sobs.

Out of doors the rain is falling.

50年后的忏悔

这件事发生在英国利奇菲尔德市的一家小书店里。地板刚擦过，百叶窗已从一扇小窗上取下来。时间还早，顾客还没开始进来。门外正下着雨。

在靠近门口的一张小桌子边，一个瘦弱的白发老人正在打点几包书。他在往一个大篮子里装这几包书时,不时停下来,好像因疼痛而焦虑。他将一只手放在身体一侧,非常痛苦地咳嗽着,随后双肘支在桌上,坐下来休息。

"塞缪尔!"他喊道。

在房间远处的角落里,有一个年轻人正在忙着看面前打开的一本大书。他的视力一定很差,因为他看书时弯下腰,脸离书页相当近。

"塞缪尔!"老人又喊道。

可是,塞缪尔没有回答。他正看得津津有味,所以没有听到。老人休息了一会儿,然后打好了包裹。

他提起沉重的篮子,放在桌子上。因为用力,他又咳嗽了一阵;之后,他第三次喊道:"塞缪尔!"

"父亲,什么事?"这次他听见了喊声。

"塞缪尔,你知道,"他说,"明天是尤托克西特集市日,我们的书摊必须有人照看。我们的一些朋友会到那儿去看他们希望我带去的新书。我们俩今天早晨必须有一个乘公共马车去那里,把一切准备停当。可是,我觉得不能去那里了。我咳嗽得很厉害。再说,你看,雨下得很大。"

"是的,父亲,对不起。"塞缪尔答道;随后,他的脸又俯向了那本书。

"塞缪尔,你这次不愿替我到集上去吗?"

老人在穿着大衣。

他伸手去拿帽子。

篮子挎在了胳膊上。

他向儿子投去恳求的目光,希望儿子在最后一刻会发发慈悲。

"马车来了,塞缪尔。"老人又咳嗽得喘不过气来。

塞缪尔仍在看书,既没表示,又没行动。

马车沿街咔嗒咔嗒过来了。

老人挎着书篮,蹒跚着走出了门。马车停了一会儿,老人爬进了马车。随后,赶车人挥动鞭子,车子走远了。

塞缪尔待在店里,仍然俯首看书。

门外正下着雨。

整整50年过去了,又到了尤托克西特集市日。

街上正下着雨。卖东西的人纷纷挤在屋檐下,挤在有顶棚的摊子和棚子里。

从利奇菲尔德来的一辆轻便两轮马车在市场入口停了下来。

一位老人下了车。人们会以为他有70岁了。他身材高大,样子并不好看,脸上有不少疤痕。他从车里出来时愁眉苦脸,让人感到奇怪。他呼哧呼哧地喘气,好像患有哮喘病。他拄一根粗手杖走着。

他步履缓慢而沉重地走进了市场,环顾四周。他仿佛不知道正在下雨。

他看着沿市场墙边摆的一些小货摊。有些摊子有顶棚,是热闹的买卖中心。其他一些则无人使用,空荡荡的。

这个陌生人在一个空摊子前站住。"对,就是这个,"他说,"我记得很清楚。在那些集市日里,我父亲就是在这里把书卖给这个郡的牧师的。那些好人从各个教区来看他的书,听他讲书里的内容。"

他突然转过身。"对,就是这地方。"他重复道。

他一动不动直挺挺地站在这个小小的旧摊子前。他脱下帽子,夹在腋下。他的大手杖已经掉到了路沟里。他低下头,紧握双手,似乎不知道正在下雨。

市场上方塔楼的钟敲了11下。过路的人停下来,注视着这个陌生人。集市上的人从他们的货摊里看着他。有些人看到雨水从他带有疤痕的老脸上滚滚流下,就笑出了声。是雨水?还是眼泪?

孩子们对他发出了嘲笑声。一些比较粗鲁无礼的孩子甚至示意向他扔泥块;可是,因为感到羞耻,他们就没有动手。

"他是个可怜的疯子,随他去吧。"比较有同情心的人说。

雨落在他的光头上和宽宽的肩膀上。他被雨淋透了,冷飕飕的。可是,他站在那里一动不动,一声不吭,也不左右张望。

"那个老傻瓜是谁?"一个轻率的年轻人碰巧路过这里时问道。

"你问他是谁?"一个从伦敦来的绅士回答说,"哎呀,他是塞缪尔·约翰逊博士,英国最著名的人。我们当代最伟大的大英语词典就是他编写的。他是英国的文学巨匠。"

"那他为什么来尤托克西特,这样站在倾盆大雨中?"

"我无法告诉你;但毫无疑问,他这样做是有原因的。"说完,这位绅士就继续赶路了。

最后,暴风雨暂时停息。鸟儿在屋顶上叽叽喳喳叫个不停。

市场塔楼的钟敲了12下。这位著名的陌生人在这集市上一动不动地站了整整一个小时。雨又下了起来。

这时,他慢慢地戴上帽子,找到了掉落的手杖。他谦恭地抬头看了一会儿，然后迈着气派而迟缓的步子沿街而行，迎向那辆准备返回利奇菲尔德的马车。

我们尾随他冒着哗哗大雨回到了他的故乡。

"哎呀，约翰逊博士！"女主人大声叫道，"我们整整一天都没见到你了。你都淋成了这个样子，冻坏了吧！你到哪里去了？"

"太太，"这个伟人说，"50年前，就是这一天，我默不作声拒绝给父亲帮忙，也没有听从他的吩咐。从那时起，我就一直想着自己给他造成的痛苦，这使我心神不安。为了结束那时的罪过，我今天早上乘马车去尤托克西特，在父亲从前用过的摊子前当众忏悔。"

这个伟人低下头，双手掩面，哭了起来。

门外正下着雨。

Love Is a Two-Way Street

A father sat at his desk poring over his monthly bills when his young son rushed in and announced, "Dad, because this is your birthday and you're 55 years old, I'm going to give you 55 kisses, one for each year!" When the boy started keeping his word, the father exclaimed, "Oh, Andrew, don't do it now; I'm too busy!"

The youngster immediately fell silent as tears welled up in his big blue eyes. Apologetically, the father said, "You can finish later." The boy said nothing but quietly walked away, disappointed. That evening the father said, "Come and finish the kisses now, Andrew!" But the boy didn't respond.

Unluckily, a few days later, the boy had an accident and was drowned. His heartbroken father wrote, "If only I could tell him how much I regret my thoughtless words, and could be assured that he knows how much my heart is aching."

Love is a two-way street. Any loving act must be warmly accepted or it will be taken as rejection and can leave a scar. If we are too busy to give and receive love, our life will lose its true significance. Nothing is more important than responding with love to the cry for love from those who are near and precious to us.

爱是一条双行道

一位父亲坐在书桌边全神贯注地看每月的账单，这时他的小儿子跑进来大声说道："爸爸，因为今天是你的生日，你55岁了，我要给你55个吻，一年一个！"当男孩准备兑现诺言时，他的父亲大声说道："噢，安德鲁，现在不行，我太忙了！"

小男孩马上静了下来,蓝蓝的大眼睛涌起了泪水。父亲抱歉地说:"你待会儿来吻吧。"男孩一声不吭,默默地走开了,感到非常失望。那天晚上,父亲说:"来吧,安德鲁,现在来吻吧!"但小男孩没有回答。

不幸的是,几天后,小男孩发生了意外,被淹死了。他的父亲伤心地写道:"如果我能告诉他,我是多么后悔自己那些有欠考虑的话,并能确信他知道我现在心里有多么痛苦,该多好啊!"

爱是一条双行道。任何爱的行为都必须热情接受,否则对方会以为你在拒绝而留下伤疤。如果我们太忙而不能给予和接受爱,那我们的生活就失去了真正的意义。对我们身边那些亲近和珍爱的人,用爱去回应他们爱的呼唤,比什么都重要。

I Hear the Love

When I was growing up, I didn't recall hearing the words "I love you" from my father. When your father never says them to you when you are a child, it gets tougher and tougher for him to say those words as he gets older. To tell the truth, I couldn't honestly remember when I had last said those words to him either. I decided to set my ego aside and make the first move. After some hesitation, in our next phone conversation, I blurted out the words, "Dad…I love you!"

There was a silence at the other end and he awkwardly replied, "Well, same back at you!"

I chuckled and said, "Dad, I know you love me, and when you are ready, I know you will say what you want to say."

Fifteen minutes later, my mother called and nervously asked, "Paul, is everything okay?"

A few weeks later, Dad concluded our phone conversation with the words, "Paul, I love you." I was at work during this conversation and the tears were rolling down my cheeks as I finally heard the love. As we both sat there in tears we realized that this special moment had taken our father-son relationship to a new level.

A short while after this special moment, my father narrowly escaped death following heart surgery. Many times since, I have pondered the thought if I didn't take the first step and Dad didn't survive the surgery, I would have never heard the love.

我听到了爱

我渐渐长大后,想不起来曾听到过爸爸说"我爱你"这三个字。你小时候,你爸爸从来不你不说"我爱你,"那随着他年纪越来越大,他会越来越难开口。说实话,我确实想不起上次我对爸爸说"我爱你"是什么时候了。我决定放下自我,主动表白。犹豫了一阵后,我在我们下一次通话时脱口说道:"爸爸……我爱你!"

电话那端沉默了一会儿后,他难为情地答道:"噢,对你也一样!"

我暗自笑道:"爸爸,我知道你爱我,等你准备好时,我知道你会说出你想说的话的。"

15分钟后,妈妈打来了电话,不安地问道:"保罗,一切正常吧?"

几周后,爸爸在通话结束时说:"保罗,我爱你。"通话时我正在上班,听到爱的声音,泪水顺着我的脸颊滑落下来。我们俩都坐在那里热泪盈眶,意识到这种特殊的时刻将我们的父子关系带到了一个新的水平。

在这个特殊时刻过后不久,爸爸做了心脏手术,勉强死里逃生。从那以后,我多次想到,如果我没有迈出第一步,爸爸的手术没有成功,那我就再也听不到爱的声音了。

Homework of Love

In a class I teach for adults, I recently did the "unpardonable." I gave the class homework! The assignment was to "go to someone you love within the next week and tell them you love them. It has to be someone you have never said those words to before or at least haven't shared those words with for a long time."

Now that doesn't sound like a very tough assignment, until you stop to realize that most of the men were over 35 and were raised in the generation of men that were taught that expressing emotions is not "macho." Showing feelings or crying was just not done. So this was a very threatening assignment for some.

At the beginning of our next class, I asked if someone wanted to share what happened when they told someone they loved them. I fully expected one of the women to volunteer, as was usually the case, but on this evening one of the men raised his hand. He appeared quite moved and a bit shaken.

As he unfolded out of his chair, he began by saying, "Dennis, I was quite angry with you last week when you gave us this assignment. I didn't feel that I had anyone to say those words to, and besides, who were you to tell me to do something that personal?"

"But as I began driving home my conscience started talking to me. It was telling me that I knew exactly who I needed to say I love you to.

"You see, five years ago, my father and I had a vicious disagreement and really never resolved it since that time. We avoided seeing each other unless we absolutely had to at Christmas or other family gatherings. But even then, we hardly spoke to each other.

"So last Tuesday by the time I got home I had convinced myself I was going to tell my father I loved him.

爱 的 作 业

我最近在教的一个成人班里做了一件"不可宽恕的事情",给班上学生布置了课外作业!作业是"下周内走到你所爱的人面前,告诉他们你爱他们。必须是以前你从未说过,或至少很久没和他们分享过这些话的人"。

听起来这不像是一份非常费力的作业,而你要认识到这个班里大多数男生已经超过了35岁,而且他们这一代受的教育是在表达情感时缺乏"阳刚之气"。人们不会太流露感情和哭泣。因此,对有些人来说,这是一项让人生畏的作业。

第二次上课时,我首先问:当他们告诉某个人他们爱他/她时,是否有想一同分享。我满以为像平常一样,某位女士会自告奋勇,但这天晚上,一位男士举起了手。他好像很受感动,有点儿颤抖。

他从椅子上直起身来,开始这样说道:"丹尼斯,上周你给我们布置这项作业时,我非常生你的气。我认为我没有什么人需要我说那些话,再说,你是谁,凭什么让我去做这种私事?

"但我驱车回家时,我的良心开始和我对话。它告诉我说,我确实知道需要向谁说'我爱你'。

"你明白,5年前,我和父亲发生了一场严重的争执,从那以后确实再也没有消除隔阂。除非必须参加圣诞节或其他家庭聚会,我们都互相回避。但即使在那时,我们彼此几乎也不说一句话。

"因此,上周二到家时,我终于说服自己准备告诉父亲说我爱他。"

Daddy's Advice

When I was about 12, I had an enemy, a girl who liked to point out my shortcomings. Week by week her list grew: I was very thin, I was not a good student, I talked too much, I was too proud, and so on. I tried to bear all this as long as I could. At last, I became very angry. I ran to Daddy with tears in my eyes.

He listened to me quietly. Then he asked, "Are the things she says true-or not?

Allen, didn't you ever wonder what you're really like? Well, you now have that girl's opinion. Go and make a list of everything she said and mark the points that are true. Pay no attention to the other things she said."

I did as he told me. To my great surprise, I discovered that about half the things were true. Some of them I couldn't change (like being very thin), but a good number I could—and suddenly I wanted to change. For the first time I got a fairly clear picture of myself.

I brought the list back to Daddy. He refused to take it. "That's just for you," he said. "You know better than anyone else the truth about yourself. But you have to learn to listen, not just closing your ears in anger and feeling hurt. When something said about you is true, you'll find it will be of help to you. Our world is full of people who think they know your duty. don't shut your ears. Listen to them all, but hear the truth and do what you know is the right thing to do."

Daddy's advice has returned to me at many important moments. In my life, I've never had a better piece of advice.

爸爸的忠告

大约12岁时,我有了一个对手,那是一个喜欢指出我缺点的女孩。随着一周周过去,她给我列的缺点越来越多:我很瘦,我不是好学生,我太爱说话,我太骄傲。我尽量长时间地忍受这些。最后,我变得非常生气,就眼含泪水跑去见爸爸。

爸爸静静地听我说。随后,他问道:"她说的这些是不是真的?爱琳,难道你不想知道自己的真实模样吗?那么,你现在有了那个女孩的意见。去把她所说的一切都列下来,在对的上面打分,对她所说的其他事情不要在意。"

我按照爸爸说的去做了。令我大为惊讶的是,我发现大约一半都是对的。其中有些我无法改变(比如很瘦),但好多我可以改变——而且突然我想改变。我第一次对自己有了一个相当清晰的印象。

我将这个清单送给了爸爸。他没有去接。"那只是送给你的,"他说,"你比任何人都更清楚自己真实的一面。但你必须学会去听,不要生气地闭上耳朵,感觉受到了伤害。当说到有关你的事情是对时,你会发现那会对你有帮助。我们的世界充满了自以为他们知道你的责任的人。不要闭上耳朵,要听他们所有的人的话,但要听真话,做你知道是正确的事情。"

爸爸的建议在很多重要的时刻都回到了我的耳边。在我的一生中,我从来没有听过比这更好的建议了。

My Father's Music

That day Dad gathered my mother and me in the living room and opened the case as if it were a treasure chest. "Here it is," he said. "Once you learn to play, it'll stay with you for life."

For the next two weeks, the accordion was stored in the hall closet. Then one evening Dad announced that I would start lessons the following week. In disbelief I shot my eyes toward Mom for support. The firm set of her jaw told me I was out of luck.

Shortly after, my lessons began with Mr. Zelli at the Allegro Accordion School, tucked between an old movie theatre and a pizza parlor. On my first day, with straps straining my shoulders, I felt clumsy in every way. "How did he do?" my father asked when it was over. "Fine for the first lesson," said Mr. Zelli. Dad glowed with hope.

I was ordered to practice half an hour every day, and every day I tried to get out of it. My future seemed to be outside playing ball, not in the house mastering songs I would soon forget. But my parents hounded me to practice.

Gradually, to my surprise, I was able to string notes together and coordinate my hands to play simple songs. Often, after supper, my father would request a tune or two. As he sat in his easy chair, I would fumble through "*Lady of Spain*" and "*Beer Barrel Polka*".

"Very nice, better than last week," he'd say. Then I would segue into a medley of his favorites, "*Red River Valley*" and "*Home on the Range*", and he would drift off to sleep, the newspaper folded on his lap. I took it as a compliment that he could relax under the spell of my playing.

One July evening I was giving an almost flawless rendition of "*Come Back to Sorrento*", and my parents called me to an open window. An elderly neighbor, rarely seen outside her house, was leaning against our car humming dreamily to the tune. When I finished, she smiled broadly and called out, "I remember that song as a child in Italy. Beautiful, just beautiful."

Throughout the summer, Mr. ZelII's lessons grew more difficult. It took me a week and a half to master them now. All the while I could hear my buddies outside playing heated games of stickball.

The fall recital was impending.

"I don't want to play a solo," I said in a car one Sunday afternoon.

"You have to," replied my father.

"Why?" I shouted. "Because you didn't get to play your violin when you were a kid? Why should I have to play this stupid instrument when you never had to play yours?"

Dad pulled the car over and pointed at me.

"Because you can bring people joy. You can touch their hearts. That's a gift I won't let you throw away." he added softly, "Someday you'll have the chance I never had: you'll play beautiful music for your family. And you'll understand why you've worked so hard."

The evening of the concert Mom wore glittery earrings and more makeup than I could remember. Dad got out of work early, put on a suit and tie, and slicked down his chair. They were ready an hour early. I got the unspoken message that playing this one song was a dream come true for them.

At the theater nervousness overtook me as I realized how much I wanted to make my parents proud. Finally, it was my turn. I walked to the lone chair on stage and performed *Are You Lonesome Tonight?* without a mistake. The applause spilled out.

After the concert Mom and Dad came backstage. The way they walked—heads high, faces flushed—I knew they were pleased. My mother gave me a big hug. Dad slipped an arm around me and held me close. "You were just great," he said. Then he shook my hand and was slow to let it go.

As the years went by, the accordion drifted to the background of my life. Dad asked me to play at family occasions, but the lessons stopped. When I went to college, the accordion stayed behind in the hall closet next to my father's violin.

A year after my graduation, my parents moved to a house in a nearby town. Dad, at 51, finally owned his own home. On moving day, I didn't have the heart to tell him he could dispose of the accordion, so I brought it my own home and put it in the attic.

There it remained, a dusty memory, until one afternoon several years later when my two children discovered it by accident. Scott thought it was a secret treasure; Holly thought a ghost lived inside. They were both right.

When I opened the case, they laughed and said, "Play it, play it." Reluctantly, I strapped on the accordion and played some simple songs. I was surprised my skills hadn't rusted away. Soon the kids were dancing in circles and giggling. Even my wife, Terri, was laughing and clapping to the beat. I was amazed at their unbridled glee.

My father's words came back to me: "Someday you'll have the chance I never had. Then you'll understand."

I finally knew what it meant to work hard and sacrifice for others. Dad had been right all along: the most precious gift is to touch the hearts of those you love.

Later I phoned Dad to let him know that, at long last, I understood. Fumbling for the right words, I thanked him for the legacy it took almost 30 years to discover. "You're welcome," he said, his voice choked with emotion.

Dad never learned to coax sweet sounds from his violin. Yet he was wrong to think he would never play for his family. On that wonderful evening, as my wife and children laughed and danced, they heard my accordion. But it was my father's music.

父亲的音乐

那天父亲把我和母亲叫到了客厅，打开了那个百宝箱似的盒子。"给，"他说，"一旦你学会弹奏，它就会伴随你的一生。"

接下来的两个星期，手风琴一直放在门厅的壁橱里。后来的一天晚上，父亲宣布我下星期开始学习手风琴课程。我将信将疑地把目光投向妈妈寻求支持。她坚定的下巴告诉我，我并不走运。

不久以后，我便跟着泽利先生在位于一家旧电影院和比萨馆之间的阿里格罗手风琴学校开始了学琴。上课的第一天，带子勒得我的肩膀紧绷绷的，处处使我感到笨笨的。"他做得怎么样？"上完课时，父亲问，"第一次上课，不错。"泽利先生神采奕奕、充满希望地说。

泽利先生要求我每天得练习半小时，而每天我都想竭力从中摆脱。我的未来似乎是在外面打球，而不是待在屋子里掌握我总是很快就会忘记的歌曲。但我的父母亲硬是逼着我去练习。

渐渐地，让我吃惊的是，我已经能将音符拉到一起，协调双手弹奏出简单的歌曲了。晚饭后，父亲总是时不时地要我拉一两首曲子。他坐在安乐椅里，我总是笨拙地拉《西班牙女郎》和《啤酒桶波尔卡》。

他总是说："非常不错，比上星期好。"随后，我会接着拉起他最喜欢的《红河谷》和《山上人家》的混合曲。之后，他总会慢慢地睡去，报纸叠放在他的膝间。我把这看成是一种赞美：他能在我拉手风琴时得以放松。

7月的一个傍晚，我正拉着几乎无可挑剔的《回到索伦托》，父母亲把我叫到了一个敞开的窗前。一位上了年纪、很少出门的邻居正靠在我们家的汽车上合着旋律如梦般哼唱着。我拉完后，她露出了灿烂的微笑，大声说道："我记得小时候是在意大利听的这首歌曲。真美妙，美妙极了。"

整整一个夏天，泽利先生的课变得越来越难了。我现在要花一个半星期才能掌握。与此同时，我总能听见外面我的小伙伴们在热火朝天地打棍球。

然而，秋季独奏会马上就要到了。

"我不想去演独奏曲。"一个星期天的下午，我在汽车里对父亲说。

"你必须去演奏。"父亲答道。

"为什么?"我嚷道,"就是因为你小时候没学会拉小提琴吗?你从来不必拉小提琴,我为什么必须拉这愚蠢的乐器?"

父亲停住车,指着我。

"因为你能给人们带来快乐,触动他们的心灵。那是我不愿意让你抛弃的天赋。"他轻轻地补充说,"终有一天,你会获得我从未抓住的机会:为你的家人演奏美妙的音乐。而且你会明白你曾如此努力的理由。"

独奏会那天晚上,母亲戴着亮闪闪的耳环,用的化妆品比我能记得的任何时候都多。父亲早早下班,穿上西装,打上领带,将头发梳得溜光水滑。他们提前一小时就准备停当。我感到此时无声胜有声:拉这首歌曲是实现他们的一次梦想。

一到剧院,我一想到我多想让父母亲骄傲,就感到一阵紧张。最后,终于该我上台了。我走向台上那张孤零零的椅子,分毫不差地演奏了《今晚你孤单吗》。全场爆发出了阵阵掌声。

独奏会后,爸妈来到了后台。一瞧他们走路的姿态——昂首阔步、红光满面——我就知道他们非常高兴。母亲紧紧地拥抱了我一下。父亲伸出一只胳膊抱住我,将我紧紧地搂住。"你真了不起。"他说,随后握住我的手久久不肯松开。

随着岁月流逝,那只手风琴渐渐退到了我生活的背后。每逢家庭聚会,父亲总是要让我拉几段,但不再上手风琴课了。我上大学时,那只手风琴退到了门厅壁橱里,与父亲的小提琴放在了一起。

我毕业一年后,父母亲搬到了附近城镇的一座房子里。51岁的父亲最后终于拥有了自己的家。搬家那天,我不忍心对他说,他可以处理掉那把手风琴,所以我把它带到了我自己的家里,放在了阁楼上。

那成了一段尘封的记忆,直到几年后的一天下午,我的两个孩子无意间发现了它。斯科特认为它是一笔秘密财宝,赫利想着里面住着一个幽灵。他们俩都猜对了。

我打开箱子时,他们都大笑着说:"拉一段,拉一段。"我勉强挎上手风琴,拉了一些简单的歌曲。让我吃惊的是,我的演技并没有荒废。很快,孩子们便围成圈翩翩起舞,咯咯直笑。就连我的妻子泰丽也随着节拍拍手大笑。我对他们无拘无束的欢快劲儿感到惊喜。

父亲的话语又回荡在我的耳边:"终有一天,你会获得我从未抓住的机会,以后你会明白的。"

我终于懂得了为他人做出努力和牺牲意味着什么。父亲一直都是对的：最珍贵的礼物是触动你所爱的那些人的心灵。

后来，我给父亲打电话说，我终于懂了。我字斟句酌感谢他让我花了差不多30年才发现的遗产。"别客气。"他说，他的声音因激动而哽咽。

父亲从未学会用小提琴奏出甜美的旋律。然而，他错误地认为他永远都不会为他的家人演奏曲子。在那个美妙的夜晚，当我的妻子和孩子们欢笑起舞时，她们听到了我拉的手风琴曲。不过，那是父亲的音乐。

The Unlighted Candle

A man had a little daughter—an only and much-loved child. He lived for her—she was his life. So when she became ill, he became like a man possessed, moving heaven and earth to bring about her restoration to health.

His best efforts, however, proved unavailing and the child died. The father became a bitter recluse, shutting himself away from his many friends and refusing every activity that might restore his poise and bring him back to his normal self. But one night he had a dream.

He was in Heaven, witnessing a grand pageant of all the little child angels. They were marching in a line passing by the Great White Throne. Every white-robed angelic child carried a candle. He noticed that one child's candle was not lighted. Then he saw that the child with the dark candle was his own little girl. Rushing to her, he seized her in his arms, caressed her tenderly, and then asked, "How is it, darling, that your candle alone is unlighted?" "Daddy, they often relight it, but your tears always put it out."

Just then he awoke from his dream. The lesson was crystal-clear, and its effects were immediate. From that hour on he was not a recluse, but mingled freely and cheerfully with his former friends and associates. No longer would his darling's candle be extinguished by his useless tears.

点不亮的蜡烛

一个男人有一个小女儿，那是唯一的孩子，他深深地爱着她，为她而活，她就是他的生命。所以，当女儿生病时，他像疯了一般竭尽全力想让她恢复健康。

然而，他所有的努力都无济于事，女儿还是死了。父亲变得痛苦遁世，避开了许多朋友，拒绝参加一切能使他恢复平静、回到自我的活动。但有一天夜里,他做了一个梦。

他到了天堂,看到所有的小天使正在举行盛大的游行。她们列队经过大白宝座,每一个小天使都身穿白色天使衣,手里拿着一根蜡烛。他注意到有一个小天使的蜡烛没有点亮。随后,他看到那个拿着没有点亮烛的小天使是自己的小儿。他奔过去,一把将女儿抱在怀里,亲切地爱抚着她,然后问道:"宝贝儿,为什么只有你的蜡烛没有点亮呢?""爸爸,他们经常重新点亮蜡烛,可你的眼泪总是把它熄灭。"

就在这时,他从梦中醒来。梦给他上的一课像水晶般透明,而且立竿见影。从那个时刻起,他再也不消极遁世了,而是自由自在、兴高采烈地回到了从前的朋友和同事们中间。宝贝女儿的蜡烛再也没有被他无用的眼泪熄灭过。

第七卷

相信爱就会有奇迹

Love Is Understanding

As a new bride, one woman moved into the small home on her husband's ranch in the mountains. She put a shoebox on a shelf in her closet and asked her husband never to touch it.

For 50 years he left the box alone until his life partner was old and dying. One day, when he was putting their things in order, he found the box again and thought it might hold something important. Opening it, he discovered two doilies and $82,500 in cash. He took the box to her and asked about the two things.

"My mother gave me that box the day we married," she explained. "She told me to make a doily to help ease myself every time I got angry at you."

Her husband was touched, for in 50 years she'd only been angry enough to make two doilies.

"What's the $82,500 for?" he asked.

She explained, "Oh, that's the money I've made selling the doilies."

Marge Piercy beautifully said, "Everyone will get three gifts in life. Life is the first gift, love is the second and understanding is the third." But it is love that gives us life and understanding that brings about love.

爱就是谅解

一位女人刚做新娘,搬到了丈夫位于山里的牧场。她将一只鞋盒放到了壁橱里的一个架子上,请丈夫千万不要动它。

50年来,他没有动过那只盒子,直到他的人生伴侣老态龙钟、奄奄一息。有一天,他在整理他们的东西时,又发现了那只盒子,想着那里面可能会装有一些重要东西。他打开盒子,发现有两块花边桌垫和82500美元现金。他把盒子拿到她跟前,问这些东西是怎么回事。

"那个盒子是咱们结婚那天母亲送给我的,"她解释说,"她让我每次生你的气时做一块花边桌垫来帮我消气。"她的丈夫很受感动,因为50年里她只做了两块花边桌垫。"这82500美元是做什么用的?"他又问道。她解释说,"噢,那是我卖花边桌垫赚的钱。"

玛奇·皮尔西说得好:"每个人一生都会收到三件礼物。生命是第一件礼物,爱是第二件礼物,谅解是第三件礼物。"而正是爱给了我们生命,正是谅解产生了爱。

Roses for Paradise

Red roses were her favorites, her name was also Rose. And every year her husband sent them, tied with pretty bows. The year he died, the roses were delivered to her door. The card said, "Be my Valentine," like all the years before.

Each year he sent her roses, and the note would always say, "I love you even more this year, than last year on this day." "My love for you will always grow, with every passing year." She knew this was the last time that the roses would appear. She thought, he ordered roses in advance before this day. Her loving husband didn't know, that he would pass away. He always liked to do things early. Then, if he got too busy, everything would work out fine. She trimmed the stems, and placed them in a very special vase. Then, sat the vase beside the portrait of his smiling face. She would sit for hours, in her husband's favorite chair, staring at his picture with the roses sitting there.

A year went by, and it was hard to live without her mate. With loneliness and solitude, that had become her fate. Then, the very hour, as on Valentines before, the doorbell rang, and there were roses, sitting by her door. She brought the roses in, and then just looked at them in shock. Then, she went to get the telephone, to call the florist shop. The owner answered, and she asked him, if he would explain why would someone do this to her, causing her such pain.

"I know your husband passed away, more than a year ago," The owner said, "I knew you'd call, and you would want to know. The flowers you received today were paid for in advance. Your husband always planned ahead, he left nothing to chance.

"There is a standing order that I have on file down here. And he has paid, well in advance, you'll get them every year. There also is another thing that I think you should know. He wrote a special little card…he did this years ago.

"Then, should ever, I find out that he's no longer here. That's the card…that should be sent, to you the following year."

She thanked him and hung up the phone, her tears now flowing hard. Her fingers were shaking as she slowly reached to get the card. Inside the card, she saw that he had written her a note. As she stared in total silence, this was what he wrote: "Hello my love, I know it's been a year since I've been gone. I hope it hasn't been too hard for you to overcome. I know it must be lonely, and the pain is very real. For if it was the other way, I know how I would feel. The love we shared made everything so beautiful in life. I loved you more than words can say. You were the perfect wife.

"You were my friend and lover. You fulfilled my every need. I know it's only been a year, but please try not to grieve. I want you to be happy, even when you shed your tears. That is why the roses will be sent to you for years.

"When you get these roses, think of all the happiness that we had together, and how both of us were blessed. I have always loved you and I know I always will. But, my love, you must go on, you have some living still.

"Please…try to find happiness, while living out your days. I know it is not easy, but I hope you find some ways. The roses will come every year, and they will only stop when your door's not answered, when the florist stops to knock.

"He will come five times that day, in case you have gone out. But after his last visit, he will know without a doubt. To take the roses to the place where I've instructed him, and place them where we are, together once again."

天堂玫瑰

红玫瑰是她的最爱，她的名字也叫Rose。每年她的丈夫都要送她系有漂亮蝴蝶结的红玫瑰。他去世那年，玫瑰花送到了她的门口，卡片上像往年那样写着："做我的爱人吧。"

每年他送给她红玫瑰，字条上总是这样说："今年我更爱你，比去年的今天更爱。""随着岁月的流逝，我对你的爱总是与日俱增。"她知道这是她最后一次收到玫瑰花。她想，他是提前订了玫瑰花。她亲爱的丈夫不知道，他将离去。他总喜欢提前做事。这样，如果他太忙，一切都会搞定。她整理好花茎，然后把它们插进一只非常特别的花瓶里，然后将花瓶放在了他微微含笑的相片旁边。她常常在丈夫最喜欢的椅子上坐上几个小时，望着他的相片，玫瑰花就放在那里。

一年过去了，没有他的日子很难过。孤独和寂寞成了她的生活。随后，在情人节这天那个非常时刻，门铃像以前一样响了起来，她的门边放着玫瑰花。她将玫瑰花拿进屋里，然后就那样震惊地看着它们。接下来，她走到电话边，给花店打去了电话。她问店主能否向她解释一下，为什么有人要这样做，引起她如此的痛苦。

"我知道你的丈夫一年多前就去世了，"店主说，"我就知道你会打电话，而且你想知道是怎么回事。今天你收到的那些鲜花已经提前付了钱。你的丈夫总是提前计划，从来不去碰运气。

"我的档案里有一个长期订单，他早已提前付了钱，你每年都会收到玫瑰花。还有一件事，我想你应该知道。他写了一张特别的小卡片……是他几年前就写好的。

"这样，如果我发现他已不在人世，这张卡片……这张卡片将会在下一年送给你。"

她向他表示感谢,就挂了电话,此时她泪如泉涌。她一边慢慢伸手去拿卡片,手指一边在颤抖。他在卡片里看到了他写给她的短信。她默默地看着,信是这样写的:"喂,我的宝贝,我知道我离去已经一年了,我希望你度过的这段日子不是太难。我知道这段日子肯定很孤独,而且确实非常痛苦。因为如果这种事发生在我身上,我知道我会有怎样的感受。我们曾经分享的爱使生命中的每件事都是那样美好。我对你的爱难以言表,你是最完美的妻子。

"你是我的朋友和爱人,你满足我的每个需要。我知道才过了一年,请尽量不要悲伤。我想让你快乐,即使你流着泪。这就是今后的岁月每年都会给你送玫瑰的原因。

"你收到这些玫瑰花时,想一想我们一起度过的所有幸福时光,还有我们俩是何等幸福。我一直爱着你,我知道我永远爱你。可是,亲爱的,你必须继续下去,你还有一些时日。

"请……在你的生活中努力找到欢乐,我知道并不容易,但我希望你能找到一些方法。玫瑰花每年都会送来,只有花店店主停下来去敲门,你不再开门,它们才会停止。

"这天他会来5次,以防你出门。你是不是还在,他最后一次拜访就会明白。他会将那些玫瑰花送到我指定的地方,并将它们放在我们再次相聚的地方。"

The Unopened CD

There was once a kid who suffered from an incurable cancer. He was 18 years old and he could die anytime.

One day he was walking down his block when he noticed a beautiful girl about his age in a CD store and he knew it was love at first sight. He opened the door and walked in, not looking at anything else but her.

She looked up and asked, "Can I help you?"

She smiled and he thought it was the most beautiful smile he has ever seen before.

He said, "Uh…Yeah…I would like to buy a CD."

He picked one out and gave her money for it.

"Would you like me to wrap it for you?" she asked, smiling her cute smile again.

He nodded and she went to the back. She came back with the wrapped CD and gave it to him.

From then on he went to that store every day and bought a CD, and she wrapped it for him. He took the CD home and put it in his closet. He was still too shy to ask her out and he really wanted to but he couldn't.

His mother found out about this and told him to just ask her. So the next day, he took all his courage and went to the store as usual. He bought a CD like he did every day and once again she went to the back of the store and came back with it wrapped. He took it and when she was not looking, he left his phone number on the desk and ran out.

One day the phone rang, and the mother picked it up and said, "Hello?"

It was the girl! The mother started to cry and said, "You don't know? He passed away yesterday…"

The line was quiet except for the cries of the boy's mother. Later in the day, the mother was surprised to find piles and piles of unopened CDs in the boy's closet and inside the wrappers, she found a piece of paper saying, "Hi…I think you are really cute. Do you wanna go out with me? Love, Jocelyn."

没有打开的CD

有一个少年患了无法医治的癌症。他才18岁，随时都可能会死去。

一天，他正沿着街区走，突然注意到一家CD店里有一个漂亮的同龄女孩，他知道他对她是一见钟情。他打开门，走了进去，始终望着她一个人。

女孩抬起头，问道："你想要买什么？"

她微微一笑，他认为这是他以前从未见过的最美丽的微笑。

他说："呃……是的……我想买一张CD。"

他选了一张CD，然后向她付了钱。

"你想让我为你包起来吗？"她又露出可爱的微笑问道。

他点点头，她走到后台。她出来时，手里拿着包装好的CD，递给了他。

从那以后，他每天都会去那家CD店买一张CD，她每次都为他包好。他把CD带回家，将它放进自己的壁橱。他仍然太害羞，不敢请她出来，他真的很想这样做，却又不能。

他的母亲发现了他这个秘密，告诉他去请她就行了。于是，第二天，他鼓足勇气，像往常一样走进了那家CD店，他像每天所做的那样买了一张CD。她再一次到后台，为他包装好交给他。他接过CD，趁她不注意时，他把自己的电话号码留在柜台上，跑了出去。

一天，电话铃响了，母亲拿起电话，说："喂？"

正是那个女孩！母亲开始哭了起来，她说："你不知道吗？他昨天走了……"

电话线那端沉默了，只听到男孩母亲的哭声。那天晚些时候，男孩母亲吃惊地发现儿子的壁橱里有一大堆一大堆没有打开的CD，在这些包装纸里，她发现了一张纸，上面写道："嗨……我想你确实可爱。你想和我一起出去吗？爱你的乔斯林。"

A Gift of Light

The passengers on the bus watched sympathetically as the attractive young woman with the white cane made her way carefully up the steps. She paid the driver, and using her hands to feel the location of the seats, walked down the aisle and found the seat he'd told her was empty. Then she settled in, placed her briefcase on her lap and rested her cane against her leg.

It had been a year since Susan, thirty-four, became blind. Due to a medical misdiagnosis she had been rendered sightless, and she was suddenly thrown into a world of darkness, anger, frustration and self-pity.

Once a fiercely independent woman, Susan now felt condemned by this terrible twist of fate to become a powerless, helpless burden on everyone around her. "How could this have happened to me?" But no matter how much she cried or ranted or prayed, she knew the painful truth—her sight was never going to return.

A cloud of depression hung over Susan. Just getting through each day was an exercise in frustration and exhaustion. And all she had to cling to was her husband Mark.

Mark was an Air Force officer and he loved Susan with all his heart. When she first lost her sight, he watched her sink into despair and was determined to help his wife gain the strength and confidence. Mark's military background had trained him well to deal with sensitive situations, and yet he knew this was the most difficult battle he would ever face.

Finally, Susan felt ready to return to her job, but how would she get there? She used to take the bus, but was now too frightened to get around the city by herself. Mark volunteered to drive her to work each day, even though they worked at opposite ends of the city. At first, this comforted Susan and fulfilled Mark's need to protect his sightless wife.

Soon, however, Mark realized that this arrangement was not working—it was hectic, and costly. Susan is going to have to start taking the bus again, he admitted to himself. But just the thought of mentioning it to her made him cringe. She was still so fragile. How would she react?

Just as Mark predicted, Susan was horrified at the idea of taking the bus again. "I'm blind!" she responded bitterly. "How am I supposed to know where I'm going? I feel like you're abandoning me." Mark's heart broke at these words, but he knew what had to be done. He promised Susan that each morning and evening he would ride the bus with her until she got the hang of it.

For two solid weeks, Mark accompanied Susan to and from work each day. He taught her how to rely on her other senses especially her hearing, to determine where she was and how to adapt to her new environment. He helped her befriend the bus drivers who could watch out for her and save her a seat.

He made her laugh. Each morning they made the journey together, and Mark would take a cab back to his office.

Although this routine was even more costly and exhausting than the previous one, Mark knew it was only a matter of time before Susan would be able to ride the bus on her own. He believed in her, in the Susan he used to know before she'd lost her sight, who was not afraid of any challenge and who would never, ever quit.

Finally, Susan decided that she was ready to try the trip on her own.

Monday morning arrived, and before she left, she threw her arms around Mark. Her eyes filled with tears of gratitude for his loyalty, his patience and his love. She said goodbye, and for the first time, they went their separate ways.

Monday, Tuesday, Wednesday and Thursday—each day on her own went perfectly, and Susan had never felt better. She was doing it! She was going to work all by herself!

On Friday morning, Susan took the bus as usual. As she was paying for her fare to exit the bus, the driver said, "Boy, I sure envy you."

Susan was not sure if the driver was speaking to her or not. Who would ever envy a blind woman who had struggled just to find the courage to live the past year?

Curious she asked the driver, "Why do you say that you envy me?"

The driver responded, "It must feel so good to be taken care of and protected like you are."

Susan had no idea what the driver was talking about, and asked again, "What do you mean?"

The driver answered, "You know, every morning for the past week, a fine-looking gentleman in a military uniform has been standing across the corner watching you when you get off the bus. He makes sure you cross the street safely and he watches you until you enter your office building. Then he blows you a kiss, and gives you a little salute and walks away. You are one lucky lady."

Tears of happiness poured down Susan's cheeks, for although she couldn't physically see him, she had always felt Mark's presence. She was lucky, for he had given her a gift more powerful than sight, a gift of love that can bring light where there had been darkness.

光明的礼物

　　一个年轻漂亮的女人拄着一根白色拐杖,小心翼翼地迈上公共汽车时,车上的乘客都同情地望着。她给司机付了钱,双手摸着找到了座位的位置,然后顺着过道走到司机说的空位上坐下来,把公文包放在腿上,将拐杖靠在了她的腿边。

　　苏珊今年34岁,已经失明一年了。误诊导致她失明,她被突然甩进了一个黑暗、愤怒、沮丧和自怜的世界。

　　苏珊曾是一个特立独行的女人。她现在感到,命运的阴差阳错使她成了一个无能为力、无依无靠的人,成了周围每个人的负担。"为什么这种事会发生在我身上?"但不管她怎样哭叫、咆哮或祈祷,她都明白一个痛苦的事实——她将无法重见光明。

　　沮丧之气笼罩在苏珊头上。她每天都在挫折和疲惫中度过,她唯一的依靠就是丈夫马克。

　　马克是一名空军军官,他一心一意爱着苏珊。苏珊刚失明时,马克看到她陷入了绝望。他决心帮助妻子获得力量和自信。马克受过军事训练,懂得如何处理各种敏感情况,但他知道这次是他最难面对的一次战役。

　　苏珊终于感到可以重新工作了,可她如何去上班呢?以前她是坐公共汽车上班,现在她非常害怕,不敢自己一个人在市里走动。马克主动提出每天开车送她上下班,纵使他们分别在城市两端上班。起先,这样做让苏珊很舒心,同时也了却了马克需要保护失明妻子的心愿。

　　然而,不久马克认识到这样安排不行——既紧张又浪费。他承认,苏珊必须重新坐公共汽车上班。但一想到要向苏珊提这件事,马克又退缩了。她仍是那样脆弱。她会作何反应呢?

　　正如马克所料,听到要再次坐公共汽车上班,苏珊目瞪口呆。她痛苦地说:"我是瞎子,怎么知道我要去哪里呀?我感到你是要抛弃我。"听到这些话,马克伤心欲裂,但他知道必须这样做。他答应苏珊每天早上和傍晚都会陪她一起坐公共汽车,直到她习惯坐公共汽车。

　　整整两周,马克每天都陪苏珊上下班。他教苏珊如何依靠自己的其他感官(尤其是听力),去确定自己所在的位置,如何去适应新环境。他让苏珊和公共汽车司机成为朋友,因为司机可以关照她,给她留座位。

马克总是逗她笑。每天早上他们都一起坐公共汽车,然后马克乘出租车回办公室。

虽然这个程序比先前那个更贵、更累人,但马克知道苏珊能独立坐公共汽车,只是时间问题。他相信她,相信以前那个没有失明的苏珊,一个不怕任何挑战的苏珊,一个绝不放弃的苏珊。

终于,苏珊决定准备试着独自坐车上下班了。

星期一早上到了,苏珊离开前,抱住马克。她的眼里充满了感激的泪水,她对丈夫的忠诚、耐心和爱感激不尽。她道别后,他们第一次走向了不同的方向。

星期一、星期二、星期三、星期四——她独自上班的每一天都顺顺当当,苏珊从来没有感觉这么好过。她成功了!她要独自坐公共汽车上班了!

星期五早上,苏珊跟往常一样坐公共汽车,当她要付费给司机准备下车时,那位司机说:"噢,我真羡慕你。"

苏珊拿不准司机是不是跟她说话。谁会去羡慕一个过去一年都在苦苦挣扎寻找勇气的盲女人呢?

出于好奇,苏珊向司机问道:"你为什么说羡慕我呢?"

司机回答说:"像你那样得到照顾和保护感觉一定很棒。"

苏珊不明白司机在说什么,又问道:"你这话什么意思?"

司机回答说:"你知道,在过去的一周里,有一个穿军服的英俊先生一直站在街角对面,目不转睛地望着你下车。他确保你安全穿过马路,直到目送你走进办公楼,才给你一个飞吻,向你微微敬一下礼,走开。你真是一个幸运的女人。"

幸福的眼泪顺着苏珊的脸颊滚滚而下。因为尽管她无法用肉眼看见马克,但她总能感觉到他的存在。她很幸运,因为马克给了她一件比视觉更有效的礼物———一件能在黑暗处带来光明的爱的礼物。

Love Is a Telephone

Love is a telephone which always keeps silent when you are longing for a call, but rings when you are not ready for it. As a result, we often miss the sweetness from the other end.

Love is a telephone which is seldom program-controlled or directly dialed. You cannot get an immediate answer by a mere"Hello", let alone go deep into your lover's heart by one call. Usually it has to be relayed by an operator, and you have to be patient in waiting. Destiny is the operator of this phone, who is always irresponsible and fond of playing practical jokes to which she may make you a lifelong victim intentionally or unintentionally.

Love is a telephone which is always busy. When you are ready to devote yourself to or even ready to die for love, you only find, to your disappointment, the line is already occupied by someone else, and you are greeted only by a busy line. This is an eternal regret handed down from generation to generation and you are only one of those who languish for flowers.

Love is a telephone which is sometimes so sensitive that you are put through by a single dial and responded to as soon as you say "Hello". But, more often than not, you only hang it up and turn away sadly just because of its lack of challenge and effort. Once you realize your mistake, no one is available at the other end.

Love is a telephone, but it is difficult to seize the right time for dialing, and you will let slip the opportunity if your call is either too early or too late.

Love is a telephone which is not always associated with happiness. Honeyed words are transmitted by sound waves, but when the lovers are brought together, the phone serves no purpose. No wonder that many lovers observe that marriage is the doom of love.

Love is a telephone which, when you use it for the first time, makes you so nervous and excited that you either hold the receiver upside down or dial the wrong number. By the time you've calmed down, you will be at a loss to whom you should make the call.

Love is a telephone which often has crossed lines. And this usually happens to you unexpectedly. Your line will either cross or be crossed. Both cases are referred to as "triangles". Fortunately, all such occurrences are transient.

爱情是一部电话

爱情是一部电话,当你渴望它响起时,它却总是悄无声息;但你不乐意去接时,它却又丁零零响起。因此,我们常常错过另一端传来的甜蜜。

爱情这部电话通常不是程控或直拨,并不是仅仅说声"喂"便能马上得到回音,更不要说呼唤一声就能深深打动你的爱人的心。它通常必须由接线员转接,你得耐心等待。命运是这部电话的接线员,她总是不负责任,喜欢搞恶作剧,她也许有意无意地使你成为终生的牺牲品。

爱情是一部总是忙碌的电话。当你准备为爱献身,甚至为爱而死时,令你失望的是,你却发现有人已经占线,迎接你的只是忙音。这是一种代代相传的永恒的遗憾,你仅仅是又一个为鲜花而憔悴的人。

爱情是一部有时非常灵敏的电话，一拨即通，一喂就应。可是，你常常只是因为它缺乏挑战、不费气力而挂机，伤心地转身离去。一旦你认识到自己的错误，另一端却无人接听。

爱情是一部电话，但很难抓准拨号时机。无论拨得太早还是太晚，你都会错失良机。

爱情是一部电话，它并不总是和幸福息息相关。尽管甜言蜜语由声波传送，但当相爱的人守在一起时，电话便发挥不了作用。难怪好多相爱的人说婚姻是爱情的末日。

爱情是一部电话，你第一次使用，会让你感到紧张激动，不是拿倒了话筒，就是拨错了号码。等你平静下来时，常常不知道该给谁打电话。

爱情是一部电话，它经常串线。而且串线常常是在你意想不到时发生。不是你的电话与别人的串线，就是别人的电话与你的串线。这两种情况都被称为"三角串"。幸运的是，所有这些串线都是瞬时现象。

The Red Rose and the White Rose

My mother and father were about to celebrate their 50th anniversary. Mother called, all excited. "He got me a dozen white roses!" She sounded like a teenager who'd been asked to the prom.

This anniversary brought out a side of my parents that I never knew. For instance, that their wedding rings are each inscribed with a line of poetry: "I send you a cream-white rosebud." My father told me this in the kitchen one day. My mother said, "Oh, John," as if to stop him. My father said, "Oh, Claire."

That's the way my parents have always been about their relationship: private. There was never any mushy stuff going on that we kids could see. What we did see was buddies, a team.

"Do you remember the poem?" I asked my dad that day in the kitchen. He looked at me, took a breath and started reciting "*A White Rose*" by the Irish-American poet John Boyle O'reilly.

"The red rose whispers of passion, /And the white rose breathes of love," he began.

My mother said, "Oh, John!"

"O, the red rose is a falcon, /And the white rose is a dove."

"Oh, John!" my mother said. Then she left the room.

"But I send you a cream-white rosebud, /With a flush on its petal tips," he went on, standing there by the sink. "For the love that is purest and sweetest, /Has a kiss of desire on the lips." My father stopped. "Isn't that beautiful?" he said, smiling. We went to find my mother, who was in the den, her head in her hands. "It's beautiful!" I said to her.

"It's embarrassing," she said.

This is a woman who in her youth had never seen a happy marriage and wondered why anyone would bother. Instead, she imagined a future as a Chaucer scholar. In university she found dating only amusing. But then she met my father.

He was the most fundamentally decent man she had ever met. It was the man, not the institution of marriage, that drew her. She went to the altar, she would tell us, feeling as if she were jumping off a cliff.

In their first year, my father went off to war. My mother was five months pregnant, and terrified. She had the baby and waited. She ate chocolate-nut sundaes to soothe her heart.

My father returned, said hello to his seven-month-old son and, with my mother, soon bought a house. Then they had a daughter, then another daughter and then me.

Even as a kid, I could tell my parents were different. Dad preferred being with Mom. And when he was not around, she didn't roll her eyes and make jokes at her husband's expense as other wives did. Instead, she'd say, "You know, he's never disappointed me."

To celebrate their 50th anniversary, my parents renewed their wedding vows in church. Some 75 friends were watching. When my father repeated his vows, he choked up and had to pause. My mother said hers with more passion. Staring into his eyes, she proclaimed, "…all the days of my life I love you…till eternity."

Then she added, "This is the happiest day of my life, better than my wedding day! Because now I know how it all works out."

红玫瑰与白玫瑰

父母亲打算庆贺他们喜结良缘50周年。母亲打来电话时激动万分。"他给我买了一打白玫瑰！"听上去她就像一名应邀参加舞会的妙龄少女。

这次纪念将我从不知道的父母亲的一面展现了出来。比如，他们的结婚戒指上分别镌刻着一句诗行："我送给你一朵乳白色的玫瑰花蕾。"这是有一天父亲在厨房里告诉我的。母亲说："噢，约翰，"好像是要阻止他。父亲说："噢，克莱尔。"

父母亲一向就是这样处理他们之间的关系：秘而不宣。我们做儿女的从未能见到他们之间多愁善感过，我们见到的就是他们的恩爱、和谐。

"你还记得那首诗吗？"那天我在厨房里问爸爸。他看了看我，吸了口气，开始背诵起爱尔兰籍美国诗人约翰·鲍埃尔·奥雷利作的那首《白玫瑰》。

"红玫瑰窃窃情语/白玫瑰爱声息息。"他开始吟诵道。

母亲说:"噢,约翰!"

"噢,红玫瑰是猎鹰/白玫瑰是鸽子。"

"噢,约翰!"母亲说着,便离开了厨房。

"可我送给你的是一朵乳白色玫瑰花蕾/它的花瓣尖上含着羞红。"他站在水池边,接着吟咏道,"为了那最纯最甜的爱情/多想在那芳唇上吻上一下。"父亲就此停住,面含微笑说:"这首诗很美吧?"随后,我们走进小屋,发现母亲正两手抱头坐在那里。我对她说:"这首诗真美!"

"真难为情。"她说。

母亲在少女时代从未见过一次幸福的婚姻,心想为什么大家要操这个心呢。于是,她便想将来当一名研究乔叟的女学者。在大学里,她发现男女约会只是为了解闷逗乐。但后来,她遇到了我的父亲。

父亲是她平生遇到的最最体面的男人。她结婚是为了这个男人,而不是什么女大当嫁的习俗。她常常告诉我们说,她走到圣坛前时,就像从悬崖上跳下来似的。

新婚第一年,父亲就离开她奔赴战场。当时,母亲已经怀孕5个月,心里非常害怕。她生下孩子后,苦苦等待,总是靠吃带巧克力豆的圣代冰淇淋安抚自己的心。

父亲归来时,向已经7个月的儿子问好,不久同母亲一道买了一座房子。随后,他们就有了一个女儿,又有了一个女儿,然后又生下了我。

甚至小时候,我就能看出父母亲不同凡响。父亲总是喜欢和母亲厮守在一块。而当他不在时,母亲从来不会像别人的妻子那样拿自己的丈夫寻开心。相反,她总是说:"你们知道,他从来都不会让我失望。"

为了庆贺金婚,父母亲在教堂里重温了他们当初的结婚誓言。当着75位朋友的面,父亲重叙他的婚誓时,声音哽咽,不得不中断;母亲说时更加富有激情,她目光炯炯地望着父亲的眼睛,郑重其事地说:"……在我生命中的每一天,我都爱你,直到永远……"

接着,她又补充道:"这是我一生中最幸福的日子,比我婚礼那天还精彩!因为现在我知道我们终于说到做到。"

At the Small Café

Can it really be sixty-two years ago that I first saw you?

It is truly a lifetime, I know. But as I gaze into your eyes now, it seems like only yesterday that I first saw you, in that small café in Hanover Square.

From the moment I saw you smile, as you opened the door for that young mother and her newborn baby. I knew that I wanted to share the rest of my life with you.

I still think of how foolish I must have looked, as I gazed at you, that first time. I remember watching you intently, as you took off your hat and loosely shook your short dark hair with your fingers. I felt myself becoming immersed in your every detail, as you placed your hat on the table and cupped your hands around the hot cup of tea, gently blowing the steam away with your pouted lips.

From that moment, everything seemed to make perfect sense to me. The people in the café and the busy street outside all disappeared into a hazy blur. All I could see was you.

All through my life I have relived that very first day. Many, many times I have sat and thought about that first day, and how for a few fleeting moments I am there, feeling again what is like to know true love for the very first time. It pleases me that I can still have those feelings now after all those years, and I know I will always have them to comfort me.

Not even as I shook and trembled uncontrollably in the trenches, did I forget your face. I would sit huddled into the wet mud, terrified, as the hails of bullets and mortars crashed down around me. I would clutch my rifle tightly to my heart, and think again of that very first day we met. I would cry out in fear, as the noise of war beat down around me. But, as I thought of you and saw you smiling back at me, everything around me would become silent, and I would be with you again for a few precious moments, far from the death and destruction. It wouldn't be until I opened my eyes once again, that I would see and hear the carnage of the war around me.

I cannot tell you how strong my love for you was back then, when I returned to you on leave in September, feeling battered, bruised and fragile. We held each other so tightly I thought we would melt. I asked you to marry me the very same day and I whooped with joy when you looked deep into my eyes and said, "yes" to being my bride.

I'm looking at our wedding photo now, the one on our dressing table, next to your jewelry box. I think of how young and innocent we were back then. I remember being on the church steps grinning like a Cheshire cat, when you said how dashing and handsome I looked in my uniform. The photo is old and faded now, but when I look at it, I only see the bright vibrant colors of our youth. I can still remember every detail of the pretty wedding dress your mother made for you, with its fine delicate lace and pretty pearls. If I concentrate hard enough, I can smell the sweetness of your wedding bouquet as you held it so proudly for everyone to see.

I remember being so overjoyed, when a year later, you gently held my hand to your waist and whispered in my ear that we were going to be a family.

I know both our children love you dearly; they are outside the door now, waiting.

Do you remember how I panicked like a mad man when Jonathon was born? I can still picture you laughing and smiling at me now, as I clumsily held him for the very first time in my arms. I watched as your laughter faded into tears, as I stared at him and cried my own tears of joy.

Sarah and Tom arrived this morning with little Tessie. Can you remember how we both hugged each other tightly when we saw our tiny granddaughter for the first time? I can't believe she will be eight next month. I am trying not to cry, my love, as I tell you how beautiful she looks today in her pretty dress and red shiny shoes, she reminds me so much of you that first day we met. She has her hair cut short now, just like yours was all those years ago. When I met her at the door her smile wrapped around me like a warm glove, just like yours used to do, my darling.

I know you are tired, my dear, and I must let you go. But I love you so much it hurts to do so.

As we grew old together, I would tease you that you hadn't changed since we first met. But it is true, my darling. I don't see the wrinkles and gray hair that other people see. When I look at you now, I only see your sweet tender lips and youthful sparkling eyes as we sat and had our first picnic next to that small stream, and chased each other around that big old oak tree. I remember wishing those first few days together would last forever. Do you remember how exciting and wonderful those days were?

I must go now, my darling. Our children are waiting outside. They want to say goodbye to you.

I wipe the tears away from my eyes and bend my frail old legs down to the floor, so that I can kneel beside you. I lean close to you and take hold of your hand and kiss your tender lips for the very last time.

Sleep peacefully, my dear.

I am sad that you had to leave me, but please don't worry. I am content, knowing I will be with you soon. I am too old and too empty now to live much longer without you.

I know it won't be long before we meet again in that small café in Hanover Square.

Goodbye, my darling wife.

相约小咖啡馆

我第一次看见你真的可能是62年前吗?

我知道,这是真正的一生。但此刻我凝视你的眼睛,就像我昨天在汉诺威广场小咖啡馆第一次看见你一样。

从那一时刻起,我就看见你面带微笑,为那位抱着新生儿的年轻母亲开门。我知道我想和你共度余生。

我仍想起我第一次凝视你的样子一定很傻。我记得我目不转睛地望着你摘下帽子用手指抖松短短的黑发。我感到自己对你的一举一动都心醉神迷,望着你把帽子放在桌上,双手捧起那杯热茶,噘起嘴唇轻轻地吹去热气。

从那一时刻起,一切对我似乎有了完美的意义。咖啡馆里与熙熙攘攘的街道上的人们都消失在烟雾朦胧中。我所能看到的只有你。

我这一生都在不断回味着初次相遇的那一天。我好多好多次坐在那里想着那一天,回味稍纵即逝的几个瞬间,再次感受一见钟情是什么样子。多年之后,我仍有那些感觉,我知道我永远都会拥有它们来安慰我。

即使在战壕里浑身颤抖,我也没有忘记过你的脸。我常常惊恐地蜷缩在湿泥中,周围子弹呼啸,炮声轰鸣。我将步枪紧握在胸前,又一次想起了我们第一次相遇的那一天。四周枪炮齐鸣,我常常惊恐地喊叫。但当我想起你,看到你向我微笑时,我四周的一切都会沉寂下来,我会在那些宝贵的瞬间和你又在一起,远离死亡和毁灭。直到再次睁开眼,我才会看到血流成河的战场、听到枪炮齐鸣。

9月休假,我伤痕累累,虚弱不堪,回到你身边,说不出对你的爱有多么强烈。我们相互紧紧地拥抱,我想我们会融为一体。就在那天,我请你嫁给我,你深情地望着我的眼睛说愿做我的新娘,我高兴得大声叫喊起来。

现在,我望着梳妆台上你的首饰盒边我们的结婚照。我想我们那时是多么青春天真。我还记得在教堂的台阶上笑得是那样开心,你说我穿着制服是多么勇敢英俊。照片现在已经陈旧褪色,但当我看着它时,我只看到我们青春勃发的光彩。我仍能清晰地记得,当时你妈妈为你做的配着精致花边和漂亮珠宝的新婚礼服。如果我聚精会神,还能闻到你的婚礼花束的芬芳,你举着花非常自豪地让每个人都看到。

我还记得,一年后,你把我的手轻轻地放在你的腰间,在我耳旁低声说我们快有孩子了,我听到后欣喜若狂。

我知道,我们的两个孩子都深深地爱着你,他们现在就在门外等候。

你还记得乔纳森出生时我惊慌失措的样子吗?我现在还能想起你笑话我的样了,当时我笨手笨脚地第一次把他抱在怀里。我目不转睛地望着你,你的笑声渐渐变成了泪水;我望着他,也高兴得笑出了眼泪。

今天早上,莎拉和汤姆带着小泰西也赶来了。你还记得第一次看到小孙女时我们俩紧紧拥抱的情景吗?我简直无法相信,她下个月就8岁了。亲爱的,我忍着泪告诉你,她今天穿着漂亮的连衣裙和闪亮的红鞋有多美,她使我浮想联翩记起了第一次相遇时你的样子。她现在剪了短发,就像你多年前那样。亲爱的,当我在门口遇到她时,她的微笑像暖暖的手套一样裹住了我,就像你当初的样子。

亲爱的,我知道你累了,我必须放你走。但我是多么爱你,这样做是多么心痛。

当我们一起渐渐变老,我常常逗你说,自从我们第一次相遇以来你什么也没有改变。亲爱的,事实确实如此。我看不到别人所看到的你的皱纹和华发。我现在看着你,只看到你鲜嫩的香唇和青春闪亮的眼睛,当时我们坐在那条小溪边第一次野炊,绕着那棵高大的老橡树追逐。我真想让那些最初的时光永远持续下去。你还记得那些时光是多么激动和美妙吗?

亲爱的,我现在必须走了。我们的孩子们在外面等着。他们想和你道别。

我抹去眼角的泪水,弯曲弱不禁风的老腿,跪在地板上,以便我能跪在你身边。我贴向你,握住你的手,最后一次吻你的香唇。

亲爱的,安心睡吧。

我很伤心你离我而去,但请别担心。我知足了,明白自己很快会跟你在一起。没有你,我垂垂老矣、精神空虚,活不了多久。

我知道,我们不久就又会在汉诺威广场那家小咖啡馆见面。

再见,我的爱妻。

I'm Going with You

In 1959, in a small town in California, a young couple had been married a few short and disappointing months.

He had never dreamed there were so many ways to ruin friend chicken. She couldn't imagine why she ever thought his jokes were funny. Neither one said aloud what they were both thinking—the marriage was a big mistake.

One hot afternoon, they got into a terrible argument about whether they could afford to paint the living room.

Tempers flared, voices were raised, and somehow one of the wedding gift plates crashed to the floor. She burst into tears, called him heartless and a cheapskate. He shouted that he'd rather be a cheapskate than a nag, and then grabbed the car keys on his way out. His parting words, punctuated by the slam of the door, were, "That's it! I'm leaving you!"

But before he could coax their rickety car into gear, the passenger door flew open and his bride landed on the seat beside him. She stared straight ahead, her face tear-streaked but determined.

"And just where do you think you're going?" he asked in amazement.

She hesitated a moment before replying, just to be sure of the answer that would decide the direction of their lives for the next forty-three years.

"If you're leaving me," my mother said, "I'm going with you."

跟你一起走

1959年，在加州的一个小镇上，一对年轻夫妇结婚才短短几个月，就心灰意冷。

他从来没想到会有那么多方法能把炸鸡做得一塌糊涂。她难以想象她以前为什么认为他的笑话那么逗人。他们俩谁也没有大声说出来——这场婚姻是个大错。

一个炎热的午后，他们为能不能负担得起粉刷客厅的费用可怕地争吵起来。

他们火气冲天，提高嗓门，而且不知怎么的，一只婚礼礼物盘子也摔碎到了地板上。她痛哭失声，大声说他无情、小气。他大声喊着他就是做小气鬼，也不愿唠叨，随后抓起车钥匙，就出了门。他临走时说："够了！我要离开你！"随后就砰地关上了门。

但还没等他来得及发动他们那辆老爷车，乘客门就飞快地打开了，新娘坐到了他的旁边，直视前方，泪水涟涟，但意志坚定。

"你想要去哪里呀？"他惊讶地问道。

她回答前，迟疑了一会儿，只是想确定一个答案，以决定他们后来43年的生活方向。

"如果你要离开我，"我的母亲说，"我就跟你一起走。"

Salty Coffee

In the first meeting, a boy invited a girl to drink a coffee, which he was too nervous to say anything, so that she was very uncomfortable. Suddenly, he said to the waiter, "Please allow me a little salt, okay? I would like to put it in coffee."

She was surprised and asked him, "How do you have such love?"

He replied, "Every time when I drink salty coffee, I always think of my childhood, think of my hometown, I miss my hometown too much, and my parents live there, I miss them very much."

When he said these words, tears were in his eyes. She was deeply moved. Then, she began to talk about her faraway hometown, her childhood and family. This was indeed a wonderful conversation, beginning from a beautiful love story.

They continued dating. She found that, in fact, he satisfied all her requirements: he was tolerant, good-hearted, warm and careful. Then, they got married and lived a happy life…

Making coffee for him every time, she always put some salt in it because she knew he liked it.

40 years passed, he passed away and left her a letter, which said: "My beloved, please forgive me, forgive my whole-life lie. This is my only lie to you—salty coffee."

"In my lifetime, how many times had I tried to tell you the truth, but I worried too much and I didn't do that because I swore to you that I would never lie to you. I'm dying now, no longer have any scruples, so I will tell you the truth, I don't like salty coffee, which flavor is very strange, but I have it during my whole lifetime! Since meeting you, I have never felt regretted for what I have done for you. My greatest happiness in my life is you around me. If I can have a second life, I still would like to meet you and own your life, even if I would also like to enjoy salty coffee."

Her tears soaked the letterheads.

One day, someone asked her, "How about the flavor of salty coffee?"

She replied, "Sweet."

This is just like the magic power between lovers; two people will always make sacrifices for each other. This kind of sacrifice will bring pain to the one who pays, but he or she will still feel sweet.

A sincere love is not for obtaining something from the opposite, but sincerely pay for each other. Although sometimes this devotion will bring suffering to your body, in the process of devotion, you will feel that your body is filled with tremendous sweetness and happiness. Such love is often more profound and worthy of cherishing.

咸 咖 啡

初次相会时,男孩邀请女孩喝咖啡。他太紧张了,说不出话来,所以她很不舒服,突然,他对服务员说:"请给我点盐,好吗?我想把它放在咖啡里。"

她吃了一惊,问他:"你怎么有这种爱好?"

他回答说:"我每次喝咸咖啡时,总会想起童年,想起家乡,我太想家乡了,我的父母亲住在那里,我非常想念他们。"

他说这些话时,热泪盈眶。她被深深地感动了。随后,她开始谈起了她遥远的故乡、她的童年和家人。这真是一场美妙的谈话,从此开始了一个美丽的爱情故事。

他们继续约会。她发现他其实符合她所有的要求:他宽容善良、热情细心。后来,他们就结为夫妻,过起了幸福生活……

她每次为他沏咖啡,总是要在咖啡里放些盐,因为她知道他喜欢。

40年过去了,他离开了人世,留给她一封信,信上说:"我的爱人,请原谅我,原谅我一生的谎言。这是我对你唯一的谎言——咸咖啡。"

"在我有生之年,有多少次我试图告诉你真相,但我太担心,就没有那样做,因为我向你发过誓绝不对你撒谎。我现在要死了,不再有什么顾忌,所以我要告诉你真相,我不喜欢咸咖啡,那种味道很怪,但我却喝了一生的咸咖啡!自从认识了你,我就从来没有对我为你做过的事情遗憾过。有你在身边是我一生最大的幸福。假如我能有第二次生命,我还是想认识你,一生拥有你,即使我还要享用咸咖啡。"

她的泪水浸透了信纸。

有一天,有人问她:"咸咖啡的味道怎么样?"

她回答说:"甜。"

这就像情侣之间的魔力一样;两个人总会为对方做出牺牲。尽管这种牺牲会给付出的一方带来一些痛苦,但他或她仍会感觉甜蜜。

真挚的爱情不是向对方索取,而是互相真心付出,虽然有时这种付出会给身体带来痛苦,但在付出过程中,你会觉得你的身体充满无比的甜蜜和幸福。这种爱往往更深邃、更值得珍爱。

Words from the Heart

Most people need to hear these three little words "I love you." Once in a while, they hear them just in time.

I met Connie the day she was admitted to the hospital ward, where I worked as a volunteer. Her husband, Bill, stood nervously nearby as she was transferred from the gurney to the hospital bed. Although Connie was in the final stages of her fight against cancer, she was alert and cheerful. We got her settled in. I finished marking her name on all the hospital supplies she would be using, then asked if she needed anything.

"Oh, yes," she said, "would you please show me how to use the TV? I enjoy the soaps so much and I don't want to get behind on what's happening." Connie was a romantic. She loved soap operas, romance novels and movies with a good love story. As we became acquainted, she confided how frustrating it was to be married 32 years to a man who often called her "a silly woman."

"Oh, I know Bill loves me," she said, "but he has never been one to say he loves me, or send cards to me." She sighed and looked out the window at the trees in the courtyard. "I'd give anything if he'd say 'I love you,' but it's just not in his nature."

Bill visited Connie every day. In the beginning, he sat next to the bed while she watched the soaps. Later, when she began sleeping more, he paced up and down the hallway outside her room. Soon, when she no longer watched television and had fewer waking moments, I began spending more of my volunteer time with Bill.

He talked about having worked as a carpenter and how he liked to go fishing. He and Connie had no children, but they'd been enjoying retirement by traveling, until Connie got sick. Bill couldn't express his feelings about the fact that his wife was dying.

One day, over coffee in the cafeteria, I got him on the subject of women and how we need romance in our lives; how we love to get sentimental cards and love letters.

"Do you tell Connie you love her?" I asked, knowing his answer, and he looked at me as if I was crazy.

"I don't have to," he said. "She knows I do!"

"I'm sure she knows," I said. "But she needs to hear it, Bill. She needs to hear what she has meant to you all these years. Please think about it."

We walked back to Connie's room. Bill disappeared inside, and I left to visit another patient. Later, I saw Bill sitting by the bed. He was holding Connie's hand as she slept. The date was February 12.

Two days later I walked down the hospital ward at noon. There stood Bill, leaning up against the wall in the hallway, staring at the floor. I already knew from the head nurse that Connie had died at 11 a.m.

When Bill saw me, he allowed himself to come into my arms for a long time. His face was wet with tears and he was trembling. Finally, he leaned back against the wall and took a deep breath.

"I have to say something," he said. "I have to say how good I feel about telling her. I thought a lot about what you said, and this morning I told her how much I loved her…and loved being married to her. You should have seen her smile!"

I went into the room to say my own good-bye to Connie. There, on the bedside table, was a large Valentine card from Bill. You know, the sentimental kind that says, "To my wonderful wife…I love you."

爱，就要说出来

大多数人都需要听到"我爱你"这三个微不足道的词语。偶尔，他们听到的会非常及时。

我看到康妮那天，她刚被送到医院的病房。我在那里做志愿者。她被从装有轮子的金属担架移到病床上时，她的丈夫比尔不安地站在旁边。尽管康妮已到了与癌症对抗的最后的阶段，但她仍然活跃开心。我们把她安顿好。我在她要用的所有东西都标上她的名字后，又问她是否还需要什么东西。

"噢，是的，"她说，"请你告诉我怎么使用这电视好吗？我喜欢看肥皂剧，不想错过任何情节。"康妮是一个浪漫主义者，爱看肥皂剧、言情小说和带有精彩爱情故事的电影。随着我们渐渐熟悉，她吐露说，她真失望，竟然嫁给一个常称她"傻女人"的男人32年。

"噢，我知道比尔爱我，"她说，"但他从来没有说过他爱我，也从来没有给我寄过贺卡。"她叹了口气，望着窗外庭院里的那些树。"如果他说'我爱你'，我愿意付出一切，但那恰恰不是他的本性。"

每天比尔都来看望康妮。开始，康妮看肥皂剧时，他坐在床边。后来，她睡觉的时间越来越多，他就在病房外的走廊上踱来踱去。不久，康妮不再看电视，清醒的时刻越来越少，我开始有了更多作为志愿者的时间和比尔在一起。

他说他是做木匠的，很爱钓鱼。他和康妮没有孩子，便以旅行来享受退休时光，直至康妮病倒。面对妻子病危的这个事实，比尔无法表达这种感受。

有一天，在自助餐厅喝咖啡时，我和他谈起了女人的话题，谈起了生活中我们如何需要浪漫，谈起了我们如何喜欢收到柔情的贺卡和情书。

"你告诉康妮你爱她了吗？"我明知故问。他看着我，好像我疯了一样。

"我觉得没必要,"他说,"她知道我爱她!"

"我确信她知道,"我说,"但她需要听到,比尔。她需要听到这些年她对你意味着什么。请想一下这件事。"

我们走回康妮的病房。比尔走了进去,我离开去看另一个病人。随后,我看到比尔坐在床边,握着入睡的康妮的一只手。那天是2月12日。

两天后的中午,我顺着医院病房走廊走着,看到比尔靠墙站在那里,盯着地板。我已经从护士长那里得知,康妮上午11点已经去世。

比尔看到我,扑到我的怀里很久。他泪流满面,浑身颤抖,最后靠回墙上,深深地吸了口气。

"我必须说点什么,"他说,"我必须说把那句话告诉她感觉真好啊。我对你说的话想了很多。今天早上我告诉她我是多么爱她,非常喜欢和她结为了夫妻。你真该看看她的微笑!"

我走进病房,和康妮告别。只见床头桌上放着比尔送的一张大大的情人节贺卡。你知道,贺卡上写着那种情意绵绵的话语:"献给我的爱妻……我爱你。"

The Shared Love

One afternoon I toured an art museum while waiting for my husband to finish a business meeting. I was looking forward to a quiet view of the masterpieces.

A young couple viewing the paintings ahead of me chattered nonstop between themselves. I watched them a moment and decided she was doing all the talking. I admired his patience for putting up with her constant parade of words. Distracted by their noise, I moved on.

I encountered them several times as I moved through the various rooms of art. Each time I heard her constant gush of words, I moved away quickly.

I was standing at the counter of the museum gift shop making a purchase when the couple approached the exit. Before they left, the man reached into his pocket and pulled out a white object. It was a long cane. He tapped his way into the coatroom to get his wife's jacket.

"He's a brave man," the clerk at the counter said. "Most of us would give up if we were blinded at such a young age. During his recovery, he made a vow his life wouldn't change. So, as before, he and his wife come in whenever there's a new art show."

"But what does he get out of the art?" I asked. "He can't see."

"Can't see! You're wrong. He sees a lot. More than you or I do," the clerk said.

"His wife describes each painting so he can see it in his head."

I learned something about patience, courage and love that day. I saw the patience of a young wife describing paintings to a person without sight and the courage of a husband who wouldn't allow blindness to alter his life.

And I saw the love shared by two people as I watched this couple walk away with their arms intertwined.

同 心 爱

一天下午，我的丈夫参加一个商务会议。我等他时，到一家美术馆参观，想静静地欣赏那些名画。

我前面有一对看画的年轻夫妇喋喋不休说个没完。我看了他们一会儿，断定是那个女的一直在说。我钦佩那个男人真有耐性，居然可以忍受她的滔滔不绝。他们的说话声让我心烦意乱，我就继续向前走。

我走过不同的艺术品陈列室时碰到了他们好几次。每次听到她喋喋不休，我就马上离开。

我站在美术馆礼品店的柜台前买东西，这时这对夫妇靠近了出口。他们离开前，男人把手伸进口袋，掏出一个白色东西。那是一根长长的手杖。他轻轻叩着地板，到衣帽间去拿妻子的短上衣。

"他是个勇敢的人，"柜台店员说，"如果我们这样年轻就失明，大多数人会放弃。他在康复期间，发誓他的生活不会改变。所以，和以前一样，只要有新的美术展，他都会和妻子来。"

"可他能从美术品中获得什么呢？"我问，"他无法看见啊。"

"无法看见！你错了。他看到的东西多着呢。比你我看到的都多，"店员说，"他的妻子给他描述每一幅画，这样他就可以在脑海里就看到了。"

那天，我明白了什么是耐性、勇气和爱。我明白了年轻妻子为盲人丈夫描述一幅幅画的耐心和丈夫不让失明改变自己生活的勇气。

随后，我目送这对夫妇手挽着手离开时，明白了两人共享的那份爱。

See How Much I Love You

My grandparents were married for over half a century, and played their own special game from the time they had met each other. The goal of their game was to write the word "shmily" in a surprise place for the other to find. They took turns leaving "shmily" around the house, and as soon as one of them discovered it, it was their turn to hide it once more.

They dragged "shmily" with their fingers through the sugar and flour containers to await whoever was preparing the next meal. They smeared it in the dew on the windows. "Shmily" was written in the steam left on the mirror after a hot shower, where it would reappear bath after bath.

At one point, my grandmother even unrolled an entire roll of toilet paper to leave "shmily" on the very last sheet.

There was no end to the places "shmily" would pop up. Little notes with "shmily" scribbled hurriedly were found on dashboards and car seats, or taped to steering wheels. The notes were stuffed inside shoes and left under pillows.

"Shmily" was written in the dust upon the mantel and traced in the ashes of the fireplace. This mysterious word was as much a part of my grandparents' house as the furniture.

It took me a long time before I was able to fully appreciate my grandparents' game. Skepticism has kept me from believing in true love—one that is pure and enduring. However, I never doubted my grandparents' relationship. They had love down pat. It was more than their flirtatious little games; it was a way of life. Their relationship as based on a devotion and passionate affection which not everyone is lucky enough to experience.

Grandma and Grandpa held hands every chance they could. They stole kisses as they bumped into each other in their tiny kitchen. They finished each other's sentences and shared the daily crossword puzzle and word jumble. My grandma whispered to me about how cute my grandpa was, how handsome and old he had grown to be. She claimed that she really knew "how to pick 'em". Before every meal they bowed their heads and gave thanks, marveling at their blessings: a wonderful family, good fortune, and each other.

But there was a dark cloud in my grandparents' life: my grandmother had breast cancer. The disease had first appeared ten years earlier. As always, Grandpa was with her every step of the way. He comforted her in their yellow room, painted that way so that she could always be surrounded by sunshine, even when she was too sick to go outside.

Now the cancer was again attacking her body. With the help of a cane and my grandfather's steady hand, they went to church every morning. But my grandmother grew steadily weaker until finally she couldn't leave the house anymore. For a while Grandpa would go to church alone, praying to God to watch over his wife.

Then one day, what we all dreaded finally happened. Grandma was gone.

"Shmily." It was scrawled in yellow on the pink ribbons of my grandmother's funeral bouquet. As the crowd thinned and the last mourners turned to leave, my aunts, uncles, cousins and other family members came forward and gathered around Grandma one last time. Grandpa stepped up to my grandmother's casket and, taking a shaky breath, he began to sing to her. Through his tears and grief, the song came, a deep and throaty lullaby.

Shaking with my own sorrow, I will never forget that moment. For I knew that, although I couldn't begin to fathom the depth of their love, I had been privileged to witness its unmatched beauty.

知道我有多么爱你

我的祖父母结婚已经半个多世纪了，从他们认识以来就玩起了特殊的游戏。游戏的目的是在一个意想不到的地方写下"shmily"这个词让对方去发现。他们轮流在屋前房后留下"shmily"，对方一发现，就开始新的一轮让另一方藏着写。

他们用手指在糖盒和面盆上写下"shmily"，等着准备下顿饭的对方发现。他们在沾着露水的窗户上写下"shmily"；一次又一次的热水澡后，总会在雾气蒙蒙的镜子上留下"shmily"。

有时，祖母甚至打开一整卷卫生纸，在最后一张纸上留下"shmily"。

没有"shmily"不可能出现的地方。匆匆写下的"shmily"的小字条会出现在汽车仪表板和车座上，或是粘贴在方向盘上。这些字条会被塞进鞋子里或留在枕头下面。

"Shmily"会写在壁炉架上的尘埃上、勾画在壁炉的炉灰上。这个神秘的词像祖父母的家具一样成了他们房子的一部分。

过了好久，我才完全明白祖父母之间游戏的意义。我疑神疑鬼不相信真爱——那种纯洁持久的爱。然而，我从未怀疑过祖父母之间的关系。他们彼此相爱。那不仅仅是轻浮的小游戏，而是一种生活方式。他们的关系是基于投入和深爱，这不是每个人都有幸体验到的。

祖父母一有机会就握着手。他们在小厨房里相遇时偷吻。他们说完彼此说了一半的句子，每天一起玩纵横拼字和字谜游戏。祖母低声对我说祖父老当益壮、好酷好帅。她宣称自己的确明白"如何选择"。每次吃饭前他们低头致谢，对自己的种种福佑大为惊奇，因为家庭幸福、好运相伴和相亲相爱。

但祖父母的生活中出现了一片乌云：祖母乳腺癌复发。第一次出现是在10年前。像往常一样，祖父总是和她走完人生的每一步。为了安慰祖母，祖父将室内涂成黄色，这样在祖母病重不能外出时，也总能感受到周围的阳光。

现在癌症再次侵袭着她的身体。在拐杖和祖父的可靠帮助下，他们每天早上去教堂。但祖母日渐消瘦，直到最后她再也不能离开家。有一阵子，祖父常常独自去教堂，向上帝祈祷照顾他的妻子。

后来有一天，我们都担心的事还是发生了。祖母撒手而去。

"Shmily"用黄色字写在祖母葬花的粉色缎带上。当人群渐渐散去、最后的哀悼者转身离去时，叔伯姑姊和其他家庭成员走上前来最后一次围聚在祖母四周。祖父走向祖母的灵柩，颤抖声音开始向她歌唱。透过悲泪，这歌声低沉轻柔，犹如催眠曲。

我因悲痛而颤抖，永远无法忘记那个时刻。因为我知道，尽管我无法测量他们爱的深度，但我有幸目睹了这无与伦比的美。

The Wings of Love

No one knows where love's wings will land. At times, it turns up in the most unusual spots. There was nothing more surprising than when it descended upon a rehabilitation hospital in a Los Angeles suburb—a hospital where most of the patients can no longer move of their own accord.

When the staff heard the news, some of the nurses began to cry. The administrator was in shock, but from then on, Harry MacNarama would bless it as one of the greatest days in his entire life.

Michael strapped in his wheelchair and breathing through his ventilator, appeared at Harry's office door one morning.

"Harry, I want to get married," Michael announced.

"Married?" Harry's mouth dropped open. "To whom?"

"To Juana," Michael said. "We're in love."

Love. Love had found its way through the hospital doors, over two bodies that refused to work for their owners and penetrated their hearts—despite the fact that the two patients were unable to feed or cloth themselves, required ventilators just to breath and could never walk again. Michael had spinal muscular atrophy; Juana had multiple sclerosis.

Just how serious this marriage idea was, became quite apparent when Michael pulled out the engagement ring and beamed as he hadn't done in years. In fact, the staff had never seen a kinder, sweeter Michael, who had been one of the angriest men Harry's employees had ever worked with.

The reason for Michael's anger was understandable. For twenty-five years, he had lived his life at a medical center where his mother had placed him at age nine and visited him several times a week until she died. He was always a raspy sort of guy, who cussed out his nurses routinely, but at least he felt he had family at the hospital. The patients were his friends.

There even had been a girl once who went about in a squeaky wheelchair who he was sure had eyed him. But she hadn't stayed long at the center. And after spending more than half his life there, now Michael was not going to get to stay either.

The center was closing, and Michael was shipped to live at the rehabilitation hospital, far from his friends and worse, far from Betty.

That's when Michael turned into a recluse. He wouldn't come out from his room. His friends drove more than two hours to see him. But Michael's spirits sagged so low, no one could reach him.

And then, one day, he was lying in bed when he heard a familiar creaking sound coming down the hall.

The squeaking stopped at his door, and Juana peered in and asked him to come outdoors with her. He was intrigued and from the moment he met Juana again, it was as though she breathed life back into him.

He was staring at the clouds and blue skies again. He began to participate in the hospital's recreation programs. He spent hours talking with Juana. His room was sunny and light. And then he asked Juana, who'd been living in a wheelchair since age twenty-four, if she would marry him.

Juana had already had a tough life. She was pulled out of school before finishing the third grade, because she collapsed and fell a lot. Her mother, thinking she was lazy, slapped her around. She lived in terror that her mother wouldn't want her anymore, so on the occasions when she was well enough, she cleaned house "like a little maid".

Before the age of twenty-four, like Michael, she had a tracheotomy just to breathe and that was when she was officially diagnosed with multiple sclerosis. By the time she was thirty, she had moved into a hospital with round-the-clock care.

"He told me he loved me, and I was so scared," she said. "I thought he was playing a game with me. But he told me it was true. He told me he loved me."

On Valentine's Day, Juana wore a wedding dress made of white satin, dotted with pearl beads and cut loose enough to drape around a wheelchair and a ventilator. Juana was rolled to the front of the room, assisted by Harry. Her face streamed with tears.

Michael wore a crisp white shirt, black jacket and a bow tie that fit neatly over his tracheotomy. He beamed with pleasure.

Nurses filled the doorways. Patients filled the room. An overflow of hospital employees spilled into the halls. Sobs echoed in every corner of the room. In the hospital's history, no two people—living their lives bound to wheelchairs—had ever married.

Janet Yamaguchi, the hospital's recreation leader, had planned everything.

Employees had donated their own money to buy the red and white balloons, matching flowers, and an archway dotted with leaves. Janet had the hospital chef make a three-tiered, lemon-filled wedding cake. A marketing consultant hired a photographer.

The final touch-the kiss-couldn't be completed. Janet used a white satin rope to tie the couple's wheelchairs to symbolize the romantic moment.

After the ceremony, the minister slipped out trying to hold back her tears. "I've performed thousands of weddings, but this is the most wonderful one I've done so far," the minister said. "These people have passed the barriers and showed pure love."

That evening, Michael and Juana rolled into their own room for the first time together. They knew they had moved many people with their love, and they had been given the greatest gift of all. They had the gift of love. And it's never known where it will land.

爱的翅膀

无人知道爱的翅膀会落在哪里。有时，它会出现在最不寻常的地方。令人吃惊的是，它降临在洛杉矶郊区的一家康复医院——这里大多数病人行动无法自理。

医护人员听到这个消息时，一些护士开始哭了起来，院长哈里·麦克南拉默也大为震惊，但从那时起，哈里就把这看作是他一生中最伟大的一天。

一天早晨，迈克尔出现在哈里的办公室门口，他的身体用带子缚在轮椅上，借助呼吸器呼吸。

"哈里，我想结婚。"迈克尔宣布说。

"结婚？"哈里张大了嘴，"和谁？"

"胡安娜！"迈克尔说，"我们在恋爱。"

爱情，爱情穿越了医院之门，降临在两个完全瘫痪的人身上，穿透了他们的心灵——尽管两位病人衣食无法自理，需要呼吸器才能呼吸，而且再也不能行走。迈克尔得了脊髓肌肉萎缩症，胡安娜身患多发性硬化症。

结婚的念头是多么认真，当迈克尔拿出结婚戒指，露出多年不见的笑容时，越发明显了。事实上，医护人员从未见迈克尔这样善良温柔过，他一直是哈里的职员们公认的脾气最暴躁的人。

迈克尔的暴躁情有可原。他在医疗中心已经住了25年。9岁时，妈妈把他送来后，每周来看几次，直到去世。他总是大发雷霆，骂走护士，但至少他觉得医院是他的家，病人们都是他的朋友。

曾有一个女孩，坐在吱吱作响的轮椅里。迈克尔敢肯定她已经注意到了他。但她在中心并没有待多久。迈克尔在那里度过了大半生后，现在再也不想待下去了。

中心快要关门了，迈克尔被转移到了康复医院，远离了他的朋友们，而且更糟的是，远离了贝蒂。

迈克尔就是这个时候变得寂寞的，他不愿走出房间。朋友们驱车两个多小时来看他。但他还是垂头丧气，没人能影响他。

后来，有一天，他躺在床上，突然听到走廊传来一阵熟悉的嘎吱声。嘎吱声在他的门口停住了，胡安娜凝视着里面，请他和她一起出门。他一下子来了兴致。从再次见到胡安娜的那一刻起，好像她让他焕发了生机。

他又仰望起了蓝天白云，开始参加医院的娱乐节目，连续几个小时与胡安娜聊天。他的房间阳光明媚。不久，他向从24岁起就一直在轮椅上生活的胡安娜求婚，问她是否愿意嫁给他。

胡安娜曾度过一段艰苦日子。她没上完三年级就辍学了，因为她身体虚弱，经常昏倒。母亲以为她懒，总是打她。她生活在恐惧中，害怕母亲不要她。所以，她身体好些时，就会"像小女佣一样"打扫房间。

24岁前，她和迈克尔一样做过一次气管切开手术，以使呼吸畅通。也就是在那个时候，她被正式确诊患有多发性硬化症。30岁时，她被送进医院接受全天护理。

"他说爱我时，我非常害怕，"她说，"我想他是在跟我开玩笑。但他对我说是真的。他对我说他爱我。"

情人节那天，胡安娜穿着一件白色绸缎结婚礼服，上面缀满珍珠，而且宽松得足以遮住轮椅和呼吸器。哈里帮着把她推到房门前。她泪流满面。

迈克尔穿着挺括的白衬衣和黑夹克，打着蝴蝶结，刚好盖在切除的气管上。他面带幸福的微笑。

门口挤满了护士，房间里都是病人，就连大厅里也满是医护人员。房间的每个角落都传来呜咽声。有史以来，医院还没有两个在轮椅上生活的人结婚的呢。

医院的娱乐节目主持人珍妮特·山口安排好了所有的一切。医护人员用捐来的钱买了红气球和白气球，同时配上鲜花，然后在拱门上点缀上绿叶。珍妮特请医院厨师做了一个三层柠檬味的结婚蛋糕。一个营销顾问请来了摄影师。

最后一项——接吻——无法完成。珍妮特用白绸缎把这对新人的轮椅系在一起,以此来象征这浪漫的时刻。

婚礼结束后,牧师强忍眼泪,悄然而出。"我已经主持了几千次婚礼,但这次是迄今为止最棒的一次。"牧师说,"这对人已经越过了障碍,展示了真爱。"

那天晚上,迈克尔和胡安娜第一次双双进入自己的房间。他们知道他们已经用爱情打动了很多人,而且收到了最伟大的礼物。他们收到了爱的礼物,而且谁也无法知道爱会落在哪里。

100/0 Love

As a teenager I had certain ideas in my mind that constituted the idyllic life of love and marriage. In Home Economics, our teacher had us plan the perfect wedding and the perfect reception, right down to the throwing of rice and driving away in a limousine. It was just like the movies where the nice guy gets the beautiful girl and they live happily ever after. Reality was not a part of the picture.

After high school, I went to college and was determined to become a nurse. I forgot about marriage. Surprisingly, two years later I met the man I would marry.

He was from a small town in Idaho and farmed with his father.I was from a Southern town, which had a greater population than the entire state of Idaho. I had always been emphatic that I didn't know whom I would marry, but one thing was for sure—he wouldn't be a farmer or dairyman! Well, I was wrong in both cases. They were not only farmers but dairymen as well.

We were married in October just prior to the beginning of heavy snowfalls. It would snow heavily throughout the whole winter. Our only entertainment was listening to the radio or the local high school sporting events. My new husband was a lover of sports. He had been a champion boxer and also participated in most sports. I was a lover of the arts. Speech, drama and dance were my first love. The nearest town with this kind of entertainment was forty miles away and the highway was closed off and on all winter.

We had only been married seven months when I received word that my mother, who was battling cancer, wouldn't live much longer. Even though there was the dairy with 75 cows and 1,400 acres to farm, as soon as my husband read the telegram, he sadly said, "Honey, get your bags packed while I make reservations for you. Your place is with your mother and your father right now." To him there had been no other decision to make. Every week I would receive a letter telling me all about how the farm was doing and inquiring about my parents and how we were all doing. Little was said about his sadness of being alone, or of missing his new bride, except at the very end of his letters where an unmistakable "I love you" was written. Teenage dream letters would have been filled with remarks of undying love and pain of missing me, but his letters were simple words of reality.

Four months later, after the funeral, I returned to Idaho where I knew my husband would be at the airport to meet me.

The look in his eyes told me more than any dream letter could. On the 80-mile drive to our home, I talked incessantly while he quietly listened. When he finally had a chance to respond, he asked me to open the glove compartment of the car and take out an envelope with my name on it. "I wanted to give you something special to let you know how much I missed you," he said quietly.

I opened the envelope to find season tickets, for both of us, to all of the area's fine art functions. I was stunned. "I don't believe this," I cried. "You don't enjoy these things!"

He reached out, hugged me and quietly said, "No, but you do, and I will learn."

In that moment I realized marriage was not 50/50, but real love was made of 100/0 sometimes. Love means putting the other one first. His example taught his young wife a great lesson—a lesson that has made a happy marriage for 51 years.

100比0的爱

少女时代，我在脑海里对爱情和婚姻所想象的是诗情画意的生活。在家政学课上，老师让我们策划完美的婚礼、完美的婚宴，一直到撒大米、新郎新娘开着豪华轿车离去。这就像电影里帅哥赢得美人归，他们从此幸福生活在一起。现实并不是这样的景象。

中学毕业后，我上了大学，决心要成为一名护士。我把婚姻忘在了脑后。让人吃惊的是，两年后我遇到了我愿意嫁的男人。

他来自爱达荷州的一个小镇，和他父亲一起经营农场。我来自南方的一个城镇，那里的人口比整个爱达荷州的人口都多。我总是强调我不知道要嫁给什么男人，但有一点是肯定的——他不会是农场主或奶牛场主！嗨，我两个都错了。我遇到的这个男人和他的父亲不仅是农场主还是奶牛场主。

我们在10月大雪开始前结了婚。大雪会下整整一冬天。我们唯一的娱乐就是听收音机或观看当地中学体育比赛。我的新婚丈夫是一个体育爱好者，他曾是拳击冠军，也参加过大多数的体育活动。我是一个艺术爱好者，演讲、戏剧和舞蹈是我的最爱。有这种娱乐活动的城镇距离我们最近的有40英里，而且整个冬天公路时开时关。

我们结婚才7个月时，我就得到消息说我母亲在与癌症抗争，活不了多久了。即使有75头奶牛要喂养和1400英亩地要耕种,我丈夫一看完电报就伤心地说:"亲爱的,收拾好行囊,我去给你订票。你马上和你父母亲在一起。"在他看来,没有什么别的决定可做。每周我会收到他的来信,告诉我农场的所有情况,询问我父母亲,我们全家人怎样。他很少说他独处的悲伤,也很少说他思念新婚妻子,只是在每封信的结尾都明确无误地写上"我爱你"。我少女时代的梦中情书应该是写满诉说永恒的爱和思念我的痛苦,但他的信却是简单叙述现实生活的几行字。

4个月后,举行完葬礼,我返回爱达荷州。我知道丈夫会到机场去接我。他的眼神告诉我的要比任何梦中情书所能表达的多。在驱车80英里回我们家的路上,我说个没完,他静静地听着。当他最后有机会应答时,他让我打开汽车仪表板上的小柜,拿出一个上面写有我名字的信封。"我想送给你一件特别的东西,告诉你我有多么想你。"他平静地说。

我打开信封,发现有好多张参加该地区所有艺术活动的季票,是我们两个人的。我大吃了一惊。"我不相信,"我叫道,"你不喜欢这些东西!"

他伸出手臂,抱住我,平静地说:"是的,但你喜欢,所以我一定要学会。"

此时此刻,我意识到婚姻不是50比50,真正的爱有时是100比0。爱就是把对方放在首位。他率先垂范,给他年轻妻子上了重要的一课——这一课促成了51年的幸福婚姻。

The Essence of Love

At a weekend gathering, the friends talked about the true meaning of love.

One of his friends asked how he felt.

Thinking for a while, he told a story:

After work that day, he stopped on the way home to buy two blocks of glass for his bookcase. Walking to the doorway, without taking care he staggered a few steps and almost fell over himself while the glass in his hands fell to the ground with a thump shattering into pieces instantly.

His wife who was cooking in the kitchen heard the sound, hurried out to hold his hands and asked him gently, "Are your hands cut? First come in and have a rest. The meal is ready in a moment. I clean the pieces."

He said nothing, but gazed at his wife affectionately.

爱 的 真 谛

周末聚会,朋友们谈论爱的真谛。

有朋友问他的感受。

他略一思忖,讲了一个故事:

那天下班,他顺道去为书柜配了两块玻璃。走到家门口,他没留神,一个趔趄,踉跄几步,险些摔倒,手中的玻璃"哗"地掉到地上,立时碎片四溅。

正在厨房里做饭的妻子闻声赶来,拉起他的手,柔声问道:"手划破了没有?你先进屋去休息,过一会儿饭就做好了,我来清扫一下玻璃碴。"

他什么话也没说,只是深情地看了妻子一眼。

A Letter to Sophie

Dear Sophie,

I cannot leave this place without saying a few words to you. So, my pet, you expect a good deal from me. Your happiness, your life, even depend, you say, upon my ever loving you!

Never fear, my dear Sophie, that will endure, and you shall live, and be happy. I have never committed a crime yet, and am not going to begin. I am wholly yours—you are everything to me. We will sustain each other in all the ills of life it may please fate to inflict upon us; you will soothe my troubles; I will comfort you in yours. Would that I could always see you as you have been lately! As for myself, you must confess that I am just as I was on the first day you saw me.

This is no merit of my own, but I owe it in justice to myself to tell you so. It is one effect of good qualities to be felt more vividly from day to day. Be assured of my constancy to yours, and of my appreciation of them. Never was a passion more justified by reason than mine. It is not true, my dear Sophie, that you are very amiable? Examine myself—see how worthy you are of being loved, and know that I love you very much. That is the unvarying standard of my feelings.

Good night, my dear Sophia. I am as happy as man can be in knowing that I am loved by the best of women.

Yours forever,
Dennis

写给索菲的信

亲爱的索菲：

不对你说几句话，我舍不得离开此地。你看，我的宝贝，你对我抱有多大期望。你说，你的幸福，甚至你的生命，都取决于我对你一如既往的爱！

亲爱的索菲，千万别担心，你将永远拥有我的爱，你会幸福地活下去。我从未犯过罪，也不会去犯罪。我完全属于你——你是我的一切。在人生将要经历的苦难中，我们要同甘共苦；你要除去我的烦恼，我要为你排忧解闷。但愿我能看见你永远像现在这样。至于我自己，你得承认，我就是你第一天见到我时的那个样子，没有任何改变。

这不是我的优点，但确实是我的心声，它表现出一种美好的品质，而且日复一日，你将感受更深。相信我会对你忠贞不渝，我将把你的美德铭刻在心。没有人像我这样合乎情理地对你痴迷。亲爱的索菲，难道你不亲切可人吗？看看自己吧——看你多么值得爱慕，我又是多么爱你。这就是我永恒不变的感情。

晚安，亲爱的索菲，一个男人得知自己拥有世界上最好的女人的爱，这是多么幸福啊。

你永远的
丹尼斯

The Sign Language of Love

From the very beginning, the girl's family argued against her dating this guy. They said that she would suffer for the rest of her life if she insisted on being with him.

The girl indeed was in love with the guy. She always asked him, "How much do you love me?"

A few years later, the guy graduated from college and decided to go abroad for further study. Before leaving, he proposed to the girl, "I'm not a smart mouth. All I know is that I love you. If you allow me, I will take care of you for the rest of my life. As to your family, I'll try my best. Will you marry me?" The girl said yes.

The guy kept his words and made her parents accept the fact.

They got engaged before the guy set off.

Then the girl stayed and started working while the guy focused on his study in another country. They sent their love through emails and phone calls. It was hard, but neither of them ever wanted to quit.

One day when the girl was on her way to work, a car lost control and knocked her down. Waking up and seeing her parents standing beside her bed, the girl realized that she was badly injured. Her mother kept crying. She wanted to comfort her. But all that could come out of her lips was just a sigh.

The doctor diagnosed that the girl had lost her voice due to the injury in her brain. She broke down. She wept all day, without a word.

When she got back home from hospital, she didn't feel herself deserving him anymore. So she wrote to him and told him that she hated to be kept waiting and returned the engagement ring to the guy.

He called and wrote, trying to get her back to him, but he was always refused by her parents.

Her parents decided to move away with the hope that she would forget everything and be happy. This decision really helped the girl start a new life. She began learning sign language and told herself to forget him every day.

One day her good friend dropped by and told her that he was back home and looking for her everywhere. She asked her friend not to tell him what happened to her and for his own good, to forget about her. Then, nothing new about him came.

Another year passed. Her friend came with a wedding invitation from the guy. She was shattered. Opening the invitation, she saw her name went after the "bride". Just about to ask her friend what was going on, she saw him standing in front of her.

He spoke in sign language, "I've spent a year learning sign language, just to let you know that I never wanted to break my promise. Please give me a chance. Let me speak for you. I can be your voice."

He slipped the ring back into her finger. She finally smiled.

爱 的 手 语

女孩的家人一开始就反对她和这个男孩约会。他们说,如果她坚持要和男孩在一起,就会吃一辈子苦。

女孩确实爱这个男孩,总是问他:"你有多爱我?"

几年后,男孩大学毕业,决定出国留学。出国前,男孩向女孩求婚。"我不会花言巧语,只知道我爱你。如果你愿意,我会照顾你一辈子。至于你的家人,我会竭尽全力。你愿意嫁给我吗?"女孩答应了。

男孩说话算数,终于使女孩的家人接受了这个事实。

于是,在男孩出国前,他们就订了婚。

后来,女孩留在国内开始工作。男孩在异国他乡精心学习。他们通过电邮和电话传递爱情。尽管日子难熬，但他们俩谁也没有想过放弃。

有一天，在女孩上班的路上，一辆汽车失控，把她撞倒在地。女孩醒来后看到父母站在病床边，才明白自己受了重伤。她母亲哭个不停。女孩想安慰母亲，但嘴唇里所能发出的仅仅是一声叹息。

医生诊断说因为大脑受伤，女孩丧失了说话能力。她一下子就垮了，成天以泪洗面、一声不吭。

出院回家后，她觉得自己再也配不上他了，就写信告诉他说她不喜欢再等了，把订婚戒指也退给了男孩。

他又是打电话又是写信，想设法让她回心转意，但总是被她的父母亲拒绝。

她的父母亲决定搬家，希望女孩忘记一切、开心起来。这个决定确实帮助女孩开始了一种新的生活。她开始学习手语，每天都告诉自己要忘记他。

有一天，她的好友来访，告诉她男孩已经回国了，在四处找她。她请好友不要把她的事告诉他，为了他好，就忘了她吧。之后，就再也没有他的任何消息。

又一年过去了。女孩的好友带来了男孩的结婚请帖。她顿时心碎。打开请帖后，她看到自己的名字出现在"新娘"栏中。她正要问好友是怎么回事，只见他站在了她面前。

他用手语说："我花了一年时间学手语，就是想告诉你，我从来没有想违背诺言。请给我一个机会，让我替你说话。我可以成为你的声音啊。"

他重新将戒指又戴回了她的手指。她终于露出了微笑。

Written in the Stars

Ted went away to school, and we wrote letters to each other quite often at first. Then as the days passed, we wrote less and less. And that was the beginning of the end. He couldn't come home for Thanksgiving; and when he was home for Christmas, I had the measles.

We didn't get to see each other until spring vacation. But then we had been apart so long that we spent the whole week getting to know each other again. Ted was as good and sweet and wonderful as ever, but somehow he seemed different. When he went back to school, he said, "don't forget me."

"Of course not," I said, but this time I was not so sure.

As it worked out, it was Ted who met somebody else. She was a student at

Tulane. Ted wrote me a letter telling about her. He said he was sorry, and he knew I would understand.

It was raining the day the letter came. I read it in the living room and then gave it to Mother to read and went upstairs to my room.

I laid on the bed and listened to the sound of the rain. I didn't hate Ted, but I couldn't believe what had happened. I didn't even hate the girl. I couldn't believe that he was now gone and he would never come back again. Never!

I was still lying there when Mother came in. Before she spoke, I knew what she was going to say.

"There are other boys," she said. "You may not believe it now, but there will be."

"I suppose so," I said, "but Ted was the one. I can never fall in love again!"

Mother was silent a moment. Then she said, "Do you have the locket I gave you?"

"The locket? Yes, of course, it's in the top drawer of the dresser."

Mother got the locket. "Put it on," she said.

I sat up and put the locket around my neck.

"You see," she said, "the locket was given to me by a special person when we were engaged."

Then I held the locket lovingly, remembering Daddy. What a happy life he and Mother had had.

"You see," she said, "he was kind, sweet, and wonderful. I was sure he was written for me in the stars." Then she added slowly, "He was killed in a train wreck three weeks after we became engaged."

"He what!" I exclaimed. "But I thought—you mean you loved somebody before Daddy—somebody you thought was The Special One?"

"Yes, that is it. If I'd married him, I'm sure that I would have been very happy. As it worked out, three years later I married your father. We loved each other, and I was happy with him."

"I don't understand," I said.

Then Mother replied, "What I'm trying to tell you, honey, is that there is no one special person who alone can make us happy. There are many fine people in the world. Ted is one of them, but he came along too soon."

I almost cried because I thought I was losing the dream of my childhood.

Then Mother said gently, "One of these days a good man will come along at the right time—he will be the one written for you in the stars."

She went out and closed the door softly and left me alone, listening to the rain.

I looked at the door Mother had just closed behind her, and I thought about the other door, the door of Hope that she had just opened.

命中吉星

特德离开家上学去了,起初我们经常写信。后来,随着一天天过去,我们写得越来越少了。而那正是结局的开始,他无法回家过感恩节;等他回家过圣诞节时,我又患上了麻疹。

我们直到第二年春假才见面。但那时我们已经分开了很久,所以我们花了整整一周来再次了解对方。特德还和以前一样善良、可爱,令人愉快,但不知何故他好像不大一样了。他返校时,说:"别忘了我。"

"当然不会。"我说,但这次我却没有把握。

结果是特德遇上了另一个女孩,她是图兰学院的学生,特德在给我的信里提到了她。他说他很抱歉,并说他知道我会理解。

信来时,天正下着雨。我在客厅里看了信,又把它给妈妈看,然后就回楼上自己的房间去了。

我躺在床上,听着窗外的雨声。我不恨特德,但我无法相信发生的一切。我甚至不恨那个女孩。我无法相信,他现在飘然而去,再也不会回来了。再也不会!

妈妈进来时,我仍躺在那里。还没等她开口,我就知道她要说什么。

"男孩有得是,"她说,"现在你也许不相信,但将来会有的。"

"我想是吧,"我说,"但特德就那一个。我再也不会堕入情网了!"

妈妈沉默了一会儿,然后说道:"我给你的小盒子还在吗?"

"小盒子?在,当然在,它在梳妆台最上面的抽屉里。"

妈妈拿出小盒子。"戴上吧。"她说。

我坐起身,把小盒子戴在脖子上。

"你明白,"她说,"这小盒子是一个心上人在我们订婚那天送给我的。"

于是,我爱抚着小盒子。想起了爸爸。他和妈妈曾过着多么幸福的生活啊。

"你明白,"她说,"他善良可爱、令人愉快。我确信他就是我的命中吉星。"接着,她又慢慢补充道,"我们订婚三周后,他却在一次火车失事中死去了。"

"他什么!"我惊叫道,"可我还以为——你是说你在爸爸之前还爱过别人——你原来认为另一个人是心上人?"

"是的,就是这样。如果嫁给他,我肯定自己会很幸福。结果是,3年后我嫁给了你父亲。我们相亲相爱,我和他也很幸福。"

"我不明白。"我说。

随后,妈妈回答说:"亲爱的,我想告诉你的是,我们的幸福并不仅仅是某个心上人给我们的。世界上有许多好人。特德是其中的一个,但他来得太早了。"

我差点儿失声痛哭,因为我认为自己正在失去童年的梦想。

接下来,妈妈柔声说道:"总有一天,一个好男人会在适当时候出现——他将是你的命中吉星。"

她走了出去,轻轻地关上门,留下我独自听雨。

我看着妈妈身后刚刚关上的那扇门,随后想到了另一扇门,一扇妈妈刚刚为我打开的希望之门。

第八卷

只要心中有爱

The Remembrance of Lilacs

The family had just moved to Rhode Island, and the young woman was feeling a little melancholy on that Sunday in May. After all, it was Mother's Day—and 800 miles separated her from her parents in Ohio.

She had called her mother that morning to wish her a happy Mother's Day, and her mother had mentioned how colorful the yard was now that spring had arrived. As they talked, the younger woman could almost smell the tantalizing aroma of purple lilacs hanging on the big bush outside her parents' back door.

Later, when she mentioned to her husband how she missed those lilacs, he popped up from his chair. "I know where we can find you all you want," he said. "Get the kids and c'mon."

So off they went, driving the country roads of northern Rhode Island on the kind of day only mid-May can produce: sparkling sunshine, unclouded azure skies and vibrant newness of the green growing all around. They went past small villages and burgeoning housing developments, past abandoned apple orchards, back to where trees and brush have devoured old homesteads.

Where they stopped, dense thickets of cedars and junipers and birch crowded the roadway on both sides. There was not a lilac bush in sight.

"Come with me," the man said. "Over that hill is an old cellar hole, from somebody's farm of years ago, and there are lilacs all around it. The man who owns this land said I could poke around here anytime. I'm sure he won't mind if we pick a few lilacs."

Before they got halfway up the hill, the fragrance of the lilacs drifted down to them, and the kids started running. Soon, the mother began running, too, until she reached the top.

There, far from view of passing motorists and hidden from encroaching civilization, were the towering lilacs bushes, so laden with the huge, cone-shaped flower clusters that they almost bent double. With a smile, the young woman rushed up to the nearest bush and buried her face in the flowers, drinking in the fragrance and the memories it recalled.

While the man examined the cellar hole and tried to explain to the children what the house must have looked like, the woman drifted among the lilacs. Carefully, she chose a sprig here, another one there, and clipped them with her husband's pocketknife. She was in no hurry, relishing each blossom as a rare and delicate treasure.

Finally, though, they returned to their car for the trip home. While the kids chattered and the man drove, the woman sat smiling, surrounded by her flowers, a faraway look in her eyes.

When they were within three miles of home, she suddenly shouted to her husband, "Stop the car. Stop right here!"

The man slammed on the brakes. Before he could ask her why she wanted to stop, the woman was out of the car and hurrying up a nearby grassy slope with the lilacs still in her arms.

At the top of the hill was a nursing home and, because it was such a beautiful spring day, the patients were outdoors strolling with relatives or sitting on the porch.

The young woman went to the end of the porch, where an elderly patient was sitting in her wheelchair, alone, head bowed, her back to most of the others. Across the porch railing went the flowers, into the lap of the old woman. She lifted her head, and smiled.

For a few moments, the two women chatted, both aglow with happiness, and then the young woman turned and ran back to her family.

As the car pulled away, the woman in the wheelchair waved and clutched the lilacs.

"Mom," the kids asked, "who was that? Why did you give her our flowers? Is she somebody's mother?"

The mother said she didn't know the old woman. But it was Mother's Day, and she seemed so alone, and who wouldn't be cheered by flowers?"Besides," she added, "I have all of you, and I still have my mother, even if she is far away. That woman needed those flowers more than I did."

This satisfied the kids, but not the husband. The next day he purchased half a dozen young lilacs bushes and planted them around their yard, and several times since then he has added more.

I was that man. The young mother was, and is, my wife.

Now, every May, our own yard is redolent with lilacs. Every Mother's Day our kids gather purple bouquets. And every year I remember that smile on a lonely old woman's face, and the kindness that put the smile there.

紫丁香的回忆

5月的那个星期天，一家人刚移居罗德岛，那个年轻女人感到有点儿忧伤。毕竟，这一天是母亲节，而她却与俄亥俄州的父母亲相距800英里。

她那天早上给母亲打去电话，祝母亲节日愉快。随后，她的母亲向她提到，因为春天已经来临，所以院子里的色彩是多么绚丽。在她们通话时，年轻女人几乎可以闻到悬垂在父母亲后门外大灌木丛上的紫丁香醉人的芬芳。

后来，当她向丈夫说起她是如何怀念那些丁香时，他突然从椅子上一跃而起。"我知道我们可以在哪里找到你想要的东西，"他说，"带上孩子们，走吧。"

于是，他们就出发，驱车行驶在罗德岛北部的乡村小路上，那种天气只有5月中旬才会有：闪闪发亮的阳光、蔚蓝色的晴空，以及生机勃勃、随处可见的鲜嫩青草。他们穿过一座座小村庄和一座座拔地而起的房屋，穿过废弃的苹果园，来到了树林和灌木丛掩映的老农场。

他们停下车。车道两边长满了茂盛的雪松、杜松和白桦树，连一棵紫丁香也没有看到。

"随我来，"那个男人说，"翻过那座小山，有个老地窖，几年前是一个人的农场，四周长满了紫丁香。这块地的主人说我可以随时到这里来闲逛。我相信，我们要是采几束紫丁香，他是不会介意的。"

还没等他们到达半山腰，紫丁香的芬芳已经向他们飘了过来。于是，孩子们开始奔跑。不久，那位母亲也开始跑了起来，直至到达山顶。

那里，远离了过往汽车司机的视野，避开了纷扰的文明世界，高耸的丁香花丛开满了硕大的圆锥形的串串花束，几乎把花茎都压弯了。那个年轻女人微笑着冲到离得最近的那处花丛，把脸埋在鲜花中，啜饮着芳香，它重新唤起了她的记忆。

在那个男人察看地窖试图向孩子们解释这个房子必定是什么样子时，那个女人不由自主地走进了丁香花丛。她小心翼翼地从这里摘一枝，在那里采一束，然后用丈夫的折刀将它们剪下来。她不慌不忙，像欣赏稀有珍宝似的欣赏着每一朵花。

然而，他们最后还是返回汽车，走在了回家的路上。孩子们叽叽喳喳说个不停，那个男人驾着车，那个女人坐在那里面带微笑，她周围放满了鲜花，眼里充满着向往。

当他们离家不足3英里时，她突然向丈夫大声喊道："停车，就在这里停车！"

那个男人嘎地刹住车。还没等他问为什么要停，那个女人就已经下了车，匆匆走向附近的草坡，怀里仍然抱着那些丁香花。

山顶上是一家疗养院，而且因为这是一个美丽的春日，所以病人正在室外和亲友漫步或坐在门廊上。

那个年轻女人走到门廊尽头，只见那里有一个上了年纪的病人正坐在轮椅里，独自一人，低着头，背对着其他大多数人。年轻女人越过门廊栏杆，将鲜花放在了老太太的膝间。老太太抬起头，露出了笑脸。

两个女人聊了一会儿，都兴高采烈的。随后，那个年轻女人转身跑回家人的身边。

汽车开动时，坐在轮椅里的那个女人挥动着手，手里紧握着那束丁香。

"妈妈，"孩子们问，"那人是谁？你为什么把我们的花送给她？她是谁的母亲？"

他们的母亲说，她不认识那个老太太，但今天是母亲节，她看起来是那么孤独，谁不情愿用鲜花为自己喝彩呢？"再说，"她补充道，"我拥有你们所有的人，而且我还有自己的母亲，即使她离我很远。那个女人比我更需要那些鲜花。"

她这一席话使孩子们都很满意，但她的丈夫却不是这样。第二天，他买了半打丁香幼苗，栽到了院子四周；而且，从那以后，每隔一段时间，他就会增加一些。

我就是那个男人，那个年轻母亲是我的妻子。

如今，每年5月，我们自家的院子都会散发出紫丁香的浓郁芬芳。每逢母亲节，我们的孩子都要采撷紫丁香花束。而且，每年我都会记起那位孤独的老太太脸上露出的那种笑容，以及笑容里呈现出的那种慈祥。

The Envelope on Christmas Morning

It's just a small, white envelope stuck among the branches of our Christmas tree. No name, no identification, no inscription. It has peeked through the branches of our tree for the past 10 years or so.

It all began because my husband Mike hated Christmas—oh, not the true meaning of Christmas, but the commercial aspects of it—overspending…the frantic running around at the last minute to get a tie for Uncle Harry and the dusting powder for Grandma—the gifts given in desperation because you couldn't think of anything else.

Knowing he felt this way, I decided one year to bypass the usual shirts, sweaters, ties and so forth.

Our son Kevin, who was 12 that year, was wrestling at the junior level at the school he attended; and shortly before Christmas, there was a non-league match against a team sponsored by an inner-city church. These youngsters dressed in sneakers so ragged that shoestrings seemed to be the only thing holding them together, presented a sharp contrast to our boys in their spiffy blue and gold uniforms and sparkling new wrestling shoes.

As the match began, I was alarmed to see that the other team was wrestling without headgear, a kind of light helmet designed to protect a wrestler's ears. It was a luxury the ragtag team obviously couldn't afford. Well, we ended up walloping them. We took every weight class. And as each of their boys got up from the mat, he swaggered around in his tatters with false bravado, a kind of street pride that couldn't acknowledge defeat.

Mike, seated beside me, shook his head sadly. "I wish just one of them could have won," he said. "They have a lot of potential, but losing like this could take the heart right out of them."

Mike loved kids—all kids—and he knew them, having coached little league football, baseball and lacrosse. That's when the idea for his present came. That afternoon, I went to a local sporting goods store and bought an assortment of wrestling headgear and shoes and sent the anonymously to the inner-city church.

On Christmas Eve, I placed the envelope on the tree, the note inside telling Mike what I had done and that this was his gift from me. His smile was the brightest thing about Christmas that year and in succeeding years.

For each Christmas, I followed the tradition—one year sending a group of mentally handicapped youngsters to a hockey game, another year a check to a pair of elderly brothers whose home had burned to the ground the week before Christmas…

The envelope became the highlight of our Christmas. It was always the last thing opened on Christmas morning and our children, ignoring their new toys, would stand with wide-eyed anticipation as their dad lifted the envelope from the tree to reveal its contents.

As the children grew, the toys gave way to more practical presents, but the envelope never lost its allure. The story doesn't end there. You see, we lost Mike last year due to dreaded cancer. When Christmas rolled around, I was still so wrapped in grief that I barely got the tree up. But Christmas Eve found me placing an envelope on the tree, and in the morning, it was joined by three more.

Each of our children, unbeknownst to the others, had placed an envelope on the tree for their dad. The tradition has grown and someday will expand even further with our grandchildren standing around the tree with wide-eyed anticipation watching as their fathers take down the envelope. Mike's spirit, like the Christmas spirit, will always be with us.

圣诞节早晨的信封

卡在我们的圣诞树枝上的仅仅是一个小小的白色信封。没有姓名，没有身份证明，也没有题字。放在我们树枝上的这封信已有10年左右了。

开始都是因为丈夫迈克不喜欢圣诞节——噢，并不是真的指圣诞节，而是指它的商业方面——花费超支……为了给哈利叔叔买领带，给奶奶买爽身粉，他拼命地跑前跑后，只能送这些礼物，因为你想不出别的东西。

有一年，我知道他也这样想，就决定不再像以往那样买衬衫、毛线衫、领带等东西。

我们的儿子凯文那年12岁，正在学校练习初级摔跤。圣诞节前不久，他们要举行一项不结盟比赛，他们的对手由市里一家教堂赞助。这些少年穿的运动鞋破旧，似乎脚上就剩鞋带了。我们这边的孩子身穿漂亮的金蓝色制服和新灿灿的摔跤鞋，和他们形成了鲜明的对比。

比赛开始，我看到对方没有戴那种保护摔跤选手耳朵的浅色护头。对他们这样的乌合之众来说是一种奢侈，显然他们买不起。那么，最终我们以击败他们而告终，而且打败了每一个举重班。那些男孩从垫子上站起来时，穿着破旧的衣服，虚张声势地走来走去，带着一种不承认失败的街头傲气。

迈克坐在我旁边，伤心地摇着头，说："我真希望他们能有人赢，他们很有潜力，但这样输了，可能会使他们失去信心。"

迈克喜欢小孩——喜欢所有的小孩——他了解他们，他曾担任过小足球队、垒球队和长曲棍球队的教练。那天下午，我去附近的一家体育用品店买了一套摔跤护头和鞋子，匿名把东西送给了市里的教堂。

圣诞节前夕，我把信封放在了圣诞树上，信的内容是告诉迈克我所做的事儿，这就是我送给他的礼物。那年和接下来几年的圣诞节，他的笑容是最灿烂。

每年圣诞节，我都遵循这个传统——有一年是送一些残障少年参加一场曲棍球比赛，还有一年是看望了两位上年纪的兄弟，他们的房屋在圣诞节前烧成了平地……

信封渐渐成为我们圣诞节时最重要的部分。圣诞节早上，信封总是最后一个拆开。我们的孩子们对他们的新玩具熟视无睹，而是常常瞪大眼睛，站在那里，期待着爸爸把信封从圣诞树上摘下来，披露其中的内容。

随着孩子们渐渐长大，他们都要更实用的礼物，但信封从来没有失去吸引力。故事并未到此结束。你明白，去年迈克因可怕的癌症离开了我们。圣诞节来临时，我还处在悲伤中，几乎没有装饰圣诞树。但在圣诞节前夕，我在树上放了一封信，到了第二天早上，又多了三封。

趁大家不注意时，我们的每个孩子都在圣诞树上放了一封写给爸爸的信。这个传统一直延续着，有一天我们的孙子也会站在圣诞树边，瞪大眼睛盼望着他们的父亲取下信封。迈克的灵魂，就像圣诞精神一样，永远和我们同在。

The Heart-Shaped Pillow

Valentine's Day had arrived and like every other day of the year, I was very busy.

My romantic husband, Roy, planned a date like we had never had before. A reservation at an expensive restaurant was made. A beautifully wrapped present had been sitting on my dresser for a few days prior to the heart-filled holiday.

After a hard day at work, I hurried home, ran into the bathroom and jumped into the shower. When my sweetheart arrived, I was dressed in my finest outfit and ready to go. He hugged me, just as the sitter arrived. We were both excited.

Unfortunately, the littlest member in our household was not so happy.

"Daddy, you were going to take me to buy Mamma a present," Becky, my eight-year-old daughter said, as she sadly walked over to the couch and sat down beside the babysitter.

Roy looked at his watch and realized that if we were to make our reservations, we had to leave right away. He didn't even have a few minutes to take her to the corner drugstore, to buy a heart-shaped box of chocolate candy.

"I'm sorry, I was late getting home, honey," he said.

"That's OK," Becky replied. "I understand."

The entire evening was bittersweet. I couldn't help being concerned about the disappointment in Becky's eyes. I remembered how the joyful Valentine's Day glow had left her face, just before the door closed behind us. She wanted me to know how much she loved me. She didn't realize it, but I already knew it very well.

Today, I can't remember what was wrapped in that beautiful box, which I swooned1 over for several days, but I'll never forget the special gift, which I received when we arrived, back home.

Becky was asleep on the couch, clutching a box, which was sitting on her lap. When I kissed her cheek, she awoke. "I've got something for you, Mamma," she said, as a giant smile covered her tiny face.

The little box was wrapped in newspaper. As I tore the paper off and opened the box, I found the sweetest Valentine gift that I have ever received.

After Roy and I left for our date, Becky got busy. She raided my fabric and cross-stitch box. She stitched the words "I Love Ya" on a piece of red fabric, cut the fabric in the shape of a heart, stitched the two pieces together, adorned it with lace and stuffed it with cotton. It was a heart-shaped pillow, filled with love, which I'll cherish forever.

My wonderful Valentine gift has a special place in my bedroom today, some thirteen years later. As she was growing up into a young woman, many times I held that pillow close to my heart. I don't know if a pillow can hold magic, but this pillow has surely held a great deal of joy for me over the years. It has helped me through several sleepless nights since she left home for college. I not only cherish the gift, but the memory, as well.

I know that I am a very lucky mother, indeed, to have such a wonderful little girl, who wanted so desperately to share her heart with me. As long as I live, there will never be another Valentine's Day, which will be any more special to me.

心形枕头

情人节已经到了，和一年中的其他日子一样，我都很忙。

我的丈夫罗伊非常浪漫，他安排了一个我们以前从未有过的约会，在一家豪华饭店预订了座位。在充满爱心的日子到来的前几天，一件包装精美的礼物一直放在我的梳妆台上。

一天辛劳后，我匆匆赶回家，跑进浴室，进行淋浴。等爱人回来时，我穿好了最漂亮的衣服，准备出发。他紧紧地抱住我，临时保姆也刚好赶到。我们俩都非常高兴。

不巧的是，我们家里最小的成员却不高兴。

"爸爸，你说过要带我去给妈妈买礼物。"说着，8岁的女儿贝基伤心地走到了沙发边，在临时保姆身边坐下来。

罗伊看了一下手表，意识到如果我们要按时到达预订的饭店，不得不立刻动身。他甚至抽不出几分钟时间带女儿到街角小店买一盒鸡心形巧克力糖。

"对不起，我今天回家晚了，宝贝儿。"他说。

"没关系，"贝基回答说，"我明白。"

整个夜晚苦甜参半。我总会情不自禁地想起贝基失望的眼神。我想起了房门在我们身后关闭之前，贝基因情人节而兴奋的光芒从脸上已经消失了。她想让我知道她是多么爱我。尽管她没有意识到，但我心里已经非常清楚。

如今，那个漂亮盒子里装了什么礼物我无法记得了。虽然我因它兴奋了好几天，但那晚回到家时收到的另一件特殊礼物，我却永远难忘。

贝基在长沙发上睡着了，手里还紧紧地抱着一个盒子，盒子放在她的膝间。当我吻她的脸颊时，她醒了。"妈妈，我要送给您一件东西。"她说着，灿烂的笑容绽开在了她的小脸上。

小盒子用报纸包裹着。我撕开报纸，打开盒子，发现了我迄今为止收到过的最甜美的情人节礼物。

在我和罗伊离开家去约会后，贝基就忙了起来。她把我的织品和十字绣盒都翻出来。她在一块红织品上绣上了"我爱你",把布料剪成心形,将两块布缝到了一起,缀上了花边,并在里面塞满了棉花。这是一个充满爱的心形枕头,我会永远珍惜它。

大约13年后,那件奇妙的情人节礼物在我的卧室里仍占一席之地。女儿渐渐长大成人,这期间我多次将枕头紧紧地贴在心口。我不知道这个枕头是否藏有魔力,但我确信,这么多年来它曾给我带来了很多快乐。女儿离开家去上大学时,它帮助我度过了好几个不眠之夜。我不仅珍爱这件礼物,而且珍爱这份记忆。

我知道我确实是一位非常幸运的母亲,能有这样一个了不起的可爱女儿,她是那样渴望与我分享她的心。在我看来,只要我活着,绝不会再有比这更特殊的情人节礼物了。

The Seed of Love

I saw my six-year-old son wrestling with a limb of my azalea bush. By the time I got out side he'd broken it. "Can I take this to school today?" he asked.

With a wave of my hand, I sent him off. I turned my back so he wouldn't see the tears gathering in my eyes. I loved that azalea bush. I touched the broken limb as if to say silently, "I m sorry."

I wished I could have said that to my husband earlier, but I'd been angry. The washing machine had leaked on my brand-new linoleum. If he'd just taken the time to fix it the night before when I asked him instead of playing checkers with Jonathan. What are his priorities anyway? I wondered. I was still mopping up the mess when Jonathan walked into the kitchen. "What's for breakfast, Mom?" I opened the empty refrigerator. "Not cereal," I said, watching the sides of his mouth drop. "How about toast and jelly?" I smeared the toast with jelly and set it in front of him. Why was I so angry? I tossed my husband's dishes into the sudsy water.

It was days like this that made me want to quit. I just wanted to drive up to the mountains, hide in a cave, and never come out.

Somehow I managed to lug the wet clothes to the laundromat. I spent most of the day washing and drying clothes and thinking how love had disappeared from my life. As I finished hanging up the last of my husband's shirts, I looked at the clock. 2∶30. I was late. Jonathan's class let out at 2∶15. I dumped the clothes in the back seat and hurriedly drove to the school.

I was out of breath by the time I knocked on the teacher's door and peered through the glass. With one finger, she motioned for me to wait. She said something to Jonathan and handed him and two other children crayons and a sheet of paper.

What now? I thought, as she rustled through the door and took me aside. "I want to talk to you about Jonathan," she said.

I prepared myself for the worst. Nothing would have surprised me.

"Did you know Jonathan brought flowers to school today?" she asked. I nodded, thinking about my favorite bush and trying to hide the hurt in my eyes. I glanced at my son busily coloring a picture. His wavy hair was too long and flopped just beneath his brow. He brushed it away with the back of his hand. His eyes burst with blue as he admired his handiwork.

"Let me tell you about yesterday," the teacher insisted. "See that little girl?"

I watched the bright-eyed child laugh and point to a colorful picture taped to the wall. I nodded.

"Well, yesterday she was almost hysterical. Her mother and father are going through a nasty divorce. She told me she didn't want to live, and she wished she could die. I watched that little girl bury her face in her hands and say loud enough for the class to hear, 'Nobody loves me.' I did all I could to console her, but it only seemed to make matters worse."

"I thought you wanted to talk to me about Jonathan," I said. "I do," she said, touching the sleeve of my blouse. "Today your son walked straight over to that child. I watched him hand her some pretty pink flowers and whisper, I love you."

I felt my heart swell with pride for what my son had done. I smiled at the teacher. "Thank you," I said, reaching for Jonathan's hand, "you've made my day."

Later that evening, I began pulling weeds from around my lopsided azalea bush. As my mind wandered back to the love Jonathan showed the little girl, a biblical verse came to me: "…these three remain: faith, hope and love. But the greatest of these is love." While my son had put love into practice, I had only felt anger.

I heard the familiar squeak of my husband's brakes as he pulled into the drive. I snapped a small limb bristling with hot pink azaleas off the bush. I felt the seed of love that God planted in my family beginning to bloom once again in me. My husband's eyes widened in surprise as I handed him the flowers. "I love you," I said.

爱的种子

我看见6岁的儿子在使劲攀折我的一大枝杜鹃花丛。等我走到外面时,他已经把它折断了。"我今天能把这个带去学校吗?"他问。

我挥了挥手,让他上学去。我转过身,这样他就看不见我眼里涌起的泪水了。我爱那棵杜鹃花。我抚摸那被折断的枝条,好像默默地说:"对不起。"

我真希望能早一点对丈夫这样说,但当时我很生气。洗衣机里的水漏在了我崭新的油毯上。如果他前一天晚上听我的话，不和乔纳森下跳棋，而是花点时间把它修好，就不会发生这种事了。我不知道，对他来说什么事更重要。当乔纳森走进厨房时，我仍在拖地上的水。"早饭吃什么，妈妈？"我打开空空的冰箱。"没有麦片粥了，"我话音刚落，就看见他的嘴耷拉了下来。"吐司面包和果酱怎么样？"我把果酱涂在吐司面包上，放在他面前。我为什么这样生气？我把丈夫的碟子扔进冒着泡沫的水里。

这样的日子常使我想离开。我只想驱车上山，躲在一个洞穴，再也不出来。

不管怎么说，我还是设法把那些湿衣服费力弄到了自助洗衣店。我花了大半天时间在那里把那堆衣服洗净烘干，一边洗一边想着爱是怎样从我的生活中消失的。我把丈夫的最后一件衬衫收好时，看了看时钟。2点30分。我迟到了。乔纳森2点15分放学。我把衣服丢在后座上，慌忙开车向学校驶去。

待赶到教室门敲门，透过玻璃向里张望时，我已是气喘吁吁。老师用一根手指示意我等一会儿。她对乔纳森说了些什么，然后递给他和另两个孩子每人一些蜡笔和一张纸。我心里想，现在怎么了？她快步走出教室，把我拉到了一边，说："我想跟你谈谈乔纳森。"

我做好了最坏的准备。什么都不会让我吃惊。

"你知道乔纳森今天带花到学校里来了吗？"她问。我点了点头，同时想到了我心爱的杜鹃花丛，竭力隐藏起眼里的受伤神情。我瞥了一眼正在忙着给一幅图画上色的儿子。他的鬈发太长了，耷拉到了眉毛下。他用手背把它拂到了一边。他欣赏自己的作品时，眼睛里突然流露出了沮丧的神色。

"让我告诉你昨天的事吧，"老师强调说，"看见那个小女孩了吗？"

我发现那个眼睛明亮的孩子笑出了声，指着贴在墙上的一幅鲜艳的图画。我点了点头。

"噢，昨天她差不多歇斯底里了。她的父母正在闹离婚。她告诉我她不想活了，她希望一死了之。我看着那个小女孩把脸埋进小手里，大声说：'没有人爱我。'她的声音大得足以让全班同学听见。我竭力安慰她，但那似乎只能让事情变得更糟。"

"我以为你想跟我谈有关乔纳森的事。"我说。"是的，"她抚摸着我的衬衫袖说，"今天，你的儿子径直走到那个女孩身边。我看着他把一些漂亮的粉红色杜鹃花递给她，低声说，我爱你。"

我感到心里涌起一种自豪感，为儿子所做的事感到骄傲。我对老师笑了笑。"谢谢你,"说着,我伸手去拉乔纳森的手,"你让我今天很开心。"

那天晚上晚些时候,我开始为倒向一边的杜鹃花拔去了杂草。当我回想起乔纳森向那个小女孩展示爱时,我的脑海里浮现起了《圣经》里的一句诗:"……这三点保持不变:信任,希望和爱。但其中最重要的是爱。"当我的儿子把爱付诸实践时,我却只感到生气。

我听到外面车道上传来了丈夫开进车道时的汽车刹车声。我从花丛中折下了一小枝开着火红色的杜鹃花。我感到上帝种在我家里的爱的种子又开始在我的心里盛开了。当我把花递给丈夫时,他惊讶得睁大了眼睛。"我爱你。"我说。

Tomorrow Shining Ahead

Jennifer Paige was halfway down the stairs, her hand trailing lightly along the banister, when she turned and went back to the door of her room. Though she knew it all by heart, she wanted to take one last look. Good-bye, room…She lingered over the soft and faded quilt that lay folded at the foot of bed…the window curtains tied back, framing a view of the elm top…Oh, the wide-awake dreams that had often drifted through her head as she gazed out that window.

Not that she was sentimental about such things. Not now. She couldn't afford to be. Certainly there was no reluctance in her farewell. It was like the brief pause at the ending of a chapter in a good book, and she was eager to turn the page. All spring she had waited for this day. Longer than that, really. Finishing high school and going away to school was so much more than just going away to school…

Jennifer went down the stairs again to where her mother and father, strangely quiet, were waiting. Mother was sitting on the little chair that no one ever sat on, her head tilted to one side, and Dad just standing there with his hands thrust into his trouser pockets. The best parents in the world—she knew it—if you didn't consider the few occasions when they were completely unreasonable about some small matter. Sometimes she wondered if they loved her too much. A twinge of guilt stirred deep within her when she admitted to herself how longingly she had looked forward to getting "out from under."

"It seems like only yesterday you were starting to kindergarten," her mother said.

Jennifer had heard those words at least a half dozen times a day in the last week. "Mother, do you realize how many times you've said that lately?" she asked.

"I may say it again before you're on the train," her mother said. "I can't promise that I won't, dear."

"Be patient with your mother," Dad said, winking. "It isn't every day she loses a daughter to higher education and a career."

Jennifer smiled in acknowledgment and then paused. In front of the hall mirror for a quick glance. The dark cotton dress looked just appropriate for a warm day, serious enough for someone who was going to be a nurse.

Her raincoat lay across the luggage stacked beside the front door. "I keep asking myself if we've forgotten anything," her mother said. "I know, the camera! I want a snapshot of you getting on the train."

"I thought of that," her father announced proudly. "I put it in the car last night. Just to be sure."

As they were going out the front door, her mother said, "Around the world would only be a trip…This is a milestone, Jenny."

Dad put the suitcases in the back. Of the car, and then came forward to hold the front door open. "Sit in the middle, dear," her mother suggested, touching Jennifer's arm gently, and Jennifer noticed her mother was wearing one of those sad-looking smiles. Her mother had enjoyed talking about all of it—the school catalogue, how lucky Jennifer was to have only one roommate in the dormitory, which clothes to take along. But in the last few days, as the time drew nearer, she had reflected less and less of her early enthusiasm. In fact, Jennifer was afraid her mother might even get weepy at the station.

Her father pulled out of their driveway and Jennifer turned for one last look at the house.

Her father pulled out of their driveway and Jennifer turned for one last at the house.

"Do you know what just came to my mind?" Her mother said. "The hanky. Do you remember when you were in kindergarten all the children were supposed to wear a handkerchief pinned to their clothes?"

"Oh, Mother!" Then she caught her mother's teasing glance and she had to laugh. She kissed her mother on the cheek and then leaned head back against the seat. "You know something?" she said. "I love you both very much."

They pulled up at the station then, and suddenly there was no more time. They walked across the gravel to the platform. Dad checked the luggage and placed the ticket in Jennifer's hand. The train was coming. There were last-minute reminders and questions…last-minute words of advice…and then last-minute embraces.

"Well, I'm on my way," Jennifer said brightly.

When her father snapped the picture, she noticed her mother was not weepy at all-the smile on her face was not even sad-looking.

Through the window, Jennifer held them with her eyes as the train moved slowly from the station. They were standing close together, and somehow it brought back the memory of that day when she was seven…maybe eight—when she had persuaded them to let her ride the big county-fair Ferris wheel "all by myself." They had stood the same way then, close together, waiting…and she had sat rigidly still in the exact middle of the seat, but certain that even if she fell, even if the Ferris wheel itself tumbled, even if…she had known they would catch her.

And now they began to blur before they were out of sight. "Jennifer Paige, don't you know you'd bawl," she whispered, fumbling for a tissue. She wiped her eyes and thought: isn't this the weirdest thing? The beginning of something bright and wonderful and she was crying. Tomorrow was shining ahead of her. She wiped her eyes one last time and when she looked again, her parents were out of sight.

明天就在眼前

詹妮弗·佩奇轻轻地扶着楼梯扶手下楼，走到半道，又转身返回了房门口。尽管她悉数在心，但她还想最后再看一眼。再见了，房间……她的目光慢慢扫过床头叠好的柔软褪色的被子……束起来的窗帘，显出窗外风景的榆树梢……噢，还有她凝望窗外时常浮现在脑海里的漫无边际的梦想。

并不是因为她正在为这些东西感伤，现在不行，她没有时间。当然，她的告别没有勉强的成分。这就像一本好书中某一章结尾时的短暂停顿一样，她急于想翻到下一页。整个春季，她都在等待着这一天。真的，时间比那还要长。中学毕业离家上学比平时上学大不一样……

詹妮弗又下了楼梯，来到了父母亲那里。他们正在等着她，出奇的安静。妈妈坐在一把从来没人坐过的小椅子上，头歪向一边；爸爸站在那里，两手插在裤袋里。她知道，如果不计较他们偶尔在一些小事上完全不讲道理的话，他们是世界上最好的父母亲。有时她想知道他们是否爱她爱得过分。当她自己承认她曾多么渴望从父母亲的"羽翼下钻出来"时，她内心深感内疚。

"就像昨天你才开始上幼儿园似的。"她妈妈说。

上周，詹妮弗每天至少听妈妈这样说过五六次。"妈妈，你知道这话你最近说了多少遍吗？"她问。

"在你上火车前我可能还会说，"妈妈说，"我不能保证我不说，亲爱的。"

"对你妈妈要有耐心，"爸爸眨了眨眼说，"并不是每天都有高等教育和事业来让她失去女儿的。"

詹妮弗默然一笑，然后在大厅镜子前暂时停住脚步，飞快地瞥了一眼。黑棉布裙看上去正合适——适合暖和天穿，而且对一个即将当护士的人来说，这套衣服也足够庄重。

她的雨衣搭在堆在前门旁边的行李上。"我一直在问自己是否我们忘记了什么，"妈妈说，"我知道了，照相机！我要抓拍一张你上火车的照片。"

"我早就想到了，"爸爸得意地说，"昨晚我就把它放在汽车里了，一定不会忘的。"

他们一边走出前门，她妈妈一边说："周游世界只是一次旅行……这是一个里程碑，詹妮。"

爸爸把皮箱放进车后面，然后走过来，打开车前门。"亲爱的，坐在中间，"妈妈建议道，轻轻地抚摸着詹妮弗的胳膊。詹妮弗注意到妈妈脸上带着伤心的微笑。妈妈曾热衷于谈论大学简要说明中所有的内容，詹妮弗多么走运，宿舍里只有一个室友，要带哪些衣服。但最近几天，随着日期越来越近，她早些日子的那种热情变得越来越少。真的，詹妮弗真怕妈妈甚至会在车站流泪。

爸爸将车驶出车道，詹妮弗转身最后看了一眼房子。

"你知道我突然想起了什么吗？"妈妈说，"手帕。你还记得当初你在幼儿园时，所有的孩子都应该在衣服上别上一块手帕吗？"

"噢，妈妈！"这时，她看到妈妈取笑的眼神，便忍不住笑了起来。她亲了亲妈妈的脸颊，然后仰头靠在座位上，说："你们知道吗？我非常爱你们俩。"

他们驱车来到了车站。这时，他们突然发现时间已经不多了。他们走过碎石路，来到站台，爸爸托运了行李，将车票放到詹妮弗手里。火车来了。于是，他们再做临别的提醒和询问……临别的嘱咐……然后是临别的拥抱。

"好了，我走了。"詹妮弗兴高采烈地说。

当爸爸按动快门时，詹妮弗看到妈妈一点没有流泪——她带着笑容的脸上甚至看不出伤感。

火车慢慢地驶离了车站。詹妮弗透过车窗目送着父母亲，只见他们紧紧地站在一起。不知怎么的，这使詹妮弗想起她七八岁时的一天，那时她说服父母同意让她"独自一人"去坐当地博览会上的空中大转轮，他们那时就是这样站着，紧紧地靠在一起，等待着……她当时坐在座位的正中央一动都不敢动，但心里确信：即使她摔下去，即使转轮翻倒，即使……她知道父亲一定会上来接住她。

此时，詹妮弗泪眼模糊地望着父亲，他们依然站在那里。"詹妮弗·佩奇，你不知道会哭出声来吧。"她低声说着，摸出一张纸巾，擦了擦眼睛，心里想：这是不是世界上最不可思议的事儿？辉煌而精彩的事情有了开端，她却在哭泣。明天在她面前是那样灿烂。她最后一次擦去眼中的泪水，又去看父母亲时，他们已经不见了踪影。

Christmas Present

Paul received an automobile from his brother as a Christmas present. On Christmas Eve when Paul came out of his office, a street boy was walking around the shiny new car, admiring it. "Is this your car, Mister?" he asked.

Paul nodded. "My brother gave it to me for Christmas." The boy was shocked. "You mean your brother gave it to you and it didn't cost you anything? Boy, I wish…" He hesitated.

Of course Paul knew what he was going to wish for. He was going to wish he had a brother like that. But what the lad said shocked Paul all the way down to his heels.

"I wish," the boy went on, "that I could be a brother like that."

Paul looked at the boy in surprise, then impulsively he added, "Would you like to take a ride in my automobile?"

"Oh yes, I'd love that."

After a short ride, the boy turned and with his eyes aglow, said, "Mister, would you mind driving in front of my house?"

Paul smiled a little. He thought he knew what the lad wanted. He wanted to show his neighbors that he could ride home in a big automobile. But Paul was wrong again.

"Will you stop where those two steps are?" the boy asked.

He ran up the steps. Then in a little while Paul heard him coming back, but he was not coming fast. He was carrying his little crippled brother. He sat him down on the bottom step, then sort of squeezed up against him and pointed to the car. "There she is, Buddy, just like I told you upstairs. His brother gave it to him for Christmas and it didn't cost him a cent. And some day I'm gonna give you one just like it, then you can see for yourself all the pretty things in the Christmas windows that I've been trying to tell you about."

Paul got out and lifted the lad to the front seat of his car. The shining-eyed older brother climbed in beside him and the three of them began a memorable holiday ride.

On that Christmas Eve, Paul learned what it means by "It is more blessed to give…"

My wish for the world is that we all could be brothers like that.

圣诞礼物

保罗从哥哥那里得到一辆新车,作为圣诞礼物。圣诞节前夜,保罗离开办公室的时候,街道上的一个小男孩绕着那辆闪闪发亮的新车,羡慕地问道:"先生,这是你的车吗?"

保罗点点头说:"这是我哥哥送给我的圣诞礼物。"男孩满脸惊讶:"你是说这是你哥哥送的礼物,你没有花一分钱?嗨,真希望……"他欲言又止。

保罗当然知道他希望什么:他是希望也能有个那样的哥哥送给他一辆车。但男孩的话却让保罗非常震惊。

"我希望自己也能成为那样的哥哥,送一辆车给弟弟。"男孩继续说。

保罗惊讶地看着男孩,然后脱口而出:"愿意坐我的车兜风吗?"

"噢愿意,我非常乐意。"

车子开了一小段路后,小男孩转过身,两眼熠熠生辉:"先生,你能把车子开到我的家门前吗?"

保罗微微一笑,心想自己知道小家伙有什么打算:他是想向邻居们炫耀一番,他能坐一辆大汽车回家。但保罗又错了。

"你能把车子停在那两级台阶前面吗?"男孩问道。

男孩跑上台阶。过了一会儿,保罗听到他返回的脚步声,但动作有些缓慢。他搂着跛脚的弟弟,把他安顿在最底下一级台阶上坐下,然后紧贴着他,指着那辆新车说:"看见了吧,弟弟,刚才我在楼上全告诉你了。这是保罗的哥哥送给他的圣诞礼物!没有花他一分钱。将来有一天,我也要送给你一辆这样的车子。到时候,你就能亲眼去看那些我总是对你说起的挂在橱窗里的漂亮东西了。"

保罗走下车,将跛脚的弟弟抱到了车子的前座。满眼发亮的哥哥也爬上车子,坐在弟弟的身边。三个人开始了一次令人难忘的节日之旅。

那个圣诞节前夜,保罗才真正体会到"施与比接受更有福"这句话的含义。

但愿世界上的人都能成为那样的哥哥。

Don't Wait Till the Flowers Wilt

Each spring brings a new blossom of wildflowers in the ditches along the highway I travel daily to work.

There is one particular blue flower that has always caught my eye. I've noticed that it blooms only in the morning hours, for the afternoon sun is too warm for it. Every day for approximately two weeks, I see those beautiful flowers.

This spring, I started a wildflower garden in our yard. I can look out of the kitchen window while doing the dishes and see the flowers. I've often thought that those lovely blue flowers from the ditch would look great in that bed alongside other wildflowers.

Every day I drove past the flowers thinking, "I'll stop on my way home and dig them." "Gee, I don't want to get my good clothes dirty…" Whatever the reason, I never stopped to dig them. My husband even gave me a folding shovel one year for my trunk to be used for that expressed purpose.

One day on my way home from work, I was saddened to see that the highway department had mowed the ditches and the pretty blue flowers were gone. I thought to myself, "Way to go, you waited too long. You should have done it when you first saw them blooming this spring."

A week ago we were shocked and saddened to learn that my oldest sister-in-law has a terminal brain tumor. She is 20 years older than my husband and unfortunately, because of age and distance, we haven't been as close as we all would have liked.

I couldn't help but see the connection between the pretty blue flowers and the relationship between my husband's sister and us. I do believe that God has given us some time left to plant some wonderful memories that will bloom every year for us.

And yes, if I see the blue flowers again, you can bet I'll stop and transplant them to my wildflower garden.

莫等到花儿都谢了

在我每天上班沿途公路的那些沟渠里，每年春天都会绽放野花。

有一种独特的蓝花总是吸引我的注意。我注意到，它只在早晨开放，午后阳光对它太热了。大约两周时间，我每天都看到那些美丽的花朵。

今年春天，我在我们的院子里着手建了一个野花园。我在做菜时，通过厨房窗口可以看到那些鲜花。我常常想，沟渠里那些可爱的蓝花在沟底其他野花的衬托下看上去一定会很棒。

每天我开车经过那些花朵就会想："我要在回家的路上停下来，把它们挖走。""哎呀，我不想把好衣服弄脏……"无论什么原因，我从来没有停下来挖那些花。有一年，丈夫甚至曾特地为我的汽车尾部行李箱配了一把折叠铲。

有一天，下班回家途中，我非常伤心地看到，公路部门已经填平了那些沟渠，漂亮的蓝花不见了踪影。我想："你等得太久了，你应该在刚看到它们开花的这个春天就挖的。"

一周前，我们既震惊又悲痛地获悉，年龄最大的姐姐得了脑瘤晚期。她比我的丈夫大20岁。不幸的是，由于年龄和距离远，我们都没有像以前那样密切联系了。

我不禁明白了那些漂亮蓝花的联系以及丈夫的姐姐和我们的关系。我确实相信，上帝已经给了我们一些时间来种植一些美好的回忆，这些回忆每年都会为我们开放。

是的，如果我再次看到那些蓝花，你可以断定，我会停下来，把它们移栽到我的野花园里。

I Love the Blue Flowers

I ran into a stranger as he passed by. "Oh, excuse me, please," was my reply.

He said, "Please excuse me, too; I just was not watching for you."

We were very polite, this stranger and I.

We said good-bye and went on our way.

But at home, a different story is told: how we treat our loved ones.

That day, when I was cooking the supper, my son stood beside me, very still.

When I turned, I nearly knocked him down.

"Move out of the way," I said with a frown.

He walked away, his little heart broken.

I didn't realize how harshly I'd spoken.

While I lay awake in bed, God's small voice came to me and said, "While dealing with a stranger, you're very polite, but the family you love, you seem to abuse. Go and look on the kitchen floor; you'll find some flowers there by the door. Those are the flowers he brought for you. He picked them himself: pink, yellow and blue. He stood very quietly not to spoil the surprise; you never saw the tears that filled his eyes."

By this time I felt very small. And now my tears began to fall.

I quietly went and knelt by his bed. "Wake up, little one, wake up," I said. "Are these the flowers you picked for me?"

He smiled. "I found them, out by the tree. I picked them because they're pretty like you. I know you'd like them, especially the blue."

I said, "Son, I'm sorry for the way I acted today; I shouldn't have yelled at you that way."

He said, "Mom, that's okay. I love you, anyway."

I said, "Son, I love you, too. And I do like the flowers, especially the blue."

我 爱 蓝 花

我和一个过路的陌生人撞在一起。"噢,请原谅。"我回答说。

他说:"也请原谅;我确实没有注意到你。"

我和这个陌生人都彬彬有礼。

我们彼此道别,继续前行。

但在家里,我们对待我们所爱的人,情况却不一样。

那天,我正在做晚饭时,儿子站在我身边,一动不动。

我转身时,差点儿把他撞倒。

"一边去,别碍事。"我皱着眉头说。

他走开了,幼小的心灵受到了伤害。

我没有注意到我说的话是多么严厉。

我睁眼躺在床上,上帝小声对我说:"对待一个陌生人,你彬彬有礼,但对你所爱的家人,你似乎出言不逊啊。去看看厨房的地板,你会发现门边有一些花朵。那是他为你采的花儿。是他亲自去采的,有粉红的、黄的和蓝的。他静静地站着,不想破坏了那份惊喜。你压根就没有看到他眼里含的泪花。"

此时,我感到自己非常渺小,泪水开始流了下来。

我悄悄地来到他的床边跪下来,说:"醒一醒,小宝贝,醒一醒。这些花是你为我采的吗?"

他微笑着说:"我在外面的树边发现了它们。我摘它们,是因为它们像你一样漂亮。我知道你会喜欢它们,特别是那些蓝花。"

我说:"儿子,我对自己今天的所作所为感到抱歉。我不该对你那样大喊大叫。"

他说:"妈妈,没事儿。不管怎样,我都爱你。"

我说:"儿子,我也爱你。我真喜欢那些花,特别是那些蓝花。"

Grandma's Love Letters

I was only seventeen when Grandma Elsie died. She was my last living grandparent and I was her only grandchild. It was until the lawyer read her will that I never fully appreciated the depth of the old lady's love. It was a moment I will never forget—a day that made me the richest kid in town.

Mom, Dad, Aunt Sophie, Uncle Bill and I sat around a small conference table in her attorney's office. She wanted her daughters and their husbands to share what little monetary wealth she left-the proceeds of her small insurance policy, an antique cameo, a few bracelets, some costume jewelry and her wedding band. She also bequeathed them the deed to her house, her bank account, a few shares of stock in the local Gas and Electric Company, as well as the American flag she was presented with at Grandpa Edwin's military funeral.

As we rose to leave, the attorney said, "There are three more things." He reached into his briefcase and brought out a small jewelry box, a letter, and a stack of envelopes neatly wrapped in tissue paper and tied with a fading pink ribbon. "Jeffrey, your grandmother left you her diamond engagement ring, hoping you'll make good use of it soon." Everyone smiled.

"These are also for you, Jeffrey," he said. "It may be the most precious legacy of all—a letter and this stack of love notes."

Grandma's letter began, "Dear Jeffrey, I am leaving you one of my most precious treasures—my memories. These memories are the letters your grandfather Edwin wrote when he was away from me. Please read them. They are both priceless and valuable—a guidebook that will teach you how to love a woman, how to understand people, and how to respect and maintain your integrity.

"When you read them, you will share the longing and passion a good man feels for a good woman, and you will also discover the empowering enchantment they will give you. You will also understand the fears and tears of war. And you will realize the differences between right and wrong. You will learn to trust the people you love and keep you distance from those you mistrust. You will learn about mature friendship and how true love can become the core of your life.

"I have been fortunate, Jeffrey. I loved a wonderful man. And he loved me. While his love is now a memory, it is also a real dream that never ends. Love is like a beautiful photograph you treasure in an album. You can enjoy its beauty each time you stare at its wonderment. It stops time. And, it makes you young again—forever! Grandpa Edwin was a professional Army officer who chased Pancho Villa back to Mexico with John J. Pershing. He also served under General Pershing in the trenches in France during World War II. To understand your grandfather's soul, read his loving letters to me. You'll learn how romantic and beautiful a real man can be. To truly understand Grandpa's character, read the personal note Jack Pershing wrote me when he heard that Edwin was killed in action.

"Jeffrey, I said this packet of notes was priceless and valuable. I've just shown you how priceless his love notes are. Please learn from them. Then find the right girl to love and love her ardently. This love will enrich both your lives and make you both happier.

"As for being valuable, save the envelopes. An appraiser at Sotheby's said the old stamps are worth far more than the rest of my estate. And, the personal handwritten note from General Pershing is even more valuable than the stamps. Have a loving, bountiful life. God bless you.

"I love you, Grandma Elsie."

外婆的情书

外婆埃尔希去世时，我才17岁。她是我最后一位在世的祖辈，我是她唯一的外孙。直到律师宣读她的遗嘱，我才完全意识到外婆对我的爱有多深。那是一个我永远难忘的时刻，因为那天我成了城里最富有的男孩。

我和爸爸、妈妈、索菲姨妈、比尔姨父坐在外婆的律师办公室的一张小会议桌边。她想让她的女儿们、她们的丈夫分享她留下的一点财富：一小笔保险单收益、一块刻有浮雕的古宝石、几只镯子、一些人造宝石和她的结婚戒指。她还把房契、银行存款、在当地天然气和电力公司的几个股份，以及外公埃德温军事葬礼时获赠的美国国旗留给了他们。

我们起身离开时，律师说："还有三件东西。"他从公文包里拿出一个小珠宝盒、一封信和一叠用棉纸整洁包着、用褪色的粉红缎带扎着的信封，"杰弗里，你外婆把她的订婚钻戒留给了你，希望你不久好好利用它。"大家都露出了微笑。

"杰弗里，这些也是给你的，"他说，"也许是所有遗物中最珍贵的——一封信和一叠情书。"

外婆的信这样写道："亲爱的杰弗里：我要把最珍贵的财富——我的回忆留给你。这些回忆是你外公不在我身边时写给我的信。请你读一下这些信，它们是无价之宝，是一本教会你如何去爱一个女人、如何去理解他人以及如何自尊和保持气节的人生指南。

"看完后，你会分享到一个好男人对一个好女人的思念和深情，你也会发现它们将给你无穷的魅力。你还会明白战争带来的恐惧和眼泪。然后，你会明辨是非。你会学会去信赖所爱的人，远离不信任的人。你还会得知什么是成熟的友谊，真爱怎样才能成为你生命的核心。

"我很幸运，杰弗里。我爱上了一个了不起的男人。他也爱我。尽管他的爱现在成了一种回忆，但它也是一个永无止境的真实的梦。爱就像你珍藏在相册里的一张美丽的照片。每次凝视它，你都能欣赏到它的精彩和美丽。它让时光停住，并会让你青春焕发，永远年轻！埃德温外公是一名职业陆军军官。他和约翰·J.珀欣把潘乔·维亚追赶回了墨西哥。二战期间，他又在珀欣将军领导下转战法国。如果想了解你外公的为人，就看一下他写给我的情书。你会明白一个真正的男人可以多么浪漫和温文尔雅。如果想真正了解他的性格，就看一下杰克·珀欣得知你外公阵亡后写给我的私人信件。

"杰弗里，我说过这包信是无价之宝。我刚才给你看了他的情书是多么珍贵。请向它们学习，然后找一个合适的姑娘，好好爱她。这种爱将会丰富你们彼此的人生，也会让双方更加幸福。

"信件非常珍贵，要保存好那些信封。索思比的一位鉴定师说，这些旧邮票比我剩余的财产要值钱得多。而且，珀欣将军的亲笔信比那些邮票还要珍贵。度过一场相亲相爱、丰富多彩的人生。上帝保佑你！

"我爱你，埃尔希外婆。"

The Sweet Memory

It had been a long year for me, and the drive past the maturing vineyard, brought back memories of the many previous seasons that we had worked, to harvest the ripe Concord grapes. The memory of the taste itself brought back thoughts of my childhood, on a cool, fall afternoon, when I had first picked grapes.

As my grandma and I stepped out of the old, rusty, green pickup, we reached for the baskets that showed the age of many harvests. Soft, woven wood, stained in black-purple, from the many bunches of Concord grapes they had held in previous years. Now that the baskets were ready, we headed towards the seemingly endless rows of grapes.

With every visit to the vineyard, I was always over-awed by the way the grapevines grew and trailed off into the horizon. In every direction around me, there were rows upon rows of grapes, twinkling, as the morning sun glimmered its glow off the dew, still balancing on each tiny, round grape. It was as if the bunches of grapes were diamonds sparkling in the light.

As we continued to walk, further into the vineyard, I could hear the birds chirping their soft sounds, as they warned each other that we were approaching. I paused for a moment as my grandma continued ahead of me by a few feet. I watched her as she reached out to touch the ripening grapes, as if the coolness from the shimmering dew would let her know that this is where we were to begin.

We knelt on the ground and laid our baskets down at our sides as the birds began a different message in a much louder pitch, quite different from their first sounds. It was as if they were now accepting us and allowing us into their area. You could hear the rustling of the leaves, as the cool morning breeze swept past our faces and brought the fresh smell of the ripening grapes. The sweetly delicious smell would penetrate your senses.

I reached out delicately and removed one single grape from its bunch of many. Looking at this grape as if it were a perfect piece of art, I turned it around in my fingers, from side to side. The skin was cool and soft, more blue in color than black. I could smell and feel the juice dripping from the opened top, from where it had been attached to the bunch.

Slowly I brought the single grape closer to my mouth. I could feel my mouth filling with moisture. I brought the grape to the edge of my mouth and quickly squeezed it, so that the juicy, middle portion popped out of the smooth skin and into my mouth. The grape was even sweeter than I had hoped for and I enjoyed the texture of the smooth, meaty wetness inside my mouth. As my mouth enjoyed the motion of chewing this fruit, slowly swallowing it down my throat, I took the remaining skin of the grape, still positioned in my fingers.

Afterwards, I began to fill my basket with the wonders of nature. The bunches of grapes were plump and heavy to the touch, yet as delicate as small vulnerable creatures in your trusting care. I carefully piled them one on top of another, taking a moment, here and there, to taste another of these perfect fruits.

I knew that the taste would soon be another memory and I hoped that I would be available for the next harvest season.

甜蜜的回忆

这对我来说是漫长的一年,驱车驶过成熟的葡萄园,多年前在康科德葡萄园一季季采摘熟葡萄的情景又浮现在眼前。葡萄的美味使我的思绪回到了童年,那个凉爽的秋日午后是我第一次摘葡萄。

我和祖母从一辆又旧又锈的绿色敞篷小货车上下来,去取放葡萄的篮子,可以看出,那些篮子已经历了很多收获季节,软软的,木条编制,已被康科德前些年的葡萄染成了紫黑色。篮子准备好后,我们走向那仿佛一望无际的葡萄园。

每次来到葡萄园,面对这茁壮成长直至天际的葡萄藤,我总是诚惶诚恐。我身边四周各个方向都有一排排葡萄。在晨光照耀下,每颗小圆葡萄上都有露珠闪耀,一串串的葡萄像灯光中的钻石一样波光闪闪。

我们继续向前走,听到小鸟轻柔的啁啾声,它们是相互提醒同伴我们正在走近。祖母向前继续走了几英尺,我暂停了一会儿,看到她伸手去摸成熟的葡萄,葡萄上闪耀凉爽的露水似乎告诉她,我们该从这里开始。

我们跪在地上,把篮子放在身边,鸟儿们开始以响亮得多的音高发出不同的消息。好像现在它们正在接待我们并允许我们进入它们的领域。清晨的凉风拂面，树叶沙沙作响，葡萄成熟的清香随风飘来。甜美的气息会渗透你的各个感官。

我小心翼翼地伸出手，摘下其中一颗葡萄。我看着这颗葡萄，在手指间翻来覆去把玩着，就像它是一件完美的艺术品似的。葡萄的外皮清凉柔软，蓝色比黑色多。我可以闻到并感觉到连接着葡萄串的开口处滴下的汁液。

我慢慢地把那颗葡萄送到嘴边，可以感受到嘴里充满了润泽。我把葡萄放在嘴边，飞快地一挤，于是汁液和果肉脱离光润的果皮滑进了我的嘴里。葡萄比我希望的还要香甜。我享受着嘴里咀嚼的鲜润和果肉，慢慢咽下喉咙，然后开始吮吸留在手里的葡萄皮。

品尝过后，我开始向篮子里装这一个个自然的奇迹。一串串葡萄摸起来圆润厚实，而又小巧易碎，需要细心呵护。我小心翼翼地撩起一串串葡萄，不时地抽空品尝一下这完美的果实。

我知道这滋味很快会成为另一次回忆，我希望不会错过下一个丰收的季节。

A Letter to Grandpa

Dear Grandpa,

I cannot help but think about you, who have so much to give and share with me happily.

Even when I was young, you were a constant figure. You were there to see me grow up. I cried, I laughed, I learned, and you were there to guide me. With your gray hair and chunky glasses, I would watch you think and brood, and your sudden smile would light up your face as quickly as it came.

That is the very thing I love about you—your smile!

I think about the times I missed being with you. So many years have passed since I saw you again, and for a brief moment, I imagined you not being in my life. I wanted to cry. But I knew you would be there, as you always were. The gray hair has turned to white, and with that came a wiry frame that was fragile. Still the eyes were as vibrant as ever, and a mind that was well-running.

You taught me to be strong and live for my dreams. With your voracious hunger for knowledge you taught me to love learning; always telling me that knowledge is a constant thing. You were so strong, so wise and your presence was always a comfort. I always loved being by your side. You always gave me a hug when I fell down. I never loved crowds, and you always seemed to understand that, not pressuring me to join the others or to pretend to have a good time.

  I got lost in the books you taught me to read. Those books which you gave me to learn more about the world, to never give up on things, to help me know myself and more. I read them constantly, ever so often reminded of the things you taught me.

  I remember you with a teary face and a wistful smile. My pain is more insistent as I try to hold on to the hope that you will pull through this, like the strong person that you are.

  I love you, Grandpa!

Your loving granddaughter
Sylvia

写给爷爷的信

亲爱的爷爷：

  我无时无刻不在想着您，想着您对我的好，想着我们在一起分享快乐的时光。

  我小时候，您就一直守在我身边，您一直关注着我的成长，无论是我在哭泣，在欢笑，还是在学习，您都在身边引导我。我常常想起您戴着一副厚眼镜的样子，您满头灰白的头发，常常情不自禁地陷入沉思，但突然的一个微笑能让您一下子容光焕发。

  那正是我最喜欢您的东西——您的微笑！

  我想起那些我们无法在一起的时光，我们再次见面竟然间隔了好几年时间。如果我的生命里没有您，我真的会放声大哭，但我知道您会一直陪着我。灰白的头发被岁月染成了银白，让我们明白了时间的无情和生命的脆弱。尽管如此，您的眼睛仍然那样明亮，思维仍然那样清晰。

  您教我要坚强，要追求自己的梦想。您自己是那样孜孜不倦地学习，您也常常鼓励我要爱学习，因为知识是无价之宝。您是那样坚强，那样充满智慧。有您在身边总能让我感到安慰。我一直都喜欢待在您的身边。当我跌倒的时候，您会给我一个拥抱。我从来都不喜欢到热闹的人群中去，而您给了我很大程度的理解和尊重，从不勉强我去参加一些聚会或假装自己很快乐。

  我深深地迷上了那些您推荐给我的书，那些书让我更多地了解了这个世界，让我知道不能轻易放弃对理想的追求，也让我更多地了解了自己。我常常捧着那些书看，也常常想起您教我的那些事情。

您的话从来就不多,但每次我们见面,我都知道您非常开心,就像我见到您时非常开心一样。

我含着泪面带微笑地想起您。虽然我还是那样痛苦难受,但我还是期待着您能挺过这一关,因为您从来都是那样坚强。

我爱您,爷爷!

您心爱的孙女
西尔维亚

Tommy's Essay

A gray sweater hung limply on Tommy's empty desk, a reminder of the dejected boy who had just followed his classmates from our third-grade room. Soon Tommy's parents, who had recently separated, would arrive for a conference on his failing schoolwork and disruptive behavior. Neither parent knew that I had summoned the other.

Tommy, an only child, had always been happy, cooperative and an excellent student. How could I convince his father and mother that his recent failing grades represented a broken-hearted child's reaction to his adored parents' separation and pending divorce?

Tommy's mother entered and took one of the chairs I had placed near my desk. Soon the father arrived. Good! At least they were concerned enough to be prompt. A look of surprise and irritation passed between them, and then they pointedly ignored each other.

As I gave a detailed account of Tommy's behavior and schoolwork, I prayed for the right words to bring these two together, to help them see what they were doing to their son. But somehow the words wouldn't come. Perhaps if they saw one of his smudged, carelessly done papers.

I found a crumpled tear-stained sheet stuffed in the back of his desk, an English paper. Writing covered both sides—not the assignment, but a single sentence scribbled over and over. Silently I smoothed it out and gave it to Tommy's mother. She read it and then without a word handed it to her husband. He frowned. Then his face softened. He studied the scrawled words for what seemed an eternity.

At last he folded the paper carefully, placed it in his pocket, and reached for his wife's outstretched hand. She wiped the tears from her eyes and smiled up at him. My own eyes were brimming, but neither seemed to notice. He helped her with her coat and they left together.

In his own way God had given me the words to reunite that family. He had guided me to the sheet of yellow copy paper covered with the anguished outpouring of a small boy's troubled heart.

The words were, "Dear Mom…Dear Daddy…I love you…I love you…I love you."

汤米的随笔

一件灰色羊毛衫无力地挂在汤米空荡荡的书桌上，这使人想起了刚刚跟随同学们走出我们三年级教室的那个垂头丧气的男孩。很快，最近分居的汤米的父母亲就会来到这里，讨论他错误百出的作业和扰乱课堂的行为。汤米的父母亲都不知道我也叫了对方。

汤米是独生子，过去一向是快乐合作、非常优秀的学生。我怎样才能使他的父母亲相信，他最近考试屡屡不及格，是一个伤心的孩子对他心爱的父母亲分居、即将离婚做出的反应呢？

汤米的妈妈走进来，在我桌边的一张椅子上坐下。很快，他的父亲也来了。好！他们都很准时，说明都很关心。他们俩的表情既惊讶又愤怒，之后显然就不理睬对方了。

我一边详细讲述汤米的行为和作业，一边祈求合适的词语使这两个人重归于好，帮助他们明白他们正在给孩子造成怎样的影响。但是，不知何故，我没有想出合适的词语。也许他们看到他污迹斑斑、马马虎虎的作业会起作用吧。

我在他的书桌后部找到了一张皱皱巴巴、泪迹斑斑的纸，是英语作业纸。正反两面写的都是字，不是作业，而是反反复复、潦潦草草的一句话。我默默地捋平作业纸，把它递给汤米的妈妈。她看过后，什么也没说，递给了丈夫。他皱了皱眉，然后表情柔和了下来。他端详着那些潦草的字，看了好长时间。

最后，他仔细叠起了那张纸，放进了口袋里，然后去拉妻子伸出的手。她擦掉了眼上的泪水，抬头向他微笑。我也流出了眼泪，但他们好像谁也没注意到。他帮她穿上了大衣，他们一起走了。

上帝以自己的方式赐给我话语，使那个家庭破镜重圆。他指引我去拿那张流露出一个伤心小男孩痛苦情绪的黄色作业纸。

那上面的话是："亲爱的爸爸……亲爱的妈妈……我爱你们……我爱你们……我爱你们。"

The Love of a Full Moon

My daughter Kate turns the page of the kitchen calendar to a new month and motions to her sister, Kenna. Together they find "Full Moon Night" and mark it with a bright sticker. At our house, full moons signal the time for magical after-dark forays.

My inspiration for this tradition was an October canoe outing with friends years ago. I had loved the way the full moon transformed the night, making the familiar landscape serene and mysterious. By the time my daughters were both three, I was sure they would enjoy such an evening.

Our first full-moon outing as a family fell on a frosty Wisconsin evening. The birch trees in our front yard cast an intricate pattern of shadows as we stepped into our cross-country skis. Although the air was cold, our physical activity and sheer exhilaration kept us warm.

We were surprised at how bright the moonlight was as it reflected off the untracked snow. "The Indians in this region had different names for each full moon," I told the girls. This one was called Shaking Hands Moon.

Kate led the way, with Kenna close behind; my husband, Tom, and I brought up the rear. Soon we were gliding across a frozen lake, our shadows gliding beside us. Finally, we meandered back along the shoreline, toward the glow of our windows.

Inside, we celebrated our trek with hot cider and popcorn. The girls' rosy cheeks and smiles assured me we'd have more moonlit adventures.

We did, under February's Sturgeon Moon; then under full moons called Crusted Snow, Maple Sugar and Budding for March, April and May, respectively. A warm June evening proved just right for skinny-dipping under a girls—only Strawberry Moon. Father-daughter night yielded a bucketful of freshly caught lake perch, as July's Half-Summer Moon lit the sky.

Another year, on a star-filled August night, with a Blueberry Moon on the rise, we spread a blanket in the back yard. The northern lights were dancing, and questions came quickly: "What makes all the colors, Daddy?" "Where will that star land, Mommy?" The girls returned to the house bubbling with enthusiasm. Out came books on the moon, stars, planets and space exploration.

I shouldn't have been surprised when, a few weeks later, Kate looked up at a quarter moon and observed: "That's a waning moon—it's getting smaller. If it were getting bigger, it would be a waxing moon."

As the holidays neared, one of the girls asked, "Could we cut down our Christmas tree on Full Moon Night?" Why not? I thought. And it was not long before Kate and Kenna were running ahead in the woods behind our house, searching for the perfect specimen, their pink snowsuits made softer in the moonglow. "Here it is," shouted Kenna. "It's perfect," said Kate, pointing to a different tree. We finally found the right one for all of us, and with December's Night Moon smiling down, the girls made snow angels around the tree in celebration.

Another of our favorite nights of full-moon magic was spent exploring a ghost town on the Upper Peninsula of Michigan. Walking down a dusty road through a long-forgotten town can be daunting enough in daylight. At night we tiptoed around the abandoned buildings, holding hands. Ordinary sounds became extraordinary in the silent emptiness. Wispy clouds temporarily masked our moonlight. Then the hoot of an owl made us all jump—and we broke into laughter.

We have yet to run out of ideas for our adventures. The girls want to try a moonlight treasure hunt, and Kenna suggested building a snowman in her grandmother's yard. "She'd wake up and wonder how he got there."

On our most recent adventure, we packed an evening picnic and headed for an observation tower in a nearby state park. We climbed the steps until we thought we must be on top of the world: we could see the twinkling lights of towns up and down the shore and hear the lapping of waves below us. In the distance, a lighthouse cast its beam across the water.

We had gazed at the view countless times before, but this was different. The four of us were seeing it in a gloriously new light.

满 月 情

我的女儿凯特将厨房里的日历翻到了新的一月，然后向她的妹妹凯娜打了个手势。她们一起找出了"满月之夜"，用一个背面有粘胶的鲜艳标签做了个记号。在我们家，满月标志着黑暗过后神奇的短暂出游。

几年前，我与朋友们在10月一起乘着独木舟外出郊游，使我对这个传统获得了灵感。我喜欢满月改变了夜空，使熟悉的景色变得宁静而神秘。到两个女儿都3岁时，我确信她们会喜欢这样一个夜晚的。

我们第一次的满月郊游是一家人到威斯康星州度过的一个寒夜。我们跨入横穿村庄的雪橇时，我们前院的白桦树已经投下了一片斑驳的阴影。虽然空气寒冷，但身体的活动和极度的兴奋使我们都感到暖融融的。

月光反射着无人走过的雪地，明亮得使我们吃惊。我对姑娘们说："本地区的印第安人给每个满月都取有不同的名字。"本月的满月被称为"握手月"。

凯特领路，凯娜紧随其后；我和丈夫汤姆殿后。不久，我们滑行在一个冰冻的湖上，我们的身影也不离左右地滑动着。最后，我们沿着湖岸线恋恋不舍地朝我们家窗户的灯光返回。

到了家里，我们用热果汁和爆米花庆祝这次旅行。姑娘们红润的脸颊和微笑使我确信，我们还会有更多的月光冒险之行。

我们的确在2月的鲟月下，然后在3月、4月和5月分别被称为硬壳雪、槭糖和萌芽的满月下进行了冒险旅行。温暖的6月之夜正是姑娘们在草莓月下单独裸泳的好时光。当7月的仲夏月照亮天空时，父女们则在夜里呈上来满满一桶刚捉到的湖鲈。

还有一年，在星星满天的一个8月之夜，一轮蓝莓月冉冉升起。我们在后院里铺开一张毛毯。北极光在熠熠闪动。很快，姑娘们产生了疑问："爸爸，所有那些颜色是怎么来的？""妈妈，那颗星星会落到哪里？"姑娘们兴致勃勃地回到了房子里。翻翻有关月亮、恒星、行星和太空探索的书，问题就迎刃而解了。

几周后，凯特仰望一弯弦月说："那是一个亏月，它正变得越来越小。如果它变得越来越大，它就是一个盈月。"对此，我一点没有感到意外。

每当节日临近时，其中一个女儿就问："我们可以在满月之夜砍下我们的圣诞树吗？"为什么不可以呢？我想。不久，凯特和凯娜就一头钻进我们家屋后的树林里，寻找起完美的样板树。她们粉红色的风雪衣在月光下变得越发柔和。"这棵树！"凯娜大声说。"这棵完美。"凯特指着另一棵不同的树说。最后，我们找到了每个人都满意的一棵树。随后，在12月的夜月面带微笑的俯视下，姑娘们在那棵树四周堆起了几个白雪天使，以示庆祝。

我们度过的另一个最让人喜欢的神奇的满月之夜，是去密歇根州北方半岛上的一座鬼城探险。大白天沿着一条土路越过一座久被遗忘的城镇就足以让人感到胆怯了。夜里，我们蹑手蹑脚地手拉手绕着那些荒凉的建筑行走。寂静的空旷中，平常声音也变得异常起来，几缕云彩暂时遮住了我们的月光。接着，一只猫头鹰的鸦叫吓得我们都一下子跳了起来。随后，我们爆发出了朗朗的笑声。

然而，我们不得不绞尽脑汁考虑着我们的冒险旅行。姑娘们想尝试月光探宝旅行，而凯娜则建议在她外婆的院子里堆一个雪人。"外婆醒来后会纳闷雪人是怎么到那里的。"

在最近的一次冒险中，我们打点好一顿晚餐，前往附近的一家州立公园的观测塔。我们爬上台阶，直至我们认为一定站在了世界之巅：我们可以看到沿岸上下灯光闪烁，听到我们下面浪花拍岸。远处，一座灯塔的光线掠过水面。

我们曾观赏过无数次这样的情景，但这次不同。我们四人是在新的一轮灿烂月光中看的。

Love Notes

It's been over eleven years now. It was a wintry afternoon, the snow swirling around the cedar trees outside, forcing little icicles to form the tips of the deep green foliage clinging to the branches.

My older son, Stephen, was at school, and Reed, my husband, at work. My three little ones were clustered around the kitchen counter, the tabletop piled high with crayon and markers. Tom was perfecting a paper airplane, creating his own insignia with stars and stripes, while Sam worked on a self-portrait, his chubby hands drawing first a head, then legs and arms sticking out where the body should had been. The children most concentrated on their work, Tom occasionally tutoring his younger brother on exactly how to make a plane that would fly the entire length of the room.

But Laura, our only daughter, sat quietly, engrossed in her project. Every once in a while she would ask how to spell the name of someone in our family, then painstakingly form the letters one by one. Next, she would add flowers with small green stems, complete with grass lining the bottom of the page. She finished off each with a sun in the upper right-hand corner, surrounded by an inch or two of blue sky. Holding them at eye level, she let out a long sigh of satisfaction.

"What are you making, Honey?" I asked.

She glanced at her brothers before looking back at me.

"It's a surprise," she said, covering up her work with her hands.

Next, she taped the top two edges of each other of paper together, trying her best to create a cylinder. When she had finished, she disappeared up the stairs with her treasure.

It was not until later that evening that I noticed a "mailbox" taped onto the doors to each of our bedrooms. There was one for Steve. There was one for Tom. She hadn't forgotten Sam or baby Paul.

For the next few weeks, we received mail on a regular basis. There were little notes expressing her love for each of us. There were short letters full of tiny compliments that only a seven-year-old would notice. I was in charge of retrieving baby Paul's letter, page after page of colored scenes including flowers with happy faces.

"He can't read yet," she whispered. "But he can look at the pictures."

Each time I received one of my little girl's gifts, it brightened my heart.

I was touched at how carefully she observed our moods. When Stephen lost a baseball game, there was a letter telling him she thought he was the best ballplayer in the whole world. After I had a particularly hard day, there was a message thanking me for my efforts, complete with a smiley face tucked near the bottom corner of the page.

This same little girl is grown now, driving off every day to the community college. But some things about her have never changed. One afternoon only a week or so ago, I found a love note next to my bedside.

"Thanks for always being there for me, Mom," it read. "I'm glad that we're the best friends."

I couldn't help but remember the precious child whose smile has brought me countless hours of joy throughout the years. There are angels among us. I know, I live with one.

爱 的 纸 条

那已是11年前的事了。一个冬天的下午，雪在门外的雪松四周飞舞，使树枝上深绿色的叶尖挂上了小小的冰柱。

大儿子史蒂芬上学去了，丈夫里德上班去了。三个小家伙挤在橱柜边，桌面上高高地堆着蜡笔和记号笔，汤姆正用星星和条纹画徽章，让纸飞机尽善尽美。山姆正在忙着自画像。他胖胖的小手先画了一个脑袋，然后在本该是身体的位置画出了腿和胳膊。孩子们大都聚精会神忙自己的事儿。汤姆不时地教弟弟怎样正确制作一架能飞过整个房间的飞机。

我们唯一的女儿劳拉却安静地坐在那里，全神贯注地忙她的事儿。偶尔她也会询问怎样拼写我们家某个人的名字，然后一个字母、一个字母用心地拼写出来，接着又画了一些带细小绿茎的花朵，纸张底部还有一些草边。她每画完一页，都会在右上角画上太阳，周围是一两寸的蓝天。她把它们举到和眼水平的位置，然后满意地长出了口气。

"宝贝，你在做什么？"我问。

她在看我之前，瞥了一眼她的兄弟们。

"这是一个意外的惊喜。"她双手捂住自己的作品说。

接下来，她粘住每张纸的上面两边，尽力做成一个圆筒。做好后，她带着那些宝贝消失在楼梯上。

直到那天晚上晚些时候，我才注意到每个人的卧室门上都贴着一个"邮箱"。史蒂夫有一个，汤姆有一个，她也没有忘记萨姆和小保罗。

随后的几周里，我们都定期收到信件。小小的纸条表达了她对我们每个人的爱。有些短信里充满了一个只有7岁孩子才会注意到的小小问候。我负责取小保罗的信件，那是一页又一页的彩色图画，其中包括花朵和笑脸。

"他还不会念字，"她低声说道，"但他可以看这些图画。"

每次收到小女儿的礼物，我就心情愉悦。

她对我们心情的细微观察让我感动。史蒂芬输了棒球赛时，便有一封信告诉他，她认为他是全世界最好的棒球手。我哪天特别辛苦时，便会有一封信感谢我的努力，并在信封上画有一张笑脸。

如今，这个小女孩已经长大，每天开车上社区学院。但她身上的有些事从未改变。大约仅仅在一周前的一天下午，我在枕边发现了一张爱的纸条。

"妈妈，感谢您一直以来都支持我，"上面写道，"我很高兴我们是最好的朋友。"

我情不自禁想起，这些年来这个心爱的孩子的笑容带给了我无数欢乐时刻。我们中间有天使，我知道，我正和其中一位生活在一起。

Love Is Not a Single Act

It was an autumn night in my native Nova Scotia. A light rain was falling, pattering on the porch roof, and it was cool enough for a fire on the Franklin stove. My father went over to the piano and began picking out a tune with one finger. My mother smiled as though recognizing a signal, put down her sewing and joined him on the bench.

In a moment they were singing—he in his sweet high tenor, Mother in her crystal clear soprano. My brother, coming in at that moment, drifted to the piano and joined in. Finally, I, the non-singer of the family, added my voice, and for once I held a makeshift alto for a line or two. My father gave me a hug. "See, you can," he said. "That was good."

I have often remembered how warm and happy—and loved—I have felt at that moment. It took me years, though, to learn that the love surrounding our family didn't just happen. We had to learn about love from one another. In fact, love never just happen—not even to people who seem as naturally loving as my mother and father. But there is, I think, a climate that is best for love—a way of living that hastens the maturity of this matchless gift.

First, love needs time. Perhaps people can fall in love in a moment, but mature love is like a tree, moving slowly from the seed in the ground to the sheltering splendor of its prime. People need time to deepen their affection, to appreciate one another's differences, to share one another's joys and grievances. So it is sad when divorces come with small provocations, when parents and children give up on one another, when friendships falter at the first injury; for thus we forfeit a great work of art—the long love.

When we accept the differences of loved ones, we find that those very differences provide the mystery and wonder of human relationships. It's foolish to expect perfection, for it doesn't exist. The key is to recognize and enjoy our differences.

To grow, love needs another, more elusive quality—the ability to let go.

Finally, love needs words to make it real. Without words, quarrels can't be resolved, resentment can't come to the surface, we lose the power to share the meaning of our lives. There are many ways of communication. The important thing is to acknowledge and express our feelings. If we don't, we deprive others of the knowledge of our love and ourselves of the joy that comes from expressing it.

Love is not a single act, but a climate in which we live, a lifetime venture in which we are always learning, discovering, growing. It is not destroyed by a single failure, or won by a single caress.

Love is a climate—a climate of the heart.

爱不是一场独角戏

那是在我的家乡新斯科舍省的一个秋夜。细雨蒙蒙，雨水滴滴答答地打在门廊顶上。天已经很凉了，我们在富兰克林壁炉式取暖炉里生起了火。父亲走到钢琴前，用一根手指一个音节、一个音节地弹奏着一首曲调。母亲面带微笑，好像听出了约定的信号，她放下手中的针线活，挨着父亲坐到琴凳上。

他们立马唱了起来，爸爸用的是甜美的男高音，妈妈用的是清亮的女高音。此时，哥哥走进来，飘然来到钢琴边和他们一起唱。最后，就连我这个家中不会唱歌的人也加入了他们的行列，我用女低音不时地插上一两句。父亲拥抱着我说："瞧，你会唱，唱得不错。"

我时常回忆起当时的那份温暖、幸福和受到关爱的感觉。然而，我多年以后才明白我们家中那种爱的氛围不是偶然形成的。我们必须得了解彼此的爱。实际上，爱从来就不会偶然产生，即使像父母亲这样的人也是如此，尽管他们看上去是天生相爱的一对。但我想有一种氛围对爱的生长是再好不过的，那就是一种可以促进这种无与伦比的天赋成熟的生活方式。

首先，爱需要时间。也许人们可能会一见钟情，但成熟的爱情就像一棵树，由土壤里的一粒种子慢慢长成参天大树。人们需要时间加深彼此的感情，理解双方的差异，分享相互的苦乐。因此，为鸡毛蒜皮的一点小事便分道扬镳，父母和子女各自心灰意冷，以及彼此的友谊因一次伤害而发生动摇，这些都是令人伤心的事情，因为我们会因而失去一件伟大的艺术品——持久的爱。

当接受与所爱的人之间的差异时，我们发现正是那些差异造就了人际关系中的奥妙和神奇。期望尽善尽美是非常愚蠢的，因为它并不存在。关键是要认识并分享彼此的差异。

为了使爱得到升华，还需要具有另一种独有的品质——放手的能力。

最后，爱需要通过语言使它成为现实。没有语言，分歧就无法解决，怨恨也无法显露出来，我们也就失去了分享生活意义的权利。交流的方式有许多。重要的是了解并能表达我们的情感。如果不进行情感交流，我们就会剥夺别人了解我们之间爱的权利，同时也剥夺了我们自己表达爱情时的那种快乐。

爱不是一场独角戏，而是一种生活氛围，也是我们毕生所追求的，在这一过程中我们要不断学习，不断发现并逐渐成熟起来。爱不会因为一次小小的挫折而毁灭，也不会因为一次的爱抚而赢得。

爱是一种氛围，一种心灵的氛围。

Greet This Day with Love

I will greet this day with love in my heart. For this is the greatest secret of success in all ventures. Muscle can split a shield and even destroy life but only the unseen power of love can open the hearts of men. I will make love my greatest weapon and none can defend against its force.

And how will I do this? Henceforth will I look on all things with love and I will be born again. I will love the sun, for it warms my bones; yet I will love the rain, for it cleanses my spirit. I will love the light, for it shows me the way; yet I will love the darkness, for it shows me the stars. I will welcome happiness, for it enlarges my heart; yet I will endure sadness, for it opens my soul. I will acknowledge rewards, for they are my due; yet I will welcome obstacles, for they are my challenge.

And how will I speak? I will laud my enemies and they will become friends; I will encourage my friends and they will become brothers. Always will I dig for reasons to applaud; never will I scratch for excuses to gossip. When I am tempted to criticize I will bite on my tongue; when I am moved to praise I will shout from the roofs.

Is it not so that birds, the wind, the sea and all nature speaks with the music of praise for their creator? Cannot I speak with the same music to his children? Henceforth will I remember this secret and it will change my life.

And how will I act? I will love all manner of men, for each has qualities to be admired even though they are hidden. With love I will tear down the wall of suspicion and hate which they have built round their hearts and in its place will I build bridges so that my love may enter their souls.

I will love the ambitious, for they can inspire me! I will love the failures, for they can teach me. I will love the kings, for they are but humans; I will love the meek, for they are divine. I will love the rich, for they yet lonely.

I will love the poor, for they are so many. I will love the young, for the faith they hold; I will love the old, for the wisdom they share. I will love the beautiful, for their eyes of sadness; I will love the ugly, for their souls of peace.

But how will I react to the actions of others? With love. For just as love is my weapon to open the hearts of men, love is also my shield to repulse the arrows of hate and the spears of anger. Adversity and discouragement will beat against my new shield and become as the softest of rains.

And how I confront each whom I meet? In only one way. In silence and to myself I will address him and say, "I Love You." Though spoken in silence these words will shine in my eyes, unwrinkle my brow, bring a smile to my lips, and echo in my voice; and his heart will be opened.

用爱迎接今天

我要用心中的爱迎接今天，因为这是所有冒险中最大的成功秘诀。臂力能劈开盾牌，甚至毁灭生命，但只有无形的爱的力量才能打开人们的心灵。我要让爱成为无人抵御的最强大武器。

我将做什么呢？从此，我将充满爱心地看待一切，使自己重获新生。我爱太阳，因为它能温暖我的身体。我爱雨水，因为它能净化我的心灵。我爱光明，因为它能照亮我的道路。我爱黑夜，因为它使我看到满天繁星。我将迎接快乐，因为它使我心胸开阔；我将忍受悲伤，因为它将打开我的灵魂。我将接受报酬，因为它们是我应该得到的。我将迎接困难，因为我愿迎接挑战。

我将说什么呢？我赞美敌人，他们会成为我的朋友；我鼓励朋友，他们将成为我的兄弟。我总要找理由赞美别人，而绝不挖空心思找借口说三道四。当我忍不住要批评人时，就咬住舌头；当我感动得赞美别人时，就大声说出口。

小鸟、风、海浪和世间万物，不都在用美妙悦耳的歌声赞美造物主吗？难道我不能同样的歌声去赞美它的儿女们吗？从此，我要记住这个秘诀，它将改变我的生活。

我将如何行动呢？我爱所有的人，因为每个人都有值得敬佩的优秀品质,即使他们秘而不宣。我要用爱摧垮阻碍人们心灵自由沟通的怀疑和仇恨之墙,同时我要用爱在人们之间搭建一座桥梁,使我的爱能进入他们的灵魂。

我爱有抱负的人,因为他们能激励我!我爱失败者,因为他们能教育我。我爱国王,因为他们不过是凡人。我爱谦恭者,因为他们是天才。我爱富人,他们更孤独。

我爱穷人,因为他们有很多人。我爱年轻人,因为他们坚定的信念。我爱长者,因为他们睿智。我爱美人,因为他们的眼神忧郁。我爱丑人,因为他们有平和的心灵。

但我对他们的行动怎样做出反应呢?用爱。因为爱不仅是打开人们心灵的钥匙,也是反击仇恨之箭和愤怒之矛的盾牌。逆境和挫折在我的新盾面前也会变得像细雨一样柔软。

我该怎样面对和我相遇的每个人呢?只有一种办法。我将默默地一心一意地对待他,并说"我爱你"。尽管无声,但这些话语将会闪现在我的眼神中,舒展我的眉头,让我的嘴唇露出微笑,引起我的共鸣,随后将会打开他的心灵。

The Old Man with Flowers

We were a very motley crowd of people who took the bus every day that summer 3 years ago. During the early morning ride from the suburb, we sat drowsily with our collars up to our ears, a cheerless and taciturn bunch.

One of the passengers was a small gray man who took the bus to the center for senior citizens every morning. He walked with a stoop and a sad look on his face when he, with some difficulty, boarded the bus and sat down alone behind the driver. No one ever paid very much attention to him.

Then one July morning he said good morning to the driver and smiled down through the bus before he sat down. The driver nodded guardedly. The rest of us were silent.

The next day, the old man boarded the bus energetically, smiled and said in a loud voice, "And a very good morning to you all!" Some of us looked up, amazed, and murmured "Good morning" in reply.

The following weeks we were more alert. Our friend was now dressed in a nice old suit and a wide out-of-date tie. The thin hair had been carefully combed. He said good morning to us every day and we gradually began to nod and talk to each other.

One morning he had a bunch of wild flowers in his hand. They were already dangling a little because of the heat. The driver turned around smilingly and asked:

"Have you got yourself a girlfriend, Charlie?" We never got to know if his name really was"Charlie", but he nodded shyly and said yes.

The other passengers whistled and clapped at him. Charlie bowed and waved the flowers before he sat down on his seat.

Every morning after that Charlie always brought a flower. Some of the regular passengers began bringing him flowers for his bouquet, gently nudged him and said shyly: "Here." Everyone smiled. The men started to jest about it, talk to each other, and share the newspaper.

The summer went by, and autumn was closing in, when one morning Charlie was not waiting at his usual stop. When he was not there the next day and the day after that, we started wondering if he was sick or on holiday somewhere.

When we came nearer to the center for senior citizens, one of the passengers asked the driver to wait. We all held our breaths when she went to the door. Yes, the staff said, they knew who we were talking about. The elderly gentleman was fine, but he hadn't been coming to the center that week. One of his very close friends had died at the weekend. They expected him back on Monday. How silent we were the rest of the way to work.

The next Monday Charlie was waiting at the stop, stooping a bit more, a little bit more gray, and without a tie. He seemed to have shrunk again. Inside the bus was a silence akin to that in a church. Even though no one had talked about it, all those of us, who he had made such an impression on that summer, sat with our eyes filled with tears and a bunch of wild flowers in our hands.

手持鲜花的老人

3年前的夏天，我们这些芸芸众生每天乘坐同一辆公共汽车。在郊区开往市里的早班车上，我们竖起衣领盖住耳朵，坐在那里昏昏欲睡，沉默寡言，了无情趣。

其中一名乘客是一个头发花白的小个子，他每天早上乘车去老年活动中心。他走起路来弓着腰、神情忧郁，每次有些吃力地上车后，就独自坐到司机后面。没有人过多地注意过他。

后来，7月的一个早晨，他向司机说了声早安，然后向车厢里的人微微笑了一下，才坐下来。司机谨慎地点了点头，我们其他人都一声不吭。

第二天，这位老人精神饱满地上了车，微微一笑，朗声说道："大家早上好！"我们中一些人抬起头，吃了一惊，低声回答说："早上好。"

接下来的几个星期，我们更加注意起了他。我们这位朋友穿着一件漂亮的旧西装，打着一条过时的宽领带，稀疏的头发梳得一丝不苟。每天他都向我们问早安。我们渐渐开始点头，相互交谈。

一天早上，他手里拿着一束野花。因为天气炎热，它们已经有点儿耷拉了。司机微笑着转过头，问道："你自己找女朋友了吧，查理？"我们根本不知道他是不是叫"查理"，但他不好意思地点头称是。

其他的乘客对他又是吹口哨，又是鼓掌。查理鞠了一躬，挥了挥手里的鲜花，然后在座位上坐了下来。

从那以后，查理每天早上都会带一朵花，有些老乘客也开始给他带鲜花，轻轻地用胳膊肘推他一下，不好意思地说："给。"每个人都面带微笑。大家开始开玩笑、聊天，一起看报纸。

夏去秋来。一天早上，查理没在以往那个站等车。以后的两天，他都没来，我们开始纳闷他是不是病了，或者是到什么地方度假去了。

当我们的车靠近老年活动中心时，一个乘客让司机停车。当她走到门口时，我们都屏住呼吸。那个职员说：是的，他们都知道我们说的是谁。那位老先生身体很好，但他那个星期没来活动中心。上周末，他非常亲近的一个朋友去世了，他们盼望他星期一能回来。剩下的路程，我们都沉默不语。

接下来的那个星期一，查理在那个站等车，他的背更弯了，头发更白了，也没打领带。他好像又缩回了从前。车里像教堂一样寂静。即使谁都没说话，我们所有的人也都眼噙热泪、手持一束野花，因为那个夏天，是他给我们留下了那样深刻的印象。

The Chain of Love

He was driving home one evening, on a two-lane country road. Work, in this small mid-western community, was almost as slow as his beat-up Pontiac was.

But he never quit looking. Ever since the factory closed, he'd been unemployed. And with winter raging on, the chill had finally hit home. It was a lonely road. Not very many people had a reason to be on it, unless they were leaving. Most of his friends had already left. They had families to feed and dreams to fulfill. But he stayed on. After all, this was where he buried his mother and father. He was born here and he knew the country. He could go down this road blind, and tell you what was on either side, and with his headlights not working, that came in handy.

It was starting to get dark and light snow flurries were coming down. He'd better get a move on. He almost didn't see the old lady, stranded on the side of the road. But even in the dim light of day, he could see she needed help.

So he pulled up in front of her Mercedes and got out. His Pontiac was still sputtering when he approached her. Even with the smile on his face, she was worried. No one had stopped to help for the last hour or so. Was he going to hurt her? He didn't look safe; he looked poor and hungry.

He could see that she was frightened, standing out there in the cold. He knew how she felt. It was that chill which only fear can put in you. He said, "I'm here to help you, Madam. Why don't you wait in the car where it's warm? By the way, my name is Joe." Well, all she had was a flat tire, but for an old lady, that was bad enough. Joe crawled under the car looking for a place to put the jack, skinning his knuckles a time or two. Soon he was able to change the tire. But he had to get dirty and his hands hurt.

As he was tightening up the lug nuts, she rolled down the window and began to talk to him. She told him that she was from St. Louis and was only just passing through. She couldn't thank him enough for coming to her aid. Joe just smiled as he closed her trunk.

She asked him how much she owed him. Any amount would have been all right with her. She had already imagined all the awful things that could have happened had he not stopped. Joe never thought twice about the money. This was not a job to him. This was helping someone in need, and God knows there were plenty who had given him a hand in the past.

He had lived his whole life that way, and it never occurred to him to act any other way. He told her that if she really wanted to pay him back, the next time she saw someone who needed help, she could give that person the assistance that they needed, and Joe added"…and think of me."

He waited until she started her car and drove off. It had been a cold and depressing day, but he felt good as he headed for home, disappearing into the twilight.

A few miles down the road the lady saw a small café. She went in to grab a bite to eat, and take the chill off before she made the last leg of her trip home. It was a dingy-looking restaurant. Outside were two old gas pumps. The whole scene was unfamiliar to her. The cash register was like the telephone of an out-of-work actor—it didn't ring much. Her waitress came over and brought a clean towel to wipe her wet hair.

She had a sweet smile, one that even being on her feet for the whole day couldn't erase. The lady noticed that the waitress was nearly eight months pregnant, but she never let the strain and aches change her attitude.

The old lady wondered how someone who had so little could be so giving to a stranger. Then she remembered Joe. After the lady finished her meal, and the waitress went to get change for her hundred-dollar bill, the lady slipped right out the door. She was gone by the time the waitress came back. She wondered where the lady could be, and then she noticed something written on the napkin.

There were tears in her eyes when she read what the lady wrote. It said, "You don't owe me anything, I have been there too. Someone once helped me out, the way

I'm helping you. If you really want to pay me back, here is what you do: don't let the chain of love end with you."

Well, there were tables to clean, sugar bowls to fill, and people to serve, but the waitress made it through another day. That night when she got home from work and climbed into bed, she was thinking about the money and what the lady had written.

How could the lady have known how much she and her husband needed it? With the baby due next month, it was going to be hard. She knew how worried her husband was, and as he lay sleeping next to her, she gave him a soft kiss and whispered, "Everything's gonna be all right; I love you, Joe."

爱 的 链 条

一天晚上，他开车回家，行驶在一条双行道的乡村公路上。在这个中西部小镇找工作几乎就像他那辆庞帝亚克老爷车一样慢。

但他从不放弃寻找。自从工厂关门后，他就失业了。而随着冬天不断肆虐，严寒终于长驱直入。这是一条偏僻公路，除非有人正要离开，否则不会有多少人有理由出现在这里。他的大部分朋友都已经离去。他们要养家糊口，要实现梦想。但他留了下来，毕竟，这里是他安葬父母的地方。他出生在这里，他熟悉这里。这条路他可以闭着眼走下去，并告诉你道路的两边都是什么。他那辆车的前灯坏了，所以这派上了用场。

天色渐渐暗了下来，小雪正纷纷飘落。他最好赶路。他几乎没有看到困在路边的那位老太太。但即使在昏暗的暮色里，他还是能看清她需要帮助。

于是，他在她那辆奔驰车前停下来，下了车。当他走近这位老太太时，他那辆庞帝亚克老爷车还在喷气。虽然看到他脸上的笑容，老太太还是担心。在过去的一小时左右，没有人停下来帮她。他会伤害她吗？他看上去不可靠，而是又穷又饿。

他可以看到站在寒风中的她非常害怕。他明白她的感受。这种寒冷只会让你感觉恐惧。他说："我是来帮你的，太太。你何不待在车里，车里暖和？顺便说一下，我叫乔。"呃，她的车轮胎漏气了，但对一位老太太来说，这够糟了。乔爬到车底下，寻找支千斤顶的地方，他的指关节磨破一两处。很快他就能换车胎了。可是，他不得不把身上弄脏，手也受了伤。

当他在上紧接线片螺丝时，她摇下车窗开始和他聊了起来。她对他说她来自圣路易斯，只不过是路过这里。对他能赶来相助，她感激不尽。乔只是微微一笑，合上了她的汽车尾部的行李箱。

她问付给他多少钱，多少钱她都没事儿。她已经想象到了，如果他不停下来，可能会发生的种种可怕的事情。乔从来没想到过要钱。这对他来说不是工作，而是救人所急，而且上帝知道，过去曾有好多人帮助过他。

他的一生都是这样度过的，他从未想过采取其他方式。他告诉她说，如果她真的想报答他，下次看到有人需要帮助，她就可以提供那人所需的帮助。随后，乔补充说："……然后想起我。"

他一直等到她发动车子离去。这天寒冷阴沉，但他朝家驶去，消失在暮色中时，感觉良好。

沿路行驶了几英里后，老太太看到了一家小咖啡馆。她进去想吃点东西，暖暖身子，然后走完回家的最后一程。这是一家看上去寒酸的咖啡馆。外面是两台旧加油泵。她对整个场景都不熟悉，收银台像是一部失业演员的电话——总也不响。女招待向她走来，拿来了一条干净毛巾，让她擦干了湿发。

她带着甜甜的笑容，甚至跑了一整天的腿都无法抹去那笑容。老太太注意到女招待差不多已有八个月的身孕，但她却从不让疲劳和持续疼痛来改变自己的态度。

老太太纳闷，为什么一个这样穷的人却能对一个路人这样慷慨相助。接着，她想起了乔。在老太太用完餐，女招待去拿一百美元钞票找零钱时，老太太溜出了门外。等到女招待回来，老太太已经不见了。她纳闷老太太会可能去哪里呢，随后她注意到了餐巾上写着什么东西。

她念着老太太的留言，热泪盈眶。上面写道："你什么也不欠我，我也曾有过你的处境，有人帮我摆脱了困境，正如我现在帮你一样。如果你真想报答我，就这样做：别让爱的链条在你那里终止。"

噢，还有桌子需要收拾，糖碗需要加满，顾客需要招待，但女招待又坚持挺过了一天。当晚，她下班回到家里钻进被窝时，她还在想着那笔钱和老太太写下的那段话。

老太太怎么可能会知道她和丈夫多么需要钱呢？婴儿下个月就要降生了，日子会非常艰难。她知道丈夫多么为难。当他挨着她躺下睡觉时，她温柔地吻了他一下，低声说道："一切都会好起来的；我爱你，乔。"

Saving Happiness

The small, well-poised and alert 92-year-old lady, who is up and dressed each morning by eight o'clock with her hair nicely combed even though she is blind, moved to a nursing home today.

Her husband of 70 years recently died, making the move necessary. After an hour of waiting patiently in the lobby of the nursing home, she smiled when I told her that her room was ready.

As she maneuvered her walker to the elevator, I described her tiny room, including the eyelet curtains that had been hung on her window.

"I love it!" she said.

"Mrs. Jones, you haven't even seen the room…just wait."

"That doesn't have anything to do with it," she replied. "Happiness is something you decide on ahead of time. Whether I like my room doesn't depend on how the furniture is arranged; it's how I arrange my mind. I already decided to love it. It's a decision I make every morning when I wake up. I have two choices: I can spend the day in bed recounting the difficulties I have with the parts of my body that no longer work, or get out of bed and be thankful for the ones that do. Each day is a gift, and as long as my eyes open I'll focus on the new day and all the happy memories I've stored away just for this time in my life. Old age is like a bank account: you withdraw from what you've put in. Thank you for your part in filling my Memory Bank. I am still making deposits."

Please remember the five simple rules to being happy:

Free your heart from hatred.

Free your mind from worries.

Live simply.

Give more.

Expect less.

Your happiness will increase every day.

储存幸福

这位小巧、安详而机警的92岁的老太太每天早上8点起床，头发梳得一丝不乱，即使她已经失明，今天要搬到一家疗养院。

她70岁的丈夫刚刚去世，所以她必须搬过来。在疗养院的休息室耐心等待了一小时后，我告诉她房间已经准备好，这时她露出了微笑。

她一边将助步架移上电梯，我一边向她描述她的小房间，其中包括挂在她窗户上的金属挂环窗帘。

"我非常喜欢！"她说。

"琼斯太太，您还没有看到房间，请等一下。"

"那没关系，"她回答说，"幸福是你提前决定的东西。我是不是喜欢自己的房间并不取决于家具如何安排，而是取决于我如何调整心态。我已经决定喜欢它。每天早上一醒来，我都做这样的决定。我有两个选择：我是一天躺在床上数着自己因身体的一部分器官不能再工作而遇到的那些困难，还是起床对那部分能工作的器官心怀感激。每天都是一件礼物。只要我睁开眼睛，就要关注这新的一天以及我在生活中这一刻存储的所有幸福记忆。老年就像银行账户：你总是提取你存储的东西。谢谢你为我的记忆库存储的部分。我也在存储着。"

请记住幸福的五个简单原则：

让心远离仇恨。

让心远离烦恼。

简单生活。

多给予。

少期盼。

你每天的幸福就会越来越多。

As Long As You Have Love in Your Heart

It was a winter morning without the sun, the freezing cold quietly nipping to the bone of the people waiting for the bus. They were all black, sometimes raising their heads to look afar or looking up at the sullen sky.

Suddenly, the crowd stirred up. Yes, here came a bus, a minibus rolled along in no hurry. Curiously, the people still stood where they were, still raising their head and looking at the place farther away; they didn't seem to be anxious to get on the bus, still expecting something. Who were they waiting for? Did they have a partner not to come?

Sure enough, after a figure appeared from afar, the crowd stirred up once again. The figure walked hurriedly, sometimes trotted and finally drew near. It was a woman, a white woman. At this time, the crowd was on the point of cheering. Undoubtedly, she was the partner who the black people were waiting for together.

Why? You know, in this country, the white and the black were always hostile to each other. What force made them so close?

Formerly, it was a remote way station, the bus moved to and fro every two hours, and the bus drivers had a privity: the bus stopped in the presence of white people, but the people who lived nearby were almost black. It was said that the white woman was a writer who lived in a place three miles ahead, where there was also a station. But in order to make the black people ride the bus favorably, she insisted walking here for three miles to board the bus, rain or shine.

The black people almost embraced the writer to send her on to the bus.

"Hi, Susan." Before the female writer kept her legs, she heard someone call her name. Looking up, she saw her friend Jay.

"Why do you get on the bus here?" asked Jay in confusion.

"Because," the writer said, pointing to the station, "the bus doesn't stop without white people, so I come here." With that, the writer tidied up the goods in her arms.

Surprised, Jay stared at the writer and said, "Just for these black people?"

The writer also widened her eyes, "Why, is it very important?"

We were also surprised and then came to understand: as long as you have love in your heart, everything will be as pure as nature.

只要心中有爱

这是一个没有太阳的冬天的早晨，刺骨的寒气悄悄地渗进候车人的骨髓。他们都是黑人，时而翘首远方，时而抬头望着阴沉的天空。

突然，人群骚动起来，是的，车来了，一辆中巴正不紧不慢地开了过来。奇怪的是，人们仍站在原地，仍在翘首更远的地方，他们似乎并不急于上车，似乎还在企盼着什么。他们在等谁？难道他们还有一个伙伴没来？

果然，远方隐隐约约出现了一个身影后，人群又一次骚动起来。身影走得很急，有时还小跑一阵，终于走近了，是一个女人，白种女人。这时，人群几乎要欢呼了。无疑，她就是黑人们共同等候的伙伴。

怎么回事？要知道，在这个国家，白人与黑人一向互相敌视。是什么力量让他们如此亲近？

原来，这是一个偏僻小站，公交车每两小时才来一趟，而且这些公交车司机们都有一种默契：有白人才停车，而偏偏这附近住的几乎都是黑人。据说，这个白种女人是个作家，她住在前面3英里处，那里也有一个车站。可为了让这里的黑人顺利地坐上公交车，她每天坚持走3英里来这里上车，风雨无阻。

黑人们几乎是拥抱着将女作家送上了车。

"苏珊，你好。"女作家脚还没站稳，就听见有人叫自己的名字。抬头一看，是朋友杰伊。

"你怎么在这里上车？"杰伊疑惑地问。

"这个站，"女作家指了指上车的地方，"没有白人就不停车，所以我就赶到这里来了。"说着，女作家理了理怀里的物品。

杰伊惊讶地瞪着女作家，说："就因为这些黑人？"

女作家也瞪大了眼睛："怎么，这很重要吗？"

我们也惊讶了，继而又明白了：只要心中有爱，一切都会纯如天然。

Make the Love Grow in the Heart

Maybe God wants us to meet a few wrong people before meeting the right one so that when we finally meet the right person, we will know how to be grateful for that gift.

When the door of happiness closes, another opens, but oftentimes we look so long at the closed door that we don't see the one, which has been opened for us.

The best kind of friend is the kind you can sit on a porch and swing with, never say a word, and then walk away feeling like it was the best conversation you've ever had.

It's true that we don't know what we've got until we lose it, but it's also true that we don't know what we've been missing until it arrives.

Giving someone all your love is never an assurance that they'll love you back! don't expect love in return; just wait for it to grow in their heart but if it doesn't, be content it grew in yours. It takes only a minute to get a crush on someone, an hour to like someone, and a day to love someone, but it takes a lifetime to forget someone.

don't go for looks; they can deceive. don't go for wealth; even that fades away. Go for someone who makes you smile because it takes only a smile to make a dark day seem bright. Find the one that makes your heart smile.

让爱在心中成长

也许是上帝让我们在最终找到知音之前总要遇到几个不尽如意的人，这样我们才能对知音这份礼物充满感激之情。

一道幸福之门关闭时，另一扇就会打开，但我们常常久久地看着关闭的门，而看不见已经对我们开启的门。

最好的朋友就是你坐在门廊和秋千上，一句话没说，然后走开时却感到好像你曾有过最好的交谈。

的确，我们失去自己拥有的东西时，才会知道。同样，一件东西得来时，我们才知道自己一直缺少。

付出全部的爱，并不能确保你一定会得到回报！别指望爱有什么回报；耐心等待让它在他们心中成长。但如果不能成长，也要满足爱已在你的心中成长。迷恋一个人只需要一分钟，喜欢一个人需要一个小时，爱上一个人需要一天，但忘记一个人则需要一辈子。

不要追求外表，外表常会骗人。不要追求财富，财富也会散尽。追求能使你微笑的人，因为只有微笑才能使黑暗的日子变得光明。找到那个能使你的心灵微笑的人吧。

Bobby's Gift

Bobby was getting cold standing in his backyard in the snow. Bobby didn't wear boots; he didn't like them and anyway he didn't own any. The thin sneakers he wore had a few holes in them and they did a poor job of keeping out the cold.

Bobby had been in his backyard for about an hour already. And, try as he might, he couldn't come up with an idea for his mother's Christmas gift. He shook his head as he thought, "This is useless, even if I do come up with an idea, I don't have any money to spend."

Ever since his father had passed away three years ago, the family of five had struggled. It was not because his mother didn't care or try, there just never seemed to be enough. She worked nights at the hospital, but the small wage that she was earning could only be stretched so far.

While the family lacked in money and material things, they more than made up for in love and family unity. Bobby had two older and one younger sisters, who ran the household in their mother's absence.

All three of his sisters had already made beautiful gifts for their mother. Here it was Christmas Eve already, and he had nothing. Wiping a tear from his eye, Bobby kicked the snow and started to walk down to the street where the shops and stores were.

Bobby walked down from shop to shop, looking into each decorated window. Everything seemed so beautiful and so out of reach. It was starting to get dark and Bobby reluctantly turned to walk home when suddenly his eyes caught the glimmer of the setting sun's rays reflecting off of something along the curb. He reached down and discovered a shiny dime.

As he held his new found treasure, a warmth spread throughout his entire body and he walked into the first store he saw. His excitement quickly turned cold when salesperson after salesperson told him that he couldn't buy anything with only a dime.

He went into a flower shop and waited in line. When the shop owner asked if he could help him, Bobby presented the dime and asked if he could buy one flower for his mother's Christmas gift. The shop owner looked at Bobby and his dime. Then he put his hand on Bobby's shoulder and said, "You just wait here and I'll see what I can do for you."

As Bobby waited, he looked at the beautiful flowers and even though he was a boy, he could see why mothers and girls liked flowers.

The sound of the door closing as the last customer left jolted Bobby back to reality. All alone in the shop, Bobby began to feel alone and afraid. Suddenly the shop owner came out and moved to the counter. There, before Bobby's eyes, lay twelve long-stemmed, red roses, all tied together with a big silver bow. Bobby's heart sank as the owner picked them up and placed them gently into a long white box.

"That will be ten cents, young man," the shop owner said reaching out his hand for the dime. Slowly, Bobby moved his hand to give the man his dime. Could this be true? No one else would give him a thing for his dime? Sensing the boy's reluctance, the shop owner added, "I just happened to have some roses on sale for ten cents a dozen. Would you like them?"

This time Bobby didn't hesitate, and when the man placed the long box into his hands, he knew it was true. Walking out the door that the owner was holding for Bobby, he heard the shop keeper say, "Merry Christmas, son."

As he returned inside, the shopkeeper's wife walked out. "Who were you talking to back there and where are the roses you were fixing?" Staring out the window, he replied, "A strange thing happened to me this morning. While I was setting up things to open the shop, I thought I heard a voice telling me to set aside a dozen of my best roses for a special gift. I was not sure at the time whether I had lost my mind or what, but I set them aside anyway. Then just a few minutes ago, a little boy came into the shop and wanted to buy a flower for his mother with one small dime. When I looked at him, I saw myself many years ago. I too was a poor boy with nothing to buy my mother a Christmas gift. A bearded man, whom I never knew, stopped me on the street and told me that he wanted to give me ten dollars. When I saw that little boy tonight, I knew whose voice it was, and I put together a dozen of my very best roses."

The shop owner and his wife hugged each other tightly, and as they stepped out into the bitter cold, they somehow didn't feel cold at all.

博比的礼物

博比站在后院的雪地里，感觉越来越冷。他没有穿靴子；他不喜欢穿，也穿不起。他穿的薄运动鞋有几个窟窿，无法抵挡严寒。

博比已经在后院待了大约一小时。尽管他左思右想，但他拿不定主意给母亲买什么圣诞礼物。他一边想一边摇头："这没用，即使我想起来送什么，我也没钱买呀。"

自从3年前他的父亲去世以来，一家5口人就苦苦挣扎着。不是因为他的母亲不关心，也不是因为没有尽力，只是她的工资好像总不够用。她在医院上夜班，她赚的那点微薄工资仅仅能维持到现在。

尽管家里缺钱少物，但他们相亲相爱、团结和睦。博比有两个姐姐和一个妹妹，母亲不在家时，她们就管理家务。

姐妹们都已经为母亲准备好了漂亮的礼物。现在已是平安夜了，他还是两手空空。博比擦去眼角的一滴泪水，踢着地上的雪，向街上的一排排商店走去。

博比走过了一家家商店，从每个装饰的窗户往里看，里面的东西好像是那样漂亮，那样遥不可及。天渐渐黑了，博比勉为其难地转身往回走。突然，他看到了路边的一个东西在夕阳映照下闪闪发光。他伸手拿起来，发现那是一枚亮晶晶的一角硬币。

他手握新发现的宝贝，一股暖流涌遍了全身。他走进自己看到的第一家商店。当一个个店员都告诉他一角钱什么也买不到时，他的兴奋感顿时冷了下来。

他走进一家鲜花店，排队等候买花。店主问他买什么，博比拿出那枚硬币，问店主他能不能买一枝鲜花，送给他母亲作为圣诞节礼物。店主看了看博比和他那枚硬币，然后拍了拍他的肩膀说："你就在这里等一会儿，我看看能不能帮上你的忙。"

博比一边等，一边看着商店那些美丽的鲜花，即使他是个男孩，也能明白母亲们和女孩们为什么喜欢鲜花。

最后一位顾客离开时，商店关门的声音使博比醒过神来。店里只剩下博比一个人了，他开始感到孤独和害怕。突然，店主出来，走到了柜台前。博比眼前出现了12朵长茎红玫瑰。所有这些花都用一只银色大蝴蝶结束在一起。店主将这束花轻轻地放进一个白色长盒里时，博比的心沉了下来。

"小伙子，这束花10美分，"店主一边说，一边伸手去拿那一角硬币。博比慢慢地把钱递给了那个人。这会是真的吗？没有人愿意用一件东西换一角硬币呀？店主感觉到博比勉为其难的样子，便补充说："我刚好有一角钱一打的玫瑰要卖。你想买吗？"

这次，博比不再犹豫了。当店主把长盒放到他手里时，他才明白这是真的。博比向门外走去，店主为他打开了门。他听到店主说："圣诞快乐，孩子。"

店主返回店里时，他的妻子走了出来。"你刚才和谁在说话？你扎好的那束玫瑰在哪里？"店主望着窗外，回答说："今天早上我遇到了一件怪事。我收拾好东西要开门时，我想我听到有个声音在对我说，扎12朵最好的玫瑰作为一件特殊的礼物。当时我拿不准我是不是精神错乱什么的，但我还是这样做了。后来，也就是几分钟前，一个小男孩走进店里，要拿微不足道的一角钱给他母亲买一朵花。我看着他，就看到了多年前的自己。当时，我是个穷孩子，没有钱给母亲买一件圣诞礼物。我根本不认识的一个留有胡子的男子在街上拦住我，告诉我他要给我10美元。我今晚看到那个小男孩时，明白了早上那是谁的声音了。于是，我就扎了12朵最好的玫瑰。"

店主和妻子紧紧地拥抱在一起。他们走出店子，进入凛冽的寒风中时，不知何故，一点也不感觉到冷。

What Is Love

A few nights ago, my friend Lisa asked me what I thought love was. At the time I thought that there were so many different types of love that I really struggled to answer her. The love of a child, the love of a parent, the love of a friend, the love of a partner. What I did say was that I thought you had to first be truthful and show love to yourself before you could show love to another. I still believe this is true and now I have learned that there is only one type of love.

Both Lisa and I have been hurt by men who lied to us. She felt that if these men had lied to us, then they were not worthy of our love. I am now able to move on. I found my answer for her about what I think love is. So here is my letter to my friend Lisa.

Lisa,

I think I have finally found my answer to your question, "What is love?"

Real love truly is unconditional.

I have been looking back to the times I spent with my grandma. As you know, I grew up with her. I was not very nice to her at times, like most teenagers. As I was growing up, I really did some nasty things to hurt her.

You know, Lisa, she was always there to forgive me, once I realized my mistakes.

She did this openly and honestly and with her arms wide open. Her love never judged me. Her love never condemned me. Her love never knew spiteful words. She would tell me that my actions had hurt her, but she never did say mean things or even punish me. Ever.

She held me up, she let me become myself and then she let me go.

To me, if you can't love without judging, then you don't love. If you can't love without expectation, then you don't love. If you can't love just because you can, then why would you do it? Does someone have to show you love in return for you to feel it? My grandma never did. She just loved all of me, no matter what my actions were.

I believe that to love, you have to be patient. To love, you have to be kind. To love, you have to forgive. I'm not saying that you should put your life on hold, but all the same, I don't believe that you should turn your back just because that person hasn't yet found the strength to know who they are.

Sometimes people just make mistakes. This is their walk, not ours. Their life lessons, not ours. Who are we to judge? And if you truly did love in the first place, then you will be there to forgive. To me, this is real love.

爱 是 什 么

前几天夜里,我的朋友丽莎问我:爱是什么?当时我认为,爱的种类太多,各不相同,我确实得绞尽脑汁才能回答她。孩子的爱,父母的爱,朋友的爱,伴侣的爱。我对她说的是,在你对另一个人示爱之前,你得先诚实,对自己示爱。我仍然相信这话不错,现在我已经明白只有一种爱。

我和丽莎都曾被向我们撒谎的男人伤害过。她感到,如果这些男人对我们撒谎,那他们就不值得我们去爱。我现在能继续向前。我找到了她那个爱是什么的问题的答案。这是我写给朋友丽莎的一封信。

丽莎:

我想我终于找到了你问我的"爱是什么?"这个问题的答案。

真爱的确是无条件的。

我一直在回想和奶奶一起度过的那些岁月。你知道,是她看着我长大的。就像大多数青少年一样,有时我对她不是很好。我在成长过程中的确做过一些伤害她的坏事。

丽莎,你知道,一旦我认识到自己的错误,她总是原谅我。

她原谅我时坦率真诚,张开怀抱。她对我的爱从不评判,她对我的爱从不责难,她对我的爱从不恶言恶语。她常常告诉我说我的行动已经伤害了她,但从不说刻薄话,也不惩罚我。从来都不会。

她支撑着我,让我做自己的主人,然后才放我走。

对我来说,如果你无法不加评判地去爱,那你就不要爱。如果你无法不带期望地去爱,那你就不要爱。如果你不能仅仅因为爱而去爱,那你为什么还要这样做呢?难道必须有人给你回报你才能感觉到爱吗?我奶奶从不这样做。她只爱我的一切,无论我曾做过什么。

我相信,要爱,你就必须有耐心。要爱,你就必须善良。要爱,你就必须原谅。我并不是说你应该一辈子都悬在那里,但我也同样相信,不能仅仅因为你爱的人还没有找到了解自己的力量,你就应该转身离去。

有时,人总会犯错误。这是他们的道路,不是我们的。这是他们的人生教训，不是我们的。我们要去评判谁呢？如果你首先确实心中有爱，那你一定会去原谅。对我来说，这才是真爱。

The Wallet of Love

As I walked home one freezing day, I stumbled on a wallet someone had lost in the street. I picked it up and looked inside to find some identification so I could call the owner. But the wallet contained only three dollars and a crumpled letter.

The envelope was worn and the only thing that was legible on it was the return address. I started to open the letter, hoping to find some clue. The letter had been written almost sixty years ago. It was written in a beautiful feminine handwriting on powder blue stationery with a little flower in the left-hand corner. It was a "Dear John" letter that told the recipient, whose name appeared to be Michael, that the writer couldn't see him any more because her mother forbade it. Even so, she wrote that she would always love him. It was signed, Hannah. It was a beautiful letter, but there was no way except for the name Michael, that the owner could be identified. Maybe if I called information, the operator could find a phone listing for the address on the envelope.

"Operator," I began, "this is an unusual request. I'm trying to find the owner of a wallet that I found. Is there anyway you can tell me if there is a phone number for an address that was on an envelope in the wallet?"

She suggested I speak with her supervisor, who hesitated for a moment, then said, "There is a phone listing at that address, but I can't give you the number." She said, as a courtesy, she would call that number, explain my story and would ask them if they wanted her to connect me. I waited a few minutes and then she was back on the line, "I have a party who will speak with you."

I asked the woman on the other end of the line if she knew anyone by the name of Hannah. She gasped, "Oh! We bought this house from a family who had a daughter named Hannah. But that was 30 years ago!" "Would you know where that family could be located now?" I asked.

"I remember that Hannah had to place her mother in a nursing home some years ago," the woman said. "Maybe if you got in touch with them they might be able to track down the daughter." She gave me the name of the nursing home and I called the number.

They told me the old lady had passed away some years ago but they did have a phone number for where they thought the daughter might be living. I thanked them and phoned. The woman who answered explained that Hannah herself was now living in a nursing home.

I called the nursing home in which Hannah was living and the man who answered the phone told me, "Yes, Hannah is staying with us."

I thanked him and drove over to the nursing home. The night nurse and a guard greeted me at the door. We went up to the third floor of the large building. In the day-room, the nurse introduced me to Hannah. She was a sweet, silver-haired old timer with a warm smile and a twinkle in her eye. I told her about finding the wallet and showed her the letter.

The second she saw the powder blue envelope with that little flower on the left, she took a deep breath and said, "Young man, this letter was the last contact I ever had with Michael." She looked away for a moment deep in thought and then said softly, "I loved him very much. But I was only 16 at the time and my mother felt I was too young. Oh, he was so handsome."

"Yes," she continued. "Michael Goldstein was a wonderful person. If you should find him, tell him I think of him often. And," she hesitated for a moment, almost biting her lip, "tell him I still love him. You know," she said smiling as tears began to well up in her eyes, "I never did marry. I guess no one ever matched up to Michael…"

I thanked Hannah and said goodbye. I took the elevator to the first floor and as I stood by the door, the guard there asked, "Was the old lady able to help you?" I told him she had given me a lead. "At least I have a last name."

I had taken out the wallet. When he saw it, the guard said, "Hey, wait a minute! That's Mr. Goldstein's wallet. He's always losing that wallet. I must have found it in the halls at least three times."

"Who's Mr. Goldstein?" I asked as my hand began to shake.

"He's one of the old timers on the 8th floor. That's Mike Goldstein's wallet for sure."

On the eighth floor, the floor nurse said, "I think he's still in the day room. He likes to read at night. He's a darling old man."

We went to the only room that had any lights on and there was a man reading a book. The nurse went over to him and asked if he had lost his wallet. Mr. Goldstein looked up with surprise, put his hand in his back pocket and said, "Oh, it is missing!"

"This kind gentleman found a wallet and we wondered if it could be yours?" I handed Mr. Goldstein the wallet and the second he saw it, he smiled with relief and said, "Yes, that's it! It must have dropped out of my pocket this afternoon. I want to give you a reward."

"No, thank you," I said. "But I have to tell you something. I read the letter in the hope of finding out who owned the wallet." The smile on his face suddenly disappeared. "You read that letter?"

"Not only did I read it, I think I know where Hannah is." He suddenly grew pale. "Hannah? You know where she is? How is she? Is she still as pretty as she was? Please, please tell me," he begged.

"She's fine…just as pretty as when you knew her." I said softly. The old man smiled with anticipation and asked, "Could you tell me where she is? I want to call her tomorrow." He grabbed my hand and said, "You know something, mister, I was so in love with that girl that when that letter came, my life literally ended. I never married. I guess I've always loved her."

"Mr. Goldstein," I said, "Come with me." We took the elevator down to the third floor. The hallways were darkened and only one or two little night-lights lit our way to the day-room where Hannah was sitting alone watching the television. The nurse walked over to her.

"Hannah," she said softly, pointing to Michael, who was waiting with me in the doorway. "Do you know this man?" She adjusted her glasses, looked for a moment, but didn't say a word. Michael said softly, almost in a whisper, "Hannah, it's Michael. Do you remember me?"

She gasped, "Michael! I don't believe it! Michael! It's you! My Michael!" He walked slowly towards her and they embraced.

About three weeks later I got a call at my office from the nursing home. "Can you break away on Sunday to attend a wedding? Michael and Hannah are going to tie the knot!"

It was a beautiful wedding with all the people at the nursing home dressed up to join in the celebration. Hannah wore a light beige dress and looked beautiful. Michael wore a dark blue suit and stood tall. They made me their best man. The nursing home gave them their own room and if you ever wanted to see a 76-year-old bride and a 79-year-old groom acting like two teenagers, you had to see this couple. A perfect ending for a love affair that had lasted nearly 60 years.

爱 的 钱 包

一个严寒的日子，我正往家走时，有人遗失在大街的钱包绊了我一下。我捡起钱包，打开看了看里面，看有没有一些身份证明，这样我就能给失主打电话，但钱包里只有3美元和一封皱巴巴的信。

信封破旧，上面唯一能看清的就是回信地址。我打开信，希望找到一些线索。信是差不多60年前写的。粉蓝色的信纸左侧一角有朵小花，上面是娟秀的字体。这是一封绝交信，写信人想告诉收信人，因为她母亲反对，她不能再见他了。上面显示收信人是迈克尔。虽然这样，她还是写着她会永远爱他。署名是汉娜。信写得很美，但信里除了"迈克尔"这个名字，没有任何能证明失主身份的途径。也许给信息台打电话，接线员能找到信封上所写地址的电话。

"接线员，"我开口说道，"这是一个不同寻常的请求。我正在设法寻找我拾到的一个钱包的主人。钱包里有封信,上面有一个地址,你能告诉我有什么办法找到这个地址的电话号码吗?"

她建议我跟她的主管谈谈。她的主管犹豫了片刻,然后说:"那个地址列有一个电话号码,但我不能给你。"出于礼貌,她说她会打那个号码,向对方说明我的情况,询问他们是不是想让她跟我联系。我等了几分钟,随后她回电话说:"我有一个当事人愿意跟你说话。"

我问电话那端那个女的,她是否认识一个叫汉娜的人。她喘着气说:"噢!我们买的这个房子先前的房主的女儿叫汉娜。但那是30年前的事了!""那你知道那户人家现在可能住的地方吗?"我问。

"我记得几年前汉娜不得不把她母亲安置在一家疗养院。"那个女的说,"也许你跟他们联系,他们说不定能查到她女儿的下落。"她把那家疗养院的名字给了我,我就按那个号码拨了过去。

对方告诉我说老太太几年前就去世了,但他们确实有他们认为是那个女儿可能住的地方的电话号码。我谢过他们,把电话打了过去。接电话的妇女解释说,汉娜本人现在住在一家疗养院。

我给汉娜住的那家疗养所去了电话。接电话的男子告诉我:"是的,汉娜和我们住在一起。"

我谢过他,便开车前往那家疗养院。夜班护士和一名保安在门口迎接我。我们上到那座大楼的三楼。在休息室,那名护士把我引见给汉娜。她是一位和蔼可亲、满头银发的老太太。她面带亲切的微笑,眼睛炯炯有神。我对她说了我拾到那个钱包的情况,并让她看了那封信。

她一看到那个左侧有朵小花的粉蓝色信封,深吸了口气说:"年轻人,这封信是我和迈克尔的最后一次联系。"她把目光移开,沉思了片刻,接着又轻轻地说,"我非常爱他。但我当时只有16岁,妈妈觉得我太小。噢,他是那么帅。"

"是的,"她继续说道,"迈克尔·戈尔茨坦的确很帅。如果你找到他,就告诉他我时常想起他。还有,"她犹豫了一下,几乎是咬着嘴唇,"告诉他我依然爱他。你知道,"她微笑着说,眼里涌起了泪水,"我始终没有结婚。我想没有人配得上迈克尔……"

我谢过汉娜,向她道别,乘电梯来到一楼。当我来到门口时,那名保安问:"那个老太太能帮上忙吗?"我告诉他,她给了一个线索。"至少,我有了这个人的姓。"

我拿出那个钱包。保安一看,便叫道:"嘿,等一下!那是戈尔茨坦先生的钱包。他总是丢那个钱包。我在大厅里肯定拾到过至少三次。"

"戈尔茨坦先生是谁?"我一边问,手一边开始颤抖。

"他是8楼的一位老先生。那肯定是迈克尔·戈尔茨坦的钱包。"

我来到8楼,楼层值班护士说:"我想他还在休息室。他喜欢晚上看书。他是个可爱的老头。"

我们走向那个唯一亮着灯的房间。那里有一个男的正在看书。护士走到他身边,问他是不是丢了钱包。戈尔茨坦先生吃惊地抬起头,把一只手伸进后面的口袋说:"噢,就是不见了!"

"这位好心先生拾到了一个钱包,我们不知道是不是你的?"我把那个钱包递给戈尔茨坦先生。一看到钱包,他就松了口气,笑道:"是的,就是它!一定是今天下午从我的口袋里掉出来了。我要酬谢你。"

"不,谢谢,"我说,"但我必须告诉你一件事。我看了那封信,希望找到钱包的主人,"他脸上的微笑突然消失了,"你看了那封信?"

"我不仅看了信,我想我还知道汉娜在哪里,"他突然脸色煞白,"汉娜?你知道她在哪里?她怎么样?她还像过去那样漂亮吗?请、请告诉我。"他恳求道。

"她很好……就像你认识她时一样漂亮。"我轻声说道。老人满怀期望地露出微笑,问道,"你能告诉我她在哪里吗?我明天要给她打电话。"他一把抓住我的手说,"先生,你知道,我有多爱那个姑娘,收到那封信时,我觉得一生简直完了。我始终未娶。我想我会永远爱她。"

"戈尔茨坦先生,"我说,"随我来。"我们乘电梯下到3楼。走廊里昏暗。只有一两盏小夜灯为我们照亮前往汉娜正独自坐在里面看电视的那个休息室。护士向她走了过去。

"汉娜,"她指着迈克尔轻声说,迈克尔和我等在门口,"你认识这个人吗?"她调整了一下眼镜,打量了片刻,但一句话也没说。迈克轻轻地说,几乎是耳语:"汉娜,我是迈克尔。你记得我吗?"

她喘着气说:"迈克尔!我不相信!迈克尔!真是你!我的迈克尔!"他慢慢地走向她,他们拥抱在一起。

大约3周后,我在办公室接到了那家疗养院打来的电话。"星期天你能抽空参加一个婚礼吗?迈克尔和汉娜要喜结良缘!"

那是一场美丽的婚礼,疗养所所有的人都衣着盛装前来庆祝。汉娜身穿淡米黄色婚纱，非常漂亮。迈克身穿深蓝色西装，身材高大。他们让我做伴郎。疗养院给了他们一个房间。如果你想看76岁的新娘和79岁的新郎如何像青年男女那样扮相，那就来看这对伴侣。持续了将近60年的恋情终于有了一个完美的结局。

Rudy's Angel

I walked into the grocery store not particularly interested in buying groceries. I was not hungry. The pain of losing my husband of 37 years was still too raw. And this grocery store held so many sweet memories.

Rudy often came with me and almost every time he'd pretend to go off and look for something special. I knew what he was up to. I'd always spot him walking down the aisle with the three yellow roses in his hands. Rudy knew I loved yellow roses.

With a heart filled with grief, I only wanted to buy my few items and leave, but even grocery shopping was different since Rudy had passed on.

Standing by the meat, I searched for the perfect small steak and remembered how Rudy had loved his steak.

Suddenly a woman came beside me. She was blond, slim and lovely in a soft green pantsuit. I watched as she picked up a large pack of T-bones, dropped them in her basket, hesitated, and then put them back. She turned to go and once again reached for the pack of steaks. She saw me watching her and she smiled. "My husband loves T-bones, but honestly, at these prices, I don't know."

I swallowed the emotion down and met her pale blue eyes. "My husband passed away eight days ago," I told her. Glancing at the package in her hands, I fought to control the tremble in my voice. "Buy him the steaks. And cherish every moment you have together."

She nodded her head and I saw the emotion in her eyes as she placed the package in her basket and wheeled away.

I turned and pushed my cart across the length of the store to the dairy products. There I stood, trying to decide which size milk I should buy. A quart, I finally decided and moved on to the ice cream section near the front of the store. I placed the ice cream in my cart and looked down the aisle toward the front. I saw first the green suit, then recognized the pretty lady coming toward me. In her arms she carried a package. On her face was the brightest smile I had ever seen. I would swear a soft halo encircled her blond hair as she kept walking toward me. As she came closer, I saw what she held and tears began misting in my eyes.

"These are for you," she said and placed three beautiful long-stemmed yellow roses in my arms. "These are paid for." She leaned over and placed a gentle kiss on my cheek, then smiled again.

I wanted to tell her what she'd done meant to me, but still unable to speak. I watched as she walked away, tears clouding my vision. I looked down at the beautiful roses nestled in the green tissue wrapping and found it almost unreal. How did she know?

Suddenly, the answer seemed so clear. I was not alone. "Oh, Rudy, you haven't forgotten me, have you?" I whispered, with tears in my eyes. He was still with me, and she was his angel.

We should be thankful for what you have every day and love can grow in our heart.

鲁迪的天使

我走进了一家食品杂货店，但对买食物并不是特别感兴趣。我不饿。失去和我共同生活了37年的丈夫仍然非常痛心。而这个食品杂货店留下了很多很多甜蜜的回忆。

鲁迪经常常陪我一起来这里，几乎每次他都要假装离开一会儿，去找一些特别的东西。我知道他要做什么。我总是看到他手里拿着三枝黄玫瑰沿着过道走来。鲁迪知道我喜欢黄玫瑰。

我心里充满悲伤，只想买一些东西就离开，但自从鲁迪去世以来，就连到这里买东西也不一样了。

我站在肉食柜台边，寻找那种最好的小牛排，想起了鲁迪是多么喜欢吃牛排。

突然，一个女人来到了我身边。她金发碧眼，身材苗条，身穿淡绿色套装。我看到她拿起一大包丁字牛排，把它们放进购物车，犹豫了一下，然后又放了回去。她转身要离开时，又拿起那包牛排。看到我在看她，她露出了微笑。"我丈夫喜欢丁字牛排，但说实话，我不知道是这种价钱。"

我抑制住自己的情绪，望着她淡蓝色的眼睛，告诉她说："我丈夫8天前去世了，"看着她手里那包牛排，我拼命抑制自己颤抖的声音，"给他买牛排吧。珍惜你们一起相处的时光。"

她点了点头，把牛排放回购物车推走时，我看到了她眼里激动的神情。

我转过身，推着购物车，走到商店的乳制品区。我站在那里，想着自己应该买多大量的牛奶。我最后决定买一夸脱，随后又来到了商店门前的冰淇淋区。我把一支冰淇淋放进购物车里，然后顺着过道向前面望了一眼。我第一眼就看到了那个淡绿色套装,随即认出了是那个漂亮的女士正朝我走来。她怀里抱着一包东西,面带我所见过的最灿烂的微笑。我发誓,她向我走来时,一圈柔光环绕在她的金发四周。她越走越近了,我看到了她怀里抱的东西,泪水开始模糊了我的双眼。

"这是送给你的,"说着,她把三枝漂亮的长茎黄玫瑰放在了我的怀里,"这付过账了。"她侧过身,轻轻地吻了吻我的脸颊,然后又微微一笑。

我想告诉她,她做的一切对我来说意味着什么,却说不出话来。我望着她离开时,泪水模糊了我的视线。我低头看着这束用绿色棉纸包装纸包好的漂亮玫瑰,简直不敢相信是真的。她怎么会知道呢?

突然,答案好像清楚了。我并不孤单。"噢,鲁迪,你没有忘记我,对吗?"我眼含泪水低声说。他仍和我在一起,她就是鲁迪的天使。

我们应该为我们拥有的一切怀着感恩之心,爱才会在我们的心中成长。

"I Pity Them"

A poor man once undertook to emigrate from Castine, Me., to Illinois. When he was attempting to cross a river in New York, his horse broke through the rotten timbers of the bridge, and was drowned. He had but this one animal to convey all his property and his family to his new home.

His wife and children were almost miraculously saved from sharing the fate of the horse; but the loss of this poor animal was enough. By its aid the family, it may be said, had lived and moved; now they were left helpless in a land of strangers, without the ability to go on or return, without money or a single friend to whom to appeal. The case was a hard one.

There were a great many who "passed by on the other side." Some even laughed at the predicament in which the man was placed; but by degrees a group of people began to collect, all of whom pitied him.

Some pitied him a great deal, and some did not pity him very much, because, they said, he might have known better than to try to cross an unsafe bridge, and should have made his horse swim the river. Pity, however, seemed rather to predominate. Some pitied the man, and some the horse; all pitied the poor, sick mother and her six helpless children.

Among this pitying party was a rough son of the West, who knew what it was to migrate some hundreds of miles over new roads to locate a destitute family on a prairie. Seeing the man's forlorn situation, and looking around on the bystanders, he said, "All of you seem to pity these poor people very much, but I would beg leave to ask each of you how much."

"There, stranger," continued he, holding up a ten dollar bill, "there is the amount of my pity; and if others will do as I do, you may soon get another pony. God bless you." It is needless to state the effect that this active charity produced. In a short time the happy emigrant arrived at his destination, and he is now a thriving farmer, and a neighbor to him who was his "friend in need, and a friend indeed."

"我同情他们"

曾经有一个穷人,他从缅因州迁移到伊利诺伊州。当他试图渡过纽约的一条河时,马踩断了已经腐朽的木桥,掉进河里淹死了;而他只有这么一头牲口,驮着所有的财产还有家人到新家去。

然而幸运的是,妻子和孩子被救了下来,他们没有像可怜的马儿一样失去性命。但失去马匹就足够让他们烦恼的,它活着的时候帮这一家人运东运西,现在死了,只留下无助的一家人站在一片陌生的土地上。他们既不能返回,又无法继续前进,此刻他们身无分文,在这儿又没有可依靠的朋友,情况很糟糕。

有很多人从他们身边经过,一些人甚至嘲笑这一家人的处境。不过还是有同情他们的人,不一会儿便有许多人围住了他们。

一些人非常同情这个穷人,也有一些人不怎么同情他,因为他们认为他不该试图穿越那座危险的木桥,并且应该让马匹从河中游过去。然而,同情他的人还是较多。有些人同情那个穷人,也有一些人同情那匹马,更多的人则是同情那个生着病的可怜母亲和六个无助的孩子。

人群中有一个人是西部男子,他长得很强壮,深知辛辛苦苦地经过千山万水,来到草原上组建一个新家有多么难。看了看绝望的穷人,又看了看周围的旁观者,他说:"你们看起来非常同情他,那么请允许我问问你们每个人对他的同情到底有多少?"

"给你,陌生人,"他拿出一张10美元的钞票,继续说道,"这是我对你同情的数额,如果其他人也能像我一样,那么你很快就能买一匹马了。愿上帝保佑你。"无须多说,他这一施舍举动很快就有了效果。就这样,那位快乐的移民在很短的时间内就到达了目的地。现在他经营着一个兴盛的农场,而他的邻居正是那位曾帮助过他的"患难之交"。

An Old-fashioned Girl

Polly hoped the "dreadful boy" (Tom) would not be present; but he was, and stared at her all dinner time in a most trying manner.

Mr. Shaw, a busy-looking gentleman, said, "How do you do, my dear? Hope you'll enjoy yourself;" and then appeared to forget her entirely. Mrs. Shaw, a pale, nervous woman, greeted her little guest kindly, and took care that she wanted for nothing.

Madam Shaw, a quiet old lady, with an imposing cap, exclaimed, on seeing Polly, "Bless my heart! the image of her mother—a sweet woman—how is she, dear?" and kept peering at the newcomer over her glasses till, between Madam and Tom, poor Polly lost her appetite.

Her cousin Fanny chatted like a magpie, and little Maud fidgeted, till Tom proposed to put her under the big dish cover, which produced such an explosion that the young lady was borne screaming away by the much-enduring nurse.

It was, altogether, an uncomfortable dinner, and Polly was very glad when it was over. They all went about their own affairs; and, after doing the honors of the house, Fan was called to the dressmaker, leaving Polly to amuse herself in the great drawing-room.

Polly was glad to be alone for a few minutes; and, having examined all the pretty things about her, began to walk up and down over the soft, flowery carpet, humming to herself, as the daylight faded, and only the ruddy glow of the fire filled the room.

Presently Madam came slowly in, and sat down in her armchair, saying, "That's a fine old tune; sing it to me, my dear. I haven't heard it this many a day."

Polly didn't like to sing before strangers, for she had no teaching but such as her busy mother could give her; but she had been taught the utmost respect for old people, and, having no reason for refusing, she directly went to the piano and did as she was bid.

"That's the sort of music it's a pleasure to hear. Sing some more, dear," said Madam, in her gentle way, when she had done.

Pleased with this praise, Polly sang away in a fresh little voice that went straight to the listener's heart and nestled there. The sweet old tunes that one is never tired of were all Polly's store. The more she sung, the better she did it; and when she wound up with "A Health to King Charlie," the room quite rung with the stirring music made by the big piano and the little maid.

"That's a jolly tune! Sing it again, please," cried Tom's voice; and there was Tom's red head bobbing up over the high back of the chair where he had hidden himself.

It gave Polly quite a turn, for she thought no one was hearing her but the old lady dozing by the fire. "I can't sing any more; I'm tired," she said, and walked away to Madam in the other room. The red head vanished like a meteor, for Polly's tone had been decidedly cool.

The old lady put out her hand, and, drawing Polly to her knee, looked into her face with such kind eyes that Polly forgot the impressive cap, and smiled at her confidently; for she saw that her simple music had pleased her listener, and she felt glad to know it.

"You mus'n't mind my staring, dear," said Madam, softly pinching her rosy cheek, "I haven't seen a little girl for so long, it does my old eyes good to look at you." Polly thought that a very odd speech, and couldn't help saying, "Aren't Fan and Maud little girls, too?"

"Oh, dear, no! not what I call little girls. Fan has been a young lady this two years, and Maud is a spoiled baby. Your mother's a very sensible woman, my child."

"What a queer old lady!" thought Polly; but she said "Yes'm," respectfully, and looked at the fire. "You don't understand what I mean, do you?" asked Madam, still holding her by the chin. "No'm; not quite."

"Well, dear, I'll tell you. In my day, children of fourteen and fifteen didn't dress in the height of the fashion; go to parties as nearly like those of grown people as it's possible to make them; lead idle, giddy, unhealthy lives, and get blase' at twenty. We were little folks till eighteen or so; worked and studied, dressed and played, like children; honored our parents; and our days were much longer in the land than now, it seems to me."

The old lady appeared to forget Polly, at the end of her speech; for she sat patting the plump little hand that lay in her own, and looking up at a faded picture of an old gentleman with a ruffled shirt and a queue. "Was he your father, Madam?"

"Yes, my dear; my honored father. I did up his frills to the day of his death; and the first money I ever earned, was five dollars which he offered as a prize to whichever of his six girls would lay the handsomest darn in his silk stockings."

"How proud you must have been!" cried Polly, leaning on the old lady's knee with an interested face.

"Yes; and we all learned to make bread, and cook, and wore little chintz gowns, and were as gay and hearty as kittens. All lived to be grandmothers; and I'm the last—seventy next birthday, my dear, and not worn out yet; though daughter Shaw is an invalid at forty."

"That's the way I was brought up, and that's why Fan calls me old-fashioned, I suppose. Tell more about your papa, please; I like it," said Polly.

"Say, 'father.' We never called him papa; and if one of my brothers had addressed him as 'governor,' as boys now do, I really think he'd have him cut off with a shilling."

守旧的女孩

波莉希望那个"讨人厌的汤姆"不会出现在餐桌前,但他偏偏就在那儿,而且整晚都用一种不屑的眼神上下打量着她。

萧先生是一位看起来总是很忙碌的人,他打招呼说:"你好,亲爱的,希望你别客气,随便些。"说完后就好像完全忘了她这个人的存在。萧太太是个脸色苍白、有点神经质的女人,她以客礼待她,并照顾她的日常需要。萧老夫人是一位沉静的老太太,戴着一顶华丽的帽子,一见到波莉就兴奋地喊道:"上帝保佑!亲爱的,你和你妈妈简直是一个模子里刻出来的,你妈妈还好吗?"此后她就一直从厚厚的眼镜片后面不住地打量着这位新来的客人。可怜的波莉在老夫人和汤姆两人的双目夹攻下,胃口全无。

芬妮在餐桌上像个麻雀似的叽叽喳喳没完,莫迪一直吵吵闹闹,直到汤姆出主意说把她放在大餐桌底下,吓得她大哭起来,后来由好脾气的凯蒂带走了,这才算安静下来。老实说,这顿饭吃得并不是很舒服,所以在离开餐厅的时候,波莉感到很开心。大家都去做各自的事去了。芬妮向波莉说声"抱歉"之后就被裁缝叫去了,留下波莉一个人在画室里自娱自乐。

波莉很高兴自己能独处一会儿。在仔细观察了周围的各种精美饰物之后,她开始在绚丽的地毯上来回走动起来,并低声哼着小曲。此时天已逐渐暗了下来,只有熊熊的炉火映红着整个房间。

过了一会儿,老夫人慢慢地走了过来,在她的安乐椅上坐下来。她说:"那老调真不错,唱给我听听,亲爱的,我已经很久没有听过了。"

波莉其实并不喜欢在陌生人面前唱歌,但她素来尊重老人,没有理由拒绝她的请求,便径直走到钢琴前为她弹唱了一曲。

"那是一种让人听了很喜悦的曲子,再多唱几曲,亲爱的。"老夫人听完又轻声说道。

听到这样的夸奖,波莉很是开心,唱起来愈来愈有精神。她每一曲都唱得委婉动听、动人心弦。这些甜美的老歌是难不倒波莉的。她最喜欢的是苏格兰风格的,比如《祝查理王健康》等歌曲。她唱得越来越动听,一曲胜似一曲。当她唱完最后一曲时,房间里一下子变得寂静无声,整个房间回荡着优美的钢琴声和小姑娘甜美的歌声。

"这是乔治的作品,很欢快的调子!请再唱一遍。"随着说话声,汤姆那满头红发的脑袋忽然从藏身的椅子后面冒了出来。

这让波莉着实吓了一跳,她还以为除了在火炉旁打盹的老夫人以外不会有别的人听到呢。"我不能再唱了,我很累。"波莉说完,陪老夫人去另一个房间了,那个红头发的脑袋也像流星一样瞬间消失了,因为波莉说话的语气非常冷漠。

老夫人伸出手,一把将波莉搂了过来,温柔慈祥地望着波莉的脸庞,她那慈祥的目光甚至让波莉忘了那顶夸张的帽子,也望着她笑了。看到自己那简简单单的音乐竟让这位聆听者那么开心,她感到非常高兴。

"你别介意我盯着你看,亲爱的!"老夫人说着轻轻抚摸了一下波莉那玫瑰似的脸颊,"我很久没有见过你这样的女孩了,你让我这昏花的老眼一亮。" 波莉心想老夫人的话多奇怪啊,禁不住问道:"难道芬妮和莫迪不是小女孩吗?"

"噢,亲爱的,她们不是!不是我所说的小女孩。芬妮这两年已变成一个妙龄女郎了,而莫迪只是一个被溺爱的孩子。你的妈妈是一位明智的女人,我的孩子。"

"多奇怪的一个老太太啊!"波莉心想,但嘴上却恭敬地应着"是",眼睛瞧着炉火。

"你不会明白我的意思,对吗?"老夫人问道,依旧捧着她的下巴,"不,不大懂。"

"好吧,亲爱的,我来告诉你。在我们那个时代,十四五岁的孩子不能和成年人一样穿时髦的衣服或者去参加舞会。因为那样很有可能会误导她们走向游手好闲、轻率、不健康的生活,也许在20岁时就已经养成了一种养尊处优的娇惯习气。那时候,18岁以下都还是小孩子,干活、学习、穿衣和玩耍都还是小孩子的行径,而且非常尊重父母。那时候,人们的寿命也比现在长。"

老太太说着说着,好像忘了波莉的存在,只轻轻拍着自己的手,眼睛望着墙壁上挂着的一幅老先生的相片。那位老先生穿着一件带褶边的衬衣,脑后拖着一条辫子。"他是您父亲吗,老夫人?"

"是的,亲爱的,他是我尊敬的父亲。他生前都是我帮他做的褶边。我第一次挣的钱也是他作为奖励给我的。那时,我们姐妹六个比赛,看谁能把他的丝织长袜补得最精致,最后我赢了。"

"那您一定很自豪了!"波莉喊道,欣然将小脸靠在老夫人的膝盖上。

"是啊,而且当时我们还学着做面包、烹饪,穿着短小的棉布袍子,像小猫一样快活自由。现在我们都是奶奶或者祖父了。我是最小的一个,明年我就七十岁了,但你看我还精神饱满呢。而我的儿媳妇才40岁,身体就垮掉了。"

"我也是在那样的环境下长大的,我想这就是为什么芬妮说我土里土气的原因了。再告诉我一些关于您爸爸的故事吧,我很喜欢听。"波莉请求道。

"叫'父亲',我们从来不喊他'爸爸'。如果我的兄弟们像现在的男孩子一样喊父亲'长官'的话,我想他们肯定要不到零花钱了。"

The Tea Rose

There it stood, in its little green vase, on a light ebony stand in the window of the drawing-room. The rich satin curtains, with their costly fringes, swept down on either side of it, and around it glittered every rare and fanciful trifle which wealth can offer to luxury, and yet that simple rose was the fairest of them all. So pure it looked, its white leaves just touched with that delicious, creamy tint peculiar to its kind: its cup so full, so perfect, its head bending, as if it were sinking and melting away in its own richness. —Oh! when did ever man make anything to equal the living, perfect flower!

But the sunlight that streamed through the window revealed something fairer than the rose—a young lady reclining on an ottoman, who was thus addressed by her livelier cousin: "I say, cousin, I have been thinking what you are to do with your pet rose when you go to New York; as, to our consternation, you are determined to do. You know it would be a sad pity to leave it with such a scatter-brain as I am. I love flowers, indeed, —that is, I like a regular bouquet, cut off and tied up, to carry to a party; but as to all this tending and fussing which is needful to keep them growing, I have no gifts in that line."

"Make yourself easy as to that, Kate," said Florence, with a smile; "I have no intention of calling upon your talent; I have an asylum in view for my favorite."

"Oh, then you know just what I was going to say. Mrs. Marshall, I presume, has been speaking to you; she was here yesterday, and I was quite pathetic upon the subject; telling her the loss your favorite would sustain, and so forth; and she said how delighted she would be to have it in her greenhouse; it is in such a fine state now, so full of buds. I told her I knew you would like to give it to her; you are so fond of Mrs. Marshall, you know."

"Now, Kate, I am sorry, but I have otherwise engaged."

"Whom can it be to? you have so few intimates here."

"Oh, it is only one of my odd fancies."

"But do tell me, Florence."

"Well, cousin, you know the little pale girl to whom we give sewing?"

"What! little Mary Stephens? How absurd, Florence! This is just another of your motherly, old-maidish ways; dressing dolls for poor children, making bonnets, and knitting socks for all the little dirty babies in the neighborhood. I do believe you have made more calls in those two vile, ill-smelling alleys behind our house than ever you have in Chestnut Street, though you know everybody is half dying to see you; and now, to crown all, you must give this choice little bijou to a seamstress girl, when one of your most intimate friends, in your own class, would value it so highly. What in the world can people in their circumstances want with flowers?"

"Just the same as I do," replied Florence, calmly. "Have you not noticed that the little girl never comes without looking wistfully at the opening buds? And don't you remember, the other morning she asked me so prettily if I would let her mother come and see it, she was so fond of flowers?"

"But, Florence, only think of this rare flower standing on a table with ham, eggs, cheese, and flour, and stifled in that close little room, where Mrs. Stephens and her daughter manage to wash, iron, and cook."

"Well, Kate, and if I were obliged to live in one coarse room, and wash, and iron, and cook, as you say; if I had to spend every moment of my time in toil, with no prospect from my window but a brick wall and a dirty lane, such a flower as this would be untold enjoyment to me."

"Pshaw, Florence; all sentiment! Poor people have no time to be sentimental. Besides, I don't believe it will grow with them; it is a greenhouse flower, and used to delicate living."

"Oh, as to that, a flower never inquires whether its owner is rich or poor; and poor Mrs. Stephens, whatever else she has not, has sunshine of as good quality as this that streams through our window. The beautiful things that God makes are his gifts to all alike. You will see that my fair rose will be as well and cheerful in Mrs. Stephens's room as in ours."

"Well, after all, how odd! When one gives to poor people, one wants to give them something useful—a bushel of potatoes, a ham, and such things."

"Why, certainly, potatoes and ham must be supplied; but, having ministered to the first and most craving wants, why not add any other little pleasures or gratifications we may have it in our power to bestow? I know there are many of the poor who have fine feeling and a keen sense of the beautiful, which rusts out and dies because they are too hard pressed to procure it any gratification. Poor Mrs. Stephens, for example; I know she would enjoy birds, and flowers, and music as much as I do. I have seen her eye light up as she looked upon these things in our drawing-room, and yet not one beautiful thing can she command. From necessity, her room, her clothing, —all she has, must be coarse and plain. You should have seen the almost rapture she and Mary felt when I offered them my rose."

"Dear me! all this may be true, but I never thought of it before. I never thought that these hard-working people had any ideas of taste!"

"Then why do you see the geranium or rose so carefully nursed in the old cracked teapot in the poorest room, or the morning-glory planted in a box and twined about the window? Do not these show that the human heart yearns for the beautiful in all ranks of life? You remember, Kate, how our washerwoman sat up a whole night, after a hard day's work, to make her first baby a pretty dress to be baptized in." "Yes, and I remember how I laughed at you for making such a tasteful little cap for it."

"True, Kate, but I think the look of perfect delight with which the poor woman regarded her baby in its new dress and cap was something quite worth creating; I do believe she could not have felt more grateful if 1 had sent her a barrel of flour."

"Well, I never thought before of giving anything to the poor but what they really needed, and I have always been willing to do that when I could without going far out of my way."

"Ah! cousin, if our heavenly Father gave to us after this mode, we should have only coarse, shapeless piles of provisions lying about the world, instead of all this beautiful variety of trees, and fruits, and flowers,"

"Well, well, cousin, I suppose you are right, but have mercy on my poor head; it is too small to hold so many new ideas all at once, so go on your own way;" and the little lady began practicing a waltzing step before the glass with great satisfaction.

茶 玫

客厅窗台上，光滑的乌木架子上摆放着一只绿色小花瓶，一株香水玫瑰插在花瓶里。厚厚的、吊着华贵流苏的绸缎窗帘从窗户两边悬挂下来，周围是一件挨一件的稀有而珍贵的小摆设。但那株不起眼的香水玫瑰却是它们中间最美丽的。它看起来那么纯净，白色的花瓣娇嫩欲滴，色若凝脂。花萼圆润，曲线完美，微微低垂，似乎由于太过饱满而开始融化——啊！人类创造的任何东西都不能与这朵鲜活、精美的花相媲美。

阳光透过窗帘，照在一个比这株玫瑰更美的生物身上———一位年轻的女郎斜靠在一张长椅上，她活泼的表妹对她说："我说，表姐，我在想，你去了纽约后，你这株玫瑰怎么办呢？你坚持这么做，真让我们感到吃惊。你决定让我这个粗心大意的人来照料它，这可不明智啊！我是喜欢花，可我喜欢的是整齐的花束，修剪打理好了，可以带到舞会上去。至于照顾它，让它生长，我可没那个天赋。"

"放松点，凯特，"弗洛伦斯笑着说，"我不要求你发挥天赋，我会细心保护自己喜欢的东西的。"

"哦，那你知道我想说什么吗？我敢肯定，马绍尔夫人跟你谈过了。她昨天来过，我非常同情她，因为我不得不告诉她，我们不能把你最心爱的花给她。她说如果她能把它养在自己的温室里，那该是多好的事。它现在长得多好啊，有这么多花骨朵。我跟她说你本来非常愿意给她的，你很喜欢马绍尔夫人，是不是？"

"但是，非常抱歉，凯特，我已经另有打算了。"

"会是谁呢？你在这儿没几个好朋友呀！"

"哦，我只是心血来潮而已。"

"告诉我吧，弗洛伦斯。"

"嗯，表妹，你还记得那个我们为她缝补衣服的生病的小女孩吗？"

"什么！小玛丽·史蒂芬斯？太荒谬了，弗洛伦斯！你总是那么充满母性，像个老处女一样！给穷苦孩子的布娃娃穿衣服、做帽子，为邻居家脏兮兮的小孩织袜子。我敢肯定，你去拜访我们屋后那两条肮脏、臭气熏天的小巷的次数，比你去斯纳街的次数还多，尽管你知道斯纳街的人都热切希望你去那儿。现在，更糟糕的是，你最亲密的朋友、与你在同一阶层的人这么喜欢那盆花，你竟然选择把它送给一个女裁缝的女儿。那种处境的人要花究竟有什么用？"

"就跟我一样，"弗洛伦斯平心静气地回答，"你没注意到吗，每次那个小女孩来的时候，她都会满怀期待地看着待放的花苞。你难道不记得，一天早上，她轻轻地问我，可不可以让她妈妈来看看它，她可喜欢花了！"

"但是，弗洛伦斯，想象一下，这么稀有的一盆花，和一桌子火腿、鸡蛋、奶酪还有面粉在一起，憋在史蒂芬斯太太和她女儿洗衣、熨烫、做饭的小房子里。"

"好了，凯特，如果我只能住在一间简陋的屋子里，就像你说的洗衣、熨烫、做饭，假如我必须不停地干活，向窗口看去，没有别的，只有砖墙和陋巷，那么这样一盆小花对我来说，将会是无尽的享受。"

"哎，弗洛伦斯，你可真是多愁善感啊！但穷人可没那么多时间去多愁善感。再说，花儿在她们那里肯定长不好。它是温室花朵，已经习惯了温室的环境。"

"哦，这个嘛，花儿从来不在乎主人是贫是富。也许，史蒂芬斯太太别的什么都没有,但是照进她家窗户的阳光和这里的阳光一样好。上帝将他创造的美好事物,丝毫不差地馈赠给每个人。看着吧,我美丽的玫瑰在史蒂芬斯太太家,会和在这里一样快乐、健康。"

"是吗?不管怎么说,这么做太奇怪了!如果向穷人施舍,你应该给他们一些有用的东西,比如土豆、火腿呀什么的。"

"是的,土豆和火腿当然是少不了的。但是,在给了最需要的东西之后,为什么不做一些我们力所能及的事,为他们带去小小的喜悦和满足呢?我认识许多穷人,他们虽然生活贫困,但是跟我们一样对美丽非常敏锐、渴望。只不过,他们的这种渴望只是被苦难的生活埋没了。就像可怜的史蒂芬斯太太一样,我知道,她本来可以像我一样欣赏花卉、鸟和音乐。在我们的客厅里,我亲眼看到她看这些东西时,眼睛里闪闪发光。但是,这些美丽的东西,她一样都没有。生活所迫,她的房子、衣服——所有的东西——都那么简陋、朴素。你应该看看我把玫瑰送给她们的时候,史蒂芬斯太太和玛丽有多高兴。"

"天哪!这一切也许都是真的,但之前我从没有想过。我从未想过,那些辛勤工作的人会有其他的爱好。"

"为什么在穷人家的房子里,能看到被精心养在老茶壶里的天竺和玫瑰,或是种在盒子、缠绕在窗户上的牵牛花?难道这些还不能表明人们的心灵不分等级,人人渴望美丽吗?凯特,你还记不记得,那位白天忙着为我们洗衣服的妇女,一夜没睡,给第一个宝宝赶制了一件漂亮的礼服,就是为了能让他在洗礼的时候穿!""当然记得,我还取笑你为了这件事,专门做了一顶可爱的小帽子。"

"是的,凯特。但是,我觉得那样做很值得,因为那个可怜的妇女觉得她宝宝的礼服和帽子非常完美,她特别高兴。我相信,就算我送她一桶面粉,也没有这件事让她感激我。"

"嗯,我从来没想过除了给穷人需要的东西外,还应该给他们什么。如果不是太费劲的话,我还是非常乐意帮助穷人的。"

"哦,表妹,如果上帝也让我们过着那样的生活,那么我们就不会有遍地的树木、果实、鲜花,而只有粗俗、简陋的东西。"

"好了,好了,表姐!我想你是对的,但是请可怜可怜我的笨脑袋吧,它太小了,一下子容不了那么多新想法,你就按自己的方式去做吧!"说完,这个小女郎就在镜子前顾影自怜地练起了华尔兹舞步。

The Machinist's Return

On our way from Springfield to Boston, a stout, black-whiskered man sat immediately in front of me, in the drawing-room car, whose maneuvers were a source of constant amusement. He would get up every five minutes, hurry away to the narrow passage leading to the door of the car, and commence laughing in the most violent manner, continuing that healthful exercise until he observed that some one was watching him, when he would return to his seat.

As we neared Boston these demonstrations increased in frequency and violence, but the stranger kept his seat and chuckled to himself. He shifted the position of his two portmanteaus, or placed them on the seat as if he was getting ready to leave. As we were at least twenty-five miles from Boston, such early preparations seemed extremely ridiculous. He became so excited at last that he could not keep his secret. Some one must be made a confidant; and as I happened to be the nearest to him, he selected me.

Turning around suddenly, and rocking himself to and fro in his chair, he said, "I have been away from home three years. Have been in Europe. My folks don't expect me for three months yet, but I got through and started. I telegraphed them at the last station —they've got the dispatch by this time." As he said this he rubbed his hands, and changed the portmanteau on his left to the right, and then the one on the right to the left.

"Have you a wife?" said I. "Yes, and three children," was the answer. He then got up and folded his overcoat anew, and hung it over the back of the seat. "You are somewhat nervous just now, are you not?" said I.

"Well, I should think so," he replied. "I haven't slept soundly for a week. Do you know," he went on, speaking in a low tone, "I am almost certain this train will run off the track and break my neck before I get to Boston. I have had too much good luck lately for one man. It can't last. It rains so hard, sometimes, that you think it's never going to stop; then it shines so bright you think it's always going to shine; and just as you are settled in either belief, you are knocked over by a change, to show you that you know nothing about it."

"Well, according to your philosophy," I said, "you will continue to have sunshine because you are expecting a storm." "Perhaps so," he replied; "but it is curious that the only thing which makes me think I shall get through safe is, I fear that I shall not."

"I am a machinist," he continued; "I made a discovery; nobody believed in it; I spent all my money in trying to bring it out; I mortgaged my home?—?everything went. Everybody laughed at me—everybody but my wife. She said she would work her fingers off before I should give it up. I went to England. At first I met with no encouragement whatever, and came very near jumping off London Bridge. I went into a workshop to earn money enough to come home with: there I met the man I wanted. To make a long story short, I've brought home $50,000 with me, and here I am."

"Good!" I exclaimed. "Yes," said he, "and the best of it is, she knows nothing about it. She has been disappointed so often that I concluded I would not write to her about my unexpected good luck. When I got my money, though, I started for home at once."

"And now, I suppose, you will make her happy?" "Happy!" he replied; "why, you don't know anything about it! She's worked night and day since I have been in England, trying to support herself and the children decently. They paid her thirteen cents apiece for making shirts, and that's the way she has lived half the time. She'll come down to the depot to meet me in a gingham dress and a shawl a hundred years old, and she'll think she's dressed up! Perhaps she won't have any fine dresses in a week or so, eh?"

The stranger then strode down the passageway again, and getting in a corner where he seemed to suppose that he was out of sight, went through the strangest pantomime, —?laughing, putting his mouth into the drollest shapes, and swinging himself back and forth in the limited space.

As the train was going into the depot, I placed myself on the platform of the car in front of the one in which I had been riding, and opposite the stranger, who, with a portmanteau in each hand, was standing on the lowest step, ready to jump to the ground. I looked from his face to the faces of the people before us, but saw no sign of recognition. Suddenly he cried, "There they are!"

Then he laughed outright, but in a hysterical way, as he looked over the crowd in front of him. I followed his eye and saw, some distance back, as if crowded out by the well-dressed and elbowing throng, a little woman in a faded dress and a well-worn hat, with a face almost painful in its intense but hopeful expression, glancing rapidly from window to window as the coaches passed by.

She had not seen the stranger, but a moment after she caught his eye. In another instant he had jumped to the platform with his two portmanteaus, and, pushing his way through the crowd, he rushed towards the place where she was standing. I think I never saw a face assume so many different expressions in so short a time as did that of the little woman while her husband was on his way to meet her.

She was not pretty, —on the contrary, she was very plain-looking; but somehow I felt a big lump rise in my throat as I watched her. She was trying to laugh, but, God bless her, how completely she failed in the attempt! Her mouth got into the position to laugh, but it never moved after that, save to draw down at the corners and quiver, while her eyes blinked so fast that I suspect she only caught occasional glimpses of the broad-shouldered fellow who elbowed his way so rapidly toward her.

As he drew close, and dropped the portmanteaus, she turned to one side, and covered her face with her hands; and thus she was when the strong man gathered her up in his arms as if she were a child, and held her sobbing to his breast.

There were enough staring at them, heaven knows; so I turned my eyes away a moment, and then I saw two boys in threadbare roundabouts standing near, wiping their eyes on their sleeves, and bursting into tears anew at every fresh demonstration on the part of their mother. When I looked at the stranger again he had his hat drawn over his eyes; but his wife was looking up at him, and it seemed as if the pent-up tears of those weary months of waiting were streaming through her eyelids.

机械工回家

我们当时坐在一列火车上，这列火车行驶在从斯普林菲尔德到波士顿的必经之路上，一个身材结实、长着络腮胡子的男人正好坐在我前面。他每五分钟起身一次，匆忙走向通往车门的狭窄过道，然后无法抑制地放声大笑；当他要回到座位时，如果发现没有人看他的话，他会继续这种健康的锻炼方式。

当我们快到波士顿的时候，他大笑的次数和狂野的程度更加频繁和剧烈了，就连回到座位的时候，这个陌生人也忍不住哈哈大笑。他不停地移动自己的两个旅行皮箱，或者把它们放在自己座位上，看起来就好像准备要下车了。但是，当时我们离波士顿至少还有25英里远，这么早就做好下车的准备，让人觉得有些滑稽。最后，他太过兴奋，说出了自己的秘密。他必须找人倾诉，由于我正好坐在他最近处，所以他选中了我作为宣泄对象。

他猛地转过身，在自己座位上前后摇晃着身体，对我说："我离开家去欧洲已经有三年了。我一直待在欧洲。我那些朋友认为，最多不超过三个月，我就会回来，但是我撑过来了。我在最后一个车站给他们发了电报——他们现在应该已经收到了。"他边说边摩擦自己的双手，并且把左、右两边的旅行皮箱互换了位置。

"你有老婆吗？"我问道。"有，还有三个孩子。"他回答道。然后他站起来，叠好他的新大衣，并且把它放到后边的座位上。"你现在是不是有点紧张？"我问他。

"嗯，我想是的。"他答道，"我已经一个星期没有睡好觉了，你知道吗？"他用嘹亮的嗓音继续说道，"我敢说，在我到达波士顿之前，这列火车会脱轨，我的脖子也会被扭断。我最近从一个人身上得到了太多的好运。但是，你并不能总是获得好运，有时雨下得很大，就在你认为这雨不会停下来的时候，突然雨过天晴；你又认为天空总是晴朗的，当你坚信那种情况时，你就会被改变击倒，从而明白过来，其实你什么也不知道。"

"哦，依照你的逻辑推理，"我说，"你的生活还会是一片晴朗，因为你正期待一场暴风雨。""或许是吧，"他答道，"不过，听起来奇怪的是，唯一能让我认为自己平安无事的理由，居然是我害怕自己不会安全抵达。"

"我是个机械工，"他继续说，"我曾有过一个重大发现，但是没有人相信我，我用尽积蓄试图给大家呈现出来，我把自己的房子抵押了——所有的东西都没了。所有人都嘲笑我——除了我老婆。她说，只要我不放弃，她就会全力支持我。于是我去了英格兰。起初，没有任何人鼓励我，我当时真想从伦敦桥上跳下去。后来，我去了一家工厂，赚了足够带回家的钱。就在这里，我找到了我想要找的人。简短地说，我带了五万英镑回来。"

"很好！"我惊呼道。"是的，"他说，"最好的事情是，我老婆对此并不知情。她对我很失望，所以，我觉得不应该把自己出人预料的好运气告诉她。尽管这样，在我拿到钱的时候，我就已经想着回家了。"

"现在呢，我猜，你能让她过得很幸福吧？""幸福！"他答道，"为什么？你什么都不知道！自从我去了英格兰之后，她没日没夜地工作，支撑起这个家。她给人做衬衫，一件只能赚到13美分，她就是靠这点钱养活全家的。等会儿她会来车站接我，穿一件方格花布衣服，披一件有上百年历史的围巾，而她一定会认为自己打扮得很好！或许她在这一个礼拜之内都没有件像样的衣服，你明白吗？"

然后他又去了过道，来到一个他认为没人注意到他的角落，表演起了最奇怪的哑剧——他大笑着，把自己的嘴弄成最滑稽的形状，并在有限的空间里前后摇摆身体。

就在列车快要到达车站的时候，我来到列车门前的站台上。在我前面，这位陌生人两只手各拎着一个旅行皮箱，站在列车门最下面的台阶上，随时准备跳到站台上。我从他的脸看向站在我前面的其他人的脸，一点也没看出他要找的人来。突然，他大叫道："他们来了！"

然后，他歇斯底里地笑了起来，看向站在他前面的人群。我顺着他的视线，看到一个穿着褪色衣服、戴着一顶磨坏帽子的女人，她被华丽衣服的人群推挤到了外围，她的表情既痛苦又带有希望，在火车经过她身边的时候，她快速地看向从她旁边掠过的车厢窗户。

她还没有看到她丈夫，但就在她看到丈夫的时候，她丈夫已经从列车的平台上跳了下去。他拎着旅行皮箱，挤进人群，朝她站着的位置跑过去。我想，在他向老婆的位置跑过去的瞬间，再也没有人能在这么短的时间内，闪现出像她脸上那么复杂的表情。

她长得并不漂亮——恰恰相反，她长得很一般，不过当我看到她的时候，喉咙不由得一颤。她想笑，但是上帝保佑，她没能笑出来！她的嘴已经摆到了要笑的位置，但是之后就没再动过，反而嘴角下垂，颤抖起来；她的眼睛眨得很快，我猜她是在寻找那个在人群中快速朝自己跑来的、拥有宽厚肩膀的男人。

当他快要挤到老婆身边的时候，他放下了行李，她把身体转向一边，用手捂住脸，那个强壮的男人把她抱在自己怀中，她就像个孩子一样，在他胸前啜泣起来。

只有上帝知道，周围的人都在看着他们；于是，有那么一段时间，我不再看向他们。然后，我看到两个衣衫褴褛的小男孩站在附近的交叉路口边，他们用袖子擦着眼睛，每当他们的妈妈有什么新举动时，他们就会泪流满面。当我再次看向那个陌生人的时候，他将帽子遮住了眼睛；但是，他的老婆仰头看向他，焦急等待数月的泪水再也无法抑制地从眼中倾泻而出。

The Best Kind of Revenge

Some years ago a warehouseman in Manchester, England, published a scurrilous pamphlet, in which he endeavored to hold up the house of Grant Brothers to ridicule. William Grant remarked upon the occurrence that the man would live to repent of what he had done; and this was conveyed by some talebearer to the libeler, who said, "Oh, I suppose he thinks I shall some time or other be in his debt; but I will take good care of that." It happens, however, that a man in business can not always choose who shall be his creditors. The pamphleteer became a bankrupt, and the brothers held an acceptance of his which had been indorsed to them by the drawer, who had also become a bankrupt.

The wantonly libeled men had thus become creditors of the libeler! They now had it in their power to make him repent of his audacity. He could not obtain his certificate without their signature, and without it he could not enter into business again. He had obtained the number of signatures required by the bankrupt law except one. It seemed folly to hope that the firm of "the brothers" would supply the deficiency. What! they who had cruelly been made the laughingstock of the public, forget the wrong and favor the wrongdoer? He despaired. But the claims of a wife and children forced him at last to make the application. Humbled by misery, he presented himself at the countinghouse of the wronged.

Mr. William Grant was there alone, and his first words to the delinquent were, "Shut the door, sir!" sternly uttered. The door was shut, and the libeler stood trembling before the libeled. He told his tale and produced his certificate, which was instantly clutched by the injured merchant. "You wrote a pamphlet against us once!" exclaimed Mr. Grant. The suppliant expected to see his parchment thrown into the fire. But this was not its destination. Mr. Grant took a pen, and writing something upon the document, handed it back to the bankrupt. He, poor wretch, expected to see "rogue, scoundrel, libeler," inscribed; but there was, in fair round characters, the signature of the firm.

"We make it a rule," said Mr. Grant, "never to refuse signing the certificate of an honest tradesman, and we have never heard that you were anything else." The tears started into the poor man's eyes. "Ah," said Mr. Grant, "my saying was true! I said you would live to repent writing that pamphlet. I did not mean it as a threat. I only meant that some day you would know us better, and be sorry you had tried to injure us. I see you repent of it now." "I do, I do!" said the grateful man; "I bitterly repent it." "Well, well, my dear fellow, you know us now. How do you get on? What are you going to do?" The poor man stated he had friends who could assist him when his certificate was obtained. "But how are you off in the meantime?"

And the answer was, that, having given up every farthing to his creditors, he had been compelled to stint his family of even common necessaries, that he might be enabled to pay the cost of his certificate. "My dear fellow, this will not do; your family must not suffer. Be kind enough to take this ten-pound note to your wife from me. There, there, my dear fellow! Nay, do not cry; it will all be well with you yet. Keep up your spirits, set to work like a man, and you will raise your head among us yet." The overpowered man endeavored in vain to express his thanks; the swelling in his throat forbade words. He put his handkerchief to his face and went out of the door, crying like a child.

最好的报复

几年前，英国曼彻斯特的一个批发商出版了一部语言粗俗下流的小册子，他在书里不遗余力地丑化格兰特兄弟公司，致使该公司陷入被公众嘲笑的境地。威廉·格兰特就这件事发表言论，说此人会为自己的所作所为后悔一辈子。一些搬弄是非的人把这句话传给了那位诽谤者，而他却说："哦，我猜他是想说，也许有一天我会欠他的债吧。但我还是会小心的。"然而碰巧的是，一个生意人不能总是选择自己的债主。出版这个小册子的人破产了，而格兰特兄弟却持有他的一张承兑汇票，上边有同样也破产了的发票人的转让认可签名。

受到大肆诽谤的人就这样成了造谣者的债主！现在他们完全有能力让造谣者为自己的言行后悔。没有他们的签字认可，造谣者的营业执照就无法生效，如果没有营业执照，他就不能再经商了。他已经获得了破产法要求的其他签名，除了最后一个——格拉特公司的签字。想让格兰特兄弟公司为他签字？简直是痴人说梦。怎么可能，那些无辜成为公众笑柄的人怎么可能会把造谣者的恶行抛诸脑后？他绝望了，但妻子和孩子的压力，迫使他不得不再提出申请试试，于是，他愧疚不安地来到了被诽谤者的会计室。

威廉·格兰特先生独自坐在那里，他对这位犯了错的人所说的第一句话就是："先生，请关门！"语气严肃而坚决。门关上了，诽谤者战战兢兢地站在受害者的面前。他讲述了自己的情况，并递上了自己的营业执照，被诽谤的受害者一把抓过执照。"你曾写过一本诽谤我的小册子！"格兰特先生说道。诽谤者以为自己的执照会被烧掉，但事实却并非如此。格兰特先生拿出笔，在文件上写了些东西，然后把它交还给那个破产的人。这位可怜又可悲的诽谤者以为会看到"流氓、无赖、造谣"这样的话，可他真正看到的却是清晰可见的格兰特公司的签名。

"我们有一个规定，"格兰特先生说，"永远不会拒绝在一个诚实商人的执照上签字。至少我们从来没有听说过你在这方面有什么不好。"眼泪一下充满了这位可怜人的眼睛。"啊，"格兰特先生继续说道，"我的话兑现了！我说过你会为自己写那本小册子而后悔的，但我并没有威胁你的意思，我只想有一天你能更多地了解我们，从而为自己曾试图伤害我们感到难过。我看到，你现在就后悔了！""是的，确实是这样！"他感激涕零地说，"我实在太后悔了！"格兰特先生说："嗯，好，朋友，你现在了解我们了，接下来你要干什么，有什么打算吗？"这个可怜的人说，一旦他的营业执照生效，他有朋友可以帮他。"但是你现在有多少钱呢？"格兰特先生问道。

那个人的回答是，他已经把稍微值钱的东西给了债主，现在甚至减少了家里必需品的开支，这样他才能够支付得起重新启用营业执照的成本。"亲爱的朋友，这可不行，你的家人不应该遭受痛苦，请代我把这十英镑交给你的妻子！不要哭，不要这样，一切都会好起来的。打起精神来，像个男人一样，放手去做吧，很快你又会在我们中间高高地昂起头的。"这个万分感动的人想努力表达自己的谢意，可他却哽咽地说不出话来。他拿出手帕捂着脸，像个孩子似的哭着走出了门。